THE FRENCH CIVIL WARS, 1562–1598

R. J. KNECHT

An imprint of Pearson Education

Harlow, England · London · New York · Reading, Massachusetts · San Francisco
Toronto · Don Mills, Ontario · Sydney · Tokyo · Singapore · Hong Kong · Seoul
Taipei · Cape Town · Madrid · Mexico City · Amsterdam · Munich · Paris · Milan

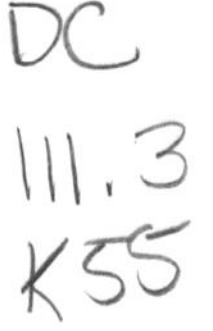

Pearson Education Limited
Edinburgh Gate
Harlow
Essex CM20 2JE
England

and Associated Companies throughout the world

Visit us on the World Wide Web at:
http://www.pearsoneduc.com

First published 2000

© Pearson Education Limited 2000

The right of R. J. Knecht to be identified as author of this work has been asserted by him in accordance with the Copyright, Designs, and Patents Act 1988.

All rights reserved; no part of this publication may be reproduced, stored in a retrieval system, or transmitted in any form or by any means, electronic, mechanical, photocopying, recording, or otherwise without either the prior written permission of the Publishers or a licence permitting restricted copying in the United Kingdom issued by the Copyright Licensing Agency Ltd, 90 Tottenham Court Road, London W1P 0LP.

ISBN 0 582 09548 4 CSD
ISBN 0 582 09549 2 PPR

British Library Cataloguing-in-Publication Data
A catalogue record for this book is available from the British Library.

Library of Congress Cataloging-in-Publication Data
Knecht, R. J. (Robert Jean)
The French civil wars, 1562–1598 / R.J. Knecht.
p. cm. — (Modern wars in perspective)
Includes bibliographical references and index.
ISBN 0–582–09549–2 (pbk.: alk. paper) — ISBN 0–582–09548–4 (cased: alk. paper)
1. France—History—Wars of the Huguenots, 1562–1598. I. Title. II. Series.

DC111.3.K55 2000
944′.029—dc21 00–026013

Typeset by 35 in 11/13pt Baskerville MT
Produced by Pearson Education Asia Pte Ltd.
Printed in Singapore

43590092

To Michael and Monique

CONTENTS

LIST OF MAPS

PREFACE

Although civil wars are in many respects similar to foreign wars, notably in their destructiveness of life and property, they are also profoundly different. A foreign war, complex as its origins may be, is fought between two or more countries, usually over some piece of disputed territory. It is fought along one or more fronts which can be easily identified on a map. Thus, in the early sixteenth century, French armies crossed the Alps into Italy in pursuit of certain claims which the kings of France laid to the kingdom of Naples or the duchy of Milan. Civil wars are fought essentially for another reason: to overthrow a government or to extract concessions from it. This aim may stem from a variety of motives – political, economic, social, religious or racial – or a mixture of some or all of these. Whereas a foreign war may start almost unexpectedly as an aggressor tries to spring a surprise, a civil war is invariably the culmination of a period of domestic unrest. The French civil wars may have begun formally in April 1562 but they were preceded by a long period of turmoil. Their outbreak can only be understood if this is taken into account. Foreign wars can involve several nations. In this respect, a civil war is no different, for the parties involved nearly always need outside assistance. Thus, during the French civil wars, the crown looked to Spain while the Huguenots turned to England and the Dutch rebels. The course of a civil war is also usually difficult to plot on a map. Fronts tend not to exist as fighting may break out anywhere in a given country. Civil wars also raise particular ethical issues. A war may be deemed 'just' if it is fought defensively by a country facing external aggression, but can it ever be 'just' if brother is expected to kill brother? As the rival French armies faced each other for the first time on the field of Dreux in 1562, the hideousness of their fratricidal plight caused them to hesitate for a moment. But once battle was joined, there was no limit to the blood-letting. And as the appetite for fighting grew, so did its fierceness. Family disputes are known to be the most bitter, and civil wars demonstrate that awful truth on a larger scale.

Perhaps for all these reasons, historians have tended to be wary of the civil wars that tore France apart during the second half of the sixteenth century. Military historians have traced the movements of armies, described the battles and sieges and considered changes of tactics and armaments. The wars have been considered within the context of the so-called 'Military Revolution'. Other historians have examined the rise of Protestantism in France and the challenge which it posed to a monarchy closely tied by tradition to the Catholic church. Others still have tried to relate religious change to underlying socio-economic developments. Traditionally the civil wars have been called 'Wars of Religion', but the label is misleading. Though undoubtedly a major source of conflict, religion was not alone. The wars may also be seen as struggles for power between rival families of noblemen. Indeed, some historians, taking their cue from a contemporary witness, have argued that the nobles were using religion as a cloak with which to cover their more selfish motives. This, however, is another simplification. Mack Holt has argued convincingly that 'the French Wars of Religion were fought primarily over the issue of religion as defined in contemporary terms: as a body of believers rather than the more modern definition of a body of beliefs'.[1] Recent research by a host of scholars, not merely focusing on the power struggles at the centre of government but also on conflicts in the provinces and in particular towns, has yielded a far more complex picture than that traditionally presented by historians. Profound disagreements over matters of faith which may or may not have been influenced by socio-economic conditions did sponsor violence of different kinds, but other factors, not least professional or personal jealousies, may have played a part. Popular hysteria, fed by rumours or incited by fanatical preachers, could unleash a massacre of innocent people, thereby provoking a response in kind.

An understanding of the French civil wars must also rest on an awareness of their evolution in time. They were spread out over half a century and we need to ask ourselves why so many peace settlements proved so short-lived. J. B. Wood has advanced the very credible thesis that the crown simply could not defeat the Huguenots because it could not afford to keep an army on a wartime footing for longer than a few months at a time. Peace settlements were accordingly dictated by economic considerations rather than by any genuine desire to overcome outstanding differences between the parties involved. The actual fighting also changed in character. At first, large pitched battles were fought, but they left so much to chance and took such a heavy toll of the officer class that both sides began consciously to avoid them. Sieges became far more important after the massacre of St Bartholomew as Huguenots sought shelter behind the walls of La Rochelle and in other strongholds of the Midi. As the main centre of operations shifted from north of the river Loire to provinces in the south, the crown found itself at a logistical disadvantage as traditionally its forces

1 M. Holt, *The French Wars of Religion, 1562–1629* (Cambridge, 1995), p. 2.

had been garrisoned in the north and its artillery based mainly in Paris. As the wars seemed to drag on for ever without resolving outstanding issues, some of the combatants grew disillusioned. A group of Catholic nobles – the so-called 'Malcontents' – began to see that if the Protestants could not be eliminated by force, some kind of settlement would have to be hammered out with them. Moderates on both sides joined forces and the wars lost something of their denominational character, becoming more political, less religious.

These are some of the issues which this study hopes to address. I have tried to understand the wars, not only as a military phenomenon, but also as the result of a multiple clash of interests. A short book such as this cannot hope to do full justice to such a vast topic. But it may at least indicate the richness of the field and point to directions for future research. Thanks to J. B. Wood, to whose work I am greatly indebted, much more is now known about the king's army during the first five civil wars, but the Huguenot armies are not so well documented.

While writing this book I have frequently sought and received valuable advice from friends. I am especially grateful to Hamish Scott, not only for his kindness in inviting me to contribute to this series of war studies, but also for his wise counsels and infinite patience. My warmest gratitude also goes to Mark Greengrass, David Potter and Penny Roberts for generously sharing their knowledge of the period with me in various ways.

Robert Knecht
Birmingham
1999

Acknowledgements

The publishers wish to thank the following for permission to reproduce the material:

Map 1 from *La France du XVI siècle*, 1483–1598, Presses universitaires de France, Paris (Arlette Jouanna, 1996); Maps 2, 4 and 5 from *The French Wars of Religion*, Macmillan Publishers Ltd., London (D. Potter, 1997); Maps 6 and 7 from *A History of the Art of War in the 16th Century*, Methuen, London (Sir Charles Oman, 1937).

Though every effort has been made to trace the owners of copyright material, in a few cases this has proved impossible and we take this opportunity to apologise to any copyright holders whose rights may have been unwittingly infringed.

LIST OF ABBREVIATIONS

A.H.R.	*American Historical Review*
A.R.	*Archiv für Reformationsgeschichte*
B.H.R.	*Bibliothèque d'Humanisme et Renaissance*
B.L.	British Library, London
B.N.	Bibliothèque nationale, Paris
B.S.H.P.F.	*Bulletin de la Société de l'histoire du protestantisme français*
C.S.P.F.	*Calendar of State Papers, Foreign Series, of the Reign of Queen Elizabeth*, 23 vols. (London, 1863–1950)
E.H.Q.	*European History Quarterly*
E.H.R.	*English Historical Review*
F.H.	*French History*
F.H.S.	*French Historical Studies*
H.	*History*
H.J.	*Historical Journal*
J.Ecc.H.	*Journal of Ecclesiastical History*
J.E.S.	*Journal of European Studies*
J.I.H.	*Journal of Interdisciplinary History*
J.M.H.	*Journal of Modern History*
P.H.S.L.	*Proceedings of the Huguenot Society of London*
P.& P.	*Past and Present*
P.R.O.	Public Record Office, London
P.W.S.F.H.	*Proceedings of the Western Society for French History*
R.H.	*Revue historique*
R.H.M.C.	*Revue d'histoire moderne et contemporaine*
R.Q.H.	*Revue des questions historiques*
R.S.	*Renaissance Studies*
S.C.J.	*Sixteenth Century Journal*
St.P.	*State Papers*, series of P.R.O.

INTRODUCTION

In April 1559 the long series of Habsburg–Valois wars between France and the Holy Roman Empire, which had been fought mainly in Italy and along France's north-east border, was brought to an end in the peace treaty of Cateau-Cambrésis. Both Henry II of France and Philip II of Spain needed a respite from war. They were running out of cash and Henry wanted to be free to deal with the growth of Protestantism in France. His most important duty as 'the Most Christian King' was to root out heresy from his kingdom. This was not only a religious obligation, but also a political one; for, in the sixteenth century, religious unity was regarded as essential to political unity. The principle of *cuius regio, eius religio*, which had been recently formulated at the Diet of Augsburg, underlined this belief by asserting that the prince determined the faith of his subjects.

The peace treaty was interpreted by many Frenchmen as a national humiliation, for France ceded most of her hard-won territorial gains in Italy. While Bresse, Savoy and Piedmont were handed back to the duke of Savoy, France retained only the small marquisate of Saluzzo and, for a time, five fortified places in Piedmont. Spain's rights to Milan and Naples were recognized and French fortresses in Lombardy were handed over to Spanish forces. In Tuscany, all French positions were ceded to the duke of Mantua or the duke of Florence. The peace was sealed by two marriages: one between the duke of Savoy and Henry's sister, Marguerite; the other, between Philip II and Henry's eldest daughter, Elizabeth.

On 30 June Henry II was fatally wounded in a tournament held in Paris as part of the celebrations for the two marriages. When the king died ten days later, his crown passed to his eldest son, Francis II, a sickly boy of fifteen, who was married to Mary Stuart, Queen of Scots. Although constitutionally old enough to rule, Francis lacked maturity of judgment and political experience. The government consequently passed into the hands of his mother, Catherine de' Medici, who had never been allowed much say in state affairs by her late husband. She relied for help on François, duc de Guise, and his brother, Charles, cardinal of Lorraine. The former was a brave soldier who had won fame by conquering Calais from the English and by successfully defending Metz against the emperor Charles V. His brother, the cardinal, was not only a leading churchman but also a wily politician and diplomat. Both were staunchly Catholic at a time when Protestantism was beginning to make significant headway in France. Excluded from the new administration was Anne de Montmorency, Constable of France, who had been Henry II's close friend and chief minister. As the richest landowner in France, however, he remained extremely powerful. Though he himself was a staunch Catholic, his three Châtillon nephews – Odet, Gaspard and François – became Protestants. Many Frenchmen questioned the right of the Guises to run the government, particularly as their family originated in the duchy of Lorraine, which had not yet become part of France. They believed that Antoine de Bourbon, king of Navarre, as first prince of the royal blood, had a better claim to administer the kingdom, but he was in Guyenne at the time of Henry II's death and took so long to reach the court that the Guises were able firmly to secure their position.

CHAPTER ONE

France around 1559

The kingdom of France in the mid sixteenth century covered an area of between 450,000 and 460,000 square kilometres. Though smaller than present-day France it was in contemporary terms a huge and diversified country which was not easy to administer.

The frontiers

Several territories, which are now part of France, lay outside its boundaries in the sixteenth century. In the north, Artois and Flanders belonged to the king of Spain. Calais, on the other hand, which had been English for centuries, had been reconquered for France by François, duc de Guise, in 1558. In the east, Alsace and Lorraine were part of the Holy Roman Empire. The city of Metz and the bishoprics of Metz and Toul were occupied by France. Franche-Comté remained imperial territory, but Charolais had reverted to France under the peace of Cateau-Cambrésis. Following this treaty the king of France retained only a few fortified places in Italy, including Pinerolo and the marquisate of Saluzzo. Within France there were still some foreign enclaves: the Comtat-Venaissin belonged to the Holy See, while the principality of Orange was ruled by the house of Nassau. In the south, Roussillon was Spanish, Béarn an independent principality and Navarre a separate kingdom.[1]

1 G. Zeller, *Les institutions de la France au XVIe siècle* (Paris, 1948), pp. 1–9.

The frontiers of France were less well defined than they are today. There was confusion in the area between France and the Empire, a situation which the inhabitants exploited to their own advantage by avoiding taxation from both sides.[2] A similar state of affairs existed in the area between Burgundy and Franche-Comté. But the kings of France had a pretty fair idea of where their jurisdiction lay. They showed this during their progresses through France by avoiding areas where any trespassing on their part might provoke a diplomatic incident. As from the second quarter of the century the kings possessed maps, which were useful if rudimentary. Speed of travel in the sixteenth century was calculated according to the number of days necessary to go from one place to another. In 1552 Henri Estienne published a guide book, *Le guide des chemins de France*, written by his son, Charles. It proved very popular and ran through many editions. It indicated major itineraries, stopping places, difficult roads and sites of interest. Such information had been garnered from merchants, pedlars and pilgrims. According to Estienne, France was '22 days' wide and '19 days' in length.[3] The time taken to cover one league (roughly four kilometres) depended, of course, on the method of travel.

A large number of people in France walked to wherever they were going. On average they covered between 20 and 30 kilometres in a day. But the favourite means of travel was the horse. Montaigne doubtless echoed a general opinion when he wrote in his *Essais*: 'Now I cannot put up for long with coach, litter or boat (and could do so less still in my youth). I loathe all means of conveyance but the horse, both for town and country.'[4] A horseman covered on average between 40 and 50 kilometres in a day. For people who preferred to be carried, various types of conveyance existed. During her grand tour of France in 1564–5, Queen Catherine de' Medici used a litter. Waggons and carts were mainly employed to transport merchandise. About the middle of the century, the coach was introduced into France from Italy. A suspension system consisting of straps attached to springs fixed to the chassis provided a measure of comfort for travellers. A coach travelled between 30 and 40 kilometres a day.[5]

Roads in sixteenth-century France were for the most part unpaved tracks which easily turned into quagmires in wet weather. They were also far from safe as they were targeted by brigands. Especially dangerous were roads

---

2 H. Stein and L. Legrand, *La frontière d'Argonne* (Paris, 1905).

3 C. Estienne, *Le guide des chemins de France de 1553*, ed. J. Bonnerot, 2 vols. (Paris, 1936); J. Boutier, A. Dewerpe and D. Nordman, *Un tour de France royal. Le voyage de Charles IX (1564–1566)* (Paris, 1984), pp. 15–16.

4 Montaigne, *Essais*, III. 6.

5 Boutier, Dewerpe and Nordman, *Un tour de France royal*, pp. 124–5.

that ran through forests, where an additional hazard was the presence of wolves. Rivers were often preferable to roads as a means of communication. Sailing boats and barges manned by oarsmen would be towed up inclines by teams of men or horses operating from towpaths. The average daily rate of travel downstream was between 35 and 65 kilometres and upstream 20 kilometres or less.[6]

Times of travel between Paris and other towns in France convey some idea of the country's apparent immensity in the sixteenth century. Thus it took two days to go on horseback from Paris to Amiens, eight to ten to Lyon and 16 to 20 to Marseille. One could travel faster by using the network of post-horses which had been set up in the fifteenth century. This allowed one to cover 90 kilometres in a day between Lyon to Roanne. Messengers bearing urgent letters or parcels could go faster still. The historian, Roland Mousnier, has tried to equate times of travel in sixteenth-century France with the present day. In his judgment a journey on an ordinary horse (not a post-horse) from Paris to Lyon in the sixteenth century would have been as long and tiring as a car journey between Paris and Moscow today.[7]

An awareness of these facts is necessary to an understanding of the problems faced by the royal administration in controlling a country as vast and diverse as was sixteenth-century France. In 1515 it had only some 5,000 officials to administer a population of about 16 million.[8] In an emergency decisions had to be taken on the spot, subject to their being approved later by the king, as communications were too slow to permit any other course of action. Thus the degree of autonomy enjoyed by a town or a province was not simply a legacy from a complex past; it was a necessity. Administrative centralization, which historians often take as the test of an absolute monarchy, was not possible in sixteenth-century France nor for some considerable time after.

In addition to being large, the kingdom of France contained territories of varying juridical status. The royal domain consisted of the lands owned by the king. The apanages were lands detached from the domain and given to the king's younger sons. They were transmissible by primogeniture but escheated to the crown in the absence of any male heir. Then there were large fiefs which were often the result of a marriage between two important noble houses. In the late sixteenth century, the most important was the

6 Ibid., pp. 120–23.
7 R. Mousnier, *Études sur la France de 1494 à 1559* (Cours de Sorbonne, Paris, 1964), pp. 9–13.
8 J. Jacquart, *François Ier* (Paris, 1981), pp. 282–3.

domain owned by Henri de Navarre in south-west France. A strange territory was the principality of Dombes, which had been confiscated from the Constable of Bourbon following his treason in 1523. It was returned to the duc de Montpensier in 1560. As prince, he could levy taxes and mint coins.

Population

No precise figure can be given for the population of France in the mid sixteenth century owing to the lack of comprehensive and reliable documentary evidence.[9] In the absence of any general census, the historian has to depend on a variety of sources, notably parish registers or tax returns, which are at best patchy. Even so, one can say with confidence that a steep rise in the population of France beginning in the late fifteenth century had largely made up the heavy losses sustained in the fourteenth century as a result of the Black Death and Hundred Years' War. But the rise was not continuous; it would level off from time to time before continuing its ascent. About 1560 it was about 18 million and larger than the population of any other European country. England, by contrast, had only about 4 million people. Of course, the density of France's population (between 35 and 40 people per square kilometre) varied from region to region.[10]

Several reasons have been adduced for the rising demographic curve: the absence of any great famine between 1470 and 1520; a lowering of the average age of marriage; a decline of infant mortality; the virtual disappearance of leprosy; fewer plague epidemics; and improved public hygiene in towns. Migration also played its part. After the Hundred Years' War, regions, such as the countryside around Bordeaux, which had been abandoned were repopulated. Peasants whose lives had been hit by bad harvests would often move to towns where they would swell the number of beggars or casual workers. Apprentices and servants would go to towns in search of employment. Such factors help to explain the growth of major towns in the sixteenth century. Lyon's population, for example, rose from around 20,000 in 1470 to 80,000 in the mid sixteenth century. The population of Paris went up from about 200,000 in the mid fourteenth century to about 300,000 in the mid sixteenth century. A document of 1538, distributing the cost of

9 P. Goubert, 'Recent theories and research on French population between 1500–1700', in D. V. Glass and D. E. C. Eversley (eds.), *Population in History* (London, 1965), pp. 56–73; F. Braudel, *The Identity of France*, vol. 2 (London, 1991), pp. 170–73.

10 B. Garnot, *La population française aux XVIe, XVIIe, XVIIIe siècles* (Gap, 1988); J. Dupâquier (ed.), *Histoire de la population française*; vol. 2: *De la Renaissance à 1789* (Paris, 1988).

infantry among the various towns in accordance with their ability to pay, enables us to rank them in order of size. After Paris were four towns (Rouen, Lyon, Toulouse and Orléans) of between 40,000 and 70,000 inhabitants; then perhaps a score of towns of between 10,000 and 30,000 inhabitants; then another forty or so between 5,000 and 10,000. Finally, there were many more small towns with fewer than 5,000 inhabitants.[11] It is often difficult to draw the line between a small town and a large village. A town was usually walled; it also had privileges and comprised a wider variety of occupational and social types than a village.

Contemporaries welcomed the rising population. Jean Bodin wrote in *Response aux paradoxes de M. de Malestroict* (1568): 'Another reason for the many blessings which have befallen us in the past 120 or 140 years is the infinite number of people which has multiplied in the kingdom since the end of the wars between the houses of Orléans and Burgundy; it has made us appreciate the delights of peace and enjoy its fruits over a long period and until the troubles over religion, for the foreign war which we have had since then has been only a purging of bad humours necessary to the whole state. Previously the countryside and to some extent the towns were abandoned [. . .] but in the last hundred years an infinite number of forests and moors have been reclaimed, many villages built, towns populated.'[12]

The economy

France was largely self-sufficient in basic necessities, grain being its principal product. Wine consumption increased significantly in the sixteenth century. Then, as now, it was produced not only for the home market but also for export. Major vineyards were developed along the Atlantic coast around Bordeaux, La Rochelle and the Basse-Loire. Salt, like wine, was produced for markets at home and abroad. For metal goods, France was largely dependent on foreign imports. As trade developed, no fewer than 344 markets and fairs were set up between 1483 and 1500. A fair was given privileges designed to attract foreign merchants. By 1500 most big towns and many smaller ones had fairs, the most famous being the four annual fairs of Lyon which drew many foreigners, especially Italians, Germans and Swiss. The fairs were also important in the history of banking. Banks first became important in France as agencies of credit and exchange in the

---

11 P. Benedict (ed.), *Cities and Social Change in Early Modern France* (London, 1989), pp. 8–10.

12 A. Jouanna, *La France du XVIe siècle, 1483–1598* (Paris, 1996), pp. 34–5. My translation.

fifteenth century. Bankers, mainly Italians, based themselves at Lyon because of the large amount of business transacted there, and threw out branches in other trading centres. Use of the bill of exchange almost eliminated the need to transport large amounts of cash, thereby minimizing the risks of interception. The Lyon fairs became a regular clearing house for the settlement of accounts. At the same time the bankers took money on deposit, lent it at interest and negotiated letters of credit. The crown was one of their major customers.[13]

French trade flourished in the sixteenth century. Though Marseille failed to wrest the monopoly of Levantine trade from Venice, it did establish useful links with parts of Italy, Spain and north Africa. Ports along the Atlantic coast and the Channel had a lively trade with England, Spain, the Netherlands and Scandinavia. As land communications were poor, harbours developed along France's navigable rivers, even far inland. Rouen was a major port used for international trade. The expansion of such trade was related to industrial growth. The most important French industry was cloth-making, which was mainly centred in the north. Most French cloth was of ordinary quality and cheap, though some luxury cloth was produced, mainly in Lyon. In order to satisfy the sophisticated taste of the court and nobility, luxury cloth also had to be imported from Italy and the Netherlands.[14] A major new industry which grew rapidly from the late fifteenth century was printing. By 1500 40 towns had presses, Paris alone boasting 75. The printers published books of many kinds for a wide clientèle, including university teachers and students, members of the clergy, magistrates and lawyers.[15] Printing was, of course, to play a leading role in the battle of minds that raged during the Reformation and the Wars of Religion.

Society

French society in the sixteenth century consisted mainly of peasants who lived in the kingdom's 30,000 villages. Each village had its own hierarchy. At the top was the lord or *seigneur*, who was usually, but not always, a nobleman, for a *seigneurie* could be purchased like any other piece of property.

13 R. Gascon, *Grand commerce et vie urbaine au XVIe siècle: Lyon et ses marchands* (Paris, 1971), vol. 1, pp. 240–63.

14 R. Boutruche, *Bordeaux de 1453 à 1715* (Bordeaux, 1966), pp. 113–38; P. Chaunu and R. Gascon, *Histoire économique et sociale de la France*, vol. 1 (1450–1660), pt. I, *L'état et la ville* (Paris, 1977), pp. 251–3.

15 L. Febvre and H.-J. Martin, *The Coming of the Book: The Impact of Printing* (London, 1986), pp. 170–77, 181–6.

It comprised a landed estate of variable size and a judicial area. The estate was usually divided into two parts: the domain, which included the seigneur's house and the tribunal as well as the lands and woods which he cultivated himself, and the *censives* or *tenures*, which he had entrusted in the past to peasants who cultivated them in return for obligations, called *redevances*. The main one was an annual rent, called *cens*. The seigneur usually retained the local mill, winepress and oven, expecting payment for their use. He took a proportion of any land sold, exchanged or inherited by a *censitaire*, and at harvest time exacted a sort of tithe, called *champart*. The seigneur also had judicial powers. He had usually surrendered his authority in criminal cases to the royal courts, but continued to judge civil suits through his *bailli* and other officials.[16]

Urban society was more varied, open and mobile than rural society. Contemporaries tended to divide it into two groups: the well-to-do (*aisés*) and the proletariat (*menu peuple*). But the reality was more complex. The well-to-do were themselves divided between merchants and office-holders. In towns, like Bordeaux and Toulouse, which were important centres of trade but also had parlements, the two groups were fairly evenly balanced; but in Lyon, where trade was all-important, merchants were pre-eminent. They lived in comfortable houses and added to the profits of their trade the revenues from their estates in the neighbouring countryside. A town's character was determined by its main activity. Trade was important to all towns, but some were also administrative, intellectual and ecclesiastical centres. Seven had parlements, about 50 were the capitals of *bailliages* or *sénéchaussées*, 15 had universities, about 110 were archiepiscopal or episcopal sees. Virtually the only industrial towns were Amiens (cloth) and Tours (silk). In towns which were primarily administrative centres, office-holders were preponderant. They were often as rich as merchants from whose ranks many of them had risen. The core of urban society was made up of artisans and small-to-middling merchants. They worked for themselves, served in the urban militia, paid taxes and took part in general assemblies of the commune, and owned enough property to guarantee their future security. Artisans were mainly of two kinds: those who employed large numbers of workmen and those who employed only members of their own family. The lower stratum of urban society, the *menu peuple*, consisted of manual workers, who were excluded from any share in local government. They included journeymen paid in money or money and kind, *manoeuvres* (paid by the day) and *gagne-deniers* (paid by the piece).[17]

16 P. Goubert, *L'ancien régime* (Paris, 1969), vol. 1, pp. 81–5.
17 Benedict (ed.), *Cities and Social Change*, pp. 11–17.

All Frenchmen in the sixteenth century were deemed to belong to one of three estates: the clergy, nobility and third estate, which were regarded as divinely ordained and fixed for all time. Each had its function, life-style and privileges, which were recognized by law and custom. Of the three estates, the easiest to define was the clergy, whose members had to be ordained or had at least taken minor orders. At the top of the clerical hierarchy were the archbishops, bishops, abbots and priors. Then came the canons of cathedrals and collegiate churches, and below them the vast mass of parish priests, unbeneficed clergy, monks, friars and nuns. In terms of wealth, the gulf separating the prelate from the parish priest or *curé* was wide. While the former often drew large landed revenues, the latter was often desperately poor. The secular clergy may have numbered some 100,000, including about 30,000 parish priests. The regular clergy cannot be quantified, but was obviously substantial. There were 600 Benedictine abbeys, 400 mendicant houses, more than 100 commanderies of St John and 60 charterhouses.[18]

The noble estate was widely envied for its prestige and life-style. The noble condition was identified with perfection while juridically and politically it implied a special status. The part played by the nobility in the Wars of Religion was so important that it is treated separately in Chapter 2. As for the third estate, it consisted of the bulk of France's population and represented widely different fortunes and occupations. Claude de Seyssel in his *La monarchie de France* (1519) drew a useful distinction, which remained valid half a century later, between middling people (*peuple moyen*) and lesser folk (*peuple menu*). The former were merchants and office-holders; the latter were people engaged in 'the cultivation of the land, the mechanical arts and other inferior crafts'.[19]

The mid-century crisis

The sixteenth century in France has been called 'the beautiful century', but it was only so for some people, usually at the top of the social pyramid. For many it was a time of worsening poverty. The activities of large gangs of vagabonds, who terrorized the countryside, loom large in contemporary chronicles and were the subject of several royal edicts and ordinances. The century also witnessed the introduction of new measures of poor

18 J. H. M. Salmon, *Society in Crisis: France in the Sixteenth Century* (London, 1975), pp. 79–83; Jacquart, *François Ier*, p. 67.

19 C. de Seyssel, *The Monarchy of France*, ed. D. R. Kelley (New Haven, Conn., 1981), pp. 60–62.

relief, notably municipal organizations, called *Bureaux des pauvres* or *Aumônes générales*.

A major reason for the increase in poverty was the impact made on rural society by the demographic explosion early in the century. This was not an unmixed blessing, for it seriously threatened the delicate balance between the food supply and the number of mouths needing to be fed. In the absence of technological improvements in arable farming, the food supply failed to cope with the rising demand. Some regions, such as Brittany, managed to survive better than others. But in general the impact of the rising population was negative. In order to meet the need for additional food, land was reclaimed and turned into arable, but all too often (notably in Languedoc) the soil was poor and the yield proved disappointing. Peasants were also tempted to turn pastures into arable. A static or declining stock of farm animals meant less manure and consequently a poorer yield. The diet of humble peasants, who had been used to eating meat in the fifteenth century, was consequently impoverished. The demographic upswing also had serious implications for landholding. As peasant holdings were subdivided among heirs they dwindled in size with the passing of each generation. Some local customs favoured the eldest son in the matter of inheritance, but the general trend was for the fragmentation of holdings. In time, many fell below the five hectares deemed essential as a guarantee of minimum self-sufficiency for a peasant household. Only a minority of peasants (estimated at between a quarter and a fifth of the entire peasant population) managed to stay above this minimum; the rest were forced to buy food at inflated prices which they could not afford. As many were driven to seek employment on other holdings, they faced a lowering of their wages. In the fifteenth century, when the labour market had been tight, employers had been forced to offer competitive wages, but the situation was now reversed. As would-be day-labourers and farm hands sought work, the big rural entrepreneurs offered them less favourable terms.[20]

Another reason for the growth of poverty was the so-called 'Price Revolution'. The sixteenth century was marked in Europe generally by a rise in prices which soon outstripped wages. In France this can be followed accurately as a result of the process of *mercuriale*, regular checks on the price of grain. Between the decades 1510–19 and 1540–49, the index figure rose for grain from 100 to 224 in Paris, to 200 in Lyon and to 173 in Toulouse. From 1558 to 1591 it rose to 481 for wheat and 530 for rye. The price of

20 G. Duby and A. Wallon (eds.), *Histoire de la France rurale*, vol. 2 (Paris, 1975), pp. 108–65; J. Jacquart, *La crise rurale en Île-de-France, 1450–1670* (Paris, 1974), pp. 41–50; F. Bayard and P. Guignet, *L'économie française aux XVIe, XVIIe et XVIIIe siècles* (Gap, 1991), pp. 89–98.

grain on the Paris market, which had gone up steadily from about 1525, accelerated after 1550 and reached a peak at the close of the century. About 1600 the average nominal price was five times as high as in 1520. Taking account of successive devaluations of the *livre*, this meant a trebling in real terms. Other goods followed the same trend. The reasons for the so-called Price Revolution were hotly debated by contemporaries. In regard to grain, of course, it could be the result of poor harvests. On the whole these were few and far between in the sixteenth century, though they got steadily worse from 1562. But, as goods generally were affected by the price rise, other factors were evidently involved. About 1560 the *Chambre des comptes* ordered an enquiry into the rising cost of commodities. Six years later M. de Malestroit argued in his *Remontrances et paradoxes . . . sur le fait des monnaies* that the rise was an illusion caused by the depreciation of the *livre*. This, however, was challenged by Jean Bodin in his *Response aux paradoxes de M. de Malestroict*. Prices, in his opinion, had truly risen. While recognizing the inflationary impact of the demographic explosion, he blamed principally the increased amount of money in circulation. Historians now believe that the Price Revolution had many causes, one of them being the importation of large quantities of bullion from the New World.[21]

Farmers were only better off as a result of the Price Revolution if their rents were fixed by custom, as they were in Languedoc. Elsewhere in France, notably in Poitou and the Île-de-France, they went up steadily from the start of the sixteenth century. About 1550 they reached a peak. Landownership consequently remained a worthwhile economic activity – hence the systematic purchase of rural estates by members of the urban bourgeoisie. Many rich bourgeois began to dominate the countryside around the towns where they lived. Owning land was a passport to social climbing; it enabled them to move out of the world of trade into that of office-holding, which itself might lead to the highest status of all, that of nobleman. While prices rose, nominal wages remained more or less fixed. Such a situation spelled poverty to the great mass of landless peasants while playing into the hands of the grain merchants. A harvester in Languedoc received as his wage 10 per cent of the yield in 1480, 9 per cent under Francis I and only 8.2 per cent under Henry II. Similarly in Poitou, a reaper, who would have received the equivalent of a hectolitre of wheat for five days' work in the fifteenth century, had to toil for two weeks in the sixteenth century to receive the same amount.[22]

---

21 Bayard and Guignet, *L'économie française*, pp. 93–8.
22 I. Cloulas, *Henri II* (Paris, 1985), p. 509.

Although some social unrest had occurred in the first half of the century, notably in Lyon in 1529 and in south-west France in 1544, it had been relatively limited in duration and extent. The situation changed significantly as the economy came under strain. Riots instigated by commoners broke out in many towns. Hunger was a common motive, but it was often tied to other causes. In 1542, for example, a ship being loaded in Rouen with grain for export was attacked by a group of townspeople. They were not all poor and 1542 was not a year of particular grain shortage. The riot was mainly caused by a war which had interrupted the town's trade with the Low Countries, causing unemployment among merchants and artisans. Three years later there was more trouble in Rouen when the *Bureau des pauvres* ran out of funds. A mob of 400 or 500 craftsmen surrounded the treasurer's home. A similar outbreak occurred in Tours in 1542 when the silk industry was paralysed by war. Food riots were not new, but a strike was an innovation. In 1539 the print-workers of Lyon went on strike over wages, working conditions and the closed shop. The strikers defied not only their employers but also the city's consuls and the king's representatives. Violence punctuated the stoppage, which lasted two years. A similar clash occurred in the Paris printing industry between 1531 and 1549.[23]

Inflation was a source of great embarrassment to the government. The military campaigns of Henry II, particularly his 'German voyage', proved hugely expensive and led to an escalation of the tax burden carried by his subjects. The *taille*, which had amounted to 4 million livres per annum under Francis I, rose to 6 million. In 1555 an additional tax, the *taillon*, raised to pay for troops, was levied for the first time on the countryside whereas previously only walled towns had been asked to pay it. Contributions were also exacted from social groups theoretically exempted from direct taxation. The nobility had to bear the cost of serving in the *arrière-ban*, which was summoned every year. Some lesser nobles faced ruin as they mortgaged their property and borrowed money at high rates of interest. The clergy were required to pay tenths. Four were levied each year from 1551 until 1558, totalling 1.6 million livres.[24] But all of this proved insufficient to meet the king's needs. Henry II vastly expanded the system of *Rentes sur l'Hôtel de Ville de Paris* which had been sparingly used under Francis I. He drew sums ranging from 550,000 to 860,000 livres a year from it. But the

---

23 H. Heller, *Iron and Blood: Civil Wars in Sixteenth-Century France* (Montreal and Kingston, 1991), pp. 5, 32–3.

24 Cloulas, *Henri II*, pp. 510–11.

crown looked for larger amounts which could be more speedily realized. Merchant bankers were ready to oblige. It drew from them enormous sums: 1.5 million livres in 1553, 2 million in 1554, another 1.5 million in 1555.

In 1555 a new system of borrowing was set up called the *Grand Parti de Lyon*. Whereas in the past various banks had offered the crown short-term loans independently of each other, they were now collectively offered a new kind of long-term contract. In return for a loan of 3.4 million livres at a rate of interest of 16 per cent, the bankers were promised reimbursements of 5 per cent (i.e. 4 per cent interest plus 1 per cent amortizing of the capital) four times a year, at each of Lyon's fairs, over a period of more than ten years. The revenues of three *généralités* were earmarked for the repayments. The *Grand Parti* proved such a success at first that many private people invested in it. However, success depended in the long term on the king exercising fiscal restraint; but he soon raised new loans and incorporated them in the *Grand Parti*. His overall debt consequently rose to almost 9.7 million livres so that he now had to reimburse more than 2 million livres per annum. By 1558 his loans exceeded 13.2 million livres and the payment due each year rose above 2.6 million livres. To make matters worse, the market value of gold tumbled as silver from the New World flooded into Europe. Greedy as ever, the Lyon bankers asked the king to reimburse them in overvalued gold while obliging him to take his loans in depreciated silver. Soon the crown was unable to meet its obligations under the *Grand Parti*. By April 1557 it had defaulted on two repayments. As confidence collapsed, the king found it harder to raise new loans. In 1557 it took another knock when Philip II defaulted on his financial obligations. Henry II tried to reassure his own creditors, but in November 1557 he failed to pay the eighth instalment due to them. In defiance of the original contract, Henry promised that future payments would come from the treasurer of the *Épargne*. In February 1558 his situation was aggravated by the cost of reconquering Calais. In 1559, as peace talks got underway at Cateau-Cambrésis, the Lyon bankers made further loans to the king. The crown's debt stood at around 12 million livres when the king was accidentally killed. This effectively marked the end of the *Grand Parti*. Interest payments ceased for a time and part of the crown's debt was only paid off in devalued money over three decades. While the banks salvaged what they could from the wreckage, many private investors went to the wall.[25]

25 Cloulas, *Henri II*, pp. 512–20; M. Wolfe, *The Fiscal System of Renaissance France* (New Haven, Conn., 1972), pp. 109–13; F. J. Baumgartner, *France in the Sixteenth Century* (London, 1995), pp. 128–9.

Government

By the sixteenth century the law regulating the succession to the throne of France was well established. The king succeeded immediately following the death of his predecessor; he did not have to wait to be crowned. Yet the *sacre*, as the coronation ceremony was called, continued to have great symbolic significance: it affirmed the king's role as God's lieutenant on earth and his close alliance with the Gallican church. During the ceremony, the king took an oath: first, he promised to protect the church's privileges and to defend each bishop and his church; and secondly, he undertook to promote peace in Christendom, to protect Christians against injustice and iniquity, to dispense justice fairly and mercifully, and to expel heretics from his dominions. The oath was followed by the king's anointing with a sacred chrism, which had allegedly been brought down from heaven by a dove at the time of Clovis' baptism in AD 496. The chrism (kept in a vessel called the Holy Ampulla) conferred on the king a semi-priestly character. He received communion in both kinds, like a priest, and was deemed able to heal victims of scrofula by touching them. Royal propagandists claimed that a special blood – clear, transparent and luminous – flowed through the veins of the king of France, who bore the title of 'Most Christian King'.[26]

The court of France, which comprised the king's household, the separate households of members of his family and an amorphous mass of hangers-on, remained nomadic in the sixteenth century, as it had been for centuries. The court was as large as a medium-sized town and fitted more easily into a rural setting than an urban one. Hunting was a favourite pastime of the court in peacetime, and the king liked to look for game in various forests. He also felt the need to know his kingdom at first hand and to be seen by his subjects. As the kingdom grew larger over the centuries, so the court moved more widely. For accommodation it used châteaux which were situated mainly in the valley of the Loire or in the Paris region. Elsewhere, it would put up in the homes of noblemen, religious houses or inns. The presence of the court was not always welcome, for its members sometimes misbehaved and prices of food and drink invariably rose as the court used up local stocks.[27] Whenever the king visited a town for the first time, he was

---

26 R. A. Jackson, *Vive le Roi! A History of the French Coronation from Charles V to Charles X* (Chapel Hill, 1984), pp. 31–3, 57–9; C. Beaune, *The Birth of an Ideology: Myths and Symbols of Nation in Late-Medieval France* (Berkeley, Cal., 1991), pp. 172–93; M. Bloch, *Les rois thaumaturges* (Paris, 1961), p. 224.

27 G. Zeller, *Les institutions de la France*, pp. 94–109; J.-F. Solnon, *La cour de France* (Paris, 1987), pp. 51–73; R. J. Knecht, *Renaissance Warrior and Patron: The Reign of Francis I* (Cambridge, 1994), pp. 117–33.

given an entry. He was met outside the town by the leading citizens and, after confirming their privileges and receiving the town's keys, he would ride through it in procession under a rich canopy. Roadside theatricals and sometimes temporary monuments, often bearing inscriptions and symbols praising the monarch, would punctuate the route leading to the main church, where the king would attend a service followed by a banquet.[28]

At the heart of the government was the king's council, which continued to follow the monarch on his travels about France. In theory it comprised the princes of the blood, the peers of the realm and the great officers of state, but, in practice, admission to the council was by royal invitation. In its widest form (*conseil d'état*) there might be as many as 20 members, but there was also an inner ring (*conseil des affaires* or *conseil secret*) consisting of the king's close friends and advisers whom he would consult on matters of special importance or requiring secrecy. As yet there was no specialization among the council's members. Part of its judicial business, however, had been transferred to the *Grand Conseil*, a tribunal of fixed membership, which like the council itself, continued to follow the king on his travels and was, therefore, susceptible to his influence. Financial technicalities also tended to be left to fiscal officials.[29]

The body responsible for turning royal decisions into laws was the chancery, headed by the Chancellor of France. Its staff of notaries and secretaries drew up enactments and had them sealed by the chancellor but, as government business increased, many conciliar decisions took the form of briefs (*brevets*) requiring only the signature of a notary or secretary to be valid. Since the king or his chancellor could not keep tabs on everything, a fair number of decrees (*arrêts*) issued 'by the king and his council' were drawn up by the masters of requests (*maîtres des requêtes de l'hôtel*).[30] Some secretaries enjoyed the king's special confidence. Known as *secrétaires des finances*, they were entrusted with the drafting of particularly important and confidential documents, and often gave evidence to the king's council. In April 1547 Henry II formally shared out government business among four *secrétaires des finances*, who were soon accorded the title of secretary of state (*secrétaire d'état*) to distinguish them from other royal notaries and secretaries.[31]

The basic unit of local government in France was the *bailliage* (sometimes called *sénéchaussée*). The kingdom comprised about 100 such units, which

---

28 J. Chartrou, *Les entrées solennelles et triomphales à la Renaissance (1484–1551)* (Paris, 1928); L. M. Bryant, *The King and the City in the Parisian Royal Entry Ceremony: Politics, Ritual and Art in the Renaissance* (Geneva, 1986).

29 Jouanna, *La France du XVIe siècle*, pp. 189–92.

30 M. Etchechourry, *Les maîtres des requêtes de l'hôtel du roi sous les derniers Valois* (Paris, 1991)

31 N. M. Sutherland, *The French Secretaries of State in the Age of Catherine de Medici* (London

could vary enormously in size. The official in charge of a *bailliage*, namely the *bailli* (or *sénéchal*), had purely honorary or military duties (he summoned the feudal levy, called *ban et l'arrière-ban*), but the tribunal of the *bailliage*, under his deputy or *lieutenant* and his staff, judged lawsuits sent up from inferior courts and, in the first instance, cases concerning privileged people and *cas royaux* (crimes against the king's person, rights and domain). The *bailliages* also published royal statutes and issued decrees of their own.[32] Above them were the *parlements*, of which there were eight in 1559. The oldest and most prestigious was the Parlement of Paris. Originally part of the king's court (*Curia Regis*), it had 'gone out of court' in the thirteenth century and had become fixed in Paris in the old royal palace on the Île-de-la-Cité. Though physically separate from the king's council, it was still regarded as part of it. Thus France had, in a sense, two capitals: the court, which remained nomadic and Paris, where the Parlement and other so-called 'sovereign courts' had become fixed.[33]

The Parlement, unlike the English parliament, was not a representative body: it was the highest court of law under the king, and its members (called 'councillors') were magistrates. Drawing a distinction between the ideal sovereign and the human being who actually occupied the throne, the Parlement saw its role as protecting the ideal king from the errors that the human king might commit. Its magistrates liked to compare themselves to the senators of ancient Rome. Originally the Parlement's area of jurisdiction (*ressort*) had been the whole kingdom, but as this had been enlarged, seven provincial parlements (Rouen, Bordeaux, Rennes, Toulouse, Grenoble, Aix, and Dijon) had been created. But the Parlement of Paris was responsible for the whole of France, excluding Brittany and Normandy, as far south as the Lyonnais and Upper Auvergne. Within this area it judged lawsuits in first instance and on appeal. It also regulated public hygiene, the upkeep of roads and bridges, ensured that Paris received enough grain and fuel, controlled the quality, weight and price of bread, fixed wages and hours of work, punished shoddy workmanship and intervened in academic matters. The Parlement also controlled the book trade. Not even the church escaped its vigilance: no papal bull was valid in France unless it had first been registered by the Parlement. The court also kept an eye on the conduct of royal officials in the provinces. Finally, the Parlement had the right to scrutinize royal legislation. If it was found to be satisfactory, it would be

32 R. Doucet, *Les institutions de la France au XVIe siècle*, vol. 1, pp. 251–64; Zeller, *Les institutions de la France*, pp. 167–75.

33 Doucet, *Les institutions de la France*, vol. 1, pp. 211–17; Zeller, *Les institutions de la France*, pp. 147–63.

registered without demur; if not, the Parlement submitted objections, called *remontrances*, to the king. He might accept them and amend the proposed legislation accordingly, or he might refuse and insist in a *lettre de jussion* on the law being registered as it stood. Such a move might lead to more remonstrances and more *lettres de jussion.* In the end, if the Parlement proved stubborn, the king would hold a *lit de justice*, that is to say, he would resume the authority he had delegated to the Parlement by attending in person and presiding himself over the registration of the controversial measure. No royal law was deemed valid until it had been so endorsed. Each parlement was sovereign within its own area in respect of registering royal enactments: thus a law registered in the Parlement of Paris could not be applied in Languedoc unless it had also the endorsement of the Parlement of Toulouse.[34]

In January 1552 Henry II introduced a new tier of jurisdiction between the *bailliages* and the parlements. This consisted of 61 courts, called *présidiaux*, each with a staff of nine. They were distributed unevenly in the jurisdictional areas of five parlements, their purpose being ostensibly to save litigants time and money by freeing them from the need to undertake long and costly journeys to the parlements. Their true purpose, however, was to bring more cash into the royal treasury by putting another 500 offices up for sale. The parlements did not welcome a change which took away part of their business and profits, and the *présidiaux* never succeeded in establishing themselves firmly within the judicial hierarchy.[35]

An exalted figure in French local government was the provincial governor. There were 11 governorships (*gouvernements*) corresponding roughly to the kingdom's border provinces. The governors were normally recruited from princes of the blood and high nobility. Although closely identified with the king's own person and authority, the governor was never more than a commissioner revocable at the king's pleasure. His powers, as defined in his letters of provision, were never clearly defined. While his military duties (see below p. 37) were usually stressed, there was also often a clause open to a wide interpretation. It could amount to a general delegation of royal authority, but there was no uniformity in the commissions of governors. As a governor was often at court or fighting for the king, he seldom resided in his province. His local duties consequently devolved on a deputy, called *lieutenant*, who was commonly a lesser noble or churchman. But even an absent governor could do much for his province by ensuring that its affairs received attention from the king's council.

34 E. Maugis, *Histoire du Parlement de Paris*, 3 vols. (Paris, 1913–16); J. H. Shennan, *The Parlement of Paris*, revised edn (London, 1998).

35 Cloulas, *Henri II*, pp. 314–15.

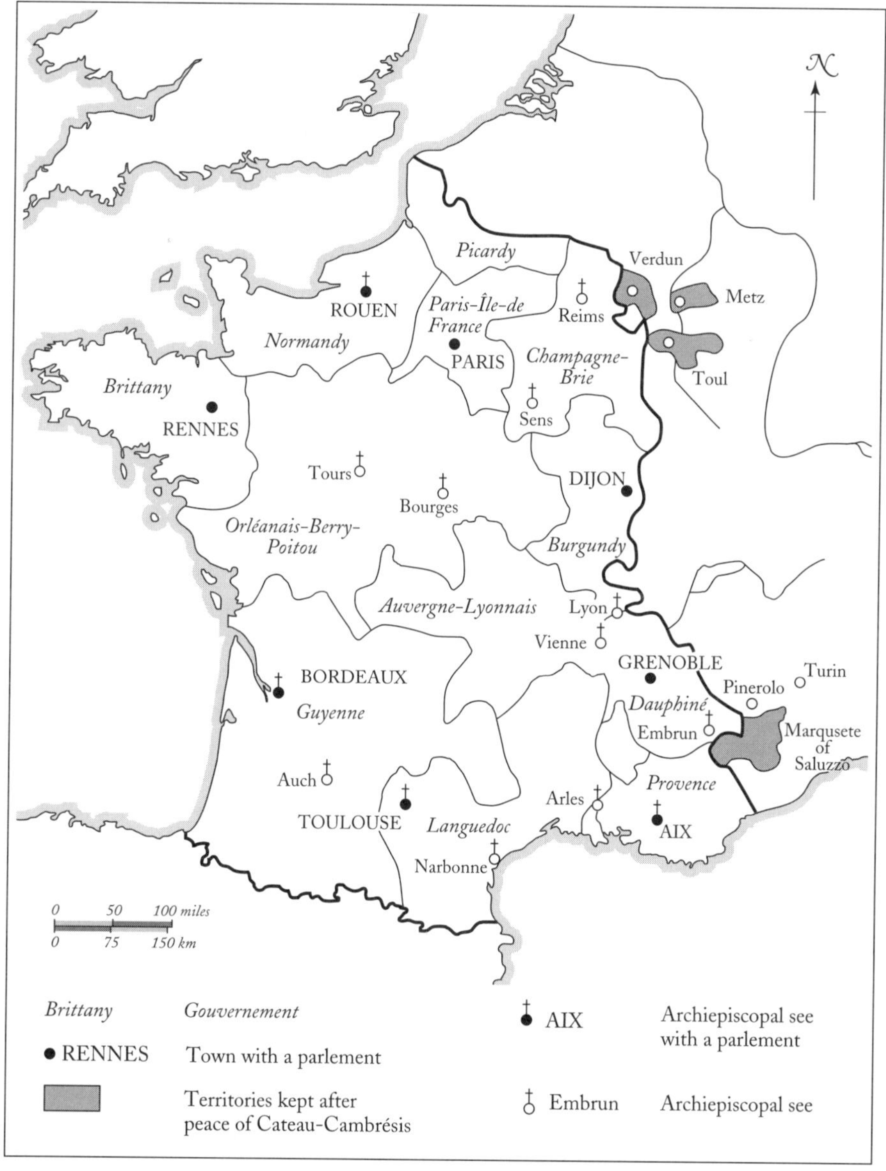

Map 1 *Gouvernements* in 1559, parlements, archbishoprics
Source: A. Jouanna, *La France du XVIe siècle, 1483–1598* (Paris, 1996).

A governor would often use his influence with the king to build up a powerful provincial clientèle. This comprised three elements: the regular army (*compagnies d'ordonnance*), household officers and servants, and local gentlemen. A governor did not have to be a captain of the heavy cavalry or *gendarmerie*, but usually was. Though officially in the king's service and paid out of his treasury, the companies were tied to their captains, who controlled their recruitment and promotion within their ranks. He would also have a large private household capable of providing employment to local noblemen and an education for their children. All of this clearly constituted a potential danger to the crown. A governor might use his personal following within his province to undermine royal authority.[36]

Taxation

Royal revenues were of two kinds: 'ordinary' and 'extraordinary'. The ordinary revenue – that which the king drew from his domain – comprised not only feudal rents, which were fixed and predictable, but a wide range of variable dues. The extraordinary revenue comprised three main taxes: the *taille*, the *gabelle*, and the *aides*. The *taille* was the only direct tax. It was levied annually, the amount being determined by the king's council. The *taille* was of two kinds: the *taille réelle* – a land tax payable by all, irrespective of social rank – and the *taille personnelle*, which fell mainly on land owned by unprivileged commoners. Though fairer, the *taille réelle* was found in only a few areas, notably Provence and Languedoc. Many people were exempt from the *taille*: not only the clergy and the nobility, but many professional groups and entire towns as well. Paris, for example, which was by far the richest town in the kingdom, was exempt. Because of these exemptions, the heaviest burden of the *taille* fell on the peasantry, the class least able to pay. The *gabelle*, a tax on salt, was levied differently in various parts of France and some regions were exempt. Francis I had planned a complete overhaul of salt taxes in France, but nothing was done till 1548 when Henry II ordered the plan to be given effect. The result was a serious revolt in south-west France, which was mercilessly crushed. The *aides* were levied on various commodities sold regularly and in large quantities (e.g. wine, livestock), but indirect taxation, like the *taille*, was subject to local variations. Several parts of France were exempt from it.

---

36 R. R. Harding, *Anatomy of a Power Elite: The Provincial Governors of Early Modern France* (New Haven, Conn., 1978).

Under Henry II taxation rose steeply. The *taille*, which had averaged 4 million livres since 1542 rose to almost 6.8 million livres in 1558. The total of all taxes, including clerical taxes and indirect taxes, which was under 5.2 million livres in 1523, exceeded 13.5 million under Henry II.[37]

The fiscal administration, which had remained virtually the same since the reign of Charles VII, underwent important changes under Francis I. It consisted originally of two administrations corresponding with the two main types of revenue, 'ordinary' and 'extraordinary'. Four *trésoriers de France* supervised the collection and disbursement of 'ordinary' revenues, while four *généraux des finances* had charge of the 'extraordinary' revenues, each being responsible for an area, called a *généralité*, which was itself sub-divided into *élections* under officials, called *élus*. The personnel responsible for administering the *gabelle* varied according to the different kinds of salt tax. Under Francis I, serious efforts were made to clean up the fiscal system and to improve its efficiency. Officials suspected of corruption were put on trial and some were severely punished. At the same time a measure of centralization was introduced with the creation of the *Trésor de l'Épargne* with powers to collect and disburse all royal revenues save those from the domain and from regular taxation. Later, the *trésorier* was given charge only of revenues from the domain and from taxation, while another official, called *Receveur des parties casuelles* was made responsible for the rest. An effect of these reforms was to undermine the power of the *trésoriers de France* and *généraux des finances*. They continued to carry out tours of inspection, but policy-making was left firmly in the hands of the king and his council. In 1532 it was decided that the coffers in which the *Trésorier de l'Épargne* kept his cash should no longer follow the court but should remain at the Louvre in Paris, but the new law was not strictly applied. In 1542 the four large *généralités* into which the old royal domain had been divided were sub-divided into 12 smaller districts called *recettes-générales*, each under a *receveur-général*, who had powers to collect all regular revenues. This amounted to the fusion of the old 'ordinary' and 'extraordinary' revenues.[38]

The army

On 8 August 1558 Henry II inspected his army at Pierrepont in Picardy. For three hours he walked through the ranks of 29,000 infantry and 11,000

---

37 Wolfe, *The Fiscal System of Renaissance France*, pp. 304–65.

38 P. Hamon, *L'argent du roi: les finances sous François Ier* (Paris, 1994), pp. 252–63, 267–75, 293–302.

cavalry. The occasion was also marked by a great display of firepower. 'Even more admired,' writes Rabutin, 'were . . . the thunder and roar of the artillery as well as the discharges of the arquebuses and the pistol volleys of the reiters. It seemed as if the heavens and the earth were exploding . . . or that the Almighty wanted . . . to blast the entire globe.'[39] Few European rulers could have put on such a display of military might, yet, as James Wood points out, the event also pointed to some grave weaknesses in the French army. In the first place, it was hardly French at all, for more than 70 per cent of the troops were foreign mercenaries: 8,000 German cavalry and 20,000 Swiss and German infantry. Their presence was in part a reflection of the crown's failure, despite several attempts, to set up a permanent native infantry. Secondly, the army was largely an *ad hoc* and temporary agglomeration of units. Many were unknown to each other, nor had they been trained together. Thirdly, the crown lacked the necessary resources to replenish the army as it suffered losses through fighting, disease or desertion. Nor could it keep the army at full strength in peacetime. When a campaign ended, a large part of the army had to be disbanded.[40]

The peacetime army was quite small. Its permanent core was the gendarmerie or heavy cavalry, which was organized in companies, called *compagnies d'ordonnance*, each comprising a number of *lances*. A *lance* consisted of a man-at-arms with four horses, two archers with two horses each, and two pages. The number of *lances* in a company varied with the social status of its commanding officer. Exceptionally a company could have 100 men, but 40 was the norm. The man-at-arms and his mount wore complete suits of armour, while the archers, who acted as scouts and skirmishers, were more lightly armoured: they wore a breastplate and an open helmet. The lance was the principal weapon, though during the 1550s most companies began to have 50 mounted arquebusiers attached to them. The equipment of a man-at-arms and that of an archer has been estimated as worth 700 livres and 400 livres respectively. Particularly expensive were the horses, which were commonly thoroughbreds imported from Spain, Denmark or Italy. A man had to be rich to serve in the gendarmerie.

Captains of companies were all members of the high nobility, while the men-at-arms and archers were mostly drawn from lower reaches of the same class. Command of a company was much sought after as it offered not only prestige but excellent opportunities for dispensing patronage and thereby creating an ever wider clientèle. For a captain, who was himself chosen by

39 F. Lot, *Recherches sur les effectifs des armées françaises des Guerres d'Italie aux Guerres de Religion, 1494–1562* (Paris, 1962), p. 179.

40 J. B. Wood, *The King's Army* (Cambridge, 1996), pp. 41–2.

the king, picked his own subordinates from among his kinsmen, neighbours, friends and clients who wore his livery. Although a captaincy was not hereditary, it often passed down from father to son. Each company included a number of officers, headed by the lieutenant who assumed command in the captain's absence.

The gendarmerie was quartered in garrison towns. These were mainly in frontier provinces for it was assumed that 'the army was not needed primarily to enforce domestic tranquility but rather was essentially a dynastic instrument to be used in adventures abroad and to defend France from foreign invasion'.[41] Leave was granted by order of seniority and in strict rotation to a quarter of the men at a time. They were paid out of taxation at musters held every three months under the supervision of royal commissioners and a treasurer. By 1549 the standard pay for a man-at-arms was 15 livres and for an archer 7 livres 10 sous, but higher payments of 20 livres and 10 livres respectively were introduced for a quarter of the men-at-arms and two-thirds of the archers in the 1540s. Until 1548 towns were meant to support the garrisons, but this became a serious cause of friction between the garrisons and the inhabitants. So in 1549 a new tax, called *taillon*, which spread the burden to all the kingdom, was created to support the gendarmerie, which was henceforth expected to pay for its food and fodder.

At the end of a war, companies were usually reduced for economic reasons. Thus, in 1559 Francis II slashed the gendarmerie from 8,800 men to 6,275, thereby relieving the royal budget of 700,000 livres per annum. Almost every company was cut down in size. Normally the crown maintained between 64 and 69 companies in peacetime or about 2,500 to 2,800 *lances* representing between 6,275 and 7,100 men. The companies were widely dispersed, albeit unevenly. They were more numerous north than south of the Loire. When a war began, provincial governors would order captains to gather their men within a fortnight and to bring them to a muster where they might be counted and paid. Locating them was not always easy, and the crown always suspected the accuracy of muster rolls.[42]

The army also comprised companies of two kinds of light cavalry though few of these were maintained in peacetime.The *chevau-légers* were noblemen who, for some reason, had not found a place in the gendarmerie. Though more lightly armoured than the men-at-arms, they were expected to serve as battle cavalry. They were organized in companies of 100 men each,

---

41 J. B. Wood, 'The royal army during the early Wars of Religion, 1559–1576', in M. P. Holt (ed.), *Society and Institutions in Early Modern France* (Athens, Ga., 1991), p. 2.

42 Ibid., pp. 44–7; D. Potter, *War and Government in the French Provinces. Picardy, 1470–1560* (Cambridge, 1993), pp. 158–66.

forming a single tactical regiment under a colonel-general. The *arquebusiers à cheval* were mounted infantry equipped with arquebuses. They rode into action but dismounted to fire their weapons. Arquebuses were still rather primitive weapons. Their rate of fire was very slow (about 20 minutes between shots) and they could not be used in the rain. Arquebusiers served in units of 50 as scouts, escorts and as mobile garrison troops.[43]

By the mid sixteenth century the main French infantry were the so-called 'old' and 'new' bands, each of 300 men. The 'old' bands were based in Picardy and Piedmont and kept on a permanent footing, unlike the 'new' bands, also called *aventuriers*, who only served in wartime. The 'old' and 'new' bands were recruited mainly from the peasantry. When they were needed blank commissions were sent out to provincial governors, who distributed them to known captains who would round up the men. Musters were held as in the case of the gendarmerie. When disbanded following a peace treaty, the *aventuriers* often became a social plague as they fed off the countryside and terrorized villagers. Many royal edicts laid down draconian, yet ineffective, measures for their suppression. An infantryman was paid 5 livres per month, though provision existed for selective double-pay. Infantry with firearms were paid 6 livres. Officers, of course, were paid considerably more. A captain received 106 livres.

The French infantry was organized in two commands, one based in Calais and the other in Pinerolo, each under a colonel-general. François, duc de Guise set up the first regiments. Each of the first three contained 12 companies of 200 men. Each regiment was commanded by a camp master (*maître de camp*), a sergeant-major and a camp marshal. The role of the camp master was to pass on the orders of the colonel-general to the captains. The sergeant-major was mainly responsible for training and discipline. There was also a small provostial and medical staff. Except for the colonels-general, who were high-ranking nobles, the captains were nearly all drawn from the lesser nobility. As from 1547 the infantry as a whole came under a single colonel-general.[44]

Foreign mercenaries formed a high proportion of the French infantry in wartime. The Swiss were excellent soldiers – brave, well-disciplined and tough – but they expected to be paid in full and regularly; otherwise they were likely to go on strike or to leave for home. Their equipment and organization also limited their usefulness on the battlefield. Almost nine out of ten were still armed with pikes and only a few wore protective armour. They were commonly relegated to guarding the artillery and trenches.

---

43 Potter, *War and Government*, pp. 167–8.

44 Ibid., pp. 168–73; Wood, *The King's Army*, pp. 47–51.

Almost as a matter of course they refused to storm breaches, although some were willing to serve as pioneers for extra pay. The French crown also employed German *landsknechts*. Surviving contracts, called *capitulations*, show how the troops were raised. A colonel, who received a pension from the French king, contacted a number of captains, who gathered troops and paid them in advance, usually for three months. The *landsknechts* were normally assembled in *bandes* or *enseignes* of 300 men. They were valued as shock troops but considered useless in sieges. They also acquired a bad name on account of their drunkenness and brutality. Brantôme describes them as 'much given to mutiny . . . great ravagers and dissipators'.[45] Not all the foreign mercenaries were infantry. From the reign of Henry II onwards the Germans sent cavalry armed with flintlock pistols. Known as *reiters*, they developed a tactic called the caracole. They would ride up to an enemy line, discharge their pistols and wheel around thereby leaving the way clear for a second wave of *reiters* to do likewise. But like the *landsknechts* they were notoriously undisciplined.[46]

The French artillery was perhaps the best in Europe. It comprised six types of guns: the cannon, great culverin, *bastarde*, *moyenne*, *faucon* and *fauconneau*. Only the first four were serviceable in the field and only the first two in siege work. Assembling an artillery train was determined by the number and size of the guns. The heavier the gun, the more men and horses were needed to man it and the higher the poundage of shot and powder required. One thousand rounds from a cannon used up 32,000 pounds of iron shot and 20,000 pounds of powder. The artillery was based mainly near the kingdom's northern frontier and in Paris where the staff of the Arsenal was headed by the Grand Master of the artillery, who was always a great nobleman. His subordinate officers were also noblemen, while the skilled workers, who looked after the artillery, and the gunners were Parisian artisans. When an artillery train was being assembled many other people were recruited for service, notably teamsters and pioneers who were not regarded as part of the army. The teamsters, who transported the guns and munitions, were mostly peasants from the provinces, while the pioneers were the army's riff-raff, poorly paid and much despised. They were formed into work-gangs of 200 or less under officers provided by the arsenal and their duties included mending potholes, assisting the movement of the guns and waggons when the going was rough, carrying munitions, putting up camps and gun emplacements, digging trenches and mining enemy fortifications. Their tasks were often extremely dangerous as they

45 Brantôme, *Oeuvres*, vol. 6 (Paris, 1873), p. 224.
46 Potter, *War and Government*, pp. 177–9; Wood, *The King's Army*, pp. 103–4, 111.

were given little protection from enemy fire. Not surprisingly, many preferred to desert.[47]

The commander-in-chief of the army was the king of France and in his absence the Constable of France. This office was held by Anne de Montmorency until his death in 1567. It was then left vacant for 30 years. The king or the Constable could delegate his authority to the Marshals of France, who were three in number under Henry II. More were appointed later. Their main responsibility was to enforce discipline and they were supposed to carry out tours of inspection, each in a third of the kingdom. They were assisted by provosts (*prévôts des maréchaux*), each with a team of subordinates. Anyone, other than the king, who commanded the army was given the title of the king's lieutenant-general (*lieutenant-général pour le roi*). The camp marshal (*maréchal de camp*) was a senior officer who assigned a place to each man when a camp was being set up. He was, in effect, the commander's principal lieutenant. The quartermaster (*maréchal des logis*) saw to the billeting of the troops with the assistance of several *fourriers*. The lieutenant-general and camp marshals dealt directly with the cavalry and infantry captains.[48]

The nature of monarchy

Historians are divided about the precise nature of French monarchy in the sixteenth century. Some see it as the first stage in the march towards the absolutism that reached its zenith under Louis XIV; others stress the limits upon its power exercised by rights and privileges surviving from its medieval past.[49] In the sixteenth century two schools of thought existed. The first, which was broadly humanistic, was represented by Claude de Seyssel's treatise, *La monarchie de France* (1515). He admired the French kings above all others because of their alleged willingness to accept three curbs (*freins*) on their authority: religion, justice and *police*.[50] The last of these meant the body of past royal ordinances as registered by the Parlement. The other school of thought, characteristic of the royal jurists, was represented by Guillaume Budé's *L'institution du prince* (1519). This argued that princes,

47 Wood, *The King's Army*, pp. 51–2, 153–83.

48 Zeller, *Les institutions de la France*, pp. 120–1, 127–9.

49 G. Pagès, *La monarchie d'Ancien Régime en France* (Paris, 1946), p. 3; J. Russell Major, *Representative Institutions in Renaissance France, 1421–1559* (Madison, Wis., 1960), pp. 3–20, 121–44.

50 C. de Seyssel, *The Monarchy of France*, pp. 82–95.

being 'perfect in prudence and nobility' stood above all other men; they owed obedience to no man and were bound by no written laws.[51]

Francis I and Henry II certainly saw themselves as 'absolute' monarchs who were responsible to no one save God. This was conceded by Charles Guillart, a president of the Parlement of Paris, in a famous speech delivered before the king in July 1527. 'We do not wish to call into question or to challenge your authority,' he declared. 'This would be a kind of sacrilege and we are well aware that you are above the laws and that laws and ordinances cannot constrain you.' But, he added: 'We wish to say that you do not wish or should not wish to do all that is in your power, but only that which is good and equitable, which is nothing other than justice.'[52] What seems abundantly clear is that political theory made little impact, if any, on the exercise of royal power. Such constraints on it as existed were structural, not theoretical; they pertained to the fabric of the state. The government of France was still evolving institutionally. Its personnel was numerically very small as compared with the population of France: perhaps 5,000 officials for about 18 million people. The standing army was also minute. Thus the king was obliged to rely heavily on the services of his more powerful subjects, namely the nobility which collectively disposed of a considerable military strength. The king also depended on the loyalty and goodwill of his subjects generally. He expected them to meet his demands for supply without which government would be forced to a standstill.

The monarchy felt sufficiently strong in the first half of the sixteenth century to dispense with the Estates-General, the only national body representing all three estates. They were suspended between 1484 and 1560, when a financial and constitutional crisis precipitated their recall. Meetings of one or two estates – usually called Assemblies of Notables – did meet occasionally, but mainly for propaganda reasons. Popular consultation survived, however, in many provinces, called *pays d'états*, in the form of local estates. But they depended on the king for their existence: he called them, fixed the date and place of their meeting, appointed their president and determined their agenda. Meeting at least once a year, the provincial estates did more than vote taxes requested by the king. For example, they raised troops, repaired fortifications, built hospitals and engaged in poor relief.[53]

The greatest constraint on royal power was financial. With a tax system that was riddled with anomalies and exemptions and an inefficient or corrupt

51 C. Bontems, L.-P. Raybaud and J.-P. Brancourt, *Le prince dans la France des XVIe et XVIIe siècles* (Paris, 1965), p. 80.

52 R. J. Knecht, 'Francis I and the *lit de justice*: a "legend" defended', *French History*, 7 (1993), pp. 53–83.

53 J. Russell Major, *Representative Government in Early Modern France* (New Haven, Conn., 1980).

fiscal administration, the king never had enough money to meet his obligations. War was becoming more expensive by the day as its technology progressed; artillery and fortifications were particularly expensive. In the absence of a large national infantry, foreign mercenaries needed to be hired and they did not come cheap. Since the traditional sources of revenue were inadequate, the king had to resort to expedients: he would sell public offices, alienate parts of the royal domain, confiscate the property of convicted criminals and borrow from merchant bankers. Though remunerative in the short term, expedients could also entail serious disadvantages in the long term. The sale of offices, for instance, encouraged their proliferation purely for profit. Nor could their purchasers be relied upon to carry out the public duties that were attached to them.[54] In time, this was to undermine royal authority. Borrowing was also a mixed blessing. In 1547 Francis I owed the bankers of Lyon as much as the entire income for that year. Henry II promptly paid off the debt, yet at the end of 1548 the debt stood at over 2.4 million livres.[55]

54 R. Mousnier, *La vénalité des offices sous Henri IV et Louis XIII*, 2nd edn (Paris, 1971).
55 Cloulas, *Henri II*, pp. 515–18.

CHAPTER TWO

Crown and nobility

The French civil wars of the sixteenth century have often been described as aristocratic conflicts sheltering under the cloak of religion.[1] There is some truth in this. The wars cannot be understood without first appreciating the crucial role played by the nobility. The king depended on the nobility for the proper execution of his policies and this is mainly why some historians have cast serious doubt on the notion, chiefly put about by the monarch himself, that his power was 'absolute'. But the dependence was not one-sided. If the monarch could do little without the support of his nobles, they looked to him for advancement. He was the great dispenser of jobs and honours. Without his leadership and patronage, nobles were likely to become disorientated.

Defining the nobility

Writing in about 1540, Guillaume de La Perrière compared the nobility to the 'butter and cream of the Republic's milk'.[2] He saw it as a natural secretion on the surface of society; but he offered no clues as to the difference between nobles and commoners. The greatest nobles were obvious enough by virtue of their considerable wealth and distinctive life-style; but how did nobles further down the social scale differ from commoners? None

1 J. W. Thompson, *The Wars of Religion in France, 1559–1576* (New York: F. Ungar, n.d.), p. 17: 'The weight of evidence is increasingly in favor of the view that the causes of the Huguenot movement were as much if not more political and economic than religious.'

2 Guillaume de La Perrière, *Le miroir politique* (Lyon, 1555), p. 44.

of the commonly cited distinguishing traits means a great deal. Nobles, for example, were theoretically exempt from taxation, but not in areas of *taille réelle* (where the main direct tax or *taille* was assessed on the status of land rather than of its owner). Many categories of commoners were also exempt. Nor does the law of inheritance offer much help, for in areas where Roman law prevailed the rule giving the lion's share to the eldest son applied equally to commoners. Certain juridical privileges claimed by nobles, such as the right to be tried in a superior court, were sometimes conceded to commoners by royal gift. Nor can we rely on such outward signs of nobility as the right to carry a sword, to have a coat of arms or to wear clothes made of silk and with gold embroidery; for they were all easily usurped, as were such titles as *écuyer* and *chevalier*.[3]

Juridically, then, the nobility of sixteenth-century France cannot be precisely defined. Nor can it be quantified, except in Normandy where enquiries aimed at discovering usurpers of noble rights (*recherches de noblesse*) existed as early as 1463.[4] Some historians have estimated that there were between 20,000 and 30,000 noble families under Henry III. If we allow an average of five persons per family, we are left with between 100,000 and 150,000 nobles; in other words less than one per cent of the kingdom's total population of between 18 and 20 million. The proportion of nobles to the rest of the population varied from one province to another: it was highest in Brittany and Normandy (2.6 per cent in 1463).[5]

Reputation was an essential ingredient of nobility. To be accepted as a noble a person needed two qualifications: an ancient family line, called *race*, and a style of living which conformed with a social ideal. To be truly ancient a family line needed to be 'immemorial': in other words, it had to stretch back beyond the memory of the oldest living witness. This meant in practice three whole generations. Rules laid down by the crown in 1484 and 1583 stipulated that a family could only be accepted as noble from the fourth generation onwards. A man could, of course, become a nobleman, but only his grandson would be a *gentilhomme*. The most respected families were those which could claim descent from a crusader or, better still, from a companion of King Clovis.

The life-style was also crucial. A nobleman had to be seen to live 'nobly'. He could not dabble in mundane occupations, such as trade or craft, which might soil his hands. He needed time to exercise his mind and body. If he

---

3 A. Jouanna, *Le devoir de révolte: la noblesse française et la gestation de l'état moderne, 1559–1661* (Paris: Fayard, 1989), pp. 16–26.

4 J. B. Wood, *The Nobility of the 'Election' of Bayeux, 1463–1666: Continuity through Change* (Princeton, N.J.: Princeton U.P., 1980), pp. 20–42.

5 Jouanna, *Le devoir de révolte*, pp. 17–18.

broke this rule, he risked losing his noble status under the law of *dérogeance*. He might, however, regain it by abstaining from those 'vile' occupations and obtaining *lettres de relief* from the king. Certain occupations, notably iron-forging and glass-making, were deemed compatible with nobility, presumably because of their close association with forests. Nobles could also enter international maritime trade. Only retail trade was regarded as beneath their dignity. A nobleman was also expected to manage his lands, but he was supposed to do so 'freely', that is to say by using servants and day-workers (*journaliers*).[6]

For a long time proof of nobility rested on the spoken testimony of elders in a community. They would focus on the battles in which a nobleman had fought and on the frontal wounds he had received. Several noblemen of the time became famous on this account. François and Henri de Guise shared the nickname of *le balafré* (scarface); Monluc wore a nose of leather after he had been disfigured at the siege of Rabastens and La Noue was known as *bras de fer* (iron arm). Death in action was, of course, the supreme proof of nobility. By comparison with such evidence, documentary proofs carried less weight, but the crown could not control verbal evidence. The idea that nobility needed only public recognition ran counter to the principle laid down by the jurist, Bartolus, in the fourteenth century that it stemmed from the prince (*nobilitas est qualitas illata per principatum tenentem*). Consequently from the sixteenth century onwards the crown began to insist on written proofs of nobility. 'Pedigree' replaced 'virtue' as the essential test.

However 'natural' and 'virtuous', nobility was not envisaged as a closed caste for this would have meant its ultimate extinction. Theorists admitted that the seed of virtue, which was normally implanted only in nobles, might also be found in the soul of a commoner. By cultivating it, he might set off an ennobling process which might in time transform his line. Such a process, however, needed to be rare and slow in order not to upset the social order. It was equated to the cultivation of an orchard or to horse-breeding; only time would yield good fruit or a fine stallion.[7]

There were various ways of entering the nobility. Most popular perhaps was assimilation (*agrégation*). A man would do all the things expected of a nobleman: he would abstain from manual work, acquire a *seigneurie* (if possible, one with judicial rights attached), bribe a fiscal official to delete his name from the tax roll, wear a sword, marry his daughter off to a nobleman or persuade a notary to add the title of *écuyer* to his name. In time people would think of him as a nobleman, but the process was necessarily tedious;

6 Ibid., pp. 18–22.
7 Ibid., pp. 22–5.

it called for patience and cunning over several generations. As a substitute for a *seigneurie*, a would-be noble might go for a military command. The Wars of Religion offered many opportunities of accelerating the process of assimilation by this route.

It has been calculated that in Provence and Beauce in the sixteenth century 30 per cent of nobles achieved their status through assimilation. One such was the Protestant poet, Agrippa d'Aubigné, who passed himself off as a nobleman although he was the grandson of a cobbler from Loudun. The truth was hidden by his friend and master, the king of Navarre, but it eventually came into the open when Agrippa's granddaughter, Madame de Maintenon, tried to get her brother admitted to the Ordre du Saint Esprit. A genealogical search was carried out and she had to admit that her proofs of nobility which she had called 'as bright as the sun' were, in fact, spurious.[8]

The king much preferred ennoblement by means of a royal grant or letter of ennoblement, which clearly implied that nobility came from him. This method was much used in Normandy, but less so elsewhere. A third way of becoming a nobleman was to acquire an office which carried the status. In Beauce, this method accounted for 17 per cent of ennoblements before 1560 and 48 per cent during the rest of the century.[9]

The concept of honour

Contemporary writers identified nobility with virtue, which was commonly seen as military virtue. This consisted of courage, endurance and strong nerves, but also of mental and visual alertness and a desire to gain renown. Members of the nobility of robe (those who acquired nobility through office) liked to think of virtue as learning and prudence, but their view never prevailed, not even in the eighteenth century. The creation of the *compagnies d'ordonnance* (see below pp. 36–8) in the second half of the fifteenth century offered the nobility opportunities of military service. It reinforced the notion that war was the ideal way of life for the nobleman, and the Italian Wars, which Charles VIII launched by crossing the Alps in 1494, offered

8 Ibid., pp. 26–7; J.-M. Constant, *La vie quotidienne de la noblesse française au XVIe–XVII siècles* (Paris: Hachette, 1985), p. 114; G. Schrenk, 'Les origines d'Agrippa d'Aubigné', *B.S.H.P.F.* (1983), pp. 489–518.

9 J.-M. Constant, 'Les structures sociales et mentales de l'anoblissement, analyse comparative d'études récentes, XVIe–XVIIIe siècles', in *L'anoblissement en France, XVe–XVIIIe siècles. Théories et Réalités* (Centre de Recherches sur les Origines de l'Europe moderne, Université de Bordeaux III, 1985), p. 52.

noblemen a wonderful chance to demonstrate their virtue. For more than 50 years Italy served as a *champ d'honneur* for anyone seeking renown at the point of a sword. Such memoirs as those of du Bellay, Monluc, Boyvin de Villars and Rabutin present the wars as contests in which each side acknowleged the other's virtue. Thus it was that the Imperialists honoured Bayard in 1522 after he had been fatally wounded. In 1584 the Protestant historian, La Popelinière, described Lombardy as 'the school of virtue, the workshop of the real business of arms, the mistress of military discipline, the theatre of honour'.[10]

Nobles did not restrict their role to fighting; they believed that they were fit to perform all the highest functions in the state. At meetings of the Estates-General they repeatedly asked that judicial offices should be reserved for them. They complained that the need to master Roman law prevented them holding offices which normally should only require common sense, honesty and *prudhomie.* They were also highly critical of venality which excluded poor nobles from office-holding. Such innovations, they believed, had split the nobility in two: the legal experts and nobles who turned their backs on professionalism. Some nobles began to say that it was dishonourable to be a judge. Since a literary education had become the badge of a new noble, they tried to differentiate themselves by making a virtue of their ignorance. Some, however, saw danger in excluding themselves from government; they urged their peers in the second half of the century to educate their sons.

Nobles who embraced a military career were never more than a minority. The vast majority preferred to live peacefully on their estates. The minority who fought did so for material gain, fun, excitement and honour. War was for them a form of exercise akin to hunting, only more dangerous and, therefore, more potentially rewarding. They were tempted to grab the attention of contemporaries and of posterity by performing some extraordinary deed. This was true especially of younger sons and of nobles who had suffered a setback in their fortunes. The defence of Christendom offered them a just cause to achieve renown.[11]

Violence was symbolic as well as real. Even as children, nobles competed against each other either one to one or as part of a team against another. As they grew up, their games assumed the appearance of combats. Tournaments, jousts, carousels and mock battles became part of the stock-in-trade of court entertainments. Half-way between such sports and war was the duel in

10 Henri Voisin, sieur de la Popelinière, *L'Amiral de France* (Paris, 1584), f. 90 recto. Cited by Jouanna, *Le devoir de révolte*, p. 43.

11 Ibid., pp. 52–5; Constant, *La vie quotidienne*, pp. 11–35.

which a nobleman obliged an opponent to acknowledge his superior valour. Lively discussions took place over the rights and wrongs of duelling.[12] Honour also played an important part in war. At the siege of Metz (1552), young noblemen could not wait to join troops planning a dangerous sortie. They were joyful, we are told, at the prospect of laying down their lives on the bed of honour (*lit d'honneur*). Even if they survived, the wounds they received were seen as decorations bearing witness to their challenging Death.

We think of war as an evil to be avoided as far as possible. But this has not always been so: in sixteenth-century France, there were noblemen who regarded war as their chance to prove their virtue. When Henry II was driven by bankruptcy to sign the peace of Cateau-Cambrésis, he dashed the hopes of many young men who longed to emulate the glorious example of their elders on the battlefield. When the king died soon afterwards, he disappointed them even more, for only the king could declare war on a foreign enemy. Francis II was too young to do so; neither his ministers nor his mother had the authority to do so. The nobles found themselves at a loose end. The outbreak of the civil wars in 1562 must have come as a welcome break to many of them.

The great nobles

At the top of the aristocratic pyramid were some 20 families preeminent on account of their landed wealth, the importance of their offices and the extent of their family ties within the kingdom and abroad. They included princes of the blood, and 'foreign' princes. The princes of the blood were the legitimate male descendants of Hugh Capet, but more realistically of Louis IX, who had a claim to the throne. The ruling family in the sixteenth century was that of Valois. Closely related were the Bourbons, who were descended from Robert, the son of Louis IX. Their head was Antoine (1518–62), king of Navarre, who had acquired an extensive landed domain by marrying Jeanne d'Albret, the niece of King Francis I. Their son was the future King Henry IV, who succeeded to the throne after Henry III's assassination in 1589.[13]

The so-called 'foreign' princes were naturalized Frenchmen who traced their family origins to a country outside France. They included the Clèves,

12 F. Billacois, *Le duel dans la société française des XVIe–XVIIe siècles. Essai de psychologie historique* (Paris: EHESS, 1986), p. 362.

13 A. Jouanna, *La France du XVIe siècle, 1483–1598* (Paris: PUF, 1996), p. 72.

Luxembourgs, Rohans, La Marck and Gonzagues; but the most famous were the Guises, a younger branch of the family that ruled the duchy of Lorraine, which at that time lay outside France. Its founder, Claude de Lorraine, who became duc de Guise in 1527, owed his advancement primarily to King Francis I. He became related to the French royal family by his marriage to Antoinette de Bourbon by whom he had six sons, all of whom became distinguished as soldiers or churchmen. Claude's eldest son, who became the second duc de Guise in 1550, was François, a fine soldier who conquered Calais from the English in 1558. His brother, Charles, cardinal of Lorraine, was a major statesman renowned for his learning and lavish life-style. The other brothers were Claude, duc d'Aumale; Louis, cardinal of Guise; François, Grand Prior and general of the galleys; and René, marquis d'Elbeuf. The extensive lands of the Guises were mainly situated in Champagne, Normandy, Picardy, Maine and Burgundy. Two other marriages brought them even closer to the royal family. François de Guise married Anne d'Este, the granddaughter of King Louis XII, while his sister, Mary, married the Scottish king, James V Stuart. The latter's daughter, Mary Queen of Scots, married the Dauphin, who became Francis II in 1558.[14]

Foremost among the other leading aristocratic houses was that of Montmorency, which traced its roots even further back than the royal line. Anne de Montmorency (1493–1567) was for many years the principal minister of Francis I and of Henry II. As Constable of France, he was in charge of the army. He was made a duke in 1551 and was also governor of Languedoc (1526–42; 1547–63). By the mid-century the Montmorencys had an extensive territorial domain, mainly situated in Île-de-France, Picardy, Normandy, Champagne, Angoumois and Brittany. Anne owned seven châteaux, including Chantilly and Écouen, and four town houses (*hôtels*) in Paris. His four sons – François, governor of Paris and Île-de-France (1556–79) and marshal of France (as from 1560); Henri de Damville, governor of Languedoc (as from 1563); Charles, seigneur de Méru; and Guillaume, seigneur de Thoré – all became important politically, as did Anne's Châtillon nephews, Gaspard de Coligny, Admiral of France, cardinal Odet (who became a Protestant and ended his life as an exile in England), and Charles d'Andelot, colonel-general of the infantry. The Montmorencys had close ties with the Dutch nobility, notably the count of Hoornes (executed in Brussels in 1568) and the baron of Montigny.[15]

---

14 Ibid., pp. 72–5.

15 Ibid., pp. 75–8. See also M. Greengrass, 'Property and politics in sixteenth-century France: the landed fortune of Constable Anne de Montmorency', *F.H.*, ii (1982), 371–98.

Relations between the king and the nobility were cemented at court, which, as we have seen, was a large and itinerant establishment. The steady rise in the number of courtiers during the sixteenth century reflected the expansion of royal patronage. Only by attending the court could nobles hope to benefit from royal gifts of offices or honours. The court was also where they could share in the king's authority by serving on his council or by drawing his officials into their clientèles. Thus in the middle of the century two secretaries of state, Fresne and d'Alluye, became clients of the Guises, while Claude de l'Aubespine served the Montmorencys.[16] It was also at court that pressure groups or factions were formed, consisting of friends, clients or allies. Royal mistresses often became the focal points of such groups. Finally, the court was the stage on which courtiers loved to show off. They advertised their prestige by the magnificence of their dress, the size of their suites or their proximity to the monarch.[17]

The crown did not have a sufficiently large civil service or standing army with which to impose its will; it needed the support of the great nobles whose prestige could be measured by the number of kinsmen, friends or clients they could mobilize. It was to them that the king looked to control the kingdom's provinces. He tied them to his service by appointing them as governors or as lieutenants-general. Thus Antoine de Bourbon was governor of Guyenne, Anne de Montmorency was governor of Languedoc, François de Guise was governor of Champagne and Jacques d'Albon was governor of the Lyonnais. Without the local knowledge and influence of such men, the king would have had difficulty raising the *compagnies d'ordonnance*, units of heavy cavalry which collectively formed the king's standing army. Historians have of late stressed the importance of clientage in sixteenth-century France. The great nobles surrounded themselves with cohorts of dependents or clients. Thus in 1551 the governor of the Île-de-France entered the Hôtel de Ville in Paris accompanied by 'thirty or forty noblemen'. Five years later, his successor came with 200 noblemen. The prince de Condé travelled in 1560 with a retinue of 500 noblemen. Anne de Montmorency turned up at Fontainebleau with 800 noblemen in his train. Clientage, as Robert Harding has shown, was 'a complex, multifaceted social institution, and far more varied than vassalage'.[18] Clients came from

16 N. M. Sutherland, *The French Secretaries of State in the Age of Catherine de Medici* (London: Athlone, 1962), pp. 82–3, 104–7, 157–9.

17 Constant, *La vie quotidienne*, pp. 36–48, 55–8.

18 R. R. Harding, *Anatomy of a Power Elite. The Provincial Governors of Early Modern France* (New Haven: Yale U.P., 1978), p. 21.

all levels of society and their relationship to a great noble varied greatly in strength, permanency and in the nature of the goods and services exchanged.

Clientage was a vertical relationship. The patron's protection took various forms, such as gifts of employment or money, intercession with the king to obtain public offices, honours or pensions, judicial assistance, or acting as godparent to the client's children. The client served his patron by performing the duties which he had received from him and by giving armed or honorific support. His service differed from vassalage in that it was not tied to land. Verbally it was often expressed in emotive language. Such words as 'love', 'passion' and 'despair' crop up frequently in the correspondence of patrons and their clients. If they were seriously meant, the client was a *fidèle* totally devoted to his master's service; if, on the other hand, they were mere rhetoric, the dependent was a *client*.

Clientage could be of three kinds: military, domestic or political. A great nobleman usually commanded one of the *compagnies d'ordonnance*. He did so by virtue of a royal commission. Although officially royal servants and paid out of the king's treasury, his men were tied to him personally; he controlled their recruitment and promotion. They wore his livery on their cassocks and were forbidden to remove it or to enlist in another company without his consent. The captain's name, reputation and colours were the focus of the company's pride and morale. If he were a provincial governor, most of his men probably hailed from his *gouvernement*. A sample of just over 1,000 troops enlisted in companies between 1568 and 1574 has shown that 75 per cent resided in their captain's governorship. The proportion was lower in Damville's company (34 per cent) probably because the Montmorency estates were widely scattered in France. Monluc drew about a third of his men from western Languedoc where he owned land, and the rest from eastern Guyenne where he lived and was lieutenant-general.

Captains normally enlisted many relatives in their companies. Seventeen per cent of the men in Gaspard de Saulx-Tavannes' company had the same surname. In Antoine de Crussol's company the proportion was 11 per cent and in Monluc's 40 per cent. In order to preserve clientage loyalties, the crown allowed a son to take over his father's company when he was old enough. If a father wished to retain his command, the son was commissioned as a captain and allowed to recruit officers and men out of his father's company. Thus the companies of Jean and Fabien de Monluc, Guillaume de Saulx-Tavannes, François de Gonzague and Henri de Montmorency resembled their fathers'. If a captain died without leaving a son, the king could appoint someone who was not a kinsman to replace him, but this could cause resentment. Monluc, for example, antagonized the d'Andelots and Montmorencys by taking over d'Andelot's company at the king's instance.[19]

The *gendarmerie* was quite different from feudal service. Whereas vassals were locked in their social position, *gens d'armes* expected to rise in the world. They picked captains who were likely to advance their careers and whose companies were unlikely to be disbanded in peacetime. As Monluc explains, 'service under a captain with a promising career cannot fail to be of a prosperous issue for them [the lesser nobles]; they think they too will succeed and will always be employed. Nothing can irritate a courageous man more than to be left at home to burn his shins by the fire while others are employed in honourable action.' By being promoted within the company and showing their valour, the *gens d'armes* could expect 'to be noticed and praised by the great nobles (*grands*) and through them become known to the king which is how we all hope to be rewarded for our service'.[20]

Clientage could also be domestic. The large household of a great nobleman provided opportunities of advancement to lesser nobles and others. Such service was viewed by contemporaries as vital to the maintenance of public order. In 1576 the Third Estate urged the wives of great nobles to maintain well-ordered households where the children of lesser nobles might be 'nourished in virtue'. Aristocratic households were seen as foster homes for aristocratic children of both sexes, who entered them at the age of ten or twelve as unpaid pages or *filles d'honneur*. The boys would eventually become pages in a *compagnie d'ordonnance* or, perhaps with the master's help, win an office at court or a commission in the army. Or they might remain in the household service in one of several capacities, such as councillor, steward, chamberlain, quartermaster or captain of a château. The cost of maintaining a large household was one of the heaviest burdens which a great nobleman had to bear. Antoine de Bourbon's household cost 27,000 livres annually in staff salaries. The household salaries of the duc de Guise rose from 9,500 livres in 1542 to 16,200 livres in 1561.

The third kind of clientage was political and consisted of local élites who owed their offices, titles or pensions to a great nobleman and who served him in various ways in return for past favours or in the hope of future patronage. This group of clients included municipal officials, members of parlements and other sovereign courts, *baillis* and *sénéchaux*, and fiscal officials. Jean Truchon, for example, owed his office of president in the parlement of

---

19 Ibid., pp. 21–31.

20 *Commentaires et lettres de Blaise de Monluc*, ed. A. de Ruble (Paris, 1864–72), i, 62. Cited by Harding, *Anatomy of a Power Elite*, p. 26.

Grenoble to the duc de Guise. He wrote to the duke, who was the governor of Dauphiné, almost every week, keeping him informed on a wide variety of local business.[21]

Clientage was not without grave risks to the monarchy. It was evidently dangerous for the king to allow the great nobles exclusive control of patronage in their areas for this might be used against his interests or those of the kingdom. The danger was particularly acute in a province like Champagne which was vulnerable to attack by a foreign power. The Guises were dominant in that province and enjoyed considerable popular support, but some parts of the province escaped their influence. They were mainly situated near the eastern border. Here were noble families which had once served the duke of Burgundy. Following the break-up of the duchy in 1477, they chose directly to become clients of the king of France. Their historian, Laurent Bourquin, has chosen to call them 'the secondary nobility' (*noblesse seconde*). Their nucleus was formed by the three ancient houses of Choiseul, Anglure and Dinteville, whose origins lay outside Champagne. Whereas clients of the Guises were reluctant to give military service far from their own estates, members of the *noblesse seconde* were, it seems, willing to venture further afield in the king's service. They were not just seeking some quick return for their services, but were prepared to take up careers in the king's army. They were rewarded with offices far beyond their station in the king's household or by membership of the exclusive Ordre de Saint-Michel. It was thanks to the *noblesse seconde*, Bourquin writes, that the crown managed to save its authority in Champagne during the Wars of Religion.[22]

The king was expected to arbitrate in quarrels among his courtiers and to exercise his patronage fairly. The great nobles wanted him to show firmness and not to allow one of their number or his family to rise at the expense of others. Their discontent was aroused if one monopolized his favours, leaving none for others, or if the king failed to strike a proper balance so that the quest for his favours turned into a wild and unpredictable scramble. Under Francis I the nobility had been reasonably content, but under Henry II relations underwent a change. This was soon made clear by the famous duel between Jarnac (backed by the Montmorencys) and La Châtaigneraye (backed by the Guises). By supporting the loser (La Châtaigneraye) and failing to stop the duel in time, the king effectively surrendered his judicial prerogative. Henceforth the rivalry between the Montmorencys and the Guises became ever more bitter.[23]

---

21 Harding, *Anatomy of a Power Elite*, p. 28. For Truchon's correspondence see B.N., ms. fr. 3948.

22 L. Bourquin, *Noblesse seconde et pouvoir en Champagne aux XVIe et XVIIe siècles* (Paris: Sorbonne, 1994), pp. 37–58.

23 Jouanna, *La France du XVIe siècle*, pp. 234–6.

The provincial nobility

The provincial nobility may be divided into three groups according to their annual incomes. At the top were the ancient families, who owned vast estates and occupied important offices in church or state. Their income amounted to 10,000 livres or more. Beneath them were nobles who earned more than 1,000 livres. Blaise de Monluc fell into this middling category. 'I was born,' he writes 'the son of a nobleman whose father had sold all his property save an income of 800 or 1,000 livres.'[24] At the lowest level were petty nobles (*petite noblesse*) earning around 100 livres per annum. The best known is Gilles, sieur de Gouberville, who kept a diary from 1549 until 1562. His family's nobility had been recognized by an enquiry in 1463, but his concerns were those of a country gentleman. He owned three *seigneuries* in Normandy, the largest covering 52 hectares. Two were let out to farmers, while Gilles himself exploited the third with the assistance of servants and of day-workers, whom he engaged for harvesting and mowing. He also benefited from peasant *corvées* (labour services due to a seigneur). He supervised the work, but where his fruit trees were concerned, he attended to the pruning and grafting himself, as these were regarded as 'noble' occupations. Gilles' annual income from the produce of his land, the sale of his animals and the sale of wool from his sheep amounted to some 200 livres, which was just enough to cover his normal expenditure. Although Gilles did not have judicial rights, he commanded a high prestige among his tenants. Each Sunday he would be invited to attend mass by the local *curé* and the service would not begin until he had taken his place in the pew reserved for him. Peasants called on him spontaneously to sort out their differences, to treat their ailments or to be godfather to their offspring. He joined them in their wakes, festivals and games. They seem to have shared his love of the soil and his literary tastes. On rainy days he would read aloud to his servants from *Amadis de Gaule*, a romance of chivalry much in vogue among nobles of his day. It shared a place on his bookshelves alongside a law book, an almanach and the *Centuries* of Nostradamus.[25]

Social relations among the provincial nobility were determined by friendship. Unlike clientage, this was horizontal, as it linked people of equal status, usually kinsmen or neighbours. It was expressed in mutual hospitality, help to arrange a marriage or to win a lawsuit, the transmission of news, intercession with a third party to secure a job, the sending of gifts and even

24 *Commentaires de Blaise de Monluc*, ed. P. Courteault (Paris, 1911), i, 29.
25 Madeleine Foisil, *Le sire de Gouberville* (Paris: Aubier, 1981), *passim*.

sometimes participation in an armed sortie against an enemy. The more friends a nobleman had, the greater his chances were of successfully overcoming hardship.

The nobility in crisis?

Historians used to believe that the nobility of sixteenth-century France experienced a serious economic decline. Their view can be summed up as follows: since nobles were forbidden to trade by the law of *dérogeance*, they were less able to adapt to economic change than members of the bourgeoisie who were not subject to such juridical restraints. Consequently, as prices rose, the nobility were unable to supplement their incomes, which they derived mainly from rents which had been fixed by custom. At the same time, the nobles made their own situation worse by living beyond their means. As they became indebted, they sold their lands to 'rising' bourgeois, who wanted to elevate themselves socially. According to Davis Bitton, the peace of Cateau-Cambrésis capped an already critical situation by obliging many young nobles who had taken up military careers to fall back on their hard-pressed family estates. As these were found wanting, 'bands of armed nobles roamed the countryside pillaging and plundering'.[26]

The traditional view has served to explain the social and political conflicts of early modern France, but it rests on sources that are literary and general rather than archival and specific. It assumes too monolithic a view of the nobility, which was not a single economic unit capable of only one response to economic pressures. Although most nobles were landlords in receipt of rents, some owned little or no land. Many had no fief or *seigneurie*, even if they had a landed income. Some, like Gouberville, worked their holdings themselves, while others never set foot in them. Moreover, office-holding nobles added wages and pensions to their income from land. While some nobles were enormously rich, others were terribly poor.

Recent research has exploded the notion of an overall economic decline of the French nobility in the sixteenth century. In the *élection* of Bayeux (Normandy), the century was marked by unprecedented expansion for the nobility: its membership doubled in less than 60 years. What is more, very few of the 'new' nobles were recent creations; the majority were 'old' nobles from other parts of the province. Nor was there a split between an 'old'

26 Wood, *The Nobility of the 'Election' of Bayeux*, pp. 7–8. For the traditional view see L. Romier, *Le royaume de Catherine de Médicis* (Paris: Perrin, 1913) i, 170–82, and D. Bitton, *The French Nobility in Crisis, 1560–1640* (Stanford, Cal.: Stanford U.P., 1969), pp. 1–2.

nobility of sword and a 'new' nobility of robe, as historians once supposed. The real division was between rich and poor. A minority of very rich nobles received more than half of all the revenue; half received less than one-tenth and an intermediate group received 40 per cent. Significantly, the proportion of poor nobles did not grow during the century. The general tendency, in fact, was towards enrichment.[27]

Recent studies in other provinces have yielded similar findings. In Beauce, where seigneurial rents were often in kind, domainial produce benefited from price inflation. Rents rose so much that landlords doubled their capital every six or seven years from 1550 onwards. In Auvergne, aristocratic wealth held its own. In Béarn, the landed income of the king of Navarre rose seven times between 1530 and 1600, while prices in Toulouse only trebled. In Dauphiné, a fall in the number of *seigneuries* held by the old nobility did not seriously damage its overall wealth. In Poitou, the picture of aristocratic decline once painted by Paul Raveau has been disproved: nobles managed to overcome a potential cash crisis by insisting on payments in kind and by cultivating their lands more efficiently. It seems that regions like Beauvaisis or Burgundy, which have yielded evidence of aristocratic decline, were exceptions.[28]

The traditional view rested on three assumptions: first, that seigneurial rents were fixed and paid in money; secondly, that war helped to ruin the nobility; and thirdly, that an extravagant life-style and a lack of business sense contributed to that ruin. All three are questionable. Many rents were paid in kind and were only a part of a seigneur's income, which was mainly raised by produce from his domain. J.-M. Constant has shown that only 40 per cent of nobles who served in the army became poorer as a result; 37 per cent grew richer and the rest did not change.[29] War was sometimes profitable. Much money could be made by capturing a man of rank and exacting a ransom in exchange for his release. Monluc once thought of raising money in this way to pay for a house in Paris.[30] Finally, the idea that noblemen ruined themselves by living extravagantly is only partly true. Those at court had to spend a great deal to justify their rank and to serve the king, but relatively few went there. Some families (notably the Nevers) did run up debts, but most important houses were surprisingly

---

27 Wood, *The Nobility of the 'Election' of Bayeux*, pp. 120–40.

28 J. Russell Major, *From Renaissance Monarchy to Absolute Monarchy: French Kings, Nobles and Estates* (Baltimore: Johns Hopkins U.P., 1994), pp. 75–86; J. Russell Major, 'Noble income, inflation and the Wars of Religion in France', *A.H.R.*, 86 (1981), pp. 21–48.

29 Constant, *La vie quotidienne*, p. 194.

30 Harding, *Anatomy of a Power Elite*, p. 150.

resilient.[31] Henri de Montmorency ran into serious difficulties at the end of the century after inheriting huge debts from his brother, but thanks to a sale of forests and to help from the crown, he succeeded in balancing his budget.[32] Another example of resilience is presented by the La Trémoïlles. In 1483 their revenues had been reduced by two-thirds and their debts were enormous, but over half a century three of their dukes managed to recover. They gave up lands in Burgundy and built up by various means an important domain in western France. After starting as a *vicomté*, it became a duchy in 1563 and a *duché-pairie* in 1595. The dukes ran their estates well and sold their produce. Louis II planted vines, built ships and took part in maritime trade and piracy. He continued the restoration of seigneurial rights begun by his father, drained marshes, and repaired mills, presses, ovens and bridges. He fought inflation by shortening leases and turning rents from money into kind. His example was followed by his son, François, who linked the family's honour with profit-making. Between 1486 and 1542 the revenues from the family's estates rose by 135 per cent and its total revenues by 99 per cent so that it ceased to depend on royal largesse.[33]

As Arlette Jouanna has written: 'It would be hazardous, given the extent of our present knowledge, to pass an overall judgment. Yet we should certainly henceforth reject the idea of a general economic decline of the nobility in the sixteenth and seventeenth centuries.'[34]

---

31 D. Crouzet, 'Recherches sur la crise de l'aristocratie en France au XVIe siècle: les dettes de la maison de Nevers', *Histoire, économie et société*, I (1984), 5–50.

32 M. Greengrass, 'Noble affinities in early modern France: the case of Henri I de Montmorency, Constable of France', *E.H.Q.*, 16 (1986), pp. 275–311.

33 W. Weary, 'La maison de La Trémoïlle pendant la Renaissance: une seigneurie agrandie', in *La France de la fin du XVe siècle. Renouveau et apogée* (Paris: CNRS, 1985), pp. 187–212.

34 Jouanna, *Le devoir de révolte*, p. 98.

CHAPTER THREE

The rise of Protestantism

Politics and religion are no longer as closely related today as they were in the sixteenth century, at least in the Christian world. The motto 'One king, one law, one faith' expressed a universal aspiration in the days before the Protestant Reformation. The ruler was God's anointed and his subjects were expected to adhere to his faith, which, in early sixteenth-century France, was the Catholic faith. The king of France proudly boasted of his title of 'Most Christian King'. He was bound by his coronation oath to protect the church and to root out heresy from his kingdom.[1] Early in the century, however, this was not a problem. Many people grumbled about abuses in the church. but this was nothing new. Moreover, not all bishops were bad: several tried to reform their dioceses. The Reformation was preceded by a period of very active Catholic reform, known to historians as the Pre-reformation.[2] But heresy – the conscious rejection of Catholic doctrine – had virtually disappeared from France since the Albigensian crusade in the thirteenth century. The great Dutch humanist, Erasmus, was broadly correct when he described France in 1517 as the only part of Christendom that was free of heresy.[3] Except in Provence, which had been infiltrated by Waldensianism, heresy was confined to a few individual cranks who were promptly silenced. This happy state of affairs, however, did not last for long.

---

1 C. Beaune, *The Birth of an Ideology: Myths and Symbols of Nation in Late-Medieval France* (Berkeley, Cal., 1991), pp. 172–81.

2 N. Lemaitre, *Le Rouergue flamboyant: le clergé et les fidèles du diocèse de Rodez, 1417–1563* (Paris: Cerf, 1988), pp. 87–119.

3 M. Mann, *Erasme et les débuts de la Réforme française* (Paris, 1934), p. 23.

In 1519, two years after Martin Luther had promulgated his famous 95 theses at Wittenberg, his creed first reached Paris. On 15 April 1521 the Faculty of Theology of the university, a widely respected institution which was often called upon to adjudicate on matters of dogma, condemned 104 Lutheran propositions as heretical, and shortly afterwards it and the Parlement assumed joint control of book censorship in and around the capital. It became an offence to sell any book which had not been authorized by the faculty. Owners of Lutheran books were ordered to hand them over on pain of imprisonment or a fine.[4] King Francis I was as strongly opposed to heresy as anyone, but, as yet, it was not easily recognized. The boundary between Christian humanism and Lutheranism was far from clear. Both emphasized the primary importance of Scripture and the role of faith in man's search for salvation, but Lutheranism rejected the Catholic doctrine of transubstantiation and papal supremacy. The king was well disposed towards humanist scholars and did not feel bound to accept any definition of heresy formulated by the University of Paris. He was encouraged in his liberal attitude by his sister, Marguerite d'Angoulême, who was the friend of Guillaume Briçonnet, the reforming bishop of Meaux. In 1523 the first signs of disagreement between the king and the faculty appeared, when it launched an attack on the *Cercle de Meaux*, a group of evangelical preachers who had gathered around the bishop in support of his reforming efforts. By now the Lutheran heresy had become so firmly entrenched in certain Parisian circles that the faculty and Parlement decided that censorship of books was not enough to check its growth; they decided to make an example of individual heretics. In August a young nobleman, Louis de Berquin, was tried for heresy, but released by royal command.[5]

Francis I's defeat at Pavia (24 February 1525) and his captivity in Spain enabled the Parlement and Paris Faculty of Theology to impose their reactionary views on the regent, Louise of Savoy. In February 1526 heresy was defined so broadly as to take in the smallest deviation from orthodoxy. Printers and publishers were forbidden to publish or stock religious books in French. The *juges délégués*, a special court exercising papal jurisdiction, renewed the attack on the *Cercle de Meaux*, forcing some of its members to flee abroad. The persecution, however, was wound up after the king's return in

---

4 J. K. Farge, *Orthodoxy and Reform in Early Reformation France: The Faculty of Theology of Paris, 1500–1543* (Leiden: Nijhoff, 1985), pp. 165–9.

5 R. J. Knecht, *Renaissance Warrior and Patron: The Reign of Francis I* (Cambridge U.P., 1994), p. 163.

March 1526. While the Parlement and faculty continued to define heresy in their own way, Francis tolerated a fair amount of evangelicalism at his court. But he drew the line at any form of religious dissent likely to disturb the public peace. As yet, iconoclasm – the destruction of religious images – had not been characteristic of dissent in France, but in 1528 a statue of the Virgin and child in Paris was mutilated by persons unknown. This was symptomatic of a shift in the nature of French dissent towards the radical doctrine of the Swiss reformer, Zwingli. Luther disapproved of the destruction of religious images, unlike the Zürich reformers who advocated it. Although the French authorities continued to refer to all dissenters as 'Lutherans', some evidently held far more extreme views. So fluid was the ideological situation that the historian, Lucien Febvre, has called this phase of the French Reformation 'a long period of magnificent religious anarchy'.[6] Francis I was angered by the incident in Paris. He immediately commissioned a new statue and took part in a public procession to invoke God's forgiveness. In October the synod of Sens, meeting under the chairmanship of Archbishop Duprat, who was also Chancellor of France, took stringent measures to suppress heresy. Meanwhile, Berquin was tried as a relapsed heretic and burnt. By August 1530 Protestantism had begun to spread into the French provinces. According to Bucer, so many people in a certain part of Normandy had taken to the Gospel that the region had become known as 'Little Germany'.[7] In November 1533, Nicolas Cop, the new rector of the University of Paris, caused a great stir by delivering a sermon containing Lutheran ideas. Members of his audience complained and he had to flee the kingdom.[8] Another fugitive was his friend, John Calvin, who may have helped him compose his sermon.

On the morning of 18 October 1534 copies of a highly inflammatory poster or placard were found displayed in the streets of Paris. They denounced the Catholic Mass as a blasphemy and the clergy as 'ravening wolves' who were leading their flocks to everlasting perdition. The author of the placard was Antoine Marcourt, a Frenchman exiled in Switzerland who had become the first pastor of Neuchâtel. The placards had been printed there and smuggled into France. Their discovery caused panic in Paris as rumours of an imminent massacre of Catholics circulated. Fear was heightened by reports that identical placards had been found in other

---

6 L. Febvre, *Au coeur religieux du XVIe siècle* (Paris: SEVPEN, 1957), p. 66.

7 A. Herminjard (ed.), *Correspondance des réformateurs dans les pays de langue française* (Geneva, 1886–7), ii, 271–2.

8 W. J. Bouwsma, *John Calvin* (Oxford U.P., 1988), pp. 15–16; F. Wendel, *Calvin* (London: Collins, 1965), pp. 40–41; T. H. L. Parker, *John Calvin* (London: Dent, 1975), p. 30.

French towns and even on the door of the king's bedchamber at Amboise. Within days a savage campaign of persecution was unleashed. By the end of November several people had been burnt at the stake. Following his return to the capital, Francis banned all religious printing for a time and took part in a huge public procession.[9] Such a demonstration 'served as a rite of purification for a city soiled by heresy, thereby conveying very clearly to the onlooking crowds the message that the Protestants formed a force within society whose polluting actions required community atonement'.[10]

The Affair of the Placards was a further indication of the distance travelled by French Protestantism since its beginnings. For the placards were vehemently 'sacramentarian' in their total rejection of the Real Presence to which Luther continued to adhere. For sacramentarians, the communion service was purely commemorative. The distinction between them and other dissenters was duly noted in the Edict of Coucy (16 July 1535), which carefully excluded 'sacramentarians' from a conditional amnesty which it offered to religious prisoners and exiles. Dissenters who refused to abjure within six months were to be hanged.

John Calvin

The credit for giving the Protestant Reformation in France some measure of doctrinal cohesion and an effective organization belongs to John Calvin. He was born at Noyon in Picardy in 1509; his father, Gérard, was clerk to the local council and the legal representative of the cathedral chapter. Gérard sent his son to Paris to study theology and got him some ecclesiastical benefices. Calvin attended the collège de Montaigu, accepting its harsh discipline without a murmur (unlike Erasmus). His education, like that of many other reformers, was a mixture of scholastic and humanistic learning. After acquiring a profound knowledge of Latin and of scholastic theology at the University of Paris, he studied law and Greek at Orléans. His interest in humanism was reflected in his earliest publication, an edition of Seneca's *De Clementia* (1532). It was soon afterwards that Calvin underwent a religious conversion, though the exact circumstances are unknown. In May 1534 he returned to Noyon to resign his benefices and in January 1535 travelled

---

9 Knecht, *Renaissance Warrior*, pp. 313–21; G. Berthoud, *Antoine Marcourt* (Geneva: Droz, 1973), pp. 174–6, 181–7, 190–95, 216–20.

10 P. Benedict, *Rouen during the Wars of Religion* (Cambridge U.P., 1981), p. 64.

to Basle. Soon afterwards he was invited by Guillaume Farel to help him win over Geneva to the Reformation, but the two men had to leave the city in 1538 after clashing with its authorities. Calvin was invited to Strassburg by the reformer, Martin Bucer, and spent a few rewarding years there. In 1541 he was recalled to Geneva, and stayed there till his death in 1564, preaching and teaching, writing innumerable letters to friends and disciples, and engaging in polemics with religious opponents.

The essence of Calvin's theology is contained in his *Institutes of the Christian Religion,* which first appeared in Latin in 1536. It was immediately successful and was published in an enlarged form in 1539. This was followed two years later by a French translation, notable for its lucid, precise and elegant style. It was promptly outlawed by the Paris Faculty of Theology and many copies were burnt outside Notre-Dame in July 1542 and again in February 1544. The final version of the *Institutes* appeared in Latin in 1559 and in French in 1560. Like Luther's theology, Calvin's is built around the idea of justification by faith alone, but he places more stress on the Fall. Rejecting completely the humanistic belief in man's free will, Calvin sees him as a perpetual sinner incapable of achieving good by his own efforts, but he is not unredeemable. God's gift of salvation is expressed in the election of certain sinners by virtue of a choice which human reason cannot explain. Some human beings have been chosen by Him for the eternal life, others for eternal damnation. The doctrine may seem unduly harsh, yet it was a source of joy, not despair, for Calvin and his followers: man may recognize the mark of his election by the faith that moves him. Calvin retains only two sacraments: baptism and communion. He sees God's presence in the Eucharist as spiritual, not corporeal; the bread and the wine are only signs of divine grace. Like Luther, he rejects purgatory, prayers for the dead and the cult of saints, who are denied any powers of intercession. He too sees Scripture as the only source of revealed truth. God communicates with man through the Bible, but His message can only be understood if one has faith, which is a divine gift reserved to the elect. The elect may be recognized by the faith displayed in their good works, but only the individual conscience can have certainty of salvation. Since the elect cannot be distinguished from the reprobate, all men (except obvious heretics) must be included within the visible church, which God has instituted to strengthen man's faith. It must be free to preach the Word of God and, therefore, cannot be subordinate to any other authority. The visible church is run by pastors and doctors, who preach and teach respectively; elders, who maintain discipline, and deacons, who care for the sick and the poor. Discipline is necessary as a defence against the enemies of Christ and as a means of leading man towards faith. At the end of the *Institutes*, Calvin discusses the role of the civil magistrate, whom he sees as divinely instituted.

He must, therefore, be obeyed unless he commands anything against the law of God. Disobedience, however, must never take the form of armed resistance.[11]

The threat from Geneva

In 1541 Calvin was given his chance to put his ideas into practice in Geneva. His first action was to draw up the *Ordonnances ecclésiastiques* (1541), which organized the Genevan church around the consistory and the Venerable Company of Pastors. The consistory consisted of ministers and 12 members of the city councils co-opted by the clergy. Their function was to maintain discipline by penalizing inhabitants of the city who violated dogma or morality. The Venerable Company comprised all the city's ministers and 12 lay elders chosen by the city councils. Its function was to prepare legislation for the consistory and to approve the appointment of teachers and ministers.

Geneva was divided into parishes, provision being made in each one for systematic worship and education. Every so often two members of the consistory, accompanied by a minister, toured the parishes, keeping an eye on the people. Every week transgressors were brought before the consistory for punishment, which was usually a public apology, public penance or a fine. Heavier penalties were sometimes inflicted: one victim was Michael Servetus, who was burnt after denying the doctrine of the Trinity. No aspect of Genevan life escaped the consistory's vigilance. Edicts were issued on all kinds of subject. Dice and card-games were banned, children were not to be given saints' names, all papist practices were suppressed, books were strictly censored. Even people who showed religious lukewarmness were liable to penalties.

Although Calvin's regime did encounter opposition, his prestige was such that he could override it. In 1555 a riot provided him with a pretext to oust his enemies from the city councils, and in 1559 his triumph was crowned by the foundation of the Academy under Théodore de Bèze. Calvin's influence was soon felt outside Geneva. His works were rapidly translated into all the tongues of the civilized world and their impact was boosted by Calvin's prolific letter-writing. When Luther died in 1546, Calvin was at once recognized as his successor as leader of the Protestant movement. People flocked

---

11 Parker, *John Calvin*, pp. 34–50; Bouwsma, *John Calvin*, pp. 172–6, 215–18; Wendel, *Calvin*, pp. 111–44, 255–84, 312–55.

to Geneva from every direction and later returned to their own countries to preach his doctrine.[12]

Calvinism in France

In 1535 Protestants still hoped for a change of heart on the part of King Francis I, a hope eloquently expressed by Calvin in the preface to his *Institutes of the Christian Religion* (Basle, 1536) which he addressed to Francis I. The evangelicals, he explained, had been falsely accused of sedition, and he should listen to what they had to say in their own defence. 'Although your heart is at present alienated from, even inflamed against us,' Calvin wrote, 'I trust that we may regain its favour, if you will only read our confession once without indignation or wrath.'[13] Protestants were encouraged in May 1536, when the Coucy amnesty was extended to all heretics provided they abjured within six months, yet they continued to be persecuted. On 1 June 1540 the Edict of Fontainebleau gave the parlements overall control of heresy jurisdiction. As the preamble explained, new measures were needed to eradicate the 'evil errors' which, having been suppressed, were reappearing in the kingdom. They were being spread, it was alleged, by exiles who had come home or by heretics who had previously lain low. All subjects were ordered to denounce heretics 'as each is bound to run in order to put out a public fire'.[14] But heresy still lacked any kind of cohesion. 'Such organisation as existed before the mid-1540s,' writes David Nicholls, 'consisted of small groups discussing Scripture in inns or private houses, and leaders were those with the prestige attached to reading ability or ownership of books.'[15]

Meanwhile, the fight against heresy intensified. The last seven years of Francis I's reign were marked by a sharp rise in the number of prosecutions for heresy by the Parlement of Paris. One victim was Étienne Dolet, the printer-publisher, who was burnt in August 1536. Outside Paris, yet within the Parlement's jurisdiction, bishops delegated their judicial powers to commissioners. Among the most active was Nicole Sanguin, who put to death 14 people at Meaux. Thousands watched the grisly spectacle which lasted

12 Parker, *John Calvin*, pp. 51–89, 97–116. R. M. Kingdon, *Geneva and the Coming of the Wars of Religion in France, 1555–1563* (Geneva: Droz, 1956), pp. 27–30.

13 Herminjard (ed.), *Correspondance des réformateurs*, iv, no. 545, pp. 3–23; Parker, *John Calvin*, pp. 34–7.

14 N. M. Sutherland, *The Huguenot Struggle for Recognition* (New Haven: Harvard U.P., 1980), pp. 33–4, 338–9.

15 A. Pettegree (ed.), *The Early Reformation in Europe* (Cambridge U.P., 1992), p. 127.

two days.[16] The commissioners were also active in the Loire valley and along the Atlantic coast. Elsewhere the response of the parlements to heresy was variable: it was lethargic in Normandy, yet fierce in Toulouse. In Provence, the parlement was even more militant: 60 people were arrested and sentenced in 15 months. But as judicial enquiries were usually slow and tentative, dissenters were often able to escape notice. Magistrates were more concerned with tangible offences than ideas. Frequent conflicts of jurisdiction between secular and ecclesiastical courts resulted in sentences being reviewed and quashed. Many heretics were lightly punished by a public penance or a fine. More serious offenders were flogged; only the incorrigible were banished or burnt. Before 1550 burnings were relatively few.[17]

Given these facts and others, such as the immunity from prosecution enjoyed by foreigners in France or the reluctance of the more liberal prelates to apply the law harshly, it is not surprising that heresy continued to thrive. So-called 'Lutherans' continued to be reported from all parts of the kingdom. In May 1542 the president of the parlement of Rouen said that the church had never been in such danger since the Aryan heresy. Now and then, an incident made the king aware of the peril. In August 1542 he admitted that heresy was growing in spite of the repressive measures. He urged the courts to redouble their efforts to discover 'the secret practices of the sectaries'. In July 1543 he decided that the power of search and arrest would be shared by the secular and ecclesiastical courts. Meanwhile, the Faculty of Theology produced clear doctrinal guidelines to assist the authorities. All the university's doctors and bachelors were ordered to subscribe to 25 articles reaffirming Catholic dogma, worship and organization. Francis ordered their publication throughout the realm; anyone teaching a different doctrine was to face prosecution.[18]

The social distribution of Calvinism in France

The origins of French Protestantism have aroused much interest among historians, but the subject is vast and requires archival documentation that is patchy at best. It is generally agreed that Protestantism was at first mainly an urban phenomenon. Consequently, some of the best studies of its origins

---

16 H. Heller, *The Conquest of Poverty: The Calvinist Revolt in Sixteenth-Century France* (Leiden: Brill, 1986), pp. 64–7.

17 D. Nicholls, 'The Theatre of Martyrdom in the French Reformation', *P.&P.*, 121 (Nov. 1988), p. 51.

18 Knecht, *Renaissance Warrior*, p. 508.

have been linked to certain towns, such as Paris, Rouen, Dijon and Troyes.[19] But the countryside, especially in the Midi, was not immune to the new faith. What is clear is that all the estates – clergy, nobility and third estate – were to some degree affected.

The Reformation began as an ecclesiastical rather than a lay movement; it sprang from the ranks of the clergy, especially the lower clergy and the regular orders. Some of the earliest French Protestants were friars, particularly the Cordeliers and Jacobins. In 1549, for example, 32 Augustinians walked out of their house in Rouen.[20] Sixty-nine members of the clergy were among 2,733 Protestants prosecuted by the parlements of Bordeaux and Toulouse.[21] Twelve bishops abandoned their sees between 1556 and 1577. Jean de Lettes, bishop of Montauban, and Jacques Spifame, bishop of Nevers, fled to Geneva with their wives. Jean de Saint-Chamond, archbishop of Aix, demonstrated his conversion in a spectacular manner on Christmas Day in 1566: after denouncing the papacy from his pulpit, he cast aside his crozier and mitre. During the civil wars, he became one of the best commanders in the Huguenot army. The most original convert among the bishops was Antonio Caracciolo of Troyes, who tried to be a pastor and a bishop at the same time. Eventually, however, he was forced to give up his see; he died alone in 1570 after an unsuccessful bid to serve as pastor in Orléans. Many bishops were understandably reluctant to surrender their temporalities. Cardinal Odet de Châtillon, count-bishop of Beauvais, who embraced the Reformation in 1561 and married in 1564, kept his episcopal revenues until he fled to England in 1568.[22]

Around 1560 Calvinism began to make deep inroads into the nobility. It has been suggested that the nobles, finding their incomes hard hit by the Price Revolution, attached themselves to the cause most likely to give them quick profits at the expense of the Catholic church; but, as we have seen, the nobility as a whole did not experience an economic decline. Some impoverished nobles undoubtedly existed, but conversion to Calvinism was not limited to them. In the *élection* of Bayeux (Normandy) more than 200 nobles, or 40 per cent of the local nobility, became Protestants in the 1560s and 41 per cent of them were comparatively rich. Most of these nobles, however, belonged to families whose status was less than a century old.

---

19 B. Diefendorf, *Beneath the Cross: Catholics and Huguenots in Sixteenth-Century Paris* (Oxford U.P., 1991); P. Benedict, *Rouen during the Wars of Religion* (Cambridge U.P., 1981); J. R. Farr, *Hands of Honor: Artisans and their World in Dijon, 1550–1650* (Ithaca, 1988); P. Roberts, *A City in Conflict: Troyes during the French Wars of Religion* (Manchester U.P., 1996).

20 D. Nicholls, 'Social change and early Protestantism in France: Normandy, 1520–62', *E.S.R.*, 10 (1980), p. 290.

21 J. Garrisson-Estèbe, *Protestants du Midi, 1559–1598* (Toulouse: Privat, 1980), p. 21.

22 A. Jouanna, *La France du XVIe siècle, 1483–1598* (Paris: PUF, 1996), p. 326.

Several had it challenged in the courts. It has been suggested that royal attempts to regulate noble status may have caused a significant part of the nobility to shelter under the banner of Protestantism, but this theory needs to be tested across the whole of France.[23]

Clientage doubtless helps to account for the rapid spread of Calvinism among the second estate. A nobleman who embraced Calvinism would carry his clients with him. This certainly occurred in south-west France where the process of aristocratic conversion to Calvinism has been compared to the spread of an oil-stain. Many of the 500 people charged with heresy by the parlement of Toulouse in 1569 belonged to the clientèle of the Gascon nobleman Pons de Polignac, sire des Roys.[24] Calvin appreciated the importance of clientage. He knew that the conversion of a single nobleman could lead to multiple conversions among his family and clients. Calvin's lieutenant, Théodore de Bèze, himself a nobleman, was well equipped to appeal to his own class. He was sent to Nérac in 1560 and may have brought about the conversion of Jeanne d'Albret, the wife of Antoine de Bourbon and the mother of the future Henry IV. A fair proportion of the exiles who went to Geneva were nobles. In 1555, Louis, prince de Condé, stopped in Geneva on his way back from a military campaign in Italy. He and his suite asked to visit the city and hear a sermon. This suggests that Condé's Protestant faith may not have been simply a matter of political convenience, as historians have often assumed.[25] The religious conscience of any historical figure is not easily probed today. Adventurism or greed may have caused some noblemen to embrace Calvinism, but sincere religious conviction cannot be ruled out as one of their motives.

Women played an important part in the conversion of many noble families around 1560. The influence of Francis I's sister, Marguerite d'Angoulême, had rubbed off on her ladies-in-waiting. Among them were Louise de Montmorency, sister of the Constable and mother of Admiral Coligny, who became leader of the Huguenots; Jacqueline de Longwy, duchesse de Montpensier, who defended Huguenots at the court of Catherine de' Medici; and Michelle de Saubonne, ancestress of the Rohans who led the Huguenots in the later civil wars. Among women of the next generation was Jeanne d'Albret, who sponsored Calvinist preaching in Béarn and Navarre even before announcing her conversion in 1560. Other important Protestant ladies included Madeleine de Mailly, comtesse de Roye, whose daughter married and converted the prince de Condé; Charlotte de Laval, the wife

23 J. B. Wood, *The Nobility of the 'Election' of Bayeux, 1463–1666: Continuity through Change* (Princeton, N.J.: Princeton U.P., 1980), pp. 156–71.

24 Garrisson-Estèbe, *Protestants du Midi*, pp. 22–8.

25 Kingdon, *Geneva and the Coming of the Wars of Religion*, p. 59.

of Admiral Coligny; Françoise de Seninghen, mother of the prince de Porcien; and Françoise du Bec-Crespin, mother of Philippe Duplessis-Mornay, a leading spokesman of the Huguenot cause.[26] Such women, it has been suggested, may have found self-fulfilment in the Calvinist faith, yet women had less scope for personal responsibility in Calvin's Geneva than in Counter-Reformation Italy.[27] Calvin and the Venerable Company of Pastors wanted their church to be run by well-trained pastors and sound male members of the consistories. They cited with approval Paul's dictum that 'women keep silence in the churches'. However, Calvin did appreciate the importance of winning noblewomen over to his cause and kept up a lively correspondence with them. They were often literate, had more time to devote to religious pursuits, and were susceptible to the influence of a Protestant tutor to their children, especially when their menfolk were absent at court or fighting in the king's wars.

In the towns Protestantism began by appealing most strongly to the lower orders of society, more particularly the artisans. One effect of the sixteenth-century Price Revolution was to depress the real wages and standard of living of urban artisans. Some historians have seen this as the explanation of religious dissent. Writing in 1899, Henri Hauser suggested that 'in Rouen in 1560 the working man's cause and the cause of the Reform were one and the same'.[28] More recently Henry Heller has argued that 'the artisans were the social base of the French Reformation. Theirs was a religious revolt founded in political and economic protest.'[29] Yet, most historians currently working on the origins of French Protestantism are sceptical about linking them rigidly to socio-economic conditions. As David Nicholls writes: 'the relationship between religious commitment and economic resentment will always remain shadowy'.[30] As more evidence comes to light, it becomes increasingly difficult to explain why certain groups in society and certain areas opted for Protestantism rather than others.

Evidence from Rouen indicates that Protestantism drew its strength from virtually all strata of society and from a wide variety of occupations, yet there are some intriguing divergences. Whereas cloth-workers and probably lawyers remained overwhelmingly Catholic, there were more Protestant hosiers than weavers. Among merchants, Protestants were usually from the main strata immediately below the wealthiest families. The more strongly

---

26 N. L. Roelker, 'The appeal of Calvinism to French noblewomen in the sixteenth century', *J.I.H.*, 2 (1971–2), pp. 391–418.
27 N. Z. Davis, *Society and Culture in Early Modern France* (London: Duckworth, 1975), pp. 65–95.
28 H. Hauser, 'La Réforme et les classes populaires', *R.H.M.C.*, I (1899–1900), p. 31.
29 Heller, *The Conquest of Poverty*, p. 69.
30 Pettegree (ed.), *The Early Reformation*, p. 132.

Protestant trades were those with a relatively high standard of literacy. This would explain why, generally speaking, fewer women than men converted to Protestantism as they were generally less literate than men.[31]

The printing industry in Lyon offers some interesting pointers to socio-religious relations in that city. Protestantism seems to have had a particularly strong appeal to printers' journeymen. As wage-earners and outsiders, working in a relatively new industry without traditions, they felt the need to band together in defence of their interests. Protestantism offered them a new kind of worship with congregational participation and a liturgy in the vernacular. Proud of their skills, they felt undervalued by the local Catholic clergy. They organized public processions in which they sang the psalms in French and hurled insults at the canons of the cathedral of Saint-Jean.[32]

Protestantism was not confined to the lower orders of urban society. In Toulouse, Grenoble and Montpellier between 55 and 65 per cent of Protestant suspects in the 1560s were 'notables', but some occupations were better represented than others. For example, they included more merchants than bankers. In Paris, a high proportion of Protestant merchants were engaged in international trade. In Lyon, the Italian bankers remained loyal to Catholicism, while the merchants turned to Protestantism.[33]

Rural folk were not immune to Protestantism. The Cévennes, for example, became a stronghold of Protestantism from the 1530s. Huguenot peasants and rural artisans also existed elsewhere, notably in Dauphiné, the Midi and Normandy. Villages in contact with towns through the putting-out system were easily penetrated and the states of Protestant nobles offered safe places for worship to Huguenots of the surrounding countryside. Yet, for the most part, peasants 'stood on the sidelines of religious division' unless forced to defend themselves against marauding troops or noble bandits.[34]

The Genevan missionaries

French dissenters, who followed Calvin to Geneva, were not content simply to practise there faith there; they wanted to bring it home, confident in the belief that its truths would eventually be accepted by their compatriots. In 1555 missionaries trained in Geneva began to slip across the border into France. Research into the archives of the Geneva Company of Pastors has

---

31 Benedict, *Rouen during the Wars of Religion*, pp. 79–80.
32 Davis, *Society and Culture*, pp. 1–16.
33 M. Greengrass, *The French Reformation* (London: Historical Assoc., 1987), p. 56.
34 Pettegree (ed.), *The Early Reformation*, p. 130.

yielded information about 88 of those sent to France between 1555 and 1562. Sixty-two were French by birth, almost every province being represented among them, particularly Guyenne and Dauphiné. The social background of 42 missionaries is also known: they comprised 14 nobles (mostly younger sons), 24 bourgeois and 14 artisans, but not a single peasant. The missionaries underwent a very thorough training in Geneva. They had to learn Latin, Greek and Hebrew in order that they should know the Bible really well. At first, no formally organized institution existed to provide this education: Calvin and Farel tried to fill the need by giving lectures themselves, but in 1559 the Genevan Academy was set up under de Bèze. Such was its success that by 1564 it had 1,500 students.

After completing their studies, the missionaries usually took up pastoral duties in Switzerland before returning home. They became thoroughly attuned to the strict collective self-discipline of the Calvinist church. Before sending a man into France, the Company of Pastors made sure of his fitness: he had to expound a selected verse from the Bible at one of its meetings. He also had to be a good speaker and his private life had to be above reproach. Once the missionary had passed all the tests, he was given a letter accrediting him to a particular church in France. Local churches were understandably reluctant to admit a minister without Genevan credentials, for all kinds of itinerant preachers, unfrocked monks and crazy heretics were roaming the French countryside. Missionaries were invariably allocated in response to a formal request from a local church. Thus the first of them, Jacques l'Anglois, was sent in response to a request from the brethren of Poitiers for 'an upright man to administer to them the word of God'. The missionaries were at first appointed secretly so as to lessen the risks to themselves and to prevent Geneva from being accused of subverting France. Once a pastor had been assigned to a church, he prepared for his journey. After arranging for the safekeeping of his property in his absence, he would set off, usually in the company of a member of the local church who acted as his guide. Some pastors crossed into France by little-known mountain tracks; others followed the big trade routes, disguised as merchants.[35]

The advent of Calvinism did not immediately impose order and coherence on Protestantism in France. In the towns 'it retained something of the nature of a religious debating society', yet the 1540s and 1550s were marked by the gradual imposition of doctrinal unity under the aegis of Geneva, culminating in the founding of Calvinist churches from 1555 onwards. Calvin distinguished between a community of believers (*église plantée*) and a 'gathered' church (*église dressée*). In 1554 he advised the faithful of Poitiers

35 Kingdon, *Geneva and the Coming of the Wars of Religion*, pp. 5–12, 14–22, 25–40.

on how to 'gather' a church. It required the 'firm foundations' of a discipline in which to elect a minister, distribute the sacraments and baptize children without fear of contamination by papal superstition. The number of missionaries sent to France was clearly inadequate given the rising demand for spiritual guidance. Calvin was overwhelmed by requests for more pastors: suppliants were clamouring for his favours, he said, like the clients of prostitutes. The needs of France could not be remotely met by Geneva's resources. Yet Calvin censured churches that tried to fend for themselves.[36]

Despite its rather messy beginnings, the Reformed church in France achieved a degree of unity around 1559. The first formal 'discipline' in the French church, drawn up in Poitiers in 1557, regulated the selection of ministers, deacons and elders as well as membership of the churches and the control of morals but failed to address several constitutional matters. At the same time Calvin drew up a confession of faith for submission to King Henry II. Two years later a gathering of representatives from various Protestant churches met in Paris in 1559. This meeting, generally regarded as its first national synod, endorsed a 'Confession of Faith' and a 'Discipline'. Calvin was told that the synod had made very few changes to his confession of 1557, but, in fact, it had made several additions. Six dealt with relations between the churches and with their government, but they failed to choose between congregationalism and firm consistorial and synodical direction. The former was implicit in the development of the French church so far, while the latter was urged by Calvin and de Bèze. For them the church was a corporate unity to be directed and represented by those best fitted to do so. Subsequent synods removed the ambiguities contained in the 1559 Confession and Discipline, and consistently upheld the principle of conformity as against congregationalism. They knew that this offered the best chance of facing up to the secular power.[37]

French Calvinism: geographical distribution and population

The geographical distribution of Protestant churches in France was uneven. The majority were situated south of the river Loire in a broad sweep of territory stretching from La Rochelle in the west to the foothills of the Alps in the east, which has come to be known as 'the Huguenot crescent'.

36 Greengrass, *The French Reformation*, pp. 29–32.
37 H. A. Lloyd, *The State, France and the Sixteenth Century* (London: Allen & Unwin, 1983), pp. 128–30.

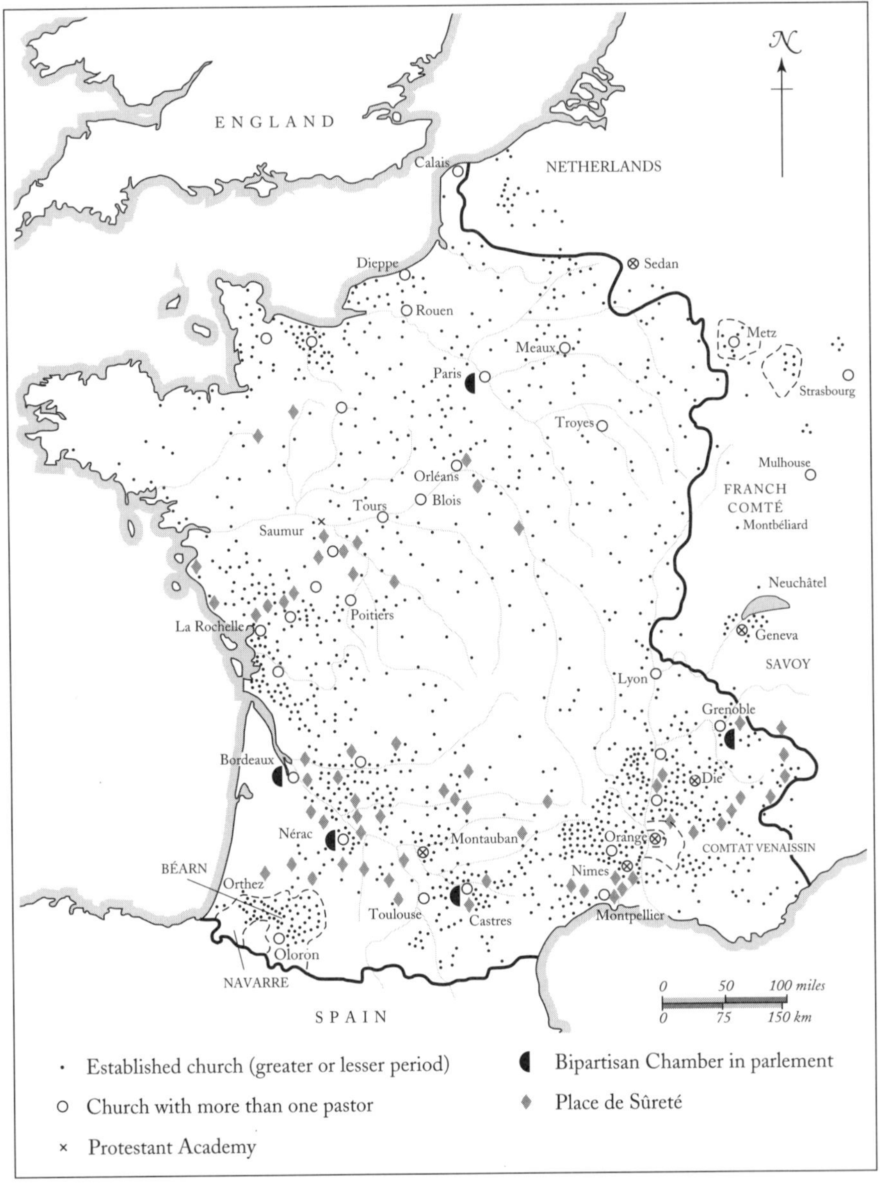

Map 2 The Reformed churches of sixteenth-century France
Source: *Histoire du Christianisme*, Vol. 8: *Le temps des confessions (1530–1620)* (Paris, 1992). Adapted from D. Potter, *The French Wars of Religion* (London, 1997).

Brittany, Picardy, Champagne and Burgundy remained dominantly Catholic. Why the south should have been more receptive to the Calvinist message is a matter for speculation. The proximity of Geneva cannot be the only explanation, for Normandy sent almost as many exiles to Geneva between 1549 and 1560 as did Languedoc. Nor can literacy be the answer, for the south was not more literate than the north, rather the reverse: the book trade was centred mainly in the north. The Midi was, of course, an area with a tradition of organized heresy reaching back to the Albigensians in the thirteenth century, but no direct link has been established between them and the sixteenth-century Calvinists. Distance from the centre of government and a strong sense of local independence may have been important determinants. As Greengrass writes: 'the Calvinist crescent is probably only explicable as an amalgam of such things as the consequences of noble patronage, its small towns with their proud elites of notaries, schoolmasters, city worthies and strong artisanal networks reaching out into the countryside, and the relatively light weight of the royal official presence.'[38]

Protestants were never more than a minority of the French population in sixteenth-century France. No precision is possible owing to a lack of essential documentary evidence: only a few baptismal registers for Protestant communities survive. A figure may be deduced from the number of Protestant churches that were set up, but even this is uncertain. Admiral Coligny submitted a list of 2,150 churches to Catherine de' Medici in 1561, but the number was almost certainly inflated in order to impress her. France probably had no more than 1,200 or 1,250 churches in the 1560s, less than 4 per cent of the number of Catholic parishes.[39] Some churches were very large in the early days of the movement. Rouen's first surviving baptismal register suggests a membership of around 16,500 in 1565; that is to say, 15 to 20 per cent of the city's population.[40] Assuming an average communicant membership of 1,500 per church across the kingdom, we are left with an adult Protestant population of less than two million; in other words, 10 per cent or more of the total population of between 16 and 20 million.[41]

Henry II and Calvinism

Following his father's example, Henry II became involved in a long and costly war with the Emperor Charles V which facilitated the progress of

38 Greengrass, *The French Reformation*, p. 46.
39 Garrisson-Estèbe, *Protestants du Midi*, pp. 64–7.
40 Benedict, *Rouen during the Wars of Religion*, p. 53.
41 Greengrass, *The French Reformation*, p. 43.

heresy in France by diverting his attention from domestic affairs. As alarming reports about the activities of heretics reached him from various corners of his kingdom, Henry admitted to the imperial ambassador that other business had prevented him from dealing with the problem. He denounced Geneva as 'the source of much evil because many heretics are received there and thence disseminate their errors into France'. He was profoundly disturbed to learn that Protestantism, which he had come to regard as a religion of the lower orders of society, was making inroads among the nobility. In February 1557 he asked Pope Paul IV for a brief establishing the Holy Office in France. Three cardinals were appointed as inquisitors of the faith, but the papal brief was never given effect. On 24 July 1557 Henry issued the Edict of Compiègne, which increased the penalties which secular courts could impose for heresy. The preamble noted that earlier edicts had failed to restore religious uniformity. The death penalty was accordingly mandated for obstinate or relapsed sacramentarians, for people who went to Geneva or had books published there, for blasphemers against images of Christ and the saints, and for illegal preaching and participation in religious gatherings, public or private. The act identified heresy with sedition. Henry gave notice that he would use force of arms and the law courts to suppress it. The edict has been aptly described as 'a declaration of war', but fierce resistance by the Parlement prevented its application.[42]

The Genevan missionaries, meanwhile, continued to make converts in France. At first they tried to operate as secretly as possible: they held services in the homes of prominent Calvinists at night and in heavily curtained rooms. If houses were not available, barns or secluded spots in woods were chosen. Sooner or later, however, their activities were bound to come to light. One of the earliest incidents took place in Paris on 4 September 1557, when an angry mob broke up a Calvinist meeting in a house in the rue Saint-Jacques. The congregation included nobles of both sexes, their children, royal officials, artisans and servants. The noblemen, who had swords, were able to fight their way out of the mêlée, but about 132 people, including several women and children, were arrested and thrown into prison. The German Protestant princes, responding to an initiative by the Geneva Company of Pastors, sent an embassy to the king of France. They appealed to his clemency and assured him that the Protestants were neither seditious nor fanatical, but Henry told them to mind their own business. The prisoners were eventually released, but only after they had endured harsh questioning and other forms of legal intimidation.[43]

---

42 Sutherland, *The Huguenot Struggle for Recognition*, pp. 55–6, 344–5.

43 Kingdon, *Geneva and the Coming of the Wars of Religion*, pp. 62–3; I. Cloulas, *Henri II* (Paris: Fayard, 1985), pp. 556–9; Diefendorf, *Beneath the Cross*, pp. 50–51.

The affair of the rue Saint-Jacques happened less than one month after the French army under Montmorency had suffered a crushing defeat at Saint-Quentin (10 August 1557). In the absence of the king who was in Italy with the bulk of his army, the Parisians feared that Spain might attack them next. The threat to the capital became entwined with Calvinist activities in the popular mind. The worshippers of the rue Saint-Jacques were even blamed for France's defeat. Thereafter, they had to meet for a time in small groups, but gradually they recovered their courage and came out into the open. In May 1558 the Calvinists, taking advantage of an apparent softening of the king's attitude, staged a public demonstration in Paris. A crowd of between 4,000 and 5,000 people gathered to sing psalms in the Pré-aux-Clercs – a meadow on the left bank of the Seine within sight of the Louvre. Some important nobles, including the king of Navarre, were reportedly among them. Henry was furious when he was told that 800 armed 'Lutherans' (as all Protestants were still called) had gathered. He ordered the gatherings to stop, yet his anger did not abate when the Huguenots complied. He ordered stiffer penalties for heresy and redoubled his efforts to make peace with the emperor.[44]

The treaty of Cateau-Cambrésis allowed Henry to give more attention to the religious problem in France. It was taken up by the Parlement at a special weekly session, called a *mercuriale*, some of whose members were accused of treating heretics too leniently. On 10 June 1559 Henry II attended such a meeting himself and was dismayed by the opinions expressed by some of the councillors. He threatened to burn one of them, Anne du Bourg, who had dared to criticize his repressive policy. But the king died soon afterwards. Protestants saw the hand of God in this event, and the succession of Henry II's 15-year-old son, Francis II, raised their hopes. The law governing the age of majority for kingship in France was ambiguous. Under an ordinance of King Charles V (1374) the age had been fixed at fourteen, but the ordinance had not been applied following the king's death in 1380. His successor, Charles VI, was only 12 when he was declared a major and crowned. The ambiguity that resulted from this enabled the Protestants in 1559 to argue that Francis II was a minor and that two steps needed to be taken: first, the Estates-General had to be summoned, and secondly, the princes of the blood had to take charge of the government. Their hopes lay in the fact that the princes of the blood were Antoine de Bourbon, king of Navarre, and his brother, Louis, prince de Condé. The former had been seen singing psalms in the Pré-aux-Clercs in May 1558, and the latter's conversion seemed genuine.

---

44 Diefendorf, *Beneath the Cross*, p. 51.

The rights of Antoine de Bourbon were taken seriously not only by Protestants but also by many other people at the French court. They expected Bourbon to return there soon from his residence at Nérac. But the situation took a very different turn. François, duc de Guise and his brother Charles, cardinal of Lorraine, were the king's uncles by virtue of his marriage to their niece, Mary Stuart. Taking advantage of this relationship, they seized control of the government with the consent of the young king and his mother, Catherine de' Medici. The duke took charge of the army and the cardinal of the royal finances. As staunch Catholics they seemed unlikely to unwind the persecution of Protestants which had gathered pace in the last years of Henry II's reign.

Although Protestants had reason to feel disappointed by this situation, they could take some comfort in the dubious legality of the authority being exercised by the Guises. They could argue that it depended upon the king's consent, which, as a minor, he was not entitled to give. This opinion was expressed by Théodore de Bèze in a letter written to his friend Bullinger on 12 September 1559: 'The king,' he wrote, 'has not yet, according to the law, the authority upon which the Guises rely.' Although related to the royal line through marriages, the blood royal did not run through their veins. Moreover, they were widely seen as foreigners in spite of the letters of naturalization which their father, Claude, had obtained in 1506. The Guises, in short, were simply favourites who ruled by the consent of a boy and his mother who were both vulnerable to exploitation.

Meanwhile, the persecution of Protestants by the crown was maintained. The short reign of Francis II was marked by a steep rise in the number of arrests and executions for heresy, and by a series of harsh new laws. Torture was used to extract information from convicted heretics. Large crowds gathered to watch public executions. To prevent the victims preaching to the spectators, the judges sometimes ordered their tongues to be cut out before they were tied to the stake. More often they were gagged. Sometimes a prisoner was strangled before being burnt, particularly if he or she had shown repentance. The crowds could be moved by the religious steadfastness of the victims, but they could also be hostile to them. Sometimes they threatened to snatch a prisoner away from the executioner and to carry out the burning themselves. As the religious conflicts escalated, mobs would cut down the bodies of Protestant martyrs and drag them through the streets before mutilating them.

New laws passed in the autumn of 1559 encouraged popular participation in the repression of heresy. The people were encouraged to inform on their neighbours in return for immunity from prosecution and a share of the property of convicted heretics. Landlords were ordered to enquire into the religious activities of their tenants. Heresy was seen by most Parisians not simply as a departure from Catholic orthodoxy, but also as immoral and seditious. Claude Haton, a Catholic priest of Provins who wrote an interesting account of events in his day, believed that Calvinists indulged in wild sexual orgies after putting out the candles at their meetings. Similar accusations were levelled at them by Antoine de Mouchy, a respected theologian, in a pamphlet. Debauchery was not the only crime imputed to the Calvinists; they were also accused of plotting treason. Haton blamed them for an attack on the king in 1558. In another work, Jean de la Vacquerie, accused them of conspiring to set fire to the capital.[45]

By 1560 the kingdom was on the brink of disaster. All the government's efforts to uphold religious unity had failed. Protestantism, now in the form of Calvinism, was spreading fast across the kingdom and penetrating all ranks of society from the nobility downwards. Although Catholics remained in the majority, they began to feel threatened in their beliefs and in their traditional monopoly of power. At a popular level, Protestantism in its outward manifestations of psalm-singing in public and abstention from Catholic processions and services was seen as a pollutant of the whole social fabric. Acts of inter-denominational violence were beginning to disfigure urban life.

45 Ibid., pp. 52–4.

CHAPTER FOUR

Opening shots (1559–1562)

The Guises soon made themselves unpopular among the nobility by their policies. Faced with a huge public deficit, they adopted a number of drastic economy measures: alienations of crown land by the two previous French kings and grants of *survivances* were revoked; interest on state loans arbitrarily reduced; and pensions, wages and bills left unpaid. Numerous troops were disbanded, payment of their wages being deferred indefinitely. On 4 July 1559, shortly before his death, Henry II had signed an order for the payment of the *compagnies d'ordonnance* at musters to be held later that month. One of Francis II's first acts was to countersign that order and to sign another assigning funds for the companies during the next two quarters, but, at the same time, he slashed their number by almost one third from 8,800 men to 6,275 men. The dismissal of 2,525 men relieved the royal budget of some 700,000 livres per year. And this was only part of a larger demobilization. The artillery train was also disbanded and numerous foreign mercenaries were paid off and sent to their own countries. Several contingents of French infantry were disbanded, while the rest were reduced to their peacetime strength and sent to guard the frontiers of the kingdom. The situation was complicated by the evacuation of the French army, including a large artillery park, from Piedmont.[1] Many demobilized and discontented troops who flocked to court demanding their wages were threatened with capital punishment by the duc de Guise. Some contemporaries saw this as one of the causes of the civil wars. Brantôme wrote: 'France made peace and that was the cause of the civil wars, for a

1 J. B. Wood, *The King's Army* (Cambridge, 1996), pp. 43–4.

Frenchman never existed who did not want to fight, if not foreigners, then his countrymen.'[2]

Unpopular as they were in themselves, the measures taken by the Guises were seen as doubly offensive on account of the exemptions granted to their own clients. The account books of the reign testify to the partisanship of their patronage.[3] They were also accused of preventing nobles outside their circle from gaining access to the king. In addition to their economic measures, the Guises pressed for the enforcement of recent anti-heresy laws and for the punishment of four councillors of the Parlement who had been charged with heresy in June 1559. One of them, Anne du Bourg, was burned at the stake in December after he had dared to complain about the policy of religious persecution and challenged the king's right to have him tried by a commission instead of by the Parlement. French nobles became the target of a skilful campaign of propaganda emanating from Protestant communities in Paris, Strassburg and Geneva. A pamphlet, which may have been written by François Hotman, called on French nobles to free the king from the tyranny of foreigners.[4]

Protestants began by looking to Antoine de Bourbon, king of Navarre and first prince of the blood, to come to their rescue. Soon after Henry II's death, John Calvin sent a pastor to Navarre to tell him that Providence had cleared his path to the regency, but he seemed more interested in reclaiming part of his small southern kingdom (annexed by Aragon in 1512) than in challenging the power of the Guises.[5] In August 1559 François Morel, another Calvinist pastor, wrote to Calvin, asking if other means existed of delivering the Protestant church from its present sufferings. The law laid down that if the king died leaving only minors, the estates should be called to appoint administrators for the realm until the children were old enough to rule. If Navarre refused to call the estates, could someone else call them, and, if peaceful means failed, could force be used to achieve the same end? Calvin replied that only the first prince of the blood could act by law.[6]

Though pressed by his friends to assume his rightful place at the head of the state, Navarre took so long to reach the French court that the Guises were firmly entrenched by the time he arrived. They allowed him to take

2 Brantôme, *Oeuvres*, vol. 4, p. 120.

3 R. R. Harding, *Anatomy of a Power Elite: The Provincial Governors of Early Modern France* (New Haven, Conn., 1978), p. 47.

4 A. Jouanna, *Le devoir de révolte: la noblesse française et la gestation de l'État moderne, 1559–1661* (Paris, 1989), p. 124.

5 N. M. Sutherland, *Princes, Politics and Religion, 1547–1589* (London, 1984), p. 56.

6 Jouanna, *Le devoir de révolte*, pp. 130–31.

his seat in the king's council, but excluded him from the innermost council which decided policy. Moreover, Navarre allowed himself to be removed from the scene by agreeing to accompany Francis II's sister, Elisabeth, to Spain for her marriage to King Philip II.[7]

The Tumult of Amboise (March 1560)

Undeterred by Calvin's advice, enemies of the Guises are said to have consulted French and German jurists about restoring 'the ancient and lawful government of France'. The jurists replied that a coup aimed at overthrowing the Guises would be lawful provided it was led by at least one prince of the blood. At this juncture the conspirators may have approached Navarre's brother, Condé, at whose suggestion an indictment of the Guises was prepared and a plan drawn up to arrest them and make them account for their administration to the Estates-General. Religious considerations may also have moved the conspirators. For Calvinists believed that the people were being 'seduced' by the Catholic church. They interpreted beliefs and practices like transubstantiation, the veneration of saints, the calendar of feasts and fasts as distractions from the central importance of Christ's sacrifice on the cross. Indulgences, anniversary masses, and dispensations were also seen by them as so much swindling of the credulous laity by an avaricious clergy. Many Calvinists believed that if only the king would read the Confession of Faith which their first national synod had recently adopted, he would see that their doctine, far from being seditious, contained the truth of the Gospel. Much of their agitation was thus aimed at presenting the Confession of Faith to the authorities.[8]

Condé's role in the events leading up to the so-called Tumult of Amboise is unclear. He certainly knew that a coup against the Guises was being prepared, but responsibility for its organization was shouldered mainly by Jean du Barry, seigneur de La Renaudie, a petty nobleman from Périgord, who had embraced Protestantism in the course of a turbulent career. In the autumn and winter of 1559 he travelled widely in France and Switzerland gathering support and recruiting mercenaries. He seems to have disposed of generous funds of unknown provenance. In Geneva, La Renaudie made a bad impression on Calvin, but he seems to have received some

7 Ibid., pp. 130, 133; Sutherland, *Princes, Politics and Religion*, p. 62.

8 J. Poujol, 'De la Confession de Foi de 1559 à la Conjuration d'Amboise', *B.S.H.P.F.*, cxix (1973), p. 171.

encouragement from Théodore de Bèze.[9] About 60 or 70 French noblemen, who had settled in Geneva as religious exiles, slipped back into France in response to La Renaudie's call.

While La Renaudie looked for support in Lyon, Périgord and Brittany, Ardoin de Maillane carried out a similar mission in Provence and Languedoc. Soon groups of men disguised as merchants or litigants converged on Nantes where, on 1 February 1560, a meeting, purporting to be the Estates-General, sought to legitimize the forthcoming coup. Its purpose was defined as the dismissal and trial of the Guises while the delegates stressed their loyalty to the king. La Renaudie was chosen as commander of the enterprise and authorized to raise an army. Moving to Paris, he dispatched orders, found more recruits and sent arms, horses, supplies and cash to Orléans and Tours, where his troops were due to assemble.

Secrecy was not easily maintained in sixteenth-century France. On 2 March, as reports of a plot reached the ears of his ministers, Francis II issued the Edict of Amboise, offering an amnesty to all religious prisoners except pastors and conspirators. Responsibility for the edict has been ascribed to the queen-mother and to Michel de l'Hôpital, soon to become chancellor.[10] But, as Evennett has argued, 'it is impossible entirely to dissociate the Cardinal of Lorraine from the Edict of Amboise': He was an astute politician, not the bloodthirsty ogre of Protestant legend. When the pope complained of the edict, Lorraine admitted that he had been its chief advocate. Two years later, Jean de Monluc, bishop of Valence, a champion of toleration, said that, persecution having patently failed, the Guises first saw the need to change their religious policy in the spring of 1560.[11]

Yet the government could not allow a challenge to its authority to go unchecked. As groups of conspirators gathered in woods around the château of Amboise, where the court was in residence, royal troops pounced. La Renaudie and some of his followers were ambushed and killed while others were rounded up, interrogated under torture and executed. Many were drowned in the Loire or hanged from the château's balconies and battlements. The corpses remained on display until April.[12] The streets of Amboise ran with blood, and corpses lay everywhere, so much so that one could not stay in the town on account of the stench and putrefaction. Among those who witnessed the grisly spectacle were Jean d'Aubigné and his eight-year-old son, Agrippa, the future poet, who happened to be travelling to Paris.

---

9 R. M. Kingdon, *Geneva and the Coming of the Wars of Religion in France, 1555–1563* (Geneva, 1956), pp. 69–70.

10 N. M. Sutherland, *The Huguenot Struggle for Recognition* (New Haven, 1980), pp. 104–5, 347–8.

11 H. O. Evennett, *The Cardinal of Lorraine and the Council of Trent* (Cambridge, 1930), p. 99.

12 L. Romier, *La Conjuration d'Amboise* (Paris, 1923), pp. 114–19.

As Jean recognized some of his former comrades in arms among the dead, he exclaimed: 'The butchers have beheaded France!' Then, placing a hand on Agrippa's head, he said: 'My son, you must not spare yourself after me in avenging these brave captains; if you do, I will curse you.' This oath was to rule Agrippa's life and to dictate the opening lines of his famous poem *Les Tragiques*, in which Hamilcar administers an oath to his son, Hannibal, to be avenged on Rome's legions.[13]

Claiming that the coup at Amboise had been aimed at the crown, the Guises also tried to implicate Condé. He had come to Amboise about 14 March and as a test of his loyalty, the Guises had required him to help defend the château. But he came under intense suspicion when a tip-off from one of his servants enabled Edme de Maligny, one of the leading conspirators who had been arrested, to escape. On 2 April Condé affirmed his innocence in the king's presence and challenged to a duel anyone who dared to accuse him. As no one took up the challenge, he left the court and rejoined his brother in Nérac.[14] Here the two men found themselves under pressure to act more vigorously against the Guises. They stood accused of failing in their duty to defend the king and the kingdom against tyranny. Condé apparently reacted more positively to this charge than did his brother. Some letters compromising him were found on one of his servants who was arrested on 26 August.[15] Five days later Francis II ordered Navarre to bring his brother to court.

The aftermath of the Amboise conspiracy is surprising. Instead of using it as a pretext for resuming the persecution of Protestants, the government stood by the Edict of Amboise. At the same time, it looked for peaceful ways of healing the religious division of France. Many people hoped that the General Council of the church, which had been meeting at Trent since 1545, would provide a solution. On past evidence, however, it seemed more likely to widen the gulf between the churches. The French crown was more favourably disposed towards a national council, which Protestants would find more acceptable, but the idea of such a council horrified the pope, who feared that it might be the first step towards an independent Gallican church.[16]

Discontent, meanwhile, continued to mount in the kingdom at large. While the release of religious prisoners was celebrated, public demonstrations against the Guises continued to take place. In Paris an effigy of the

13 M. Lazard, *Agrippa d'Aubigné* (Paris, 1998), pp. 20–24.
14 Romier, *La Conjuration d'Amboise*, pp. 120–25, 129–30.
15 Jouanna, *Le devoir de révolte*, p. 144.
16 A. Tallon, *La France et le Concile de Trente (1518–1563)* (Rome, 1997), pp. 262–9.

cardinal of Lorraine was publicly hanged and burnt. Arsonists attacked his château at Meudon and attempts were made to burn down his residences at Dampierre and in Paris. A torrent of abusive pamphlets denounced the Guises and Catherine de' Medici.[17] Fearing assassination, Lorraine sought the protection of mounted arquebusiers. For the present, however, the Guises were fairly secure. The Tumult of Amboise had shown how difficult it was to topple them by force. However, a process had begun which would transform the dissidents into an army within two years. The Edict of Amboise had banned illicit assemblies and conventicles, yet in practice such meetings continued to take place. Edicts against heresy often proved ineffective because the royal officials responsible for applying them were themselves Protestants or Protestant sympathizers. Consequently, Huguenots were able to demonstrate with impunity. In February and March 1560 Calvinists in Rouen held public meetings for the first time, and, in May, groups of people sang psalms each night in the streets. On a visit to the city in July, the Spanish ambassador was amazed to see 3,000 to 4,000 Huguenots listening to preachers outside the cathedral. In November they were holding religious services in public. When the cardinal de Bourbon visited Rouen, he was subjected to 'thousands of insults'. Calvinists mocked the host, calling it 'a god of paste' and refused to decorate the façades of their houses for the feast of Corpus Christi, as was the custom. Disrespect was also shown to images of saints and to the crucifix. Both were allegedly hung upside down from the public gallows in August 1560, and a statue of the Virgin adorning the façade of the archbishop's palace was attacked repeatedly. Immodest celebrations of religious festivals were frequently disrupted and Calvinists arrested by the authorities were often set free by their co-religionists. Like Calvin, the Reformed church in Normandy disapproved of sedition. In 1560, the provincial synod affirmed its opposition to acts of iconoclasm, while the consistory of Rouen condemned acts of violence committed by members. But the concern for public order shown by the urban élite was not always shared by its social inferiors.[18] Disturbances also occurred elsewhere. In the Rhône valley, for example, reformers attacked Catholic churches and religious houses, such acts being frequently committed by nobles over the heads of the pastors. On 18 May, the Edict of Romorantin transferred the prosecution of heresy from the royal to the ecclesiastical courts, while the punishment of illicit assemblies and seditious acts was entrusted to the presidial courts; but such was the corruption in the courts that Protestant communities were left more or less undisturbed. More public

17 Romier, *La Conjuration d'Amboise*, p. 131.

18 P. Benedict, *Rouen during the Wars of Religion* (Cambridge, 1981), p. 52.

services than ever were held by Protestants in areas where they were solidly entrenched. Conspirators who had survived the Amboise fiasco renewed their efforts. Johannes Sturm, the Strassburg reformer, wrote to the king of Denmark: 'The French conspiracy after its initial suppression, seems today to be spreading and gathering strength: the enterprise, which was once covert, will soon explode into open conflict.'[19]

In June 1560 Michel de l'Hôpital became Chancellor of France.[20] He shared the view of most of his contemporaries that two religions could not co-exist within a state without undermining its political unity, but he also knew that Protestantism was too strongly entrenched in France to be eradicated without violence, an option which he refused to contemplate. Valuing religious uniformity less than political unity, L'Hôpital believed that the best solution for France's domestic problems lay in a reform of the church and judicial system. But it was necessary, first, to restore order to the kingdom by giving the great nobles, including the Bourbons, a share in government. The people also needed to be convinced that genuine reform was on the way.[21] With these ends in mind an Assembly of Notables was called to Fontainebleau on 20 August 1560. It comprised king's councillors, princes of the blood, great officers of the crown and knights of the order of Saint-Michel. The Constable, Montmorency, turned up with a huge escort, but Navarre and Condé chose to remain in Béarn, thereby weakening their contention that they had been deliberately excluded from the government. On 21 August L'Hôpital opened the meeting with a speech in which he compared the state to a sick man whose cure depends on finding the cause of his ailment. Guise and Lorraine followed with an account of their respective ministerial responsibilities: the army and the king's finances.[22] Speaking to the assembly, Jean de Monluc, bishop of Valence, urged the government to be more tolerant towards loyal dissenters and called for a new General Council or a national council to reform the clergy. Another speaker, Charles de Marillac, archbishop of Vienne, argued that if the pope refused to call a General Council, then the king would have to summon a national one. The people's support would only be regained by calling the Estates-General

---

19 Romier, *La Conjuration d'Amboise*, p. 219.

20 Seong-Hak Kim, *Michel de l'Hôpital: The Vision of a Reformist Chancellor during the French Religious Wars* (Kirksville, Mo., 1997), p. 52. L'Hôpital was appointed in April, took up his duties in May but his letters of provision were not signed till 30 June. His salary was paid as from 1 April.

21 R. Descimon (ed.), *L'Hospital: Discours pour la majorité de Charles IX* (Paris, 1993), pp. 7–36; J. H. M. Salmon, *Society in Crisis: France in the Sixteenth Century* (London, 1975), pp. 151–62; Seong-Hak Kim, 'The Chancellor's crusade: Michel de l'Hôpital and the Parlement of Paris', *F.H.* 7 (1993), 1–29.

22 Seong-Hak Kim, *Michel de l'Hôpital*, p. 57.

so that their complaints might be heard and answered. On 23 August Admiral Coligny presented to the king and his mother two petitions from the Protestants of Normandy on behalf of all their French co-religionists. While protesting their loyalty, they begged to be allowed to worship freely pending a General Council.[23] As for the cardinal of Lorraine, he proposed that only disturbers of the peace should be prosecuted, not loyal dissenters. Backing the demand for a General Council, he offered to set up an enquiry to look into the state of the church.[24] This was approved by the assembly and the king summoned the Estates-General for 10 December.

The Huguenots, meanwhile, continued to press the claims of the princes of the blood against the Guises. Early in August, Navarre held a meeting of his council at Nérac, which was attended by François Hotman, the eminent Protestant jurist from Strassburg, and de Bèze. It drew up a remonstrance in which historical precedents were used to back up the claims of the princes of the blood and to denounce the alleged tyranny of the Guises.[25] Meanwhile, elsewhere in France, Huguenots resorted to violence. Maligny captured Lyon and might have stayed there if Navarre had not ordered him to withdraw. Condé began to levy troops and called on several great nobles to assist him. Montmorency refused, but François de Vendôme, vidame de Chartres, agreed to serve against anyone except the king and royal family. But the vidame's letter was intercepted by the authorities and he was sent to the Bastille. Francis II ordered Navarre to bring Condé to court so that he might explain himself. Forced to choose between obedience and revolt, Navarre decided to comply. On 31 October, however, Condé was arrested and put on trial. Protestant historians have alleged that he was sentenced to death but this has been disputed.[26]

On 5 December 1560 Francis II died aged only 16. He was succeeded on the throne by his brother, Charles, who was only ten. His mother, Catherine de' Medici, acted decisively to avert a political crisis. Fearing that the Estates-General might appoint Navarre as regent, she summoned him to court on 2 December, and, in front of the Guises, accused him of sedition. Protesting his innocence, he offered as a goodwill gesture, to cede his claim to the regency to Catherine. She promptly accepted and required Navarre to confirm his surrender in writing. In exchange, she promised

23 J. Shimizu, *Conflict of Loyalties: Politics and Religion in the Career of Gaspard de Coligny, Admiral of France, 1519–1572* (Geneva, 1970), pp. 41–2.

24 Tallon, *La France et le Concile de Trente*, pp. 269–71.

25 A. Jouanna, *La France du XVIe siècle 1483–1598* (Paris, 1996), p. 362.

26 Historians have often alleged that only two judges (one of them Michel de l'Hôpital) failed to sign the sentence, but this seems incorrect. According to De Thou, the sentence was drawn up, but not signed at all. See Seong-Hak Kim, *Michel de l'Hôpital*, p. 60.

him the title of Lieutenant-general of the kingdom. On 21 January the queen-mother was appointed 'governor of the kingdom' with sweeping powers. As the Guises had dominated the government since 1559, she now turned to the Bourbons to establish an equilibrium. Navarre was duly appointed Lieutenant-general of the kingdom, but given only minor responsibilities.[27]

Meanwhile, on 13 December, the Estates-General opened at Orléans with a speech from the chancellor in which he called on all parties to renounce violence. 'You say that your faith is the best,' he said. 'I stand up for mine. Which course is the more reasonable: that I should follow your opinion or you mine? And who will be the judge, if it be not a holy council? . . . Let us remove those devilish names – Lutherans, huguenots, papists – which breed only faction and sedition. Let us not change the name of Christian.'[28] To those who used religion as a cover for sedition, L'Hôpital was merciless: they deserved to be driven out of the kingdom even more than lepers or victims of plague. On 1 January 1561 the estates gave their views on how the government should deal with current difficulties. The clergy's spokesman challenged the king's right to touch the church or dogma. Instead of allowing heretics to have their own churches, he should forbid his subjects to have any dealings with Geneva or any other heretical country. The nobility's spokesman complained of abuses by the church courts and demanded freedom of worship for nobles. The third estate condemned clerical ignorance and avarice. All three orders refused to give the crown any money. On 13 January the chancellor admitted a public debt of 43.5 million livres, four times the crown's annual revenue. After debating the matter for ten days, the third estate declared itself powerless to grant any tax increases; the other orders were equally uncooperative.[29]

The growth of Calvinism

On 28 January 1561 Catherine de' Medici, using her new powers as regent, confirmed the Edict of Romorantin while modifying it. All religious prisoners were to be released and all heresy trials suspended. In effect, all participants in the Tumult of Amboise were pardoned, except the leaders, even pastors being covered by the amnesty.[30] The regent's conciliatory

27 R. J. Knecht, *Catherine de' Medici* (London, 1998), p. 73; J.-H. Mariéjol, *Catherine de Médicis* (Paris, 1920), p. 88; I. Cloulas, *Catherine de Médicis* (Paris, 1979), pp. 154–5.
28 R. Descimon (ed.), *L'Hospital*, pp. 85–7.
29 L. Romier, *Catholiques et Huguenots à la cour de Charles IX* (Paris, 1924), pp. 12–58.
30 Sutherland, *The Huguenot Struggle for Recognition*, pp. 351–2.

policy caused Huguenots to believe that she was coming over to their side. The second Calvinist synod, meeting in Poitiers on 10 March, decided to appoint representatives at court to act as a pressure group for the Reformed church. Evidence exists that such a group was formed though its impact cannot be measured. The synod also drew up a memorandum for presentation to the Estates-General. This demanded that the princes of the blood should be given power, that members of the king's council should be chosen by the estates, and that the cardinals and even the chancellor should be excluded from it.[31]

In the kingdom at large the pace of Protestant expansion quicked perceptibly. At the same time Calvinists began to come out into the open. In Rouen, for example, the number of Huguenots grew to around 15,000 (or 15 to 20 per cent of the city's population) by the end of 1561.[32] In Troyes, the arrival of the minister Jean Gravelle marked the start of the local church's 'wonder year'. In May open-air services were held in spite of attempts by the local *bailli* to stop them.[33] At Étampes, Melun, Meaux and Chartres, Calvinists held services in the open or created disturbances. The need to secure sites where Calvinists might worship in peace became one of their major demands. Here and there they were able to rely on aristocratic support. Thus, at Montargis, where Renée, duchess of Ferrara lived, her Protestant chaplain, François Morel, preached publicly in 1561.[34] Such developments were actively encouraged by the Venerable Company of Pastors in Geneva. According to R. M. Kingdon, 150 Calvinist missionaries were sent from Geneva, Neuchâtel and Berne into France in 1561 and early in 1562.[35] Works of propaganda flowed ever more swiftly into France from the Swiss presses. No less than 27,400 copies of the Psalter were printed in Geneva at the end of 1561 and early in 1562. Famous theologians also rallied to the cause. 'During 1561 and 1562, nearly every one of the Calvinist leaders, saving only Calvin himself and his lieutenant Colladon, paid at least a brief visit to France.'[36] Guillaume Farel set up a base at Gap from which the Reformation spread into Dauphiné and Pierre Viret preached at Nîmes, Montpellier and Lyon.

It was also in 1561 that Calvinists began systematically to seize churches and to destroy statues of the Virgin and saints, crucifixes and altarpieces.

31 Kingdon, *Geneva and the Coming of the Wars of Religion*, pp. 85–6.
32 Benedict, *Rouen during the Wars of Religion*, p. 53.
33 P. Roberts, *A City in Conflict: Troyes during the French Wars of Religion* (Manchester, 1996), p. 59.
34 Jouanna, *La France du XVIe siècle*, p. 376.
35 Kingdon, *Geneva and the Coming of the Wars of Religion*, pp. 79–80.
36 Ibid., p. 81.

Protestant iconoclasm in France can be traced back to 1528 when a statue of the Virgin was vandalized in Paris, but it did not become organized on a large scale until early in 1560. At first it was largely confined to the south of France. From the summer of 1561 acts of iconoclasm became more numerous and were accompanied by the occupation, peaceful or otherwise, of Catholic churches. The crowds of iconoclasts were made up not only of members of the lower orders of society but also of notables, though their respective patterns of behaviour were markedly different. The lower orders turned the destruction of images into festive occasions involving bonfires, singing and dancing. In addition to smashing images, they held banquets, dressed up in ecclesiastical vestments, fed the host to their dogs, roasted crucifixes on spits, spread excrement on the altars, and emptied reliquaries into the streets. They also helped themselves to church property in the form of treasure, provisions, fuel and furniture. Priests and monks who offered resistance were manhandled or killed. By contrast the notables wanted the destruction of images to be carried out in an orderly fashion by legally empowered officials. Inventories were drawn up, accounts carefully kept, and confiscated objects sold at auction. Treasure was melted down for the purpose of aiding the Protestant cause. At this stage, pastors and elders were most anxious to avoid any action which might be construed as rebellious or likely to endanger the social order. Thus the synod of Sainte-Foy pointed out that the removal of 'marks of idolatry' was the responsibility of magistrates, not of private individuals.[37] Various motives doubtless lay behind the iconoclasm: greed, envy, anti-clericalism, the settling of private debts and the sheer fun of pillaging all played a part, but the religious motive – the need to remove idols – was uppermost. Often it was a sermon which prompted a crowd of image-breakers to fall upon a church or religious house. Another frequent occasion was a Corpus Christi procession honouring the blessed sacrament. The iconoclasts aimed to draw the line between what they viewed as the sacred and the profane. The host, the cross and statues of saints were to them merely objects made of bread, wood or stone.[38]

As Calvinists began to worship in the open, they looked to the nobility for armed protection. Soon each church was guarded by a captain and a force of specially trained men. In November 1560 the synod of Clairac in Guyenne, presided over by the pastor Boisnormand, one of the Amboise conspirators, ordered the churches of the province to begin organizing

37 O. Christin, *Une révolution symbolique. L'iconoclasme huguenot et la reconstruction catholique* (Paris, 1991), p. 57.

38 Ibid., pp. 66–7.

military cadres, and in November 1561 the synod of Upper Guyenne meeting at Sainte-Foy completed the task. Two 'protectors' were appointed: one for the area under the jurisdiction of the parlement of Bordeaux and the other for that of the parlement of Toulouse. Colonels were chosen for each regional colloquy and captains were to organize the forces of each church. These were to be kept in a state of readiness in the event of a renewal of persecution. The ministers at Sainte-Foy were instructed to see that mustering was orderly. Some rioting took place but the mustering was generally accomplished in good order. Eventually, this form of military organization spread to every French province. A synod at Nîmes early in 1562 applied it to that area and other synods followed suit. Thus was a military infrastructure established on which the prince of Condé was able to rely when, as 'protector-general', he issued his call to arms in the spring of 1562.[39]

The Catholic backlash

The so-called 'Huguenot Lent' of 1561 was bound to provoke a Catholic backlash. A number of parlements delayed registration of the edicts of toleration or amended them so as to reduce or nullify their effectiveness. In Paris the Parlement, after tampering with the Edict of Romorantin, ordered houses used for Protestant assemblies and services to be razed to the ground. A flood of pamphlets, including some by the priest Artus Désiré, called on Catholics to rally to the defence of their faith. A kind of eschatological hysteria began to hold sway among them: the end of the world seemed nigh and Calvin was identified with the Antichrist heralded in the Apocalypse.[40] The sufferings of the church seemed like the portents of an impending divine punishment. Every Catholic was urged to arm himself and to become the arm of God in the fight against heresy. Such was the message which many preachers carried across to various parts of France. Among the most fanatical was the friar Jean de Hans. It was after one of his sermons that a so-called 'Lutheran' was murdered outside the porch of the church of the Holy Innocents in Paris. Catherine de' Medici was so alarmed by this event that she scandalized Parisians by ordering the preacher's arrest. He was soon released in triumph. He prophesied disasters for France if the king and his mother protected heretics. Preachers whipped up public hatred of the Huguenots by denouncing their nocturnal conventicles as sexual orgies.

39 Kingdon, *Geneva and the Coming of the Wars of Religion*, p. 109.
40 D. Crouzet, *Les guerriers de Dieu* (Paris, 1990), vol. 1, pp. 191–201.

They were also accused of gluttony because they denied the need for fast days and for abstinence in Lent, and charged with sedition because they boycotted ceremonies designed to promote friendship and concord. Insults soon led to blows. At Rennes a royal official warned that public order could not be guaranteed as long as a Jacobin friar was allowed to inflame the people. In several towns, notably Beauvais, Aix and Carcassonne, Protestants were massacred. In addition to committing such crimes, Catholics indulged in penitential and expiatory processions. They also had visions: at Troyes, in August 1561, an enormous cross was seen to change colour each day. Eye-witnesses saw this as a portent of the Second Coming.[41]

Early in 1561 Antoine de Navarre asked to be given more power and tried to drive the duc de Guise from the court. He threatened to leave with the Constable and his Châtillon nephews unless he got his way, but the regent stood firm. After Charles IX had persuaded Montmorency not to desert him, Navarre decided to remain at court. His brother, Condé, was pardoned, released from prison on 8 March and admitted to the king's council. On 25 March Navarre was confirmed as Lieutenant-general of the kingdom and formally renounced his claim to the regency. Angered by these developments, the Guises returned to their estates pending the king's coronation. Montmorency, too, was dissatisfied. He and Guise decided to sink their differences and were soon joined by Jacques d'Albon, marshal of Saint-André. On Easter Monday, 7 April, they formed an association for the defence of the Catholic faith, which has come to be known as the Triumvirate.[42] This was only the most dangerous among several Catholic associations or leagues that were formed about this time. In the autumn of 1561 a league of noblemen was set up in Agenais to fight heresy. At Bordeaux, a syndicate led by two *parlementaires* was created in November to protect Catholic interests. Members of the parlement of Toulouse banded together for the same purpose in the winter of 1561, and at Aix in the summer, the seigneur de Flassans gathered a force of nobles and monks to defend the old faith.[43]

In Dijon, hundreds of Protestants held public meetings in October 1561 which culminated in a riot outside the town hall. The council ordered armed guards to restore order. Catholics and Protestants were ordered home and the council banned further assemblies, but on 1 November Protestant militants gathered in the centre of the city only to be dispersed by a group of wine-growers. The Burgundian parlement ordered an enquiry and

41 Ibid., p. 217.
42 Romier, *Catholiques et Huguenots*, pp. 99–104.
43 Jouanna, *La France du XVIe siècle*, p. 385.

the arrest and prosecution of all those involved. Within months nearly all known Protestants were rounded up and banished from Dijon. This was the result, it seems, of a sense of community fostered by the élites and the large number of wine-growers in the city which bound them to the traditional church. Early appeals were made to the lieutenant-general of Burgundy, Gaspard de Saulx-Tavannes, to come to Dijon. An old campaigner who had given loyal service to the crown, he was also a zealous Catholic. In the absence of the provincial governor, the duc d'Aumale, he acted as governor, but only in a military capacity. His strength lay in his numerous and widespread clientèle. This included Bénigne Martin, the mayor of Dijon. The two men worked closely together to eliminate Protestantism in the city.[44]

On 19 April the government banned the use of the terms 'Huguenot' and 'Papist'. The right to enter houses in pursuit of illegal assemblies was restricted to magistrates and an edict reaffirmed an existing order for the release of prisoners of conscience, but it was sent to local authorities without first being submitted to the parlement for registration.[45] This offended the *parlementaires* and, far from cooling the situation, caused Catholics to think that the regent was turning Protestant.

The search for concord

On 15 May, Charles IX was crowned at Reims. The cardinal of Lorraine used the occasion to speak to the regent. He protested at the spread of Protestantism and suggested that an Assembly of Notables should be called with a view to drawing up a law forbidding religious innovations. On 11 June the Huguenots presented a petition to the king asking for permission to expound their Confession of Faith and for religious exiles to be called from abroad under a safe conduct. They also demanded an end to persecution, protection from outrages, the release of prisoners, permission to hold services in public and to have their own churches or *temples*. To show that they were not seditious, they offered to admit royal observers to their services.

Acting on a complaint from the clergy, Catherine de' Medici consulted the Parlement as well as the princes and members of the king's council in a series of meetings in Paris between 23 June and 14 July. The only tangible result was another edict which seemed to take away with one hand what it

44 M. Holt, 'Wine, community and Reformation in sixteenth-century Burgundy', *P.&P.*, 138 (Feb. 1993), 63–8.

45 Sutherland, *The Huguenot Struggle for Recognition*, p. 352.

gave with the other. It banned all Protestant worship, yet continued to deny the parlements' right to judge cases of heresy. Banishment was to be the maximum penalty for simple heresy (that is non-seditious heresy) and a complete pardon was offered for all offences committed since the death of Henry II. Not surprisingly, the edict satisfied no one and seems never to have been implemented.[46]

On 27 August 1561 the Estates-General met at Saint-Germain-en-Laye. After the opening session, the deputies split up into two groups: the nobility and third estate met at Pontoise, and the clergy at Poissy. The lay estates launched a powerful attack on the clergy's wealth: only the confiscation of the church's revenues, they believed, would serve to clear the public debt. Religious foundations, in their opinion, had been set up originally by the people and were, therefore, national assets which could be legitimately applied to state needs. A proposal was advanced for a sale of church temporalities which would yield at least 120 million livres. This money was to be used in various ways. Alarmed by this proposal, the clergy's representatives, meeting at Poissy, agreed to pay to the crown over six years 1.6 million livres for the redemption of the royal domain and of indirect taxes which had been alienated. Thereafter, over ten years, they would clear the king's debt to the tune of 7.7 million livres. In other words, the French church, for the first time in its history, committed itself to paying the crown an annual subsidy.[47]

The clergy's assembly at Poissy also offered the regent an opportunity to devise a religious settlement acceptable to all sides. It was, in effect, the national council, which the regent had had in mind for some time as an alternative to the Council of Trent. It was attended by the royal family, the princes of the blood, the king's council, six cardinals, more than 40 archbishops and bishops, 12 theologians and many canon lawyers. Most of the prelates were strictly orthodox, but five accepted the crown's proposal that Huguenots should be allowed a hearing. The national council thus became a colloquy.[48] Besides their party at court, the Protestants were represented by 12 ministers assisted by some 20 laymen. De Bèze led the Protestant delegation. Though as firm in his faith as Calvin, he was more conciliatory as to form and, at a meeting with the cardinal of Lorraine, offered some hope of compromise. The aim of the colloquy was not toleration but concord. Toleration was rarely considered in the sixteenth century

46 Ibid., pp. 352–3.
47 I. Cloulas, *Catherine de Médicis*, pp. 163–4.
48 D. Nugent, *Ecumenism in the Age of the Reformation: the Colloquy of Poissy* (Cambridge, Mass., 1974), *passim*; P. F. Geisendorf, *Théodore de Bèze* (Geneva, 1949), pp. 128–9, 136–40; M. François, *Le Cardinal François de Tournon* (Paris, 1951), pp. 411–13; Evennett, *The Cardinal of Lorraine*, pp. 295–9, 337; Tallon, *La France et le Concile de Trente*, pp. 301–15.

outside the writings of theorists such as Sebastian Castellio. Far more common was the notion of religious compromise based on mutual concessions.[49] But the Colloquy of Poissy showed that the gulf between Catholics and Protestants was too wide to be bridged. While the Catholic prelates assumed that the Protestants had come to be instructed or judged, the latter were intent on defending their doctrine. The Eucharist proved to be the main stumbling block. An attempt by Lorraine to persuade the Calvinists to subscribe to the Confession of Augsburg may have been a genuine attempt to find a middle way or a cunning ploy aimed at dividing the Protestants.[50] Either way, it failed, and on 13 October the colloquy dissolved itself.

De Bèze did not return to Geneva immediately. Instead, he preached at the French court, while other Calvinist pastors did so in the kingdom at large. They scored a notable victory by converting Antonio Caracciolo, bishop of Troyes. Their followers too became more aggressive. As both sides gathered arms, the Venetian ambassador reported that a 'great fear' was sweeping the kingdom. Yet Catherine still hoped for conciliation. Early in January 1562 a meeting of the royal council enlarged by the addition of knights of the Order of Saint-Michel and representatives of all the parlements met at Saint-Germain. The chancellor gave a clear outline of the policy which the government had in mind. Those people, he said, who were advising the king to take sides were in effect preaching civil war. Even a pagan could be a citizen. Yet, if L'Hôpital was being forced by circumstances to politicize the religious problem, he still hoped that unity would eventually be restored. On 17 January a new edict, commonly known as the Edict of January, allowed Huguenots for the first time to worship in public provided they did so in the day, unarmed and outside walled towns. Within these towns only private worship was to be allowed. Synods and consistories would be able to meet with the permission of royal officials or in their presence. In other words, the co-existence of two faiths was officially recognized by the crown. The edict, however, needed to be applied and this required more strength than the government had at its disposal.[51]

Huguenots viewed the Edict of January with mixed feelings. It fell short of what they wanted. They were still not free to worship or to have churches of their own. In the Midi they were expected to hand back Catholic churches which they had occupied. Even so, the edict seemed positive enough to be worth defending, especially as it prompted a violent response from Catholics. The parlements of Paris, Dijon and Aix refused to register it. Two *lettres de*

49 M. Turchetti, *Concordia o tolleranza? François Baudouin e i 'moyenneurs'* (Geneva, 1984).

50 Tallon, *La France et le Concile de Trente*, pp. 310–14.

51 Sutherland, *The Huguenot Struggle for Recognition*, pp. 354–6.

jussion had to be issued before the Parlement of Paris would give way and even then it issued a Declaration explaining that its action did not imply acceptance of two religions within the kingdom. A number of provincial governors refused to apply the edict. Catholic preachers also denounced it loudly. At Provins, a friar said that one might as well expect cats and rats to live together in friendship. In sermons and pamphlets Catherine de' Medici was compared to Jezebel who had worshipped false gods and corrupted her husband, King Ahab.

The Catholic reaction to the Edict of January was universally hostile. In Dijon, the mayor, Bénigne Martin, and the city council opposed it as soon as they got wind of it. When asked by the lieutenant-general, Tavannes, to require all heads of households to swear 'to live and die as Catholics', they responded with alacrity, and, when he asked for 200 men to help him evict those who refused to take the oath, they sent him 500. In July 1562 between 1,500 and 2,000 suspected Huguenots were expelled from Dijon. Many of their leaders were imprisoned and much Protestant property was confiscated. The so-called *Saint-Barthélemy dijonnaise* or *journée de Bénigne Martin* set the pattern for the 'cleansing' of Dijon during the rest of the civil wars. In the minds of the local wine-growers Protestantism was identified with the vermin, called *escripvains*, which was destroying their vines. As Mack Holt has shown, 'the particular nature of the Burgundian wine industry, especially in Dijon, had by the sixteenth century led to cultural links with the traditional church that served as a *de facto* bulwark against Protestantism'.[52]

If Catholic zealots rejected the Edict of January, Catholic moderates did not see it as the solution to the kingdom's religious problem. They were sorry that the path of religious 'concord' had been abandoned. An anonymous book, called *Mémoire sur la pacification des troubles* [*Memorandum on the pacification of the troubles*], pointed to the risk of allowing two faiths to exist side by side in France. They were bound to fight each other and to undermine royal authority. A preferable course was to bring Protestants back into the Catholic church by reforming it and offering them various concessions, such as a curb on images, prayers in the vernacular and communion in both kinds.[53]

The massacre of Vassy (1 March 1562)

Following the Edict of January, the Guises retired to their estates and immersed themselves in local politics, flatly refusing invitations to return

52 Holt, 'Wine, community and Reformation', pp. 66–9.
53 Jouanna, *La France du XVIe siècle*, pp. 392–3.

to court. But the cardinal of Lorraine, who was more determined than ever to achieve a rapprochement with the German Lutherans, contacted Christopher, duke of Württemberg, who agreed to meet the duc de Guise at Saverne in the near future. The four Guise brothers met Christopher and four Lutheran theologians at Saverne on 15 February. Christopher's only object was to commend his own faith to the Guises and to plead for toleration for French Calvinists. Lorraine, for his part, was prepared to go to almost any lengths to reach an understanding with the Lutherans. He even conceded that the Mass was merely an act commemorating Christ's sacrifice on the Cross, and not itself a sacrifice. He maintained that, if the Calvinists at Poissy had been less intransigent, an accord would have been possible. Waxing lyrical about the eirenic possibilities of the Confession of Augsburg, he proposed that another colloquy between Catholics and Lutherans should be held in Germany. At the same time, he prophesied that the victory of the Tridentine decrees would be the cause of much bloodshed.[54] As they left Saverne, the Guises solemnly promised to dedicate their energies to the cause of religious unity and to abstain from persecution.

Ten days later, François, duc de Guise set off from Joinville for Paris accompanied by members of his family, noblemen and servants. At Vassy, a small walled town situated within his domain, he stopped to attend Mass in the local church. Nearby stood a barn where many Calvinists had gathered for worship in defiance of the recent edict. What happened next is unclear, for contemporary accounts are contradictory. According to one of them, Guise, on learning that some 500 Calvinists were worshipping close by, decided to remonstrate with them. As some of his company entered the barn, they were invited to join the congregation, but instead they shouted, 'Mort-Dieu, kill them all!' and were duly thrown out. While some of the Calvinists barricaded the entrance to the barn, others climbed on to the roof and started pelting the duke and his men with stones. Some noblemen were struck, including Guise, whereupon they fired on their assailants with arquebuses. Forcing their way into the barn, they shot the worshippers 'like pigeons' as they tried to escape. Others were made to pass between two rows of Guise's men and hacked to pieces. The massacre allegedly left about 30 dead and more than 100 wounded.[55]

Writing to the duke of Württemberg, Guise described the affair at Vassy as an 'accident'. He may have been speaking the truth, for the massacre makes no sense in the light of the recent talks at Saverne. True, the duke

54 Tallon, *La France et le Concile de Trente*, pp. 332–5.

55 E. Pasquier, *Lettres historiques pour les années 1556–1594*, ed. D. Thickett (Geneva, 1966), pp. 97–104; G. Baum and E. Cunitz (eds), *Histoire ecclésiastique des églises réformées au royaume de France* (Paris, 1889), pp. 320–21.

had been under pressure for some time from his mother, Antoinette de Bourbon, who resented the presence of Huguenots at Vassy, so close to her own residence at Joinville, but he had taken no action until now. All that is certain is that for reasons best known to himself Guise failed to stop the slaughter. As far as Huguenots were concerned, Vassy was tantamount to a declaration of war. News of the event spread like wildfire, causing jubilation among militant Catholics in the capital. On 16 March they acclaimed the duke on his return to Paris as a hero. The other Triumvirs and Navarre were also there, as was Condé. The court, for its part, was at Fontainebleau. Catherine de' Medici viewed with alarm the growth of Catholic militancy among the Parisians. She tried to defuse the situation by appointing cardinal de Bourbon as governor of Paris, hoping that he would be acceptable to both Huguenots and Catholics. He ordered Guise and Condé to leave the capital, but only Condé, who felt threatened, did so. However, instead of going to Fontainebleau to protect the queen-mother and her son, he left the way clear for his enemies to go there. With the intention of legitimizing their position, the Triumvirs and Navarre descended on Fontainebleau with a thousand horse and prevailed upon Catherine and Charles IX to return with them to Paris.

The Protestants, for their part, hastily completed the military preparations which had first been envisaged at the synod of Sainte-Foy. The Huguenots' purpose was 'to be on their guard and to defend themselves should their adversaries continue their massacres and undertake to hunt them down as was being frequently rumoured'.[56] This meant gathering funds and raising troops everywhere. In principle each parish was to provide one *enseigne* and all the *enseignes* from the same colloquy were to form a regiment. An army corps was to be made up of all the regiments from a particular province. In other words, the system of recruitment was based on the same principle as had been adopted by the national synod of 1559 for the organization of the church. Levies were to be proportionate to the population, but no strict rule seems to have been followed. According to Claude Haton, all 'who were fit to carry arms and who could afford to equip themselves as infantry or cavalry went to serve the Huguenots'.[57] Michel de Castelnau affirms in his memoirs that the aim of the Huguenot captains was 'to recruit all who could carry arms'. On 25 March 1562 a Calvinist assembly at Saint-Jean d'Angély passed a resolution 'that in good conscience one could and must take up arms for the deliverance of the king

56 M. de Castelnau, *Mémoires*, in Nouvelle collection de mémoires pour servir à l'histoire de France (Paris, 1838), ix, 459.

57 C. Haton, *Mémoires*, vol. I, p. 264.

and queen-mother, and defence of the religion oppressed by those of Guise and their adherents against the edicts solemnly made and published'.[58]

Soon after Vassy, Protestant nobles and their families left the court to gather at Meaux. Condé then marched south to Orléans, capturing the city on 2 April. For Catholics this marked the start of the religious wars. On 7 April the prince ordered the Huguenot army to join him at Orléans. At the same time, he asked the ministers and elders of the Calvinist church to hasten the dispatch of troops for 'the defence of the faith', but some churches at least had anticipated his call to arms. On 3 April the nobility of Saint-Jean d'Angély elected the sire de Saint-Martin de la Coudre as their leader, collected equipment and departed as a force of 300 cavalry to join the nobility of Poitou and Angoumois on the way to Orléans. Charles Léopard, a pastor from Geneva, was chosen to accompany the force as chaplain. Six thousand infantry and two thousand cavalry very soon arrived. The intellectuals of the war party, Théodore de Bèze and François Berauld, also came. Elsewhere, zealous ministers, like Jacques Ruffy at Lyon, set about seizing places of worship. Augustin Marlorat and Martin Tachard did likewise at Rouen and Montauban respectively. Even Calvin entered into the spirit of the struggle: he wrote to the churches requesting funds to pay for the mercenaries d'Andelot had hired in Germany.

58 Kingdon, *Geneva and the Coming of the Wars of Religion*, p. 109.

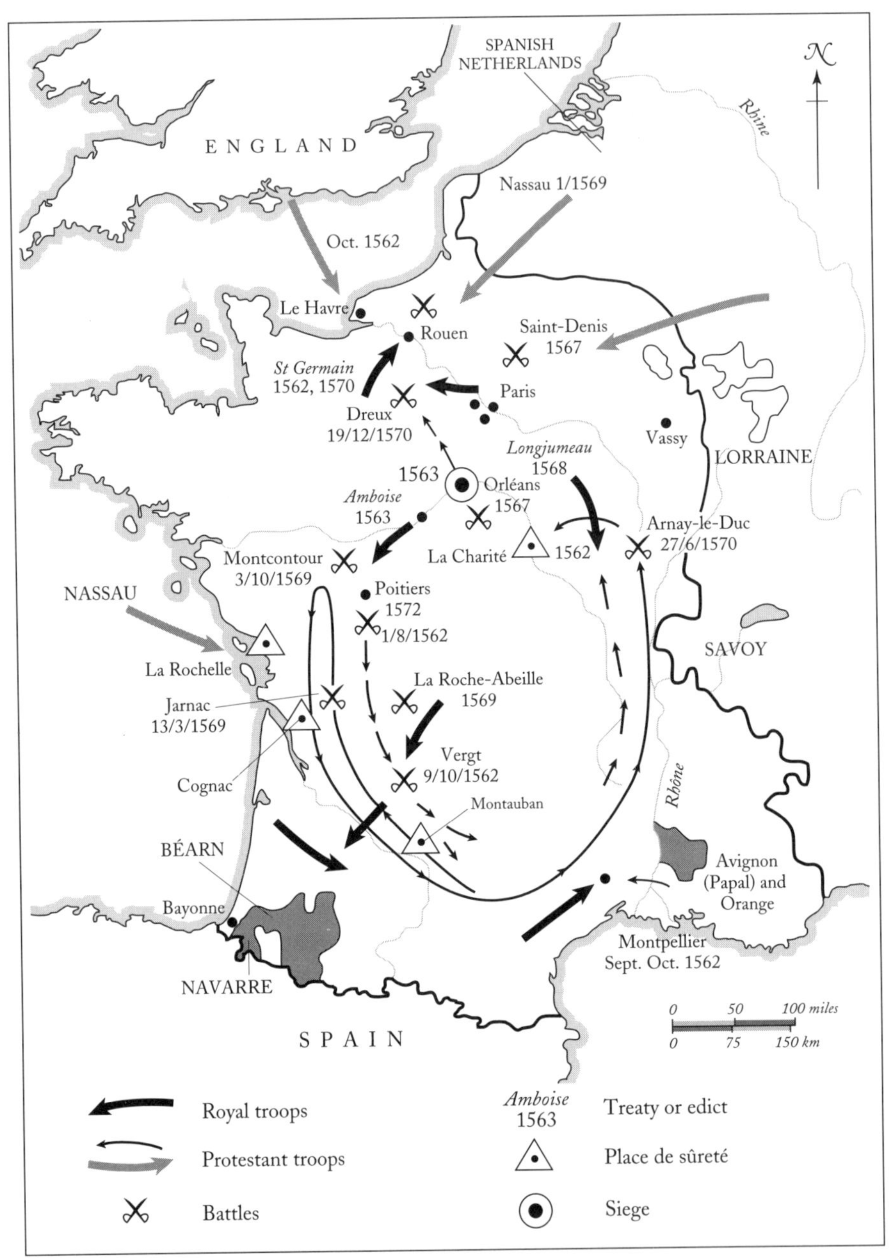

Map 3 The first wars, 1560–72

Source: Based on Michel Péronnet, *Le XVIe siècle, 1492–1620* (Paris, 1995), map 9. Adapted from D. Potter, *The French Wars of Religion* (London, 1997).

CHAPTER FIVE

The first civil war (April 1562–March 1563)

On 8 April 1562, six days after capturing Orléans, Louis, prince de Condé issued a manifesto which was almost certainly drafted by François Hotman and Théodore de Bèze. The prince needed to convince others, and perhaps himself, of the justice of his cause. Thus he claimed that Charles IX was being held prisoner by the Catholic leaders, who were using him to cover their misdeeds. Since Antoine de Bourbon had joined them, it had become necessary for another prince of the blood to take up arms with a view to freeing the king. The manifesto also claimed that Condé was upholding the Edict of January, which had been devised by a large assembly, against three men who had demonstrated their wickedness at Vassy and were now imposing their will upon the king. In seeking to preserve the freedom of conscience which the edict had granted to Protestants, Condé was affirming his adherence to French legal tradition as well as his hatred of tyranny. But the Parlement rebutted his claim by explaining that the Edict of January and its predecessor of July 1561 had been provisional: their purpose had not been to bring about permanent religious change but only to prevent religious troubles. If they had been disobeyed, it was up to the king to put things right and not for subjects to do so on their own authority and by force of arms.[1] On 19 May Condé responded to a new royal edict, imposing religious uniformity, by comparing the Catholic leaders to the Triumvirs of ancient Rome, Augustus, Mark Anthony and Lepidus, who had subverted the Roman republic and its laws. Their power, he argued, had been

1 J.-H. Mariéjol, *La Réforme, la Ligue, l'Édit de Nantes, 1559–1598* (Paris, 1983), p. 77; N. L. Roelker, *One King, one Faith: The Parlement of Paris and the Religious Reformations of the Sixteenth Century* (Berkeley, Cal., 1996), pp. 278–9.

usurped, whereas his was 'God-given and natural'. Unfortunately for Condé, the queen-mother denied that she and her son were being held prisoners. She also declared that the Catholic leaders had acted in the kingdom's best interest. Whereas Vassy might be dismissed as an unfortunate accident, Condé's seizure of Orléans could not be construed as anything other than an attack on the king's authority. By her action, Catherine effectively turned the prince and his followers into rebels.[2]

Condé's manifesto was favourably received by the German Protestant princes. The duke of Württemberg, the Elector Palatine, the Landgrave of Hesse and others assured him of their sympathy. Jacques Spifame, the former bishop of Nevers, who acted as spokesman for the Huguenots at the Diet of Frankfurt, produced letters from Catherine de' Medici asking Condé for military assistance. Her recent volte-face could be taken as evidence that she was no longer a free agent. If so, Condé's call to arms could be construed as legitimate and the German Protestants need have no compunction about helping him and their French co-religionists.[3]

Although the Huguenots had started mobilizing before the Vassy massacre, it seems that their response to Condé's call to arms was largely spontaneous and based on ties of friendship. Haton describes how people of all walks of life, from noblemen to artisans, rallied to the prince's cause. Those who could carry arms or could afford the necessary equipment set off to serve as infantry or cavalry. Others who could not serve in a military capacity, gave money to the cause, making it 'marvellously rich'. A certain André de Gramont rounded up as many soldiers as he could find in the area around Provins and after giving them cash sent them to Orléans in groups of no more than five at a time in order that they should pass unnoticed.[4] La Noue writes in his *Discours*: 'Noblemen arrived unexpectedly from every side without having been called so that within four days more than five hundred were there . . . And in this way the most renowned left the provinces with ten, twenty or thirty of their friends carrying arms secretly and lodging in hostelries or paying to camp out until they met the army and the occasion together.'[5] Each of Condé's 'friends' brought his own 'friends' with him. Sixty out of the 73 who signed a treaty of association, which was published on 13 April, have been identified: one-third came from Condé's *gouvernement* of Picardy and from Valois and Brie, where

2 R. M. Kingdon, *Geneva and the Coming of the Wars of Religion in France, 1555–1563* (Geneva, 1956), pp. 107–8; A. Jouanna, *La France du XVIe siècle, 1483–1598* (Paris, 1996), pp. 397–9.

3 Mariéjol, *La Réforme, La Ligue et l'Édit de Nantes*, pp. 77–8.

4 F. Bourquelot (ed.), *Mémoires de Claude Haton* (Paris, 1857), vol. 1, pp. 264–5.

5 F. de La Noue, *Discours politiques et militaires*, ed. F. E. Sutcliffe (Geneva, 1967), p. 613.

most of his lands were situated. Others came from the west and south-west of France, the Île-de-France and Normandy. However, as they were only 'friends', not 'clients', they retained a certain freedom of action. Two subsequently left Condé's army because they disapproved of his appeal for help from England, another after talks with the king had broken down. The nobility, of course, provided the heavy cavalry; for infantry Condé relied largely on volunteers, who were recruited mainly in the Midi. They were joined later by 3,000 *reiters* and 4,000 *landsknechts* whom François d'Andelot recruited in the German Protestant principalities. The army was funded by the sale of confiscated Catholic property and by tax revenues diverted from the king's coffers.[6]

Mobilizing for war

Condé's choice of Orléans as the rallying point for his supporters posed a serious logistical problem to the crown. For, as we have seen, it did not dispose of a large standing army. Such troops as it had in peacetime were mainly heavy cavalry, who were scattered about the kingdom in garrison towns. These were mainly situated along France's northern and north-eastern borders. They faced outward rather than inward, towards France's neighbours and potential or actual enemies. The crown had not envisaged using them against its own subjects. Removing them from their garrisons in order to bring them to Paris or some other venue within the kingdom not only exposed the kingdom to the threat of foreign invasion but was also an operation fraught with practical difficulties. In the first place, all the members of a garrison had to be located, as at least a quarter would be in their homes on leave at any given time. Once assembled, they had to march to Paris, which was difficult in itself, given the poor state of the roads at the time. In addition, the crown needed to raise infantry. The bulk of the infantry in wartime – the 'new bands' or *aventuriers* – were recruited in the provinces by captains commissioned to do so by the provincial governors. The troops, once raised, had to be equipped, mustered and paid. But the French infantry, precisely because it was a temporary force, lacked training and expertise. These qualities were only to be found abroad, mainly in Germany or the Swiss cantons. Negotiating the hire of mercenaries, however, was usually a lengthy process, as was the movement of the troops into France. Furthermore, the crown needed to assemble a proper artillery train.

---

6 Jouanna, *La France du XVIe siècle*, pp. 406–7.

It had a good store of guns in Paris and other depots as well as skilled technicians to man them, but a train also required the services of hundreds of teamsters with waggons and carts to carry the munitions, and of thousands of pioneers. All of these needed to be recruited. Satisfying these wartime requirements consumed many weeks, allowing the Huguenots to seize the initiative. While the crown painfully gathered its army, they gained control of a number of important towns and applied their resources to their own war effort.[7]

Less is known about the Huguenot army than about the king's because the relevant documentation is more elusive. The Huguenot army, however, was clearly far from negligible. In leadership, morale and even sometimes numerically it compared well with its rival. A solid military infrastructure already existed by the spring of 1562. The foundations having been laid at the synod of Sainte-Foy in 1560, it was funded by gifts from Protestant churches, by property confiscated from the 'Papists' and by tax revenues diverted from the royal coffers. The Huguenot army, like the king's, comprised cavalry and infantry. In 1562 François d'Andelot, colonel-general of the king's infantry, defected, bringing with him part of his clientèle. The infantry companies consisted of 100 to 150 men. Only about one-fifth were pikemen; the rest were arquebusiers. By 1562 it seems that some companies were made up entirely of arquebusiers. The nucleus of the heavy cavalry consisted of four companies of the king's army, who went over *en masse* to the Huguenot side. The rest were volunteers raised by the Huguenot leaders among their friends and dependents.[8]

Charles IX's captains dismissed the Huguenot army as a gathering of ragtag and bobtail who had to learn the *métier* of arms. Some of the soldiers may have been raw recruits, but the army also included many professional soldiers, who had fought for the crown in earlier wars. According to Haton, when the first civil war began 'many companies instead of going to the towns assigned to them for the king's service, went to Orléans to serve the Huguenots against the king'.[9] Individual members of other companies which remained loyal to the crown left of their own accord to join Condé. Among soldiers raised by Jacques de Crussol d'Acier in 1568 were 5,000 pikemen

---

7 J. B. Wood, *The King's Army: Warfare, Soldiers, and Society during the Wars of Religion in France, 1562–1576* (Cambridge, 1996), pp. 55–66, 98–102; J. B. Wood, 'The royal army during the early Wars of Religion', in *Society and Institutions in Early Modern France* (Athens, Ga., n.d.), pp. 8–14.

8 A. Jouanna, J. Boucher, D. Biloghi and G. Le Thiec, *Histoire et dictionnaire des Guerres de Religion* (Paris, 1998), pp. 672–3; J. de Pablo, 'Contribution à l'étude de l'histoire des institutions militaires huguenotes: l'armée huguenote entre 1562 et 1573', *A.R.*, 48 (1957), pp. 192–215.

9 Bourquelaut (ed.), *Mémoires de Claude Haton*, vol. 2, pp. 263–4.

and halberdiers. Handling a pike was a skill that required a long period of training. Thus, the idea that the Huguenot army was a scratch force of amateurs cannot be endorsed.

The Huguenot take-over of towns

Catherine de' Medici could not allow the Huguenots to mount a rebellion. She, therefore, took steps to increase the size of the king's army. *Reiters* and *landsknechts* recruited in Germany and 6,000 Swiss infantry were added to existing companies of native French infantry. The commander-in-chief was Antoine de Bourbon, who had under him the Triumvirs: Constable Montmorency, Marshal Saint-André and the duc de Guise. While preparing for war, Catherine still hoped to defuse the situation. She retired to Montceaux in May 1562 and negotiated with the Huguenot leaders, but they demanded nothing less than the removal of the Triumvirs from power and the enforcement of the Edict of January. Trusting in her diplomatic skills, Catherine then engaged in face-to-face talks with Condé. Jean de Monluc suggested that the prince might prove the purity of his motives by offering to go into exile with his followers until the king's majority. The prince seemed ready to oblige but his followers indignantly refused to quit the land of their birth.[10]

Huguenot troops, meanwhile occupied a number of towns in the Loire valley: Tours, Blois, Angers, Beaugency fell between April and May 1562. Elsewhere, too, they made significant gains: Lyon was taken over on 29 April. A chain of command was established at the same time: Jacques de Crussol became Condé's lieutenant-general in Languedoc, Symphorien de Duras in Guyenne, the baron des Adrets in Dauphiné, and the comte de Tende and Paul de Mouvans in Provence. They raised troops and appointed governors in the more important towns. Elsewhere, the citizens themselves chose a local nobleman as 'protector'. These moves were followed by what one historian has described as 'an incredible tornado'.[11] Some towns fell to Condé as their officials rallied to his cause; others were taken over by armed bands usually with the assistance of an urban fifth column. Blaise de Monluc, the king's lieutenant in Guyenne, was bewildered by the speed of the take-overs. 'The Huguenots took us by surprise,' he writes, 'so that it is a miracle that this country has survived given the

10 La Noue, *Discours*, pp. 625–9.
11 J. Garrisson, *Protestants du Midi, 1559–1598* (Toulouse, 1980), p. 168.

secret intelligence which they had in all the towns.'[12] Monluc marched on Montauban, hoping to capture it before it could rebel, but, on hearing that Agen had fallen, he went first to Villeneuve d'Agen, then to Port-Sainte-Marie, only to find them in rebel hands. In April 1562 'all of Guyenne', writes Monluc, 'was lost to the king and the pope'. The same situation was repeated elsewhere: in Angoumois and Saintonge, towns abolished the Mass more or less and appointed Huguenot administrators. In Dauphiné they all went over to Condé, including Valence, whose royal governor was murdered. The new royal lieutenant, Laurent de Maugiron, roamed about the province like a lost soul, not knowing where to set up his headquarters. In Languedoc, Rouergue, the Cévennes and Vivarais, all the towns passed out of royal control. Only Provence resisted the Huguenot tide, probably because it had started there as early as 1561 and Catholic resistance had been given time to crystallize. Orange was recaptured by the royalists in June and Sisteron in September.[13]

The take-over of towns by one side or the other was usually violent. At Sens, in April 1562, Catholics destroyed a barn which the Huguenots used for worship, killing the entire congregation; and at Tours, in July, some 200 Huguenots were thrown in the Loire after they had been bludgeoned to death. Towns were commonly sacked after they had surrendered. One sack would be answered by another. Thus the sack of Blois by Catholic troops in July was answered by that of Beaugency by Huguenots in August. On both occasions the soldiers massacred indiscriminately. At Mornas, Catholics, who had had their throats cut, were put in a boat and allowed to drift down the Rhône. The boat carried the message: 'Oh you people of Avignon! Allow these merchants to pass as they have paid the toll at Mornas.'[14] Such acts of savagery caused revulsion in certain quarters. The poet Ronsard expressed his disgust in a set of poems entitled *Discours des misères de ce temps*. The first, which is dedicated to Catherine de' Medici, describes the calamities of the civil war and expresses confidence in her ability to pacify the warring parties; should she fail, it urges her to punish the rebels.[15]

For all their success in gaining control of towns, the Huguenots failed to capture Aix-en-Provence, Toulouse and Bordeaux.[16] At Aix an attempt by Mouvans to take the town by surprise in the summer of 1560 had been foiled by the citizens with the backing of the local parlement and of the papal legate based at Avignon. At Toulouse, the parlement was forewarned

12 B. de Monluc, *Commentaires*, ed. P. Courteault (Paris, 1913), vol. 2, p. 469.
13 Garrisson, *Protestants du Midi*, pp. 168–9.
14 Jouanna, *La France du XVIe siècle*, p. 408.
15 M. Simonin, *Ronsard* (Paris, 1990), pp. 237, 241–2.
16 Garrisson, *Protestants du Midi*, pp. 168–9.

of a plot to seize the city. The Huguenots seized the town hall, occupied parts of the university and erected barricades in the streets. On 13 May 1562 fighting broke out between thousands of Catholics and Protestants and soon spread to a wide area. The Catholics, who were twice as numerous as their opponents, used four mobile towers to protect themselves from Huguenot snipers. On 15 May they set a whole district alight, destroying more than 200 houses. Huguenots, who had taken shelter in a sewer, were flushed out and thrown into the river Garonne. Ten churches and religious houses fell to the Huguenots. Members of the parlement toured the streets urging the people to murder the Huguenots and to sack their homes. The burning of Protestant bookshops was licensed by the parlement while the homes of rich Protestant merchants were ransacked. On 16 May Huguenots were allowed to leave the city under safe conduct, but many were butchered by peasants outside the city. At Bordeaux, where the Huguenot minority was socially more widely spread, there was far less violence.[17]

The Huguenot seizure of towns was not confined to the south. In Normandy, Caen and Dieppe were soon conquered. In Rouen, the Protestants took steps to protect their assemblies soon after news of the massacre of Vassy had reached them. Two royal captains, who came early in April to raise troops, were driven out. On 15 April Huguenots occupied the convent of the Celestines and the town hall. The *bailli*, Villebon d'Estouteville, was besieged in the castle, then expelled. At first, the Huguenots seemed more interested in defending themselves than in bringing about any major change to the city's day-to-day life. They affirmed their loyalty to the king and explained that they had taken up arms only to prevent a repetition of the Vassy massacre. Catholic members of the town council were allowed to function, as was the parlement. Mass continued to be celebrated in the city's churches. Early in May, however, the mood changed, as gangs of armed Huguenots systematically went from church to church, seizing treasures and smashing altars and fonts. Tapestries, pews, coffers and music books were thrown onto huge bonfires. Although an *Apology of the Ministers and Elders of the Reformed Church of Rouen* claimed that children were to blame, the degree of organization displayed by the iconoclasts tells a different story: 'The destruction probably was the premeditated effort of a group within the church wishing to push through more drastic measures than the magistrates dared to undertake.'[18] The result was an exodus of Catholic merchants, officials and clergy. Catholic services ceased and Catholics

17 M. Greengrass, 'The anatomy of a religious riot in Toulouse in May 1562', *J.Ecc.H.*, 34 (1983), pp. 469–96.

18 P. Benedict, *Rouen during the Wars of Religion* (Cambridge, 1981), p. 98.

stopped attending the town council. On 4 July a new all-Protestant council was voted into office. An extraordinary 'Council established by the People' dominated by the Reformed elders was also set up.[19] Nicolas de L'Isle, the local mint-master, was ordered by this body to receive, weigh and melt down the silver and gold of the cathedral, confraternities, parish churches and other ecclesiastical establishments. This operation raised the tidy sum of 57,934 livres 10 sous 4 deniers which was used to pay for the city's defence. This cannot have been enough, however, to cover all of its defence costs during the long siege that ensued, but precious little is known about the way in which towns taken over by the Protestants were organized for war.[20]

On 13 July Protestants were outlawed by the Parlement of Paris. A decree allowed anyone to slaughter them with impunity. According to the *Histoire ecclésiastique*, peasants left their fields and artisans their workshops and turned into lions and tigers, while women took up arms alongside them. Huguenots, too, went on the rampage. On 27 May they smashed carvings of the Last Judgment framing the west door of Bourges cathedral. Wherever they got the upper hand, they destroyed religious images and stripped altars of their adornments. They melted down chalices and church bells, turning them into coin and cannon respectively. Not even tombs were spared. At Craon the entrails of Anne de La Trémoïlle were tipped out of their urn and spread over the pavement. The iconoclasts sometimes showed scant respect for the monarchy. At Cléry they vandalized the tomb of Louis XI; at Orléans they threw the entrails of Francis II to the dogs and made a fricassee of his heart; at Bourges they cut to pieces the body of Jeanne de France, the first wife of Louis XII.[21] When a nobleman warned Huguenot iconoclasts at Saint-Mézard in Guyenne that they were offending the king, they retorted, 'What king? We are the kings. He whom you call thus is but a little kinglet of shit; we will give him rods and a job to do so that he may learn to earn his living like other men.'[22] That kind of talk, Monluc tells us, was universal, but he must be exaggerating, for it seems that at this stage of the civil war the majority of Huguenots were respectful of the monarchy.

Historians used to describe the iconoclasm which accompanied the first civil war as mindless violence by the lowest orders of society, but recent research has put a different complexion upon it. In towns which Catholics

19 Ibid., pp. 96–9.

20 M. Greengrass, 'Financing the cause: Protestant mobilization and accountability in France', in P. Benedict, G. Marnef, H. van Nierop and M. Venard (eds.), *Reformation, Revolt and Civil War in France and the Netherlands, 1555–1585* (Amsterdam, 1999), pp. 235–6.

21 Jouanna, *La France du XVIe siècle*, p. 411.

22 Monluc, *Commentaires*, ii, 416–17.

recovered from the Huguenots judicial enquiries were set up to investigate such destruction as had taken place. The statements of eyewitnesses indicate clearly that it was the work of various social groups, ranging from notables to proletarians. Their motives were mixed and not always irrational. Let two examples suffice. Early in May 1562, at Saumur, a group of notables came to the abbey of Saint-Florent and began systematically to destroy the statues and altars and to remove precious objects, including the reliquary of Saint-Florent. An inventory of the objects seized was drawn up. Having completed their task, the notables withdrew, leaving the way clear for soldiers to remove or destroy the bells, the organ, the stained glass, and the lead. In their wake a second wave of local Huguenots, accompanied by their families, threw themselves into a frenzy of destruction during which they mocked the clergy by wearing their vestments and giving themselves ecclesiastical titles. They ransacked the monastic larder and gorged themselves on its food and wine. Meanwhile, in the town the notables, aided by goldsmiths, melted down their precious loot. Some of it was allegedly intended to assist the prince of Condé. The sack of Le Mans cathedral in May 1562 is another example of the decisive role played by notables. In this case, office-holders and lawyers seem to have instigated the destruction.[23]

The destruction of religious images was not simply motivated by greed. By insulting the images and by disfiguring them in various ways, the iconoclasts were, in effect, demonstrating that they were nothing but idols. By destroying them they were obeying one of the Ten Commandments, and, in a sense, acting for the king. It could be argued in 1562 that Charles IX was not free to act as his divinely ordained mission required. The iconoclasts also wanted, it seems, to sever links with the past. By inflicting irreparable material damage to church property they hoped to rule out any chance of a return to the past. When Catherine de' Medici reproved the city authorities in Rouen in May 1562 for their inactivity, she foresaw that the actions of the iconoclasts would seriously impede a future peace settlement.[24]

Foreign intervention

As the violence spread, Catherine looked to to the Catholic powers for help. She appealed to the pope, the duke of Savoy, and Philip II of Spain. On 8 May she told the English envoy, Sir Henry Sidney, that she would

23 O. Christin, *Une révolution symbolique: l'iconoclasme huguenot et la reconstruction catholique* (Paris, 1991), pp. 81–101.

24 Ibid., pp. 123–35.

suppress Condé's revolt with Spanish help unless he agreed to her peace terms. At first the Huguenots were more interested in seeking the mediation of foreign princes than in their financial or military aid. Coligny was reluctant at first to expose his co-religionists to the charge of treason. At the National Synod of Orléans on 27 April, he declared that 'he would rather die than consent to let those of the Religion be the first to bring foreign forces into France'. But Huguenot policy changed about the end of May after it had become clear that the French crown had decided to seek military aid from Spain.[25] The Huguenots did not get much help from Geneva. The official policy of the Geneva council was one of neutrality. It turned down Huguenot requests to levy troops in the city, while allowing a number of volunteers to serve in France. When Condé asked the city to pay for 2,000 'pistoleers', Calvin said that it could not afford to do so. The Huguenots were more successful in obtaining arms from Geneva. Although the city banned the sale of horses, arms and munitions without its express permission, many exemptions were granted to merchants. Two Genevan merchants – the Chautemps – supplied des Adrets with gunpowder. Some of it, however, found its way to the Catholics at Nantua. The younger Chautemps was tried for treason and executed. He admitted at his trial that he had begun selling gunpowder in Lyon in 1561, thereby showing that 'someone in southeast France must have been preparing for war long before the Massacre of Vassy posed a threat to the very existence of French Protestantism'.[26]

While d'Andelot raised troops in Germany, two Huguenot agents, the vidame of Chartres and Robert de La Haye, sought financial and military assistance from Elizabeth I of England. She proved responsive but did not allow religious sentiment to override her political interests. Her main concern was to regain Calais, which under the treaty of Cateau-Cambrésis had been returned to France for eight years. The Huguenots promised to press Charles IX for an eventual review of the treaty, but Elizabeth insisted on occupying Le Havre as a security for the return of Calais and reimbursement of a loan of 140,000 crowns. On 20 September her demand was conceded by the Huguenots in the treaty of Hampton Court. Soon afterwards English troops occupied Le Havre, which was to be exchanged for Calais before the eight years' delay specified at Cateau-Cambrésis.

In the meantime, 3,000 *reiters* and 4,000 foot, which d'Andelot had raised in Germany, arrived in France. The *reiters* soon made themselves highly unpopular even among Protestants. 'These *reiters* are always ready to fight,'

25 J. Shimizu, *Conflict of Loyalties: Politics and Religion in the Career of Gaspard de Coligny, Admiral of France, 1519–1572* (Geneva, 1970), p. 88.

26 Kingdon, *Geneva and the Coming of the Wars of Religion*, pp. 115–24.

wrote Hotman, 'but in everything else, they obey no one and show the greatest cruelty. They pillage everything, and that does not satisfy them. They devastate everything and destroy the wines and the harvests.'[27] When the Catholic leaders learnt of their approach, they sent Aumale to levy troops in Champagne, Brie and Burgundy. The *reiters* were none the less able to push westwards to Orléans, arriving there on 6 November. They were not the only foreign mercenaries to enter France at this time. One thousand horse, led by Count Roggendorf, reached Guise's camp in July to be followed on 1 August by the Rhinegrave with five ensigns of *landsknechts*. Ten days later, 1,000 Spaniards reached Burie's camp in Guyenne.[28]

Mobilizing the king's army

On 18 May 1562 Catherine de' Medici informed the French ambassador in Spain that she was assembling an army with a view to enforcing her son's authority. A document submitted to her in July by Antoine de Bourbon sets out a plan of campaign. Four armies were envisaged: one under Montpensier to march on Guyenne; another under Saint-André to recapture Lyon; a third under Aumale to retake Rouen; and the fourth, under Bourbon himself, to confront the Huguenots based at Orléans. The three smaller armies were to pick up artillery in the provinces, while Bourbon was to draw his from depots in Picardy and from the Arsenal in Paris. He explained that he needed 40 cannon, 10,000 cannon-balls and 200,000 livres of gunpowder. Bourbon hoped to have under his command some 46,000 men, excluding the artillery. Less than half were to be French; the rest foreign mercenaries. Commenting on Bourbon's proposal, Catherine warned of the difficulties attached to hiring foreign troops. She also pointed out that the Grand Master of the artillery could not supply all the guns and ammunition that Bourbon had demanded.

Assembling an army at the start of a war was no easy task for the crown. Infantry and light cavalry had to be raised in the provinces and companies of men at arms recalled from all over the kingdom. They then had to be welded together. Experienced French troops being in short supply, the crown had to look abroad for some but hiring mercenaries required lengthy preliminary negotiations and bringing the troops into the main army was subject to long delays. Poor communications within France did not help. By

27 *R.H.*, xcvii (1908), p. 311.
28 Shimizu, *Conflict of Loyalties*, p. 90, n. 28.

contemporary standards the kingdom was vast and its terrain often rough. The rivers had few crossings suitable for an army on the move. The crown needed at least two months and often longer to assemble the core of its field army. Consequently, it failed to seize the military initiative or to prevent the Huguenots from mobilizing. Yet eventually the crown did manage to assemble substantial forces. Precise figures are not available owing to the loss of key documents, but enough *états* and lists survive as well as diplomatic correspondence for some indication to be given of the size of the king's army in the early civil wars. Thus it seems that at the end of 1562 it comprised some 288 companies of all types, totalling 48,000 men. About 62 per cent were French and the rest foreign. In size and composition it closely resembled the armies that had fought in the Valois–Habsburg wars. As Wood observes, historians have often assumed that the French Wars of Religion were fought by small and unprofessional forces. In fact, they involved very large armies whose mobilization 'represented an enormous military effort by the standards of the day'.[29]

The siege of Rouen (28 May–26 October 1562)

In July the main royal army left Paris and marched south. It recaptured Blois and sent out columns under Saint-André and Montpensier to regain other towns along the Loire valley and in Poitou. The army next laid siege to Bourges, capturing it on 31 August. This effectively cut communications between the Huguenots in Orléans and those in the Midi. The Catholic leaders now decided to march on Rouen. They hoped to capture the city before the English could relieve it. This, however, was an unreal fear, as Elizabeth I was more interested in occupying Le Havre than in allowing her troops to venture deeper into Normandy. Catherine de' Medici had opened talks with the Rouennais soon after their initial uprising, but they had foundered over their insistence on the dismissal of Aumale, Guise's brother, as lieutenant-general of Normandy. On 28 May he had laid siege to the city with inadequate forces. Protestant troops were able to enter the city and carry out raids against neighbouring towns. Meanwhile, Catholic members of the parlement, who had fled to Louviers, launched a campaign of terror against Huguenots, thereby provoking retaliation against Catholics who were still in Rouen. The Huguenot defenders of Rouen looked to

29 Wood, *The King's Army*, p. 66.

England for help but they derived scant benefit from the treaty of Hampton Court. By the time 200 Scottish soldiers reached Rouen, it was surrounded by some 30,000 royal troops. Before the arrival of a second contingent of 300 English troops, the royalists captured Fort Sainte-Catherine which commanded the south-east approach to the city.

Catherine de' Medici once again pressed for a negotiated settlement, but the Rouennais were divided. While the merchants and bourgeois were prepared to compromise, other inhabitants – mainly artisans and Huguenot refugees – backed the commander, Montgomery, who wanted to resist. On 21 October the royalists launched an assault. After five days the city walls were breached. Some Huguenot leaders fled on ships; others slipped away to other towns in Normandy under Protestant control. The royal captains tried to avoid a sack by offering their troops a pay bonus, but Rouen was sacked for three days. While Huguenot houses were looted, Catholic ones were spared only in exchange for bribes. Profiteers swooped on the city from as far away as Paris to buy cheap booty from the troops.[30] According to the Spanish ambassador, Chantonnay, the sack of Rouen cost about 1,000 lives. Catholicism soon recovered its dominant position in Rouen. The *parlementaires* returned from Louviers on the heels of the royal troops, and a new city council – without any Huguenot member – was elected. Yet many Huguenots remained in the city.

The search for concord

The civil war in France did not extinguish all hope of reuniting the churches through dialogue. After the failure of her efforts at Poissy and Saint-Germain, Catherine de' Medici no longer believed that such a dialogue was possible in France, but she did not despair of a solution being found by a General Council of the church provided certain conditions were met. She believed that it should be a new council, not just a continuation of the Council of Trent; that it should meet in a venue acceptable to the Protestants; and that its agenda should not be imposed by the Holy See. Catherine rested her hopes on a reform of church discipline coupled with various concessions to the Protestants, such as communion in both kinds and prayers in the vernacular. She evidently did not understand the deep theological gulf that separated the parties.

A key figure in the search for concord between the churches was Charles, cardinal of Lorraine, whose ideas have been too often misrepresented by

30 Ibid., p. 302.

historians. Far from being the fanatical Catholic prelate of Protestant legend, Lorraine was genuinely concerned to reach a doctrinal compromise with the German Lutherans. When he returned to Paris in triumph on 23 April 1562, it seems that he was still hoping to build on the relationships which he had established at Saverne, not realizing how much they had been damaged by the massacre of Vassy. He soon acquired a major role in the government, overseeing its finances. But, attaching more importance to his ecclesiastical duties than to his political career, he suddenly decided to attend the Council of Trent. He could rely on his brother, François de Guise, who commanded the king's army, to uphold the influence of the Guise family at court. The cardinal also probably realized that the civil war precluded any possibility of further discussions on French soil between French Catholics and Protestant theologians from Germany or England. So he decided to go the General Council but with a clear agenda of his own. He wanted a reform of the church, especially of the beneficial system. He wanted the papacy to cease collating to benefices. But the instructions which Lorraine received from Catherine went much further. He was to demand communion in both kinds and the use of French in church services. He was to give his backing to the demands of the German Protestants, should they attend the council, provided they did not contradict the Word of God. Lorraine was also to seek an accord on clerical marriage and on the question of property confiscated from the church.

On 19 September Charles IX sent a circular to some 60 prelates asking them to attend the Council of Trent, but very few were prepared to face the risks and cost of such a journey in the midst of a civil war. In the end, Lorraine, who led the delegation, was accompanied by 12 bishops, three abbots and 18 theologians. The coming of the French delegation was viewed with apprehension in Rome, for Lorraine was regarded as a dangerous churchman who had talked to heretics and spoken scandalously about the papacy. But he did his best to reassure Pope Pius IV. On 23 November the cardinal addressed the fathers at Trent with his usual eloquence. He painted a grim picture of the state of his country, blaming it on the moral corruption of the church which had incurred the wrath of the Almighty. Bishops, he said, were mainly responsible for what had happened, and it was up to them to put matters right. The council should avoid starting new quarrels and new wars. Above all, it should not look like an engine of war aimed at the dissidents. Lorraine made no secret of the fact that he regarded discussions of divine law as a waste of time. Church reform, not dogma, was his top priority.[31]

31 A. Tallon, *La France et le Concile de Trente (1518–1563)* (Rome, 1997), pp. 337–71.

Lorraine's speech was aimed not only at the council, but also at the Protestant powers. Knowing how afraid they were of the council sponsoring the creation of a European Catholic League, he wanted to reassure them. He still hoped that the German Protestants and the English would attend the council. On 23 November he wrote to Montmorency still hoping that the council would find a solution to the religious troubles in France and elsewhere. But a dramatic turn of events in France was soon to alter the situation.

The battle of Dreux (19 December 1562)

The most important Catholic victim of the siege of Rouen was Antoine de Navarre, the royal commander, who was fatally wounded on 15 October. He lived just long enough to taste his victory, but died a few days later at Les Andelys. Condé declared himself Lieutenant-general of the kingdom, but the government appointed the Cardinal de Bourbon as Navarre's successor.

Once Rouen had fallen, many royal troops were sent home for the winter, though garrisons were maintained in towns around Orléans. Guise was hoping to move against the English at Le Havre, but he had to change his plan when he learnt that Condé had left Orléans and was marching on Paris. According to La Noue, the prince merely intended to frighten the inhabitants into putting pressure on the government to open talks.[32] Guise's march eastward was hampered by bad winter conditions. 'Nevertheless everyone in camp took courage, because he was returning to the good French wines and no more needed to drink the cider of Normandy.'[33] Once back in Paris, Guise ordered the suburbs to be evacuated, organized his forces behind the city walls and refurbished the fortifications. At the same time, the government entered into talks with Condé. A short truce was declared which enabled nobles from both sides to fraternize, much to the amazement of the Germans. 'Who are these madmen,' they asked, 'who fraternize one day and kill each other the next?'[34]

On 10 December the Huguenots, realizing that the royal army was preparing to attack them, broke camp and marched on Chartres, but they were slowed down by breakdowns in their artillery train. The troops were also growing restless, particularly the Germans who had not been paid.

---

32 La Noue, *Discours*, pp. 654–5.

33 Bourquelot (ed.), *Mémoires de Claude Haton*, vol. 1, p. 305.

34 La Noue, *Discours*, p. 657.

Even more serious was the lack of a clear strategy. As Chartres was too well defended, the Huguenot leaders looked for another objective. While Condé argued for a return to Paris, which had now lost its garrison, Coligny wanted to march on Normandy, hoping to link up with the English in Le Havre. In the end, his plan was chosen. The Huguenots veered towards the north-east, but, after crossing the river Eure at Maintenon, they came up against the royal army in the open country south of Dreux. It comprised some 19,000 men, but had less cavalry than the Huguenots. According to Castelnau, the Triumvirs hesitated before risking a battle. They consulted the king and his mother, who was surprised that they 'should send for the advice of a woman and a child who were full of regret to see things in such an extreme state as to be reduced to the hazards of a civil battle'.[35] The king's council left the decision to the field commanders.

Early on 19 December the royal army crossed the Eure in silence and formed a line of battle south of Dreux between the villages of Epinay and Blainville. Scouts reported hearing the drums of the Huguenots some two miles to the south, whereupon the commanders decided to force a battle. Leaving its baggage behind, the royal army moved south, forming a line with the van on the right and main battle on the left. For some two hours the two armies stood facing each other. 'Each one,' writes La Noue, 'braced himself for battle, contemplating that the men he saw coming were neither Spanish, English nor Italian, but French, indeed the bravest of them, among whom could be found his own comrades, relatives and friends, and that within the hour it would be necessary to start killing one another.'[36] Coligny then persuaded Condé to advance. Some Huguenot light cavalry and the *reiters* retreated as they came under fire from royalist guns whereupon Condé recalled his vanguard. After resuming its battle formation, the Huguenot army launched an attack.

The battle may be conveniently divided into four phases.[37] During the first, which lasted one hour, the Huguenot cavalry charged the left half of the royal army, penetrating the Swiss infantry. Coligny's cavalry routed that of the Constable, Montmorency, capturing him in the process. Within a short time, the entire left wing of the royal army, except the Swiss, fled, pursued by the Huguenots all the way to the baggage train at Nuisement and to the Eure. Some fugitives fled as far as Paris, where they reported that the Constable had been taken and his army routed. Catherine allegedly

35 *Les mémoires de Michel de Castelnau*, 3 vols. (Brussels, 1731), vol. 1, p. 122.
36 La Noue, *Discours*, p. 661.
37 Wood, *The King's Army*, pp. 191–3.

said: 'In that case we shall have to learn to say our prayers in French.'[38] Meanwhile, the right wing of the royal army under Guise and Saint-André remained in place. During the second phase, which also lasted one hour, the Swiss bore the brunt of the fighting, as they came under attack from Coligny's cavalry returning from Nuisement. The *landsknechts* of the Huguenot army's second line then joined in the fray, only to be repulsed. They barricaded themselves inside the village of Blainville. The Swiss then tried to recapture some guns, thereby inviting a new onslaught by the cavalry which managed to break up their formation. As the Swiss retreated towards the rest of the royal army at Epinay, the German *reiters*, shouting 'Victory!', streamed across the plain to Nuisement in order to loot the royal baggage train. Condé and Coligny, knowing that the major part of the royal army remained intact, attempted to rally their cavalry, which was now dispersed all over the plain. The Huguenot infantry, meanwhile, had lost its cavalry support.

During the third phase of the battle, Guise and Saint-André launched an attack which seemed to sweep the Huguenots from the field. A unit of *gendarmes* supported by Spaniards wreaked havoc among the Huguenot infantry. Condé was captured as the Huguenot cavalry retreated, tired and disorganized, through woods on the east side of the field. The royalists seemed assured of victory and Guise approached Blainville to negotiate the surrender of the *landsknechts*. However, the battle now entered its fourth and last phase, when Coligny emerged from the woods after rallying about 1,000 horse. With more cavalry than their enemy, the Huguenots seemed well placed to win, but they came under withering fire from Guise's arquebusiers. As darkness fell, it became difficult to tell friend from foe. Coligny sounded the retreat and the Huguenot horse withdrew from the field which by now was strewn with thousands of corpses. The ensuing night, which was bitterly cold, must have taken an additional toll of the wounded. Casualties among the Swiss were especially heavy. Next morning one of their officers, Hans Krieg, and some companions toured the field looking for friends. After finding their bodies, stripped naked by scavengers, they transported them to Dreux for burial in the cathedral. Another visitor to the battlefield was the famous surgeon, Ambroise Paré. 'I observed for a good league all around the ground completely covered,' he wrote, 'the estimate was twenty-five thousand dead or more, all dispatched in less than two hours.' Paré treated many noblemen and poor soldiers including many Swiss captains. 'I treated fourteen of them in a single room,' he wrote, 'all wounded by pistol shots and by other diabolical firearms, and not one of

38 C. Oman, *A History of the Art of War in the XVIth Century* (New York, 1937), p. 417.

them died.' Following his return to Paris, the surgeon met several wounded noblemen who had retired there after the battle to have their wounds dressed.[39]

For some time there was uncertainty as to who was the victor. Early reports suggested a Huguenot victory, but it soon became clear that the crown had won. 'Some were of the opinion,' writes La Noue, 'that there was no defeat because the losers had not been routed. But they were deluding themselves, for whoever gains the field, captures the artillery and the standards of the infantry, has enough evidence of victory. Even so, it can be said that the victory is not as complete as when a rout ensues.'[40] What is certain is that the battle had been one of the bloodiest of the century. No precise casualty figures can be given. Paré's estimate was evidently a gross exaggeration. Castelnau claims to have heard a report to Guise that between 8,000 and 9,000 bodies lay on the field, but notes that others present estimated the number at 6,000. The *Histoire ecclésiastique* says 5,000. A modern historian offers 6,000 deaths during the battle 'as a conservative estimate'.[41] Casualties were extremely heavy on both sides. According to De Thou, the Huguenots admitted 3,000 casualties, not counting 1,500 *landsknechts* who had surrendered to Guise. The French infantry were particularly hard hit. A Spaniard wrote: 'We pursued them and inflicted great carnage, killing them as if they had been sheep.' Another wrote: 'Without losing more than six men, we broke them and killed 3,000 of them.' Casualties on the royalist side may have been heavier still. Probably more than 1,000 Swiss died, including their colonel and most of their officers. All but one of the cavalry commanders were killed, wounded or captured. Saint-André was murdered after he had been taken prisoner. Throckmorton reported the loss of 800 nobles, about 3,000 casualties in the infantry and, including prisoners, more than 1,000 in the cavalry. Wood estimates the total number of casualties at around 9,000 to 10,000 of the slightly more than 30,000 men who had stood facing each other that morning. 'Probably one in five of those who had begun the battle had met their death in it.'[42]

Several lessons could be drawn from the battle. For the crown it had been a close run thing and underlined the terrible risk attached to fighting a pitched battle. To lose so many soldiers was bad enough, but to lose such a large number of nobles was to strike at the very heart of the nation. The political scene was transformed as the leaders on both sides were killed, maimed or captured. One may reasonably assume that neither the Catholics

39 Wood, *The King's Army*, p. 199.
40 La Noue, *Discours*, p. 666.
41 Wood, *The King's Army*, p. 200.
42 Ibid., p. 201.

nor the Huguenots would be keen to tempt fate again in the same way. At the same time, the battle had hardened sensibilities.[43] Early hesitations had been overcome and Frenchmen had fought each other to the death for the first time in recent memory. The precedent had sinister implications for the future.

Dreux also had military lessons to teach, some of which contradict historical orthodoxy. Although the Swiss pikemen were at a disadvantage in not carrying firearms, the heroism which they had displayed evidently commended them to the crown and ensured that they would be employed again. On the other hand, the cowardice of the *landsknechts* doubtless explains why the French crown virtually ceased to use them in the next civil wars. Turning to the heavy cavalry, the decisive part which it played in the battle does not support the commonly held view that it had become an anachronism. Even the heavy lance which the *gendarmes* carried proved useful in cutting through blocks of Swiss pikemen. Firearms, too, were important, but the main victims of the *reiters'* pistol fire were not the heavy cavalry but the Swiss foot soldiers.[44]

Following the Constable's capture, the army's leaders proclaimed Guise lieutenant-general by acclamation, a promotion subsequently confirmed by Catherine de' Medici at a formal investiture. The duke did not try to pursue Coligny's army after the battle. He had more pressing matters to attend to. In addition to disposing of the bodies and caring for the wounded, he had to attend a service of thanksgiving at Dreux cathedral, where the captured flags were offered up before being sent as trophies to the king. Soon after Christmas, the duke and the remnants of the royal high command rode to Rambouillet to report to Charles IX and Catherine de' Medici. In a speech describing the battle, Guise deplored the loss of so many French lives and singled out for praise the Constable, who had inspired the troops by his valour, the Swiss, who had fought so heroically, and even Condé for refusing to order anything that he would not risk himself. Afterwards the king thanked Guise for his good services and asked him to take charge of the army in the Constable's absence.[45] The duke treated Condé with the utmost courtesy, having him share his own table and even his bed. Historians have seen this as a cynical ploy aimed at detaching the prince of the blood and the legitimacy he embodied from the Huguenot cause, but Guise was almost certainly performing one of those 'noble deeds' (*beaux actes*) so highly praised by La Noue. 'They should not be buried into

43 Ibid., p. 203.
44 Ibid., pp. 203–04.
45 Ibid., pp. 201–02.

oblivion,' he writes, 'so that others following the profession of arms may learn to imitate them and to avoid the cruelties and other unworthy things which so many allow themselves to do in these civil wars.'[46]

The battle of Dreux also had a direct impact on the Council of Trent, where Guise's brother, the cardinal of Lorraine, had been pressing for a reform of the church in the face of strong resistance from the curialists. Pope Pius IV suddenly became more conciliatory and Lorraine seized the advantage to press home his demand for church reform. But the French government, as represented by its ambassadors, notably Arnaud Du Ferrier, was even more forceful. It did not altogether trust the cardinal and, on 4 January, submitted 34 articles of reform for the council's consideration. Lorraine was anxious for the council to complete its work soon so that he might help his brother fill the power vacuum which Dreux had created at the centre of government. While still believing in church reform as the cure to Christendom's problems, he wanted the war in France to be brought to a decisive conclusion. When he learnt of Condé's capture, he proudly boasted that the victory had opened up the road leading to Germany's return to Catholicism. Lorraine was keen to see the ruin of the house of Châtillon and angered by the pope's failure to institute proceedings against Odet de Châtillon. He had less confidence in his brother's ability as a politician than as a soldier and was afraid that he might lose the fruits of his victory by accepting a compromise negotiated by Catherine de' Medici and Michel de l'Hôpital.

However, Lorraine's bellicose enthusiasm soon waned. The hostility of the curial party, lack of Spanish support at Trent, and the political caution of the Emperor Ferdinand discouraged him. He was also too committed to the idea of church reform to abandon it in favour of a military solution to the religious crisis. He was encouraged in this stance by Catherine de' Medici. She wrote to him on 23 December, saying that she wished to see peace come out of the victory at Dreux 'and that we may see emerge from the place where you are a holy and serious reform of those things which have become debased in the church of God and that this should result in a general religious union and concord'.[47] Charles IX expressed the same opinion in a letter of 18 January 1563 to the Council of Trent. Du Ferrier, who presented the king's letter to the fathers on 11 February, warned them that unless they got to work the troubles afflicting France might spread to Spain and Italy. In mid-February, Lorraine went to Innsbruck to meet the

46 La Noue, *Discours*, p. 667.

47 H. de La Ferrière and B. de Puchesse (eds.), *Lettres de Catherine de Médicis*, 10 vols. (Paris, 1880–1909), vol. 1, p. 456.

Emperor Ferdinand. He had two objectives in mind: first, to win the emperor's support for his reform proposals at Trent; secondly, to arrange Habsburg marriages for his niece, Mary Stuart, and for Charles IX. He failed to get his way on the marriages, but returned to Trent believing that he could count on imperial support for church reform and became more aggressive towards the Curia, even threatening to call the pope to account if he continued to oppose reform.[48]

Funding the war

As Wood has demonstrated, a powerful incentive to peace during the civil wars was the crown's inability to fund a military effort in the long term. It could always scrape enough money together for two or three months, but it would then run into trouble. The troops would cease to be paid and this could lead to mass desertions or worse; they might even surrender to the enemy. The correspondence that survives between the queen-mother, the various captains and ministers of the crown are full of desperate appeals for cash and of dire warnings of the possible consequences of non-payment. They can be traced back to the beginnings of the first civil war. In June 1562 Catherine de' Medici warned Gonnor, the superintendant of finance, that the only veteran infantry company left in Calais had not been paid for three months. In July the French commander in Piedmont reported that his men had not been paid for six months. Cardinal de Bourbon informed Catherine that the garrisons in Picardy were owed six months' pay and that local merchants had cut off their credit. By mid-August, Catherine informed the duc d'Étampes that even the pay of the main royal army was falling into arrears. In August the treasurer, Moreau, wrote from Bourges: there was enough money, he said, to pay the month's musters. But soon after the fall of the town, the governor reported that troops coming from Moulins were owed four months' pay. He had been obliged to lend them money from his own pocket; otherwise they might have starved to death. By September, the king's army was being sustained by hope of sacking Rouen. Catherine de' Medici tried to avert this by promising extra pay if the soldiers abstained, but her offer was ignored. The town was sacked, as we have seen, and many French troops then disbanded with the loot. Guise and the Constable were hard pushed to rally enough men, first to defend Paris, then to pursue Condé. 'You must understand, Monseigneur,' wrote

48 Tallon, *La France et le Concile de Trente*, pp. 376–85.

Robertet to Nemours, 'that we are today so short of money that not a penny can be found for the army of Monseigneur de Guise . . . everyone is nearly dying of hunger.' Letters written by the duke early in 1563 describe his frantic efforts to collect funds for his men. About the same time, Marshal Brissac complained that 23 companies of French foot in Normandy were three to four and a half months behind in their pay. Outside the main area of operations the situation was even grimmer: the garrison at Montreuil, for example, had not been paid for eight months. In March 1563 Catherine asked Gonnor for 400,000 livres as not a sou was left to pay the army besieging Orléans.[49]

The Peace Edict of Amboise (19 March 1563)

After its defeat at Dreux, the Huguenot army withdrew to Orléans. Its surviving infantry provided a more than adequate garrison for the city. Within weeks Coligny had reorganized his cavalry. Ironically, the royal army took longer to recover from the battle. Though some of its units had suffered relatively few casualties, others, notably the Swiss and the French legionaries, had been almost wiped out. The heavy cavalry was so crippled that Guise had to create 17 new companies. The army needed to be rested, refitted and nursed back to health before it could see action again. Funds, too, were urgently needed. Within weeks Guise had to reduce the infantry while ordering basic items of clothing for the men. He had to pacify the Spaniards whose pay was held up at Bayonne and had to retrieve cannon which had become bogged down on roads churned up by the winter rains.[50]

Although the Catholics had been victorious at Dreux, they had suffered enormous political damage, for the Triumvirate was no more. Saint-André was dead and Montmorency was a prisoner in enemy hands. The only surviving Triumvir was François de Guise. But, as La Noue writes in his memoirs, the battle was unusual in that the commanders on both sides were taken prisoner. Louis, prince de Condé, the Huguenot leader, was also a prisoner. This new situation enabled Catherine de' Medici to seek a negotiated peace. She did not want a total Catholic victory, which would have put her at the mercy of the house of Guise, and was consequently prepared

49 Wood, *The King's Army*, pp. 275–80.
50 Ibid., pp. 15, 202–03.

to listen to overtures from Condé. He proposed that the problems that were dividing the kingdom should be submitted to a 'free, legitimate and catholic council' at Lyon, Avignon or Besançon. Such an idea was agreeable to Catherine, who had always wanted to circumvent the Council of Trent by calling an assembly of princes to which Lutherans and Calvinists would be invited. She still hoped that something positive would come from Trent, but warned that 'if through some impassioned precipitancy we were to be denied the fruit, we would look to our own safety and conservation'. The disappearance of so many men who had dominated the French political scene since 1559 gave Catherine more room to manoeuvre. She remained receptive to Huguenot demands. On 2 December Condé asked for a council to meet within six months in order to sort out the kingdom's divisions. If this proved impossible, he asked for a general assembly in France in which everyone, including foreigners, would be allowed to take part. It was accepted by the regent. As messages sent to the cardinal of Lorraine and to the Council of Trent prove, the battle of Dreux strengthened the party of compromise at the French court rather than the hard-liners. This development was viewed with so much concern in Spain that the threat of a new Franco–Spanish war was revived. There was also talk of recalling the French prelates from Trent to take part in a new national council with Protestants taking part.[51]

Many Catholics, however, did not want a settlement which would allow two religions to co-exist in the kingdom. Their mood was reflected in Paris. On 5 January the Bureau de la Ville responded to a letter from Catherine, in which she expressed her desire for peace, by begging her to use the recent victory as a lesson to the rebels that there could only be one religion in France. She was warned that as long as the new faith was tolerated, its adherents would continue to meet, gather strength and fight again. On 17 January the English ambassador informed Elizabeth I that three obstacles stood in the path of peace: Huguenot fears of being trapped, Guise ambition feeding on the troubles, and the Parisians 'who say that they will not change their religion or receive the Huguenots amongst them, whom they have expelled'. The Parisians refused to publish an edict issued soon after the battle of Dreux promising an amnesty to all Huguenots who would return to the Catholic faith. They also took steps to prevent Huguenots slipping back into the capital. Regular searches were ordered and the guard on the city gates tightened up. Huguenot suspects were murdered each day. An accidental explosion at the Arsenal on 28 January, which was followed by a fire, was seen by the people as a Huguenot plot and provoked more

51 Tallon, *La France et le Concile de Trente*, pp. 388–94.

lynchings. On 3 February the Parlement ordered an end to the violence and four days later the regent expressed her grave displeasure over events in the capital and ordered more troops to be stationed there.[52]

On the Protestant side, too, there was a war party. Admiral Coligny, who replaced Condé at the head of the Huguenot movement, set himself three aims: to continue the fight, to rebuild the Huguenot army and to seek help from England. At the end of January 1563 he left d'Andelot in charge of Orléans and went to Normandy where he regained control of a number of towns. At the same time he urged Elizabeth I to send the money which she had promised in the Hampton Court treaty. He explained that his *reiters* had not been paid for three months and were growing restless. Elizabeth complied, but demanded in return recognition of the English possession of Le Havre until Calais was restored and the loan repaid. Her money reached Coligny at Caen on 25 February.[53]

On 5 February Guise laid siege to Orléans. Thirteen days later, as he was about to launch an assault, he was shot in the back by Poltrot de Méré and died a few days later.[54] Poltrot was a Huguenot nobleman who had taken part in the Tumult of Amboise and was allegedly related to La Renaudie. By killing the duke, he served the Huguenot cause, at least in the short term. Many Huguenots now wanted peace without losing Orléans. By his action, Poltrot served both objectives, for it seems that Guise was firmly opposed to an early peace. We cannot be sure, however, that Poltrot had acted under orders. He implicated both Coligny and de Bèze when he was interrogated, but they vigorously denied any complicity on their part, and he later retracted. The Huguenot leaders were most anxious to remain on the right side of the law. They strongly disapproved of the notion that a private individual, claiming divine inspiration, could murder an alleged 'tyrant' outside a judicial process conducted by lawful magistrates. Yet Coligny did not help his own defence by admitting that he had employed Poltrot as a spy and paid him money. Worse still, he freely admitted his joy over the duke's death in a letter to the queen-mother: 'I consider this to be the best thing that could happen to this kingdom and to the church of God and especially to me and all my family and also, if your Majesty permits me to say so, it will be the means to pacify the realm.'[55] This unfortunate

52 B. Diefendorf, *Beneath the Cross: Catholics and Huguenots in Sixteenth-Century Paris* (Oxford, 1991), pp. 68–70.

53 Shimizu, *Conflict of Loyalties*, pp. 97–101.

54 N. M. Sutherland, *Princes, Politics and Religion, 1547–1589* (London, 1984), pp. 139–55; P. de Vaissière, *De quelques assassins* (2nd edn. Paris, 1912), pp. 84–92.

55 Shimizu, *Conflict of Loyalties*, p. 106.

confession only served to convince the duke's widow, Anne d'Este, and other members of the Guise family that the Admiral was to blame for the duke's death. They refused to accept royal declarations of his innocence and set themselves up as avenging angels. There are among the archives at Chantilly two documents which point to the ferocity that attended their efforts. One reads as follows: 'I the undersigned promise and swear by the living God to render such obedience and loyal service to the duc de Guise, the cardinals his uncles, and to his mother, as I had promised to the late duc de Guise, for the recovery of his property as to avenge the death of the said duke up to the fourth generation of those who committed the said homicide or connived at it and of those who are yet defending the culprits.'[56] The duke's murder thus added a new dimension to the civil war in France: an aristocratic vendetta between the houses of Guise and Châtillon as savage as it was prolonged.

The assassination of Guise destroyed the political role of his house in the short term, for his son, Henri, prince de Joinville, was only 13 and his brother, the cardinal of Lorraine was at the Council of Trent. News of the duke's death reached Trent on 8 March, shattering the hopes of the cardinal of Lorraine. No other house, he wrote, was 'as desolate and ruined' as that of Guise. It was so poor and indebted that only the king's benificence could restore its fortunes. Catherine assured him that it would retain all its privileges and that she would follow his advice in all things. But her policy was sharply different from his. He believed that a reform of the church was the essential prerequisite to religious unity, but, in the meantime, wanted the Huguenots to be crushed. Catherine was prepared to compromise with them in order to have peace. Toleration, she thought, would lead to dialogue and dialogue, in turn, to reconciliation. It has been suggested that Lorraine, as the only effective survivor of the house of Guise, now set about forming a Catholic league on a European scale. In fact, even if he had wanted this, it would not have been possible to achieve, for Pius IV and Philip II of Spain were barely on speaking terms. The cardinal was also heartily disliked at the Curia for his reformist views and obstructive tactics at Trent. As Morvillier put it: 'the Huguenots see him as their worst enemy and the pope will see him as no less odious if he continues to speak of reform'. The cardinal felt so helpless that he even turned down offers of help from the dukes of Lorraine and Ferrara to avenge his brother. Lorraine also feared for his life. There were rumours that hired assassins were looking out for him. As a way out of his predicament, the cardinal adopted

56 Chantilly: Musée Condé. Papiers de Condé, Série L, vol. xix, f. 59.

an entirely new tack at Trent which might serve to reconcile him to the papacy. By the summer of 1563 Pius IV and cardinal Borromeo were praising his piety and goodwill.[57]

François de Guise had become a national hero in France following his defence of Metz and his conquest of Calais.[58] Since Dreux he had also become a Catholic hero. News of his assassination caused dismay and anger in Paris. The queen-mother urged the municipal authorities to prevent rioting. The popular fury was directed not only at the Huguenots but also at the crown, for it was rumoured that Catherine de' Medici was negotiating a peaceful settlement harmful to the Catholic church. The English ambassador reported that 'Parisians now say themselves that they are utterly undone; and as their great champion is overthrown, the Huguenots will have all.'[59] When Poltrot de Méré was executed on the Place de Grève in Paris on 18 March, the huge crowd of onlookers fell upon his remains like wild beasts and dragged them through the streets before tearing them to pieces. Next day, the capital turned out in force for the duke's funeral. The cortège was led by 22 town criers ringing bells, and included many bourgeois and merchants carrying flaming torches. In addition to sizeable groups of clerics and nobles, numerous militiamen armed with arquebuses or pikes and wearing chain-mail escorted the duke's coffin.[60] At Notre-Dame there was much weeping and lamentation as a preacher noted for his attacks on heretics delivered Guise's funeral oration. In another pulpit, Artus Désiré put his own gloss on Christ's words to His disciples: 'Let him who has no sword sell his tunic in order to buy one.'

Peace was becoming an urgent necessity for the crown, as the Huguenots remained a serious threat to the kingdom's political unity. Coligny was still fighting, Orléans was holding out and in Languedoc, the Huguenots seemed to be laying the foundations of a separate state within the kingdom. An assembly, which met at Nîmes in November 1562 comprised a representative of the nobility of the Vivarais and 14 delegates from as many towns. They elected the comte Antoine de Crussol as 'chief, defender and conservator'. A further meeting, held at Bagnols in March and April 1563, was attended by 25 representatives of the nobility and 31 of the third estate. It formed a politico-military association of towns and dioceses in Languedoc

57 Tallon, *La France et le Concile de Trente*, pp. 394–400.

58 The duke's death was hailed as a martyrdom in Guisard propaganda. He was even compared to Christ and Poltrot de Méré to Judas Iscariot. See D. El Kenz, 'La mort de François de Guise: entre l'art de mourir et l'art de subvertir', in *Sociétés et idéologies des temps modernes. Hommage à Arlette Jouanna* (Montpellier, 1996), ii, 629–62.

59 *C.S.P.F.* 1563, p. 164.

60 Diefendorf, *Beneath the Cross*, pp. 71–2.

scheduled to last until the king's majority. Its aim was to join Condé's association and to ally with the provinces of Dauphiné and the Lyonnais. While affirming its loyalty to 'the king's majesty', the association planned the mass expulsion of Catholics from eastern Languedoc.[61]

As peace negotiators, Catherine de' Medici employed Condé and Montmorency, who had both been captured at Dreux. The Huguenots objected to releasing the Constable, but, in the end, they were persuaded to do so by Catherine and by Condé's wife, Eléonore de Roye. Condé and Montmorency met on an island in the Loire, watched by the queen-mother and royal councillors from the river-bank. They asked to be freed on parole to consult their respective sides. When they met again on 7 March they were joined by the queen-mother, cardinal de Bourbon, the duc de Montpensier and the secretary L'Aubespine.

The peace talks produced a serious rift among the Huguenots, between, on the one hand, Condé and the majority of Protestant nobles, and, on the other, Coligny and the pastors who were at Orléans. While Condé was prepared to make substantial concessions in return for peace, the pastors wanted better terms, even at the risk of continuing the war. The argument centred on the Edict of January 1562, which the Huguenots, as a party, had pledged themselves to uphold. In preliminary talks, Montmorency indicated that he would never accept a return to that edict. The talks were suspended while each negotiator consulted his advisors. Seventy-two pastors at Orléans submitted a proposal which asked for much more than confirmation and enforcement of the January edict: namely, toleration of Protestant consistories and synods, legal recognition of Protestant baptisms and marriages, the return of offices and property taken from Huguenots for religious reasons, and punishment of those responsible for the Vassy massacre and for all other crimes against the edict. The pastors also asked Condé to demand that Calvinism should be the only form of Protestantism to be legalized in France. These proposals were angrily rejected by the prince, who decided henceforth to consult only his nobles. According to De Thou, no pastors henceforth attended his council. In the end, Condé accepted the Constable's terms and the treaty was signed on 12 March. It was confirmed on 19 March by the Edict of Amboise. 'Everyone shouts Long live France from here to Bayonne,' wrote Montmorency jubilantly to Gonnor. He urged his son, the marshal, to hasten the edict's registration by the Parlement of Paris.[62]

The peace was received badly by both Catholics and Protestants. While the pope and other Catholic powers condemned it outright, many Huguenots

61 Jouanna, *La France du XVIe siècle*, pp. 412–14.
62 F. Decrue, *Anne duc de Montmorency* (Paris, 1889), 356–8.

accused Condé of betraying their cause for his own ends. Coligny said that he had done more damage to the Reformed churches than had their enemies over ten years.[63] Calvin denounced the prince as 'a wretch who had betrayed God out of vanity'.[64] Historians have often assumed that Huguenots were particularly incensed by the social discrimination embodied in the edict, which had effectively transformed their faith into an aristocratic religion; but it seems that this aspect was less important to them than the fact that the edict failed to restore the rights which they had been given by the Edict of January.[65]

63 Shimizu, *Conflict of Loyalties*, p. 113.
64 Mariéjol, *La Réforme, la Ligue, l'Édit de Nantes*, p. 91.
65 Jouanna, *La France du XVIe siècle*, p. 406.

CHAPTER SIX

The armed peace (March 1563–September 1567)

Peace is often more revealing of the causes of conflict than war. Few examples from the past bear this out more eloquently than the four years of so-called peace which followed the first of the French Wars of Religion. The Peace Edict of Amboise (19 March 1563) marked a retreat from the crown's earlier efforts to find a religious solution to the problem that divided Frenchmen. Having failed to achieve religious concord at Poissy and Saint-Germain, the crown now looked to a council, either general or national, to do so. In the meantime, it sought to impose peace by legal and essentially non-religious means.[1] It was a genuine attempt to remove the causes of civil conflict by imposing a legal compromise, but, like so many compromises, it failed in the end because it avoided facing up to the fundamental issues.

The edict's preamble is a clear statement of aims. It acknowledges that for several years God has allowed the kingdom to be afflicted with 'many troubles, seditions and tumults' stemming from religious differences. In order to remove these differences and to prevent 'the fire from burning more fiercely' several assemblies of notables have taken place which have resulted in several edicts and ordinances. Yet 'the malice of time' and God's 'unfathomable justice' have given free rein to more tumults, even to open warfare. Countless murders, acts of pillage, sacking of towns, destruction of churches and temples, battles and other calamities have ensued. Foreigners have entered the kingdom and plans are afoot to introduce more. There has also been a huge loss of life among high-ranking nobles, captains and soldiers on whom the defence of the crown depends, so that France's foreign

1 O. Christin, *La paix de religion. L'autonomisation de la raison politique au XVIe siècle* (Paris, 1997), pp. 34–8.

enemies may be tempted to invade. All these calamities serve only to weaken the kingdom, so the king has decided to act in the hope that time, the outcome of a 'good, holy and free general or national council' and his forthcoming majority will restore peace to his subjects. He has done so with the advice of his mother, princes of the blood, peers of the realm and members of his council.

The king's measures are as follows. Freedom of conscience is allowed to everyone, but Protestant worship is restricted. A nobleman who enjoys rights of high justice may worship on his estates along with his family and servants, but an ordinary fief-holder may worship only in his home with his family. For the rest of the Huguenot population worship is restricted topographically. It is banned altogether in Paris and the surrounding area. Elsewhere it is confined to the suburbs of one town per *bailliage* or *sénéchaussée*; also to towns where Calvinism was practised on 7 March 1563. All church property, goods and revenues which have been seized during the war are to be returned. Everyone is to recover his property, status, honours and offices. Condé is discharged of any obligation in respect of revenues he has seized and taxes he has levied to pay for the recent war. He is also pardoned for minting money, manufacturing artillery and munitions, and also for fortifying towns. His agents and servants are also discharged. All prisoners of war and religious prisoners are to be set free without having to pay a ransom. However, thieves, brigands and murderers are exempted from the amnesty. The edict also pardons completely all past religious injuries and offences, while prescribing the death penalty for anyone trading insults or quarrelling over religion. All 'associations' both within and outside the kingdom are banned as are the levying of funds, the raising of troops or meeting under arms.

In attempting to be fair the edict pleased no one. Protestants mourned the edict of January 1562 which had allowed them to worship anywhere outside walled towns while respecting certain conditions relating to public order. The Peace of Amboise undoubtedly took into account the failure of that edict as well as of the Catholic victory at Dreux. As the Protestant author of an appeal to the king wrote in 1563: how could a remedy applied to only part of the body cure a disease affecting the whole? By restricting Protestant worship to certain towns and people, the edict, he suggested, offered no real solution to the problem which was tearing the kingdom apart. The only remedy, in his view, was complete religious freedom publicly expressed and legally guaranteed.[2] Coligny, who joined Condé only after the peace treaty had been signed, protested vigorously about its sharp reduction of the number of places where Protestant worship was to be

2 Ibid., pp. 55–6.

allowed. He insisted that the Huguenots had a military advantage with two of the Triumvirs now dead and begged to be allowed to exploit it, but Condé was unwilling to reverse the course of events. The pastors and their followers were accordingly obliged to accept the peace, but they did so with a bad grace. Mobs in Orléans destroyed most of the churches which the treaty required them to hand back to the Catholic authorities. At a gigantic communion service de Bèze offered tepid thanks for the peace, but as he left for Geneva a few days later he spoke bitterly to the English ambassador about the conduct of the Protestant military leaders.

In the months that followed a bitter feud developed between Condé and the pastors. The prince continued to employ a chaplain, but François Perrocelli or Pérussel, also called La Rivière, had long acted independently of Geneva and the synodical organization. Condé also became involved in love affairs which earned him a written reprimand from Calvin and de Bèze. Meanwhile, the links between the pastors, Coligny and Jeanne d'Albret, the widow of Antoine de Navarre, became ever closer.

Catholic opposition to the Peace of Amboise was even more virulent than that emanating from the Protestant camp. While Claude Haton denounced it as 'an edict of Huguenot freeedom', many commentators would not admit that it offered any legal protection at all to Protestant worship. They pointed to its provisional character and to the fact that it was being contradicted daily by the king's loyalty to the Catholic faith. By far the most systematic demolition of the edict was written by Jean Bégat in the name of the Estates and Parlement of Burgundy and at the instance of the province's governor, Gaspard de Saulx-Tavannes. Basic to his argument is the principle that 'the king maketh the law' and that he cannot, therefore, have subjects who do not share his faith. Should the king accept such a situation, he would be acting against his own authority. A Christian prince, Bégat argues, has nothing to gain from the co-existence of two mutually hostile religions under the law. Far from rallying to his obedience by disarming, they will gather their own supporters and fuel their rivalry. The prince, instead of being their protector, will find that he has fallen between two stools. In all monarchies the king makes the law and imposes it on his subjects. Bégat holds that the state cannot compromise or negotiate in matters of faith. 'In religion,' he writes, 'there is neither mediation nor neutrality; the line is straight with Jesus Christ and he who is not with him is against him.' Recent history, he claims, bears him out, for the Edict of January 'which mingled in your republic all the opinions using the name of Jesus Christ' has only resulted in civil war.[3] Although unproven, the old

3 Ibid., pp. 57–9.

maxim 'one king, one law, one faith', on which Bégat's argument rests, was a powerful slogan and symbol frequently evoked by critics of the pacification. But only a quarter of Bégat's long discourse is concerned with theory; he attaches more importance to the practical difficulties of enforcing the edict.

Opposition of the parlements

Before the Edict of Amboise could become effective, it needed to be registered and published by the various parlements. Catherine de' Medici was keen that this should be done quickly as she wanted to rid the kingdom of the German *reiters*, who had come to assist the Huguenots. Christophe de Thou, the first president of the Parlement of Paris, tried to reassure her, but, anticipating trouble from Catholic hard-liners, he asked that two princes of the blood – the cardinal de Bourbon and the duc de Montpensier – should supervise the registration.[4] This was accomplished smoothly on 27 March in the presence of the two princes, but the registration was stated to be provisional pending a 'general or national council' and the king's majority. In other words, the Parlement followed to the letter the edict's purpose as stated in its preamble. But the registration, even in its qualified form, could not remove the extreme unease concerning the peace which existed among members of the Parlement.[5] Many had been compelled to take a profession of Catholic faith during the civil war or had absented themselves rather than take it. Now, under the edict, the Parlement was legally obliged to allow absent members to resume their seats and not to insist on them or anyone else taking a profession of faith. On 9 May the king ordered the Parlement to stop requiring a profession of faith from its members and not to coerce those who refused. On 17 May he came to the Parlement for the first time. He excused himself for not having come to the court sooner, blaming his tender age and many preoccupations. The chancellor, Michel de l'Hôpital, then explained the need to alienate church property worth 100,000 écus in annual income in order to meet the cost of ousting the English from Le Havre. This met with a favourable response from de Thou, the first president, and an edict was read out. An *avocat* pleaded the case, citing passages from Roman law to the effect that 'necessity knows no

4 N. L. Roelker, *One King, One Faith: The Parlement of Paris and the Religious Reformations of the Sixteenth Century* (Berkeley, Cal., 1996), p. 285.

5 L. L. Taber, 'Religious dissent within the Parlement of Paris in the mid-sixteenth century: a reassessment', *F.H.S.*, 16 (1990), pp. 695–6.

law'.[6] But, if the edict on church lands proved uncontentious, the quarrel between the crown and the Parlement over the enforcement of the Edict of Amboise rumbled on. In a remonstrance of 22 May the court argued that it had to demand a profession of faith from its members for the sake of law and order, but the king retorted that reasons of state dictated otherwise. A further remonstrance on 25 May claimed that the profession was essential to the exercise of the king's justice since it was part and parcel of his faith.[7]

Le Havre recaptured (30 July 1563)

A school of thought existed in France which argued that the religious divisions of her subjects could be healed by uniting them in one great patriotic campaign against the foreigner. The argument was used in the 1570s by Admiral Coligny when he advocated French military action against Spain in the Netherlands. The Peace of Amboise offered an opportunity of putting the argument to the test, for the English had occupied Le Havre during the first civil war under the Treaty of Hampton Court, which they had signed with Huguenot envoys. Everyone knew, however, that Elizabeth I had only agreed to assist them in her own political interest. She hoped to recover Calais sooner than the eight years stipulated in the treaty of Cateau-Cambrésis by an exchange with Le Havre.

Many Huguenots had had serious misgivings about bringing English troops on to French soil, and they now tried to clear their consciences by helping Charles IX to reconquer Le Havre. Condé and Coligny even disclaimed all knowledge of the terms of the Hampton Court treaty. It has been suggested that the envoys who had negotiated the treaty had been supplied with a blank signed in advance by the Huguenot leaders. Be that as it may, Elizabeth had good reason to feel betrayed by her erstwhile allies. After the Peace of Amboise, both the French government and the Huguenot leaders tried to persuade her to hand back Le Havre, but in vain. Force, it seemed, would have to be used. On 23 June Marshal de Brissac took charge of a large army comprising 30 French ensigns, 37 Swiss ones, two German regiments, 4,000 pioneers and 40 cannon. On 20 July the Constable assumed overall command. The English in Le Havre were an easy target, as their commander, the earl of Warwick, had done nothing to fortify the town. Plague was also decimating the garrison. While the French court took up a position near Fécamp to watch the siege of Le

6 S. Hanley, *The 'Lit de Justice' of the Kings of France: Constitutional Ideology in Legend, Ritual, and Discourse* (Princeton, N.J., 1983), pp. 155–6.

7 Roelker, *One King, one Faith*, pp. 289–90.

Havre, Montmorency and Brissac planned their attack. On 27 July, after three days of bombardment, the garrison surrendered.

Anglo–French relations now became distinctly cool. The English ambassadors, Throckmorton and Smith, were kept under detention for a time, as were their French counterparts in England. The French argued that England had forfeited any rights she had left to Calais by her seizure of Le Havre. Months of wrangling ensued. Eventually, under the Treaty of Troyes (11 April 1564) France retained Calais in return for a payment of 120,000 crowns (roughly what Elizabeth had lent Condé).[8]

Charles IX's majority declared (17 August 1563)

The Edict of Amboise, far from pacifying the kingdom, created more problems than it solved. In Rouen, for example, it was fiercely resisted, as the inhabitants feared that it would lead to the re-establishment of Protestantism in their midst. The parlement refused to register the edict and the Council of Twenty-four petitioned the queen-mother to exempt Rouen from its provisions. When she refused, the parlement passed a law banning any Huguenot who had taken part in the seizure of the city from returning. Those who were allowed to do so were to be disarmed. Late in April many of Rouen's Protestants were still hammering at the gates, asking to be let in. Two of their representatives who tried to see the royal governor, Brissac, were lynched by a mob before they could reach him. The Huguenots retaliated by destroying a church in the suburbs and attacking some houses nearby. These incidents prompted a stinging rebuke from the government. Only then was the edict registered by the parlement and given effect.[9]

During the rest of the year, inter-denominational relations continued to preoccupy the city authorities. Royal troops, who were sent to protect the Huguenots after they had been admitted, were able to contain most potential violence, but the municipal registers are full of recriminations from both sides of the religious divide. Protestants complained that they were being denied access to their goods and offices, while Catholics were alarmed by reports that the Huguenots were stockpiling arms and planning an uprising. No Huguenots were among the civic delegation which met Charles IX when he made his entry into Rouen after his victory at Le Havre. A few

---

8 W. T. MacCaffrey, 'The Newhaven Expedition, 1562–1563', *H.J.*, 40 (1997), 1–21.

9 P. Benedict, *Rouen during the Wars of Religion* (Cambridge, 1981), pp. 114–5.

days later, the Protestants were able to form their own guard of honour, when the prince de Condé and cardinal Châtillon arrived in the city. It is as well to remember these facts when considering the king's decision to hold a *lit de justice* in the parlement of Rouen. It is often assumed that he chose the parlement of Rouen because it was more likely to comply with his wishes than that of Paris. But this seems unlikely given the tense atmosphere that prevailed in the city.

It was on 17 August that Charles IX came to the parlement of Rouen accompanied by his mother, princes, peers, royal councillors and officers of the crown.[10] The king sat on a throne while members of his entourage were disposed on three or four tiers of seats below. The *lit de justice* began with a speech from Charles, who was then in his fourteenth year. Now that he was of age, he declared, he would tolerate no disobedience from his subjects. He ordered them to observe the recent pacification and forbade them to have any dealings with foreign powers without his permission or to raise taxes save by his command. The chancellor, Michel de l'Hôpital then announced the incorporation of Calais into the kingdom and, in a long speech, praised the wisdom of King Charles V for devising a law whereby regencies, which had always proved troublesome, could be terminated without waiting for the normal course of maturation to take place. He explained that Charles IX wished to be regarded as of age in all things everywhere, and in respect of everyone save his mother to whom he reserved the power to command. L'Hôpital then rebuked members of the parlements. The king, he said, wanted all his edicts and ordinances to be observed and maintained, especially the edicts of pacification, and all his officers, including members of the sovereign courts, *baillis*, *sénéchaux*, and others, to administer his justice fairly and honestly.[11] Magistrates, he stressed, should not put themselves above the law but must submit remonstrances if they objected to any piece of legislation. 'Messieurs, messieurs,' he exclaimed, 'the ordinances are above you. You are said to be sovereign courts, but the ordinance is the commandment of the king and you are not superior to the king.'[12]

The ceremony of homage followed. Catherine announced that she was handing over the government to her son. As she took a few steps towards him, he left his throne and came towards her, cap in hand. He declared that she would govern and command as much or more than she had done

10 Hanley, *The 'Lit de Justice'*, pp. 160–72.

11 M. de l'Hôpital, *Discours pour la majorité de Charles IX*, ed. R. Descimon (Paris, 1993), pp. 105–6; Seong-Hak Kim, *Michel de l'Hôpital. The Vision of a Reformist Chancellor during the French Religious Wars* (Kirksville, Mo., 1997), p. 128.

12 Seong-Hak Kim, *Michel de l'Hôpital*, p. 128; L'Hôpital, *Discours pour la majorité de Charles IX*, pp. 105–8.

before. The princes of the blood, cardinals, great officers of state and noblemen then walked up to the king, who had returned to the throne, each in turn making a deep bow and kissing his hand. The doors of the chamber were then thrown open and a proclamation of the king's majority read out, confirming the peace and calling on all the king's subjects to give up their arms.

The *lit de justice* of 17 August 1563 was interpreted by the Parlement of Paris as a deliberate snub and seen as such by at least one contemporary observer.[13] The Spanish ambassador, Chantonnay, writing to Philip II on 19 August, explained that the crown's action had been 'to frustrate the Parlement of Paris and reduce its authority and pre-eminence'.[14] The Parisian court, which considered itself superior to all the other parlements, felt that its status had been diminished by the king's decision to hold a *lit de justice* in a provincial parlement. The chancellor, Michel de l'Hôpital, was certainly intent on demonstrating that all the parlements were equally subordinate to the king's authority in legislation and justice.

Other factors, of course, may have helped to determine the king's choice of Rouen for the declaration of his majority. He and his court had gone to Normandy to be present at the siege of Le Havre. Its reconquest marked the reconciliation of the French Protestants and Catholics who had both contributed to the victory. The reconciliation needed to be sealed without delay by declaring the king's majority and confirming the Edict of Amboise. Charles IX had just entered his fourteenth year, the age of majority for a king of France under a medieval law. By declaring his majority in Rouen rather than waiting until his return to Paris, the king was advancing the peace process by several days. Rouen had endured serious disruptions, including a Huguenot take-over during the civil war. Thus a formal reassertion of the king's authority in the city's parlement must have seemed both appropriate and necessary.

The Parlement of Paris, however, was not easily placated. When on 18 August Charles IX ordered it to register the ordinance of Rouen which linked the declaration of his majority with confirmation of the Edict of Amboise, it refused. The Parlement argued that the majority had no need to be declared and that the edict of pacification had already been registered. There followed a ding-dong struggle between the king and the Parlement which need not be followed here in detail. Rather than register the ordinance of Rouen as it stood, the Parlement raised every conceivable

13 Hanley, *The 'Lit de Justice'*, pp. 172–82; Seong-Hak Kim, *Michel de l'Hôpital*, p. 129.

14 H. de La Ferrière, *Le XVIe siècle et les Valois d'après les documents inédits du British Museum* (Paris, 1879), p. 164; Seong-Hak Kim, *Michel de l'Hôpital*, p. 127.

procedural quibble. Eventually, the king got his way by threatening to suspend the court's members. On 28 September the ordinance of Rouen was at last registered.[15]

In November, Michel de l'Hôpital gave the Parlement of Paris another dressing down. He reminded the magistrates that they administered the king's justice, not their own. The magistrates had no authority to discriminate between one ordinance and another. Such behaviour would only throw justice into confusion. He accused the *parlementaires* of encouraging 'bold and wicked spirits' and expressed his fear that they were raising the hopes of disturbers of the peace by objecting to the edicts of pacification. He deplored the fact that peace had not yet returned despite the Edict of Amboise. As many crimes as before were being committed in the provinces.[16]

Enforcing the peace

The Peace of Amboise proved highly unpopular among both Catholics and Protestants. While Catholics feared the consequences of allowing two religions to co-exist and the return of Protestants to towns which had expelled them, Huguenots resented the new restrictions imposed on their worship. All over the country news of the peace prompted hostile demonstrations against one faith or the other. Opposition to the Edict of Amboise took the form of obstructionism by people occupying positions of power or influence. They would use an office, a clientèle or control of an important institution to delay, alter or stop application of the edict in its entirety. In Paris, the town criers who read out the edict were pelted with mud by an angry crowd. On 7 April the *prévôt des marchands* reprimanded the militia for failing to keep order. Murders and other atrocities were being committed each day. Two Huguenot prisoners were killed after being snatched from their guards. Neither the municipal authorities nor the Parlement lifted a finger to help Huguenots return to their homes. By ordering the gaoler of the Conciergerie to discriminate between those prisoners who performed their Easter duties and the rest, the Parlement showed its unwillingness to allow even freedom of conscience.[17]

In the provinces, too, the edict of pacification was defied generally. A few weeks after it had been registered a Catholic notary estimated that in the

---

15 A full account of the dispute is given in S. Hanley, *The 'Lit de Justice'*, pp. 184–95.

16 Seong-Hak Kim, *Michel de l'Hôpital*, pp. 130–1.

17 B. Diefendorf, *Beneath the Cross: Catholics and Huguenots in Sixteenth-Century Paris* (Oxford, 1991), pp. 72–3.

principality of Chalais, the troubles were continuing. He deplored the fact that in as many as 50 or 60 parishes Easter was not celebrated and the Mass no longer said. A year later, Charles Soudard, syndic of the diocese of Saintes, listed benefices in 95 parishes where the Catholic faith was no longer exercised and the clergy dared not reside. In towns, the peace failed to eradicate confessional disturbances and violence. In Rouen, several hundred armed Huguenots returning from services in a suburb exchanged insults with Catholic worshippers. Three days later a Catholic mob invaded the Palais de Justice demanding action against Huguenot assemblies which were allegedly being held in the city. On the same day statues were smashed in a Catholic church. In June 1564 the arrival in Rouen of the duc de Bouillon, governor of Normandy and a leading Protestant, caused an uproar among the Catholic population.[18] In Tours, trouble over the peace terms lasted well into 1564. One of the chief aims of the small band of Catholic magistrates who ran the city was to prevent the reintegration of Huguenot officers in the presidial court. They managed to do so until January 1564 and, in the meantime, instigated a campaign of terror or pressure against Huguenots found in the city and its suburbs. Protestants, for their part, complained of being denied access by the local inhabitants to the place of worship which had been assigned to them. In June 1564 violence erupted around the Corpus Christi procession. Catholics openly boasted that they would cut the throats of all Huguenots or drown them. The governor's lieutenant, Chavigny, tried to keep order by, as far as possible, excluding Huguenots from the city.[19] Finally, in Troyes, news of the edict's provision for the release of religious prisoners prompted the authorities to kill them off before the amnesty could take effect. After publication of the edict, the city council organized a door-to-door survey of religious opinion. This was to mobilize support for a petition to the king to exclude Protestant worship from Troyes and its suburbs. About 30 people indicated that they would rather die than allow Protestant services in or near the city; others said that if this happened, they would leave. Many replies revealed anxiety concerning the violence that toleration of Protestant services would provoke.[20] A comparable survey conducted in the Midi in the Protestant stronghold of Millau in June 1563 produced unanimous opposition to a restoration of the Mass.[21]

18 Benedict, *Rouen during the Wars of Religion*, pp. 114–17.

19 D. Nicholls, 'Protestants, Catholics and magistrates in Tours, 1562–1572: the making of a Catholic city during the Religious Wars', *F.H.*, 8 (1994), 17–21.

20 P. Roberts, *A City in Conflict: Troyes during the French Wars of Religion* (Manchester, 1996), pp. 123–5.

21 'Procès verbal et enquête constatant la conversion des habitants de Millau au protestantisme par votes unanimes', *B.S.H.P.F.*, 9 (1860), 382–92.

The hostility provoked by the Edict of Amboise and the open resistance to its implementation were matters of grave concern to the government, genuinely committed as it was to the restoration of peace. At first it relied on the existing administrative and judicial bodies to enforce the pacification, but they proved inadequate. On 3 May governors and lieutenants-general were asked to spearhead the process, but they too found the task beyond them. Later that month, the vicomte de Joyeuse, the king's lieutenant in Languedoc, admitted that he had failed to publish the edict in towns 'where those of the new religion have for the past fourteen or fifteen months wielded more authority than I have'.[22] By April the crown had become convinced that only someone of the highest status, such as a prince or a Marshal of France, would be able to disarm the belligerents. Charles IX, therefore, decided to send the four Marshals of France on tours of inspection. They were instructed wherever they went to call before them royal and municipal officials and to find out from them how the edict of pacification was being applied, to listen to complaints from Catholics and Protestants and to provide the necessary remedies. A marshal had the power to call the *gendarmerie* and summon the nobility with a view to imposing order.

On 28 April, the king persuaded the Constable Montmorency to hand over his *gouvernement* of Languedoc to his eldest son, François, Marshal of France and governor of Paris and Île-de-France, and on 6 May the latter was ordered to visit its towns. Two days later Marshal de Vieilleville was appointed as the king's lieutenant-general in the Lyonnais, Forez, Beaujolais and Provence. On 12 May the Constable's younger son, Henri, comte de Damville, became governor of Languedoc. With the dispatch of Marshal Bourdillon to the western provinces the new organization for enforcing the peace was completed. To assist the marshals Charles IX appointed on 18 June 28 commissioners who were members of the *conseil privé* or councillors of the Parlement of Paris. They were expected to enforce the amnesty for acts of war, to restore the property which had been arbitrarily confiscated, to find a site for Protestant worship in each *bailliage* and to inspect local crown officials.[23]

Some idea of the difficulties which the marshals encountered on their tours of inspection can be gathered from the experiences of Marshal de Vieilleville. He arrived in Lyon, which until recently had been held by the Huguenots, on 15 June 1563 and was soon followed by two commissioners. On 24 June the edict of pacification was read out in all public places along

22 C. Devic and J. Vaisette, *Histoire générale du Languedoc* (Toulouse, 1889), vol. 12, p. 669.

23 J. Boutier, A. Dewerpe and D. Nordman, *Un tour de France royal. Le voyage de Charles IX (1564–1566)* (Paris, 1984), pp. 185–6; R. R. Harding, *Anatomy of a Power Elite: The Provincial Governors of Early Modern France* (New Haven, Conn., 1978), pp. 193–4.

with another edict of 17 June calling on everyone to hand over their arms by 1 July. At the same time Vieilleville assigned two places of worship to the Huguenots. Four days later he restored Lyon's fairs and privileges in order to lure back merchants who had moved to Chalon-sur-Saône. On 18 July the Mass was restored in the cathedral of Saint-Jean. The marshal then set off on a tour of Provence. On 28 July he tried in vain to persuade the parlement of Aix to register the Edict of Amboise. After a brief visit to Marseille, he returned to Aix on 30 July and tried to get a group of local nobles to subscribe to the terms of the peace. On 5 August local representatives reaffirmed their opposition to the new religion. On 8 August an agreement was reached: Protestants would be allowed to return to their homes and be disarmed, and the ban on *prêches* would be lifted. After touring Dauphiné for a month, Vieilleville returned to Aix on 15 September and a fortnight later, after another difficult round of talks, finally secured ratification of the Edict of Amboise. But even this achievement proved short-lived, for Catholic councillors in the parlement soon insisted on their Huguenot colleagues taking a profession of Catholic faith before resuming their seats. At Lyon, it took Vieilleville one year to complete his mission. It was not until 23 December, more than five months after he had come to the city, that a new consulate was set up in which power was shared by Catholics and Protestants. The two commissioners completed their overhaul of the judicial machinery in January 1564 and gave the city new police regulations on 30 May. Yet cohabitation between Catholics and Protestants provoked more friction so that by the spring of 1564 Lyon seemed on the verge of another insurrection.[24]

The crown's reliance on the Marshals of France was not the surest way of ensuring a smooth return to peace. Thus Gaspard de Saulx-Tavannes, the king's lieutenant-general in Burgundy, authorized the Catholic inhabitants of towns to remain under arms and to continue guarding their gates day and night on the ground that national security was at stake. By so doing he retained armed control of the towns and was able to monitor the return of Huguenots. In spite of the edict, they did not find this easy. At Mâcon, for example, on 8 June a crowd of some 300 Protestants gathered outside the walls, asking to be allowed to return to their homes. The *échevins* replied that they had not the powers to do so. The Huguenots were told to apply in writing to the town's captain, enclosing a list of the people involved so that residence credentials might be vetted. When a royal official tried to speed things up by ordering the release of prisoners and the return of exiles, the town's captains refused to act without Tavannes' permission. At the same

24 Boutier, Dewerpe and Nordman, *Un tour de France royal*, 187–8.

time Huguenots were repeatedly denied access to municipal bodies or representation on them, however minimal.[25] Another marshal, who interpreted the pacification in a distinctly partisan way, was Henri de Montmorency-Damville. His tour of Languedoc in 1563 was so aggressively Catholic that the king had to ask him to temper his zeal. He was ordered to allow Protestants to have their own places of worship, to stop prosecutions for offences committed during the civil war and to let nobles of either faith come to him bearing arms. Damville's methods succeeded only in hardening antagonisms and attracting the hatred of the Huguenots.[26]

One of the most contentious issues which the royal commissioners had to deal with was the choice of sites for Protestant worship.[27] Whereas under the edict of January 1562 Huguenots had been allowed to worship anywhere outside walled towns, they were now restricted to towns where their worship was already established by 7 March 1563 or to the suburbs of one town per *bailliage*, except Paris and its surrounding area. Huguenots naturally wanted to be allocated an easily accessible site, while Catholics wanted to see their services removed as far as possible from their own. Many Catholic towns sought exemption from the edict on the ground that they were frontier towns and that confessional co-existence in their midst would threaten national security. Where sites of worship were chosen, Huguenots often complained that they were too remote, in barren locations or accessible only by dangerous roads, sometimes through bandit-infested woods. When Huguenots left a walled town, they could be at the mercy of hostile bands of peasants, and, when they returned, they might be set upon by urban mobs. Complaints over the siting of places of worship frequently resulted in prolonged litigation. Alternative sites were sometimes proposed, but not always accepted. Another contentious issue concerned burial sites. In Tours, for example, a quarrel arose over whether the Huguenots were burying their dead on land belonging to the church.[28] In November 1563, at Mâcon, they asked for the right to use a site where they might 'in all safety, peace and modesty' accompany and bury their dead. Tavannes granted them a site outside the town on certain strict conditions: no more than eight persons were to gather there; they were to abstain from all religious services, sermons and hymn singing, and were to bury their dead at dawn.[29]

---

25 Christin, *La paix de religion*, pp. 64–5.

26 F. C. Palm, *Politics and Religion in Sixteenth-Century France: A Study of the Career of Henry de Montmorency-Damville, uncrowned King of the South* (Boston, 1927), pp. 50–63.

27 P. Roberts, 'The most crucial battle of the Wars of Religion? The conflict over sites for Reformed worship in sixteenth-century France', *A.R.*, 89 (1998), 292–311.

28 Nicholls, 'Protestants, Catholics and magistrates in Tours', p. 23.

29 Christin, *La paix de religion*, p. 65.

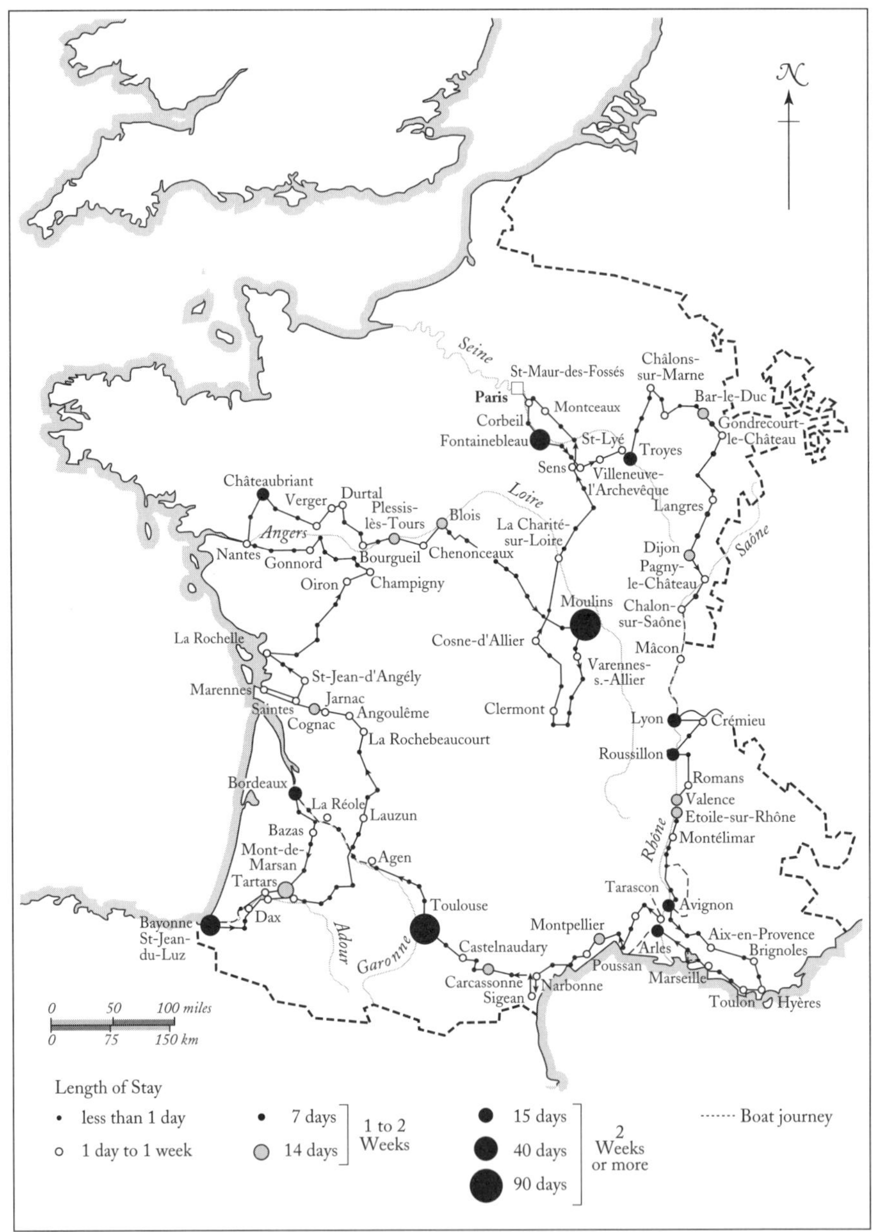

Map 4 Charles IX's 'grand tour' of France

Source: J. Boutier, A. Dewerpe, D. Nordman, *Un tour de France royal: le voyage de Charles IX (1564–1566)* (Paris, 1984).

Charles IX's 'grand tour' of France

Resistance to the pacification of 1563 was made easier in the provinces by their distance from the king and his government. The parlements, governors, and royal office-holders on whom the pacification depended often played a double game. While seeming to obey the king, they did everything they could to delay or obstruct the pacification. It was largely with a view to bringing his officials into line that King Charles IX undertook an extensive progress through France. It began on 13 March 1564, when the court, consisting of several thousand people and accompanied by a multitude of horses and mules, and a veritable army, set off from Fontainebleau. After stopping at Sens, scene of a recent massacre of Huguenots, the royal caravan travelled to Troyes, where the peace treaty with Elizabeth I was signed. Charles IX required local officials to give an account of their activities and to receive his instructions. He accused the judges of not pulling their weight and threatened to replace them unless their performance improved. After visiting Lorraine, the court moved south to Burgundy. On 22 March the king entered Dijon, whose governor, Gaspard de Saulx-Tavannes, staged an impressive military pageant in his honour.

One of the aims of the progress was to curb the independence of the provincial parlements and municipal authorities. At Dijon, on 23 May, the duc d'Orléans, acting in the name of the king, his brother, sent for the parlement's registers; he also asked the lieutenant-general of the province for information on the town council. Next day, the chancellor, Michel de l'Hôpital, checked the publication of the Edict of Amboise and examined each lawsuit recently tried by the court to ensure that its decisions were in line with its powers. The king intervened in the affairs of almost every town which he visited on his progress, and wherever possible he tried to strike a fair balance between the religious parties. From Chalon, the court travelled to Mâcon, where it was joined by Jeanne d'Albret, queen of Navarre. She was accompanied by eight Calvinist ministers and a military escort, necessitated, so she explained, by the lawless activities of Blaise de Monluc.

The next main stop was Lyon, a city with a large Protestant community. The Constable, riding ahead of the king, took charge of the city's fortifications, artillery and keys before giving it a royal garrison. As a further safeguard, Protestant services were banned for the duration of the royal visit and this was soon extended to other towns still to be visited by the court. A terrible epidemic of plague forced the court to leave Lyon on 8 July. It moved to Crémieu, where an important edict regarding towns was issued on 14 July. L'Hôpital believed that municipal independence had got out of hand. Nearly half the 'good towns' had fallen into Protestant hands in

1562, but the government was not concerned with them alone. Under the Edict of Crémieu the choice of municipal magistrates in the chief towns was given to the king. Elections were not abolished, but two lists of candidates for municipal office were to be submitted to the king, leaving him to make the final choice. This was a major step in the subordination of towns to royal control.

In the course of the progress nobles tagged on or dropped off as they pleased. Political or religious affiliations determined their movements. Thus, as long as the court was in Lorraine or territories dominated by the Guises, the principal Huguenots stayed away. Catholics consequently became dominant in the king's council, which may explain why certain measures restricting Protestant worship were enacted during the progress. Thus on 4 August, at Roussillon, a château belonging to cardinal Tournon, Charles IX issued an edict which qualified the Edict of Amboise. Heavy punishments were announced for Protestant worshippers who disregarded the limits laid down in the March edict. The new edict, as might have been expected, caused much resentment and bitterness among the Huguenots. An *Advertissement*, published in 1565, was prefaced by a letter from Condé to the queen-mother warning her that the new edict would produce unrest, if not atheism, as people turned against religion. The king and his mother were reminded that the edict was general. They should see to it, therefore, that all the king's subjects were treated equally. The king should revoke all the articles, declarations and interpretations of a discriminatory kind. The author of a *Doléance faicte au Roy* described the rights of worship given to the Protestants as 'a captive freedom'. He called on Charles IX to restore peace by suppressing the Roussillon declaration.

Resuming its journey on 15 August, the court travelled down the Rhône to Romans, then Valence. On 5 September the king's council examined a complaint from the Huguenots of Bordeaux about breaches of the peace, whereupon the king ordered his lieutenants in Guyenne to observe it. The court then visited Montélimar, Orange and Avignon, where Charles was the guest of the papal vice-legate. On 23 August the royal caravan arrived at Aix-en-Provence, whose parlement remained bitterly opposed to the pacification. It refused even to register the Edict of Amboise and Protestant worship was effectively banned within its area of jurisdiction. Charles IX asserted his authority by suspending the parlement, which he replaced by a commission of Parisian *parlementaires* and of members of the *Grand Conseil*. The next stage of the journey proved less contentious. The court visited Toulon, Marseille and Arles. As the young king visited Roman remains, his mother and the chancellor tried to persuade the local estates to accept the pacification. At Nîmes, a Protestant stronghold, the king was given an entry notable for its ingenious mechanical devices. After celebrating Christmas at Montpellier, the court set off for Toulouse on 1 January only to be held up at Carcassonne for ten days by snow.

Throughout the progress the king and his mother kept in close touch with the capital. Out of 413 letters written by Catherine during the grand tour 110 were sent to Parisians: 74 to Marshal Montmorency, governor of Paris and Île-de-France, 22 to the mayor and *échevins* and 14 to the parlement. While Catherine was in Toulouse she received alarming reports from Paris. Montmorency had refused to allow the cardinal of Lorraine (now back from the Council of Trent) to enter the capital with an armed escort. The cardinal defied the order, whereupon the marshal dispersed his escort, forcing the cardinal to take refuge in a merchant's house. The incident is significant as evidence of a reawakening of the quarrels between the houses of Montmorency and Guise, but the Parisian populace was not involved in any important way. There was much agitation in the city two weeks later when Admiral Coligny came with 500 horse in response to an appeal from the marshal for help in maintaining order. From the perspective of most contemporary observers, the crucial issues in Paris between 1563 and 1567 were not religious but economic. A severe winter in 1564 was followed by a poor harvest and a shortage of grain. In July 1566 the price of wheat topped 21 livres per *setier*, more than five times the average price for any period before 1561. The implications for public order were extremely grave.[30]

On 11 March, after 46 days spent in Toulouse, the royal caravan took to the road again. Travelling through Montauban and Agen, it reached Bordeaux. On 12 April Charles IX held a *lit de justice* in the parlement and L'Hôpital used the occasion to reprimand the judges. 'All this disorder,' he said, 'stems from the contempt in which you hold the king and his ordinances which you neither fear nor obey except at your own pleasure.' He accused the judges of allowing factional strife within the court. Debates often ended in brawls and judges were 'more afraid of the governors than of the king'. L'Hôpital urged them not to be intimidated by local lords and decided to set them an example. In Bordeaux some nobles and their armed bands frequently committed acts of pillage under the pretext of defending the Catholic faith. They openly defied the royal ban on the carrying of arms. The chancellor called their leader, the marquis de Trans, to the Parlement and scolded him harshly. When the marquis laughed, L'Hôpital roared: 'Why are you laughing? You can laugh, but I can have your throat cut the moment I give sentence. You may thank His Majesty that your

30 Diefendorf, *Beneath the Cross*, pp. 73–5.

head is still on your shoulders.' Trans almost fainted with fear. Brantôme, who witnessed the scene, wrote: 'one could not trifle with this great judge and rough magistrate'. Rarely had a chancellor spoken so harshly to a parlement. His overriding purpose was to diminish the political authority of the sovereign courts. The parlement, he explained, had no right to interpret the law; it could only remonstrate. The king, he went on, was the supreme lawgiver. As a regional body the court could not aspire to national status: its members, responsible as they were for local matters, were wrong to think of themselves as wiser than the king, the queen and the king's council who had to look after the entire kingdom. L'Hôpital reaffirmed the king's purpose to impose the pacification.[31]

On 2 May the king and his court set off for Bayonne where Catherine de' Medici had arranged to meet her daughter, Elisabeth, the queen of Spain. She had also hoped to meet her son-in-law, Philip II, believing that a tête-à-tête would serve to clear up differences which had arisen between France and Spain, but he had evaded her entreaties. In his place, he sent the duke of Alba, who was soon to demonstrate his hawkishness in the Netherlands. The duke was instructed to persuade Catherine to accept the decrees of the Council of Trent and to scrap the Edict of Amboise in favour of a policy of religious persecution. But, as far as we know, Catherine, who was more interested in arranging marriages for some of her children, refused to change her policy towards the Huguenots. Even so, the talks in Bayonne aroused the Huguenots' darkest suspicions, for they knew that the Spanish government strongly disapproved of the recent peace settlement. Their exclusion from the talks served to confirm their suspicions. Later on, after August 1572, they convinced themselves that the massacre of St Bartholomew's Day had been planned at Bayonne. Some members of Charles IX's entourage are known to have expressed hawkish sentiments in private conversations with Alba, but it seems that the queen-mother did not compromise her policy in any way.

From Bayonne the royal court travelled north to Nantes, thence to Blois by way of Châteaubriant. It then made its way across Berry to Moulins, where it remained for three months (December 1565–March 1566). The government had planned to cap its programme of administrative and judicial reform by means of a major ordinance. To this end, an Assembly of Notables was called. For the first time since 1564 the Guises and the Châtillons met face to face and Catherine de' Medici worked hard to heal

31 Boutier, Dewerpe and Nordman, *Un tour de France royal*, pp. 245–6; Seong-Hak Kim, *Michel de l'Hôpital*, pp. 132–4.

their enmity. On 29 January 1566 Charles IX finally acquitted Coligny of any part in the assassination of the second duc de Guise. The cardinal of Lorraine and Admiral Coligny were persuaded to kiss each other.

Opening the assembly, L'Hôpital pointed to judicial corruption as the underlying cause of France's domestic troubles. Private greed and ambition, he said, had taken hold of the judiciary. He complained of too many laws, of overlapping jurisdictions and of venal offices. He wanted fewer appeals and evocations, and favoured a system of ambulatory courts. The chancellor also believed that municipal bodies were abusing their powers and that these should be transferred to crown officials. Most of the points made by L'Hôpital found their way into the Ordinance of Moulins of February 1566, the 86 clauses of which covered most aspects of government. Its chief purpose was to strengthen the king's authority.[32] Two clauses were intended to diminish the political authority of the sovereign courts. The first laid down that all ordinances so far issued should be observed regardless of remonstrances or reservations attached to them; the second prescribed that parlements should register a law once remonstrance had been made and the king's wishes made known without the courts resorting to further remonstrances. In December 1566 the king withdrew the second clause after fierce opposition from the Parlement of Paris but retained the first.[33]

The chancellor's effort to tame the parlements brought him into collision with the cardinal of Lorraine at a meeting of the king's council on 16 March. The cardinal, who joined the court in Moulins after his return from Trent, presented a petition from the parlement of Dijon. It complained that a recent royal edict, which allowed Huguenots in towns to call for their ministers to console them and to teach them and their children, violated the Edict of Amboise. The cardinal de Bourbon blamed the chancellor for the edict, alleging that it had never been discussed in the council. L'Hôpital accused Lorraine of having come back to cause trouble, whereupon Lorraine retorted that he had come to prevent the chancellor from troubling the kingdom. L'Hôpital asked calmly if Lorraine wished to 'prevent those poor people, whom the king allowed to live in accordance with their conscience, from ever being consoled'. The cardinal admitted that this indeed was his purpose. He furiously accused L'Hôpital of impertinence. The cardinal of Bourbon asked the chancellor if he had issued the edict without the council's knowledge. As the meeting became chaotic, Catherine intervened.

32 J. H. M. Salmon, *Society in Crisis* (London, 1975), pp. 155–6.
33 Seong-Hak Kim, *Michel de l'Hôpital*, p. 134.

She ordered the edict to be destroyed and that Protestants should be banned from towns where they were not allowed to exercise their faith. The chancellor was forbidden to seal any religious edicts without the council's consent.[34]

With the passing of winter, the court resumed its progress. On 1 May 1566 it was back in Paris. The kingdom seemed reasonably peaceful. In March 1565 Catherine had written: 'all things are as peaceful here as one could wish; the further we go, the more is obedience established and the damage caused by disorder and confusion to the minds of the people is purged and cleansed, so I hope that with God's help all things will revert to their original state'.[35] Writing from Cognac in August 1565, she rejoiced after seeing Huguenots and Catholics dancing together at a ball. That autumn she wrote: 'How much I would like to see this kingdom revert to the state it was in when the mere sight of a white rod was enough for the whole kingdom to obey the king [. . .] The king, Monsieur my son, has the will to restore it to that state and I hope, if God allows him to live, that he will succeed.'

34 Ibid., p. 144; Louis Ier, prince de Condé, *Mémoires* 6 vols. (London, 1743), vol. 3, p. 52.
35 H. de La Ferrière and B. de Puchesse (eds.), *Lettres de Catherine de Médicis*, 10 vols. (Paris, 1880–1909), vol. 3, p. 59.

CHAPTER SEVEN

The second and third wars (1567–1570)

The phoney peace

The policy of limited religious toleration pursued by the French government since March 1563 seemed to be working quite well. By January 1567 France was more or less at peace. In the words of Claude Haton: 'it seemed as if all the affairs between the king and the princes of France were steadily improving . . . and as if the peace . . . was so consolidated that neither war nor troubles would ever arise again in France over religion'.[1] The Protestant writer, La Noue, tells the same story: 'the Edict of Pacification signed outside Orléans had given almost to the whole of France much contentment, as much in appearance as in effect, in that all misery ceasing everyone lived at peace, secure in body and free of mind.'[2] But, La Noue goes on to explain, the seeds of hatred, envy or distrust remained, albeit unseen, and in time ripened into fruits 'which returned us to our first discords'. As the Protestant leaders reflected on their past and present hardships, they concluded that their opponents were planning to undermine them gradually before suddenly striking them dead. They pointed to the dismantling of certain towns and to the building of fortresses in their places of worship; also to massacres in several places and to murders of noblemen which had gone unpunished. Among less obvious evidence, the leaders pointed to letters from Rome or Spain which had been intercepted and which clearly laid out plans directed against them. They also took seriously reports of a Franco–Spanish decision taken at Bayonne in 1565 to exterminate them

1 F. Bourquelot (ed.), *Mémoires de Claude Haton* (Paris, 1857), vol. 1, 419.
2 F. de La Noue, *Discours politiques et militaires*, ed. F. E. Sutcliffe (Geneva, 1967), p. 676.

and the Dutch 'Sea Beggars'. For these reasons the Huguenot leaders decided to act at once rather than be caught unawares.[3]

The problems facing Charles IX and his ministers were by no means unique to France. The Netherlands, too, were in turmoil as the native nobility challenged the rule of Margaret of Parma, who ruled as regent for her half-brother, Philip II of Spain. The political crisis here, as in France, was closely bound up with religion, as Calvinism made significant headway among the people of the southern Netherlands. In September 1566 Margaret informed Philip of serious riots and widespread iconoclasm. In west Flanders alone, 400 churches had been sacked.[4] The news convinced Philip that the Netherlands were going down the same path as France. He was determined to stamp out the rebellion. By December he had decided to send an army led by the duke of Alba to the Netherlands with a view to restoring order by force. Starting out from the Milanese, the army marched northwards along the so-called 'Spanish Road', which lay through Savoy, Franche-Comté and Lorraine.[5] It passed dangerously close to Geneva, causing the city council much anxiety. The French Reformed churches offered the city financial and military assistance. Three hundred troops under Paul de Richieu, sire de Mouvans, a professional plotter who had played a part in the ill-fated Amboise conspiracy, were actually sent; but they never had to fight, as Alba never attempted to attack the city.[6]

In France, too, Alba's expedition caused grave concern, not merely among the Huguenots but also in government circles. The Spanish crown had not taken Charles IX or his ministers into its confidence so that they had no clear idea of Alba's intended objective. It seemed not impossible that he would invade France, perhaps in support of the Guise faction, for Philip II strongly disapproved of the recent pacification. He hated heresy and feared its permanent establishment in France. So Charles IX took no chances. In May 1567 his ambassador in Switzerland, Pomponne de Bellièvre, hired 6,000 mercenaries.[7] Their ostensible purpose was to guard the northern frontier of France against a possible attack by Alba. But the Huguenots were not convinced by this explanation. Remembering the Bayonne meeting between Alba and Catherine de' Medici, they suspected that the Swiss

3 Ibid., pp. 676–7.

4 H. Kamen, *Philip of Spain* (New Haven and London, 1997), p. 116.

5 G. Parker, *The Army of Flanders and the Spanish Road, 1567–1659* (Cambridge, 1972), pp. 80–101.

6 R. M. Kingdon, *Geneva and the Consolidation of the French Protestant Movement, 1564–1572* (Geneva, 1967), pp. 162–3.

7 O. Poncet, *Pomponne de Bellièvre (1529–1607). Un homme d'état au temps des guerres de religion* (Paris: École des chartes, 1998), pp. 31–7.

troops were being recruited as part of a grand Franco–Spanish campaign to wipe them out. Their suspicion seemed all the more plausible when Charles IX failed to dismiss the Swiss troops after Alba had reached Brussels on 22 August, thereby lifting the immediate threat to France's borders.

Alarmed by the turn of events, the military leaders of the Huguenot movement held a series of secret meetings at the homes of Condé and Coligny at Valéry and Châtillon-sur-Loing. Some of them expressed doubts about provoking the young king unnecessarily by resorting to violence, but Coligny's younger brother, d'Andelot, made out a strong case for immediate action. He accused the crown of throwing 'six thousand foreign soldiers even unto our entrails'. Unless the Huguenots staged a pre-emptive strike he feared that their malady would no longer be curable. Rallying to d'Andelot's call, the leaders drew up a plan of action. According to La Noue, they set themselves four objectives: to seize a few important towns, to raise a strong army, to 'cut to pieces' the Swiss troops, and to drive away from court the cardinal of Lorraine, who was said to be continually pressing the king to destroy all the Protestants.[8] Orders were sent out to all the Reformed churches to raise troops and to send them to Rosay-en-Brie. Condé was put in charge of the entire operation. But its success depended on secrecy, and this proved impossible to maintain. On 4 September Catherine de' Medici was told that between 1,200 and 1,500 Huguenot cavalry had assembled near Montargis and Châtillon. Marshal Cossé was asked to investigate. On 18 September the queen-mother dismissed a report that the Huguenots were rearming as 'just a small scare'; next day she wrote to M. de Gordes, the king's lieutenant in Dauphiné, that 'everything is as peaceful now, thank God, as we could wish'.[9] Catherine refused to believe that all her peace-making efforts had been in vain.

On 24 September, however, Charles IX and his mother, who were staying at Montceaux, were told that Huguenot troops were gathered at Rosay. This time they took the report seriously. After meeting that night, the king's council ordered the Swiss troops, stationed at Château-Thierry, to come in haste. The king and his mother decided to take shelter within the walls of Meaux. The councillors then debated the pros and cons of staying put or going to Paris. The Constable Montmorency and the chancellor L'Hôpital favoured the first option, but the duc de Nemours and the Guise faction successfully argued in support of the second. Next day, at dawn, the court set off for the capital. Nemours led the march with the

8 La Noue, *Discours*, pp. 677–83.

9 H. de La Ferrière, and B. de Puchesse (eds.), *Lettres de Catherine de Médicis*, 10 vols (Paris, 1880–1909), vol. 3, pp. 53, 56–59.

cavalry while the Swiss provided cover for the court at the front and rear. At the entrance to the Lagny defile, the Huguenots appeared. Condé tried to engage the king in talks, but withdrew when confronted with the formidable array of Swiss pikes. Later, at the exit to the defile, Montmorency and the Swiss kept the Huguenots occupied, while Charles IX and his mother went on ahead to Paris.[10] The young king was angry: never again, he declared, would he allow anyone to frighten him. He swore to pursue the rebels into their houses and beds.[11] On reaching Paris, Catherine expressed both surprise at the Huguenot action and anger in several letters. Writing to Matignon on 27 September, she said that she could not understand what had prompted the Huguenot action. In a letter to Fourquevaux, the French envoy in Spain, she spoke of her sadness at seeing the kingdom revert to the troubles from which she had worked so hard to extricate it. Writing to the duke of Savoy, she described the uprising, which has come to be known as the *Surprise de Meaux*, as 'the greatest wickedness in the world'.[12] It seems not unlikely that from this time onwards Catherine's policy changed. She could not forgive the Huguenots for betraying her trust and, above all, for challenging the king's authority.

After daring to pursue Charles IX and his court as far as Paris, Condé and the other Huguenot leaders compounded their offence by blockading the capital. They encamped at Saint-Denis and on the night of 1 October burnt several windmills outside the Porte Saint-Denis. Parisians rushed to take up arms and broke into Protestant houses looking for suspected arsonists.[13] The fiery Catholic preacher, Simon Vigor, denounced the Huguenots as traitors. Their faith, he said, had been established by the sword and would be destroyed by the sword. Montmorency summoned Strozzi's infantry from Picardy and Brissac's from Lyon, while calling for funds. He expected to have under his command 18,500 infantry and 9,700 horse.[14] Meanwhile, elsewhere in France, several towns, including Orléans and La Rochelle, declared for the Huguenots. In Nîmes dozens of Catholics, including priests, were massacred and their bodies thrown into a deep well.[15] As both sides prepared for war, Condé issued a manifesto which repeated the demands he had made in 1562: namely, the expulsion of all foreigners

10 F. Decrue, *Anne duc de Montmorency* (Paris, 1889), pp. 461–3.

11 B. N., ms.fr. 3347. Bochefort to Renée of Ferrara. Cited in La Ferrière and Puchesse (eds.), *Lettres de Catherine de Médicis*, vol. 3, pp. ix–x.

12 Ibid., pp. 60–62.

13 B. Diefendorf, *Beneath the Cross: Catholics and Huguenots in Sixteenth-Century Paris* (Oxford, 1991), p. 80.

14 Decrue, *Anne duc de Montmorency*, p. 464.

15 R. Sauzet, *Chroniques des frères ennemis. Catholiques et Protestants à Nîmes du XVIe au XVIIIe siècles* (Caen, 1992), p. 23.

(that is to say, Nemours and the Guises) from the king's council, the exclusion from power of the queen-mother, and the calling of the Estates-General. By not focusing on the religious question he evidently hoped to attract non-Protestants to his side, but he also provided incriminating evidence to the crown. Two royal envoys sent to the German princes argued that the Huguenots were fighting their lawful king for political, not religious, reasons. The Elector Palatine decided to send a special envoy, named Zuleger, to France to find out the truth.[16]

On 7 October a royal herald appeared in Condé's camp. After three trumpet flourishes he called on the prince, Coligny and their associates to appear before the king or admit their rebellion.[17] Severely shaken by the challenge, the Huguenot leaders presented a shorter list of demands to Montmorency. They asked for the Edict of Amboise to be enforced without restrictions on Huguenot worship, but the Constable refused to consider a settlement which would leave France divided between two religions. As the talks once again focused on the question of religious toleration, Zuleger was able to reassure the Elector Palatine as to the religious aims of the Huguenots. The Elector consequently allowed them to levy an army of 6,500 horse, 3,000 infantry and four field cannon under the command of his son, John Casimir. He rebuffed a last-minute attempt by Charles IX's envoys to block their departure for France. But Condé had to wait several months for this German assistance to reach him.[18]

As the prospect of war drew closer, the two sides were numerically very unequal. While the Huguenots disposed of only 4,000 infantry and 2,000 horse, the royal army comprised 16,000 infantry, 3,000 horse and 18 cannon. Yet, despite their numerical weakness, the Huguenots operated on a wide front. They stopped food supplies from reaching Paris by capturing the bridge at Charenton, a move countered by Montmorency when he seized Argenteuil on 4 November. After more skirmishing, the Constable launched an attack at 3 p.m. on 10 November. The Huguenots were stretched out in a single line between the villages of Saint Ouen and Aubervilliers. Coligny and the van occupied the first village; Genlis, the second; and Condé commanded the cavalry linking the two units. The royal army was formed up for battle at La Villette: on the left were the cavalry under Nemours, Longueville and Thoré as well as the Parisian volunteers; in the centre, was the Constable Montmorency with the *gendarmerie*

16 Kingdon, *Geneva and the Consolidation of the French Protestant Movement*, pp. 170–71.

17 J. Delaborde, *Gaspard de Coligny* (Paris, 1879–82), vol. 2, pp. 490–93; Henri duc d'Aumale, *Histoire des Princes de Condé pendant les XVIe et XVIIe siècles*, 8 vols. (Paris, 1863–96), vol. 1, p. 300.

18 Kingdon, *Geneva and the Consolidation of the French Protestant Movement*, p. 171.

and the Swiss; and on the right, mainly French infantry under Brissac and Strozzi. The battle of Saint-Denis began with a bombardment by the royal guns, but Montmorency gave the order to attack before its effect could be assessed or his infantry deployed. As the left wing of the royal army advanced, Coligny threw back the inexperienced Parisian volunteers. Condé then charged the centre of the royal line, breaking through it with ease. In the ensuing scrum the 74-year-old Constable fought bravely as always. Using the pommel of his sword, he fractured the jaw of a Scotsman who had called on him to surrender; but at the same instant his own spine was shattered by a pistol shot. The old man was carried off the field by his two sons, Damville and Thoré, and died piously two days later. Although Catherine de' Medici accorded him a truly royal funeral, he was not widely mourned. Writing to Philip II, Catherine said: 'We may thank God that in so great a battle the only major loss has been his.'[19] In the south of France Protestants hailed the battle as a victory. They held services of thanksgiving and at Montauban and Saint-Antonin declared a public holiday. Montmorency's death was interpreted as a sign of divine favour.[20]

Montmorency's death left a vacancy in the army's high command. Charles IX was persuaded to appoint his younger brother, Henri, duc d'Anjou, as Lieutenant-general of the kingdom and commander-in-chief of the royal army (the office of Constable was left vacant till 1597). He was given considerable powers over all military personnel. In the campaigns that followed, Anjou addressed a flood of letters and memoranda, mostly about money, supply and personnel, to various bodies and individuals. On day-to-day matters, he was assisted by a council made up of nobles, who led the various army formations. At moments of crisis, they were expected to submit written opinions which could be forwarded to the king. One historian has described these arrangements as 'beginning an unhappy experiment in collective leadership'.[21]

Condé had emerged from the battle with honour, but as yet he disposed of too few troops to continue blockading Paris. Abandoning his camp, he made a quick dash to Lorraine with the aim of joining forces with John Casimir's German mercenaries. The king's army prepared to go in pursuit. It was 'by far the largest royal army ever put into the field during the civil wars'.[22] Its order of march is known from a surviving log-book. Two contingents – the van and the 'battle' – marched in large columns several yards

19 Decrue, *Anne duc de Montmorency*, p. 472.

20 J. Garrisson, *Protestants du Midi, 1559–1598* (Toulouse, 1980), p. 170.

21 J. B. Wood, *The King's Army: Warfare, Soldiers, and Society during the Wars of Religion in France, 1562–1576* (Cambridge, 1996), p. 18.

22 Ibid., pp. 71–2.

wide and a mile or two deep. A gap of a mile or two separated them. The van, consisting of about 15,000 troops, were led by light cavalry armed with pistols and swords. Next, in parallel columns, were several contingents of *gendarmes*, more fully armoured, mounted on sturdy horses and equipped with long wooden lances. Behind them came a column of 9,000 infantry. At its centre, grouped with the company standards, were pikemen flanked by arquebusiers. Behind the infantry were several hundred pioneers whose role was to clear a path for the substantial baggage train. This was accompanied by camp-followers of various kinds. A pair of guns, used to signal the main body, brought up the rear. The 'battle' contained 22,000 troops. Behind more contingents of *gendarmes* was the artillery comprising ornate guns of various calibres accompanied by hundreds of ammunition carts, more pioneers and hundreds of specialists – gun-loaders, blacksmiths, powderers, carpenters, wheelwrights and rope-makers; also a priest and a portable altar. Then came a huge block of 6,000 Swiss pikemen flanked by more French infantry followed by more columns of *gendarmes*, including Anjou's. Behind the Swiss came a second baggage train with camp-followers, a food convoy and commissary staff. A single company of *gendarmes* and mounted arquebusiers, who acted as scouts, brought up the rear. No place was assigned to the camp marshals and their men-at-arms, who had the duty of keeping the army on the move and of deciding the next day's camp site. Normally, the king's army consisted of 20,000 or 30,000 effectives. This one had almost 38,000 troops, two-thirds infantry and one-quarter cavalry. The rest were labourers, artillerymen and camp-followers. Taking all these into account, the army consisted of some 50,000 people and nearly 25,000 animals. Only the population of Paris and a few other towns could compare in size.

Perhaps because of its sheer size the king's army did not catch up with the Huguenots until 22 November near Châlons-sur-Marne. They managed to slip away under cover of night, however, and met up with John Casimir's force at Pont-à-Mousson on 11 January 1568. Giving up the chase, Anjou's army pitched camp at Vitry-le-François, where it was joined by forces commanded by Aumale and Nevers. The army, including garrisons, was now almost 60,000 strong, yet its commanders were reluctant to fight. They remembered all too well the losses suffered by the *gendarmerie* at Saint-Denis. 'One of the main strategic concerns of the crown and the army's leadership,' writes Wood, 'became the need to protect the nobility, that is the *gendarmerie*, from destruction.' For it was felt that this would only advantage France's traditional enemies: Spain, England and the Empire. Revoking an earlier order to bring the Huguenots to battle, Charles IX explained that 'at present, he did not wish to risk his kingdom or his nobles, who are not so strong that in risking a single battle enough of them would remain to him to fight a second in order to conserve his estate'. Anjou was prepared to fight, but, in the end, Nevers' advice not to fight prevailed. 'A country kept,' he said, 'is worth more than a country lost, as it would be, if we lost a single battle now.'[23] So the king's army, while waiting for 8,500 German cavalry of its own to arrive, engaged in Fabian tactics, hoping that the onset of winter and a lack of funds would cause the enemy to melt away.

The Huguenots, meanwhile, marched on Orléans, which had been theirs since the start of the war. As they did so, they attacked and looted villages and small towns in their path which refused to admit them. At the end of February they besieged Chartres. While part of their army functioned as a blocking force, the rest (about 9,000 men) encircled the city and used their small artillery of nine guns to breach its north wall. The Huguenots launched an assault on 7 March, but the governor, Nicolas des Essars, sieur de Linières, who had entered Chartres with 4,000 royal troops on the eve of the siege, mounted a stout defence with the help of the inhabitants. Some 600 men served in the town militia and more than 1,000 worked as pioneers. The assault was repulsed and the breach sealed off.[24] Although the siege lasted only two weeks, losses were high. Between 300 and 400 Huguenots died in the fighting and some 250 royal troops. More than 500 royal soldiers were wounded or fell sick. Civilian casualties are unknown.

Soon after the war, the city of Chartres asked the king for permission to levy a tax on the inhabitants in order to pay off debts it had incurred as a result of the war. It submitted a detailed statement of expenses. The garrison, which the city had supported during the siege, comprised 22 companies of infantry and three of cavalry – some 4,000 troops in all, equivalent to half the city's peacetime population. The soldiers remained in Chartres until mid-April, forcing it to borrow 9,000 livres. More than 11,000 royal troops, which had passed through the city or had been stationed there during the war, had cost the city 87,801 livres. Its largest expense was on food. The city had provided 263 waggon-loads of wheat, 145 of oats, 328 animals for slaughter, 10,000 gallons of wine and 624,000 loaves. Cash payments to the army amounted to 27,177 livres. Lesser items were the building and repair of walls and fortifications (11 per cent), and artillery and munitions (3 per cent).[25]

The city of Chartres was not alone in feeling the pinch of war. While the Huguenot leaders could not afford to pay their German mercenaries, the crown could no longer support its enormous army.

23 Ibid., pp. 124–5.
24 Ibid., pp. 20, 205–25.
25 Ibid., pp. 205–25.

Funding the war

As Wood has clearly demonstrated, the French crown was unable throughout the civil wars to raise enough money to pay for its army beyond the first two months or so. In the 1560s and 1570s its total cost in peacetime was 4.8 million livres. About three-quarters of this sum was spent on the *gendarmerie* and infantry. The artillery was relatively cheap. Fortifications and the royal guard accounted for 13 per cent. *Mortepayes* (permanently garrisoned infantry), the navy and the annual pension to the Swiss cantons made up another 10 per cent. Around 90 per cent of the military budget was spent on wages rather than capital improvements, equipment or supplies. During the same period, the gross annual revenues of the crown fluctuated between 10 and 14 million livres. Thus about 40 per cent of the crown's income was devoted to military purposes. But the crown also had to settle debts left over from earlier wars, which in 1560 amounted to 40 million livres. So, even in peacetime, the crown was unable to live within its means.

In wartime, as we have seen, the army was much enlarged, with inevitable consequences for the royal budget. The monthly cost in livres of various components in the army was as follows: a regiment of infantry, 20,000 (there were usually six such regiments in the main field army); the standard Swiss contingent (20 companies totalling 6,000 men), 73,000; the Rhinegrave's regiment (5,250 *landsknechts*), 67,000; a group of nine companies of 750 men-at-arms 24,000 (the army comprised between five and nine such groups); a regiment of German *reiters* (3,600 men), 130,000; the standard field artillery train of between 12 and 20 guns, 30–40,000. The total cost of the army for the month of December 1567 was almost one million livres or three times its cost in peacetime. In January 1568 it rose above 1.3 million livres per month. Additional military expenses may have totalled 192,000 livres per month. Thus the crown spent about 18 million livres per year, a sum far in excess of its normal income. In wartime, this was likely to fall sharply, as taxation became more difficult to collect. The government had to resort to various expedients, including loans which often carried exorbitant rates of interest. By such means it managed to pay most of its main army for the first two or three months of the second civil war. However, by February 1568 it faced bankruptcy.

A major reason for the crown's inability to fund its army over a longer period than two or three months was its dependence on an antiquated fiscal system. Such resources as were available were unevenly distributed across the kingdom. While some tax districts were more or less able to cope with royal demands, others were not. The distribution was skewed in favour of the northern provinces where the troops had been traditionally based in peacetime. But now that military operations were moving to other parts of France the weaknesses of the system began to tell. Even funds which existed in theory were not always easy to collect or to transport over long distances, particularly in wartime. Taxes were also diverted into the enemy's coffers. When regular revenues failed, the crown fell back on expedients which were not always dependable. And if an army was not paid, discipline soon collapsed.

The Peace of Longjumeau (23 March 1568)

Mutual exhaustion obliged both sides to negotiate.[26] A truce was declared and Condé's army, much reduced by desertions, withdrew from Chartres. On 23 March 1568 the Peace of Longjumeau was signed. This restored the Edict of Amboise without the additions restricting Protestant worship.[27] Condé and his followers were promised a complete amnesty and, in secret articles, the king undertook to help pay the wages of John Casimir's *reiters*. They were disbanded soon afterwards and left a trail of damage as they marched home through Burgundy.[28] Norris reported on 14 July that Condé had been authorized by Charles IX to levy the Huguenots for the payment of the *reiters*. Since these had already left, the levy was probably intended to reimburse the king.[29]

The settlement angered Catholics, who interpreted it as a return to the policy of limited religious toleration which the Edict of Amboise had initiated. In Paris popular resentment was encouraged by Catholic preachers in their Lenten sermons. They predicted dire consequences for the king if he did not cease supporting false prophets. The Huguenots, they warned, would destroy France unless they were exterminated by force of arms.[30] On the surface the peace seemed reasonably generous to the Huguenots but, as events were to suggest, it may have been nothing more than a deceitful ploy aimed at achieving their destruction.

---

26 Ibid., pp. 20, 208–9, 219.

27 A. Stegmann (ed.), *Édits des guerres de religion* (Paris, 1979), pp. 53–8.

28 Bourquelot, *Mémoires de Claude Haton*, vol. 2, p. 531.

29 *C.S.P.F.*, pp. 47–71, 501. A document, called 'Brief discours' in the P.R.O. London (SP 70/98) gives the following details: Condé was to pay the first month's wages of the Germans; Charles IX was to lend him 200,000 écus for the second and was to raise the rest in and around Metz. Condé was to repay his debt by levying cash from the Huguenots under the king's authority. Each month's pay for 7,860 *reiters* was 268,000 *lt.* (livres tournois) and for 3,000 *landsknechts*, 15,000 écus. I owe this information to the kindness of Dr D. Potter.

30 Diefendorf, *Beneath the Cross*, p. 82.

The true significance of the Peace of Longjumeau has not always been understood by historians. It has been called 'the little peace' and interpreted as a genuine attempt by the crown to restore peace to France whereas, in fact, it was almost certainly a trap designed to bring about the destruction of the Huguenot leadership.[31] La Noue in his memoirs calls it 'a wicked little peace', describing it as the worst for the Huguenots of all the peace treaties signed during the wars. He shows that it was forced on Condé and Coligny by their own followers. 'They were caught up,' he writes, 'in a whirlwind they could not resist.' The treaty was certainly not negotiated by the Huguenots from a position of military advantage, as some historians have suggested. Their army was melting away even during the siege of Chartres. The infantry complained of being unpaid and short of food, while the nobles were anxious to go home in order to protect their families from attacks by Catholic neighbours. Mass desertions left the leaders virtually defenceless at the start of the fighting season. They still had their German troops, but were not sure how to use them defensively. They could distribute them among various towns or put them in a fortified camp, but neither course seemed to offer any military advantage. If the Huguenots had only been able to secure surety towns (*places de sûreté*), they might have been safer, but whenever they raised the subject in their negotiations with the crown, they were charged with disloyalty. So they settled for peace and disbanded at least some of their forces, believing that the enemy would do likewise; but the Catholics did nothing of the sort: they remained under arms and continued to guard towns and river crossings. This marked a significant departure from past practice. As we have seen, it was customary for the crown to reduce its army following a peace treaty, thereby placing itself at a serious military disadvantage when the peace broke down. Mobilizing its forces was a long and complicated process during which the initiative was, as it were, handed on a plate to the Huguenots. This did not happen after Longjumeau. It is hard to imagine that this did not stem from a conscious decision not to demobilize in spite of the parlous state of the king's finances. Clearly, if there was going to be another war, it would need to be a very short one. Apparently Condé had been more favourably inclined towards the peace than Coligny, who always suspected that it might not be enforced. He thought, rightly as it happened, that it would be used to avenge the *Surprise de Meaux*.[32] In the Midi, the peace was not taken seriously. Local chroniclers viewed it with a mixture of surprise and rancour. Jacques de Gaches thought Condé had been tricked by the queen-mother, while Jean

31 N. M. Sutherland, *The Huguenot Struggle for Recognition* (New Haven, Conn., 1980), pp. 156–8.

32 La Noue, *Discours*, pp. 708–10.

Faurin treated the settlement as a trap laid for Protestants, an opinion widely shared by Huguenot notables in the region. Consequently, in the Midi at least, the Protestants did not disarm. Towns under their control maintained their garrisons, and military governors appointed by Condé remained in their posts.[33]

One historian has accused the cardinal of Lorraine of plotting to destroy the Peace of Longjumeau, but this view stems mainly from a reading of the reports of Sir Henry Norris, the English ambassador in Paris.[34] He was particularly concerned with the activities of the cardinal as he was the uncle of Mary Queen of Scots, who had sought asylum in England in May 1568. She was now effectively the prisoner of Queen Elizabeth I and the cardinal was pressing for her release. Mary was soon to become the focus of Catholic plots against the English queen which could be seen as part of an international conspiracy fomented by Rome and Spain and spearheaded by the cardinal of Lorraine. Having recently returned from the Council of Trent, he had become a powerful voice in the French king's council and was pressing for the adoption by France of the Tridentine decrees. Having once genuinely favoured a doctrinal compromise between Catholics and Lutherans, he had since become an advocate of the forceful suppression of Protestantism in France. It is not certain, however, that his views were necessarily at variance with those of Charles IX and of his mother, whatever they may have said to cover their actions. The course of events that followed the Peace of Longjumeau suggests a concerted policy of duplicity by the crown aimed at taking the Huguenot leaders by surprise and exterminating them once they had lost their forces. Significantly, the chancellor, Michel de l'Hôpital, who had consistently favoured a peaceful solution to France's religious conflict, fell from power at this moment.

In May 1568 L'Hôpital, 'finding himself striving against the stream', asked to be relieved of his office. His request was refused. About the same time papal intrusion in French affairs grew. Pius V issued a bull, allowing Charles IX to sell off church property as long as the proceeds were used to suppress heresy. At a meeting of the king's council, the chancellor argued that the bull infringed Gallican liberties. According to Norris, the cardinal of Lorraine accused L'Hôpital of hypocrisy. Their quarrel became so violent that Marshal Montmorency had to come between them. Turning to the queen-mother, Lorraine blamed the chancellor for all the kingdom's ills. If the chancellor were in the Parlement's hands, he added, 'his head should not tarry on his shoulder twenty-four hours'. L'Hôpital, for his part, said

33 Garrisson, *Protestants du Midi*, p. 171.
34 N. M. Sutherland, *The Huguenot Struggle*, p. 160.

that the cardinal was responsible for all the mischiefs in France.[35] In spite of L'Hôpital's opposition, the papal bull was confirmed by the king in letters patent which also ordered the dismissal of all Protestants holding royal offices. Refusing to seal this law, L'Hôpital again asked to be discharged. This time his request was granted. He retired to Vignay and, on 7 October, the royal seals were entrusted to Jean de Morvillier.[36] The chancellor's fall cannot be blamed on the cardinal of Lorraine alone; it was a royal decision which evidently reflected the disenchantment felt by the king and his mother with L'Hôpital's pacific policy which had failed. The crown now chose to follow the alternative policy of repression advocated by the cardinal of Lorraine and the Guises.

Wherever they looked, the Huguenots had reason to feel apprehensive about their future. In the Netherlands the duke of Alba carried out a savage campaign of repression during the summer of 1567. Many were the victims of a special tribunal called the Council of Troubles. According to recent research, out of a total of 12,000 people tried by the court, 9,000 were condemned *in absentia* and had their property confiscated, and more than 1,000 were executed, including counts of Egmont and Hoornes. The latter was related to the house of Montmorency. The Huguenots suspected that Alba's campaign of persecution was only the start of a much bigger onslaught on Protestants generally which they believed had been planned by the duke and Catherine de' Medici at Bayonne two years earlier.

As refugees from Alba's persecution poured into Picardy, Huguenots prepared to assist their Dutch co-religionists. In April 1568 the Spanish ambassador in France, Francès de Alava, got wind of an alliance between the Huguenot leaders and the Dutch rebels, known as 'Sea Beggars'. Its terms were drafted in August though the treaty may never have been signed. It provided for mutual assistance in an emergency and for the cost of such assistance to be borne by the party that requested it. Philip II viewed the prospect of a coalition between the Huguenots and the Dutch rebels with alarm. Writing to Alava on 4 May, he said that Charles IX and his mother must 'cut off the heads' of the Huguenot leaders. Unless they did so, he added, Charles would lose his throne and his life. The French government certainly had no desire to add to its current problems by provoking Spanish hostility. In the summer of 1568 it acted to prevent a force of Huguenots, led by Paul de Mouvans and François de Cocqueville, from assisting their co-religionists in Flanders. Marshal Cossé was ordered to intercept it, which he did successfully in July. The Huguenots were crushed at Saint-Valéry.

35 *C.S.P.F.*, viii, 554.

36 Seong-Hak Kim, *Michel de l'Hôpital: The Vision of a Reformist Chancellor during the French Religious Wars* (Kirksville, Mo., 1997), pp. 166–8.

On hearing the news, Catherine de' Medici instructed Cossé to hand over any Flemish prisoners to Alba and to have the French ones executed or sent to the galleys. Cocqueville, who had been captured, was summarily executed. The queen-mother now seemed committed to a policy of repression. Speaking to Alava, she described the recent execution of Egmont and Hoornes as 'a holy decision' which she hoped soon to see repeated in France.

In France the summer of 1568 was marked by a proliferation of Catholic leagues and confraternities regardless of the Peace of Longjumeau which had banned them. In addition to those which had already been set up in Burgundy, new ones were formed at Bourges, Orléans, Angers, Troyes and Le Mans. They were a response to a widespread fear of another surprise attack by the Huguenots, a fear enhanced by the fact that the provincial governors had had to disband their forces. The oath of the association founded at Troyes by the lieutenant-general, Charles de La Rochefoucauld, was evidently modelled on that of the Confraternity of the Holy Ghost in Dijon. The league at Le Mans was revived in July 1568 by the lieutenant-general, Louis d'Angennes, who was the brother of the local bishop. Its members included nobles, municipal officials, royal office-holders and bourgeois. They swore at a meeting held in the Jacobin friary outside the walls to resist Satan and the Huguenots unto death. D'Angennes admitted that he had formed the league without the king's permission, but claimed that he had been obeying a charge entrusted to him by the queen-mother.

In June Charles IX wrote to Tavannes authorizing him to keep lists of Catholics in his province who would take up arms, if ordered, in order to prevent Huguenots from doing so. The letter could be interpreted as permission to form a league, which doubtless explains why Tavannes was subsequently asked to burn it. In July Lude was ordered to prevent an association from being set up in his own *gouvernement* of Poitou. By mid-August, however, the crown tried to control Catholic militancy by placing itself at the head of the movement. It suggested that all leagues and associations should adopt the same oath. Although it included vows not to take up arms, contribute money or engage in secret enterprises without the king's permission, it does not seem consistent with the Edict of Longjumeau. Members of a league formed in Toulouse in September swore to arm themselves and die for the faith. Calling their league 'the Crusade', they identified with the defenders of Christendom against Attila the Hun and, more recently, the Albigensian heretics.

In the Midi, where Huguenots were strongly entrenched in a number of towns, Catholics were given cause to complain of breaches of the peace. At Nîmes, Montpellier and other towns where the authorities meekly complied with the military occupation prescribed by the edict, troubles soon occurred.

Lesser Protestant nobles and townsfolk committed excesses similar to those they had already committed in 1561 and 1562. Near Montpellier they carried out armed raids in the countryside. The Huguenots of Montauban ravaged the environs of Grenade-sur-Garonne after the parlement of Toulouse had ordered the arrest of the vicomte de Rapin-Thoyras, who had been sent by Condé to announce the peace. His summary trial and execution were used as a pretext for reprisals by the Montalbanais.[37]

The third war (September 1568–August 1570)

By the summer of 1568 the Huguenot leaders, Condé and Coligny, had returned to their respective homes in Burgundy fearing for their lives. In spite of the peace settlement, many of their followers were being murdered. On 6 July Coligny warned the king that mob rule was undermining the monarchy. Later that month a Calvinist nobleman serving in d'Andelot's company was shot dead outside his home near Mâcon by six armed men. Coligny blamed the crime on the confraternities of the Holy Ghost. They were responsible, he said, for 'an infinity of massacres and murders since the pacification'. He pointed an accusing finger at the king: 'It is well known,' he wrote to Charles, 'that the confraternities and leagues are planned and controlled by the provincial governors, and that means that they must have your approval or, at least, tacit consent.' Condé also blamed the government for acts of terrorism. His men, he said, had arrested two murderers who claimed to have orders from the duc de Nevers and the king to 'kill all Huguenots'.[38] On 12 July Coligny wrote to Catherine de' Medici complaining about breaches of the peace treaty. 'There is no doubt,' he wrote, 'that God will not leave unpunished so much shedding of innocent blood . . . I do not want to be so presumptuous as to judge God's actions, but I can say on the authority of His Word that all who violate public trust will be punished.' The Admiral claimed that he was passionately committed to defending the crown against its real enemies, the Guises and Spain, but, apparently unconvinced, Catherine, in her reply, urged Coligny to obey the king, assuring him that he had no cause to fear assassination.[39]

---

37 Garrisson, *Protestants du Midi*, p. 171.

38 R. R. Harding, *Anatomy of a Power Elite: The Provincial Governors of Early Modern France* (New Haven, Conn., 1978), p. 64.

39 J. Shimizu, *Conflict of Loyalties: Politics and Religion in the Career of Gaspard de Coligny, Admiral of France, 1519–1572* (Geneva, 1970), pp. 127–8.

Condé and Coligny viewed with dismay the gathering of royal troops near Paris and in Burgundy. Their fears were fuelled by meetings of the Catholic fraternities in Burgundy. According to Tavannes, he was sent by Catherine to arrest the Huguenot leaders at Noyers, but, disapproving of this mission, he arranged for a cryptic message warning them of the peril to fall into their hands. Tavannes' memoirs are far from reliable, but La Noue and De Thou mention several warnings received by Condé. The crown, for its part, viewed with intense suspicion Huguenot activities, and letters from Tavannes to the king prove that it was preparing for war. On 23 August Condé and Coligny gave their enemies the slip. They fled from Noyers to La Rochelle with their families and an escort of 150 horsemen. They compared their flight to that of the biblical tribe of Israel out of Egypt. After fording the Loire, they fell upon their knees, and sang a hymn of thanksgiving. All along the way to La Rochelle the fugitives were joined by a multitude of Huguenots with carts and waggons. They attacked Catholic communities in their path. Only by hanging a few could Condé and Coligny impose discipline. The caravan reached La Rochelle on 18 September and were soon joined by d'Andelot bringing troop reinforcements from Normandy and Brittany; also by Jeanne d'Albret and her son, Henri, with some Gascon units.

La Rochelle was an admirable base wherein the Huguenots could rebuild their fortunes. Situated as it was on the Atlantic coast, it provided easy access to their allies in England and the Netherlands and offered opportunities of privateering at the expense of Spanish and French Catholic shipping. On the landward side, the town was protected by a curtain wall and marshes beyond. During the autumn, the Huguenot leaders enlarged the buffer zone between them and the king's forces by capturing as many towns as possible in Poitou. Meanwhile, Protestants in the Midi mobilized in defence of their faith. As 25,000 troops poured out of Dauphiné, Provence and Languedoc, the commanders compared them to a whole people in search of a new home. Led by Paul de Mouvans and Jacques d'Acier, they marched on Poitou. Meanwhile, a small royal army under the duc de Montpensier launched a surprise attack near Poitiers on Huguenot troops which had become detached from the main southern army. Mouvans was killed and a number of his men were massacred by peasants, but d'Acier managed to reach La Rochelle with the bulk of the army virtually intact.

The royal artillery in 1568

As the civil wars continued, sieges became increasingly important. An immediate consequence was a growing need for artillery. Here the crown had a distinct advantage over the Huguenots who were always comparatively weak in that arm. A document of September 1568 contains interesting details of the artillery intended for use by the duc d'Anjou in the forthcoming campaign. It was to consist of 20 guns of mixed calibre, 5,000 cannonballs and 91 *milliers* of powder. A total of 1,550 horses were to draw the guns and 283 waggons of various kinds containing shot, powder, pontoon materials, workmen's tools, spare parts, forges, etc. A varied personnel, numbering 2,620, was to man the train; that is to say, an average of 131 men per gun. The personnel was made up of three groups: 233 men from the Arsenal in Paris, 367 teamsters and 2,000 pioneers. The contingent from the Arsenal comprised executive officers and their assistants, skilled workers and gunners. The teamsters, who were hired or levied, provided their own horses and carts. The pioneers, who were the lowest element in the army and the most poorly paid, performed the menial tasks of repairing roads, lending their shoulders to the waggons and guns on the road, loading, unloading and carrying the munitions, running loaded guns to their firing position, building camps and depots, digging approach trenches, mining and countermining. The pioneers were the only troops to be given uniforms in order that they should be easily recognized and, therefore, discouraged from deserting. Even so, they deserted in large numbers. Of the personnel proposed for the train of 1568 only the Grand Master of the artillery was paid 500 livres per month. His eleven principal lieutenants received a monthly wage of 100 livres. Gunners got 10 livres per month, slightly more than a pikeman or arquebusier. A pioneer was paid very little indeed for work that was often extremely dangerous.[40]

Funding the artillery was only part of a much larger problem facing the crown. As we have seen, the crown had launched the third civil war with barely enough cash to pay its army. The awful truth dawned in the course of the campaign. According to Tavannes, by August 1569 the *gendarmerie* had only been paid for one quarter and the infantry for two months since the start of the war. The troops had been kept sustained by occasional advances or loans from their officers and a fairly consistent supply of their daily rations. Even so, discipline began to crumble. An analysis of the sources from which the army was to be funded in October 1568 has revealed how much the crown depended on extraordinary, as opposed to regular, revenues. One hundred and fifty-two companies of *gendarmerie* were owed nearly 1.6 million livres. As 50,000 livres had already been paid, a sum of 974,000 livres was assigned to 107 companies which were owed over one million livres, leaving an overall deficit of 551,000 livres. The

40 Wood, *The King's Army*, pp. 160–68.

974,000 livres were raised from a variety of sources: 52 per cent from Paris, 31 per cent from Toulouse and Languedoc, and only 5 per cent from Poitou, where the campaigning was mainly centred. Only 20 per cent of the money came from the king's coffers; 72 per cent came from the clergy and the city of Paris; 10 per cent from private sources, and the rest from Languedoc in the form of a loan. The earmarking of 60,000 livres as wages due to John Casimir's German mercenaries left a deficit of 74,000 livres and no money at all for 45 companies of *gendarmerie*.

The battle of Jarnac (13 March 1569)

Following his success outside Poitiers, Montpensier was joined by Anjou with the bulk of the king's army. Winter, however, was at hand, so fighting ceased except for some skirmishing. The crown, meanwhile, reversed the edicts of pacification. The Edict of Saint-Maur, which was registered on 23 September 1568, deprived the Huguenots of their freedom of worship. They retained freedom of conscience, but all pastors were ordered to leave the kingdom. A second edict banned all non-Catholics from holding royal offices.[41] In the spring of 1569 the Catholic and Protestant armies met face to face along the river Charente. Condé and Coligny were planning to meet up in Quercy with an army which had been raised by 'the viscounts' (see p. 152). But Anjou watched their movements closely from the river's left bank. The Huguenots, for their part, remained behind the Charente in order not to provoke an engagement. They were content to guard its bridges. Tavannes, however, who was the effective commander of the king's army, crossed the river at Châteauneuf. Coligny was at Bassac with the Huguenot van, while Condé was with the 'battle' at Jarnac, a few miles away. As Tavannes attacked Coligny, Condé went to his assistance. He charged impetuously at the head of about 300 horse, but was soon overwhelmed by a much larger force of royal *reiters* and cavalry. The prince surrendered after being thrown from his horse and breaking his leg, but, recognizing him, Montesquiou, the captain of Anjou's guard, murdered him by shooting him in the head. According to Brantôme, Anjou humiliated Condé by having his corpse carried off the field 'his arms and legs dangling' on the back of an ass. Other Protestant captains had their throats cut after the battle.

41 Stegmann (ed.), *Édits des guerres de religion*, pp. 59–66; Sutherland, *The Huguenot Struggle for Recognition*, pp. 170, 358. Sutherland claims that the edict 'was prepared by the cardinal of Lorraine largely to precipitate the third civil war, which he desired'.

The Huguenots suffered few losses at Jarnac as only a part of their army had taken an active part in the fighting. Admiral Coligny, who now became the sole commander of the Huguenot army, managed to retreat westward with his infantry virtually intact. The victorious royal army set off in pursuit, but had to stop outside Cognac. As it had not yet received from Paris its heavy siege guns, it could not take the town. Meanwhile, Jeanne d'Albret presented Condé's son and her own, Henri, aged 15 and 16 respectively, to the Huguenot army. They were acclaimed as its new leaders, but everyone knew that they were only 'the Admiral's pages'. Yet, as princes of the blood, they gave to the Huguenot cause a legitimacy which the king's councillors did not possess.

In November 1568 William, prince of Orange led an army into France from Germany as if intending to join the Huguenot force in Poitou, but his troops were unpaid and poorly fed. Seeing that her son's army was engaged elsewhere, Catherine de' Medici offered William cash and Charles IX offered him free passage if he would return to Germany. Fearing mutiny among his men, William duly retreated across the Moselle on 13 January 1569, but the French crown soon had to face a far more serious threat in the form of a German mercenary army led by Wolfgang of Bavaria, duke of Zweibrücken. A royal army jointly commanded by the dukes of Nemours and Aumale waited for it on the Meuse, but Wolfgang bypassed them further south. He sacked Beaune, crossed the Loire at La Charité and pushed westward through Berry and Marche. Wolfgang died on 11 June, but, on the following day, his troops made junction with the Huguenot army at Saint-Yriex. A loan of £20,000 raised from English bankers against the security of jewels sent by the queen of Navarre arrived at the Huguenot camp later that month.[42]

The two opposing armies were now roughly equal in strength. Anjou took up a position on the heights above La Roche-l'Abeille, while two of his regiments of foot remained in the valley below. Coligny now attacked these troops and crushed them. Strozzi, the captain-general of the royal infantry, was taken prisoner. The Huguenots avenged Jarnac by taking few prisoners. Hundreds of local peasants were slaughtered on Coligny's orders as a reprisal for their treatment of Mouvans' men. On 12 July the Parlement of Paris declared the office of Admiral vacant and early in August ordered the confiscation of all the property of Huguenot leaders. In September it condemned Coligny, Montgomery and the vidame of Chartres. The sum of 50,000 gold écus was placed on Coligny's head.[43]

42 Shimizu, *Conflict of Loyalties*, p. 131.
43 Ibid., pp. 134–5.

The Admiral wanted to march north and capture Saumur as a first step towards carrying the war into the Paris region, but his German troops, keen as always to sack and loot, persuaded him to besiege Poitiers. The operation began on 24 July. The defenders, led by the comte du Lude, disposed of heavy artillery newly arrived from Paris and of a few hundred cavalry under the young Henri, duc de Guise.They flooded the meadows outside the town by diverting the course of the river Clain. A diversionary attack by Anjou on Châtellerault gave Coligny a pretext for lifting the siege of Poitiers on 7 September. When he moved against the king's army, it retreated across the Cher and set up camp at Chinon. Both armies were now in poor shape. By the end of September, however, the crown's efforts to raise more troops had begun to pay off. The king's army was now about 26,000 strong. On 3 October it engaged the enemy at Moncontour. The result was a great royal victory. Young Condé had to retire from the field after being wounded in the face. His cavalry fled and the German infantry surrendered only to be massacred by the king's Swiss troops, always their bitter rivals in war. As against a few hundred royal casualties, those suffered by the Huguenots numbered about 10,000. They lost more than 100 standards as well as most of their baggage and artillery.

Catherine de' Medici rejoiced over the Huguenot defeat. She thanked God for allowing her son to be the instrument of such a great deed. However, Charles IX's joy was tempered by jealousy of his brother's success. He lost no time in joining the army in order to share its glory. Tavannes now pressed Anjou to pursue the enemy, but the duke embarked instead on the piecemeal conquest of towns commanding the approaches to La Rochelle. He captured Niort, but Saint-Jean d'Angély resisted. Though poorly fortified, the town was well defended. The garrison threw back several assaults. Meanwhile, the king's army was reduced in size by a combination of casualties, sickness and desertion. Only a rump survived when Saint-Jean d'Angély surrendered on 2 December. As the troops dispersed for the winter, the crown was left with virtually no troops or funds.

The war in the south

After the peace of Longjumeau it seems that Huguenots in the Midi did not disarm. They were led, as they had been in the second war, by a group of viscounts who fought sometimes together and sometimes apart. The principal ones were the viscounts of Paulin, Bruniquel, Arpajon and Rapin. Their forces were now concentrated in the vicinity of Montauban. When war was resumed, Joyeuse and Gordes, the governor of Dauphiné, tried to stop the

Huguenots east of the Rhône from joining the viscounts in Languedoc. A council of war held at Millau decided that they would stay in Quercy and Languedoc while the main southern army would cross the Dordogne and seek to join Condé. On 25 October 1568, however, this army was routed by a royal force under the duc de Montpensier and Marshal Brissac. The viscounts, meanwhile, were successful in Languedoc. After destroying Gaillac on 8 September, they found the path clear when Joyeuse withdrew his force from Languedoc to assist Anjou. But on 9 June 1569 the viscounts were routed in the Ariège by Bellegarde, sénéchal of Toulouse. Their shattered bands then joined Gabriel de Montgomery, who had been detached by Coligny from his army to deal with a threat to Béarn and Navarre.[44]

The presence of Jeanne d'Albret, queen of Navarre, and her son, Henri, at La Rochelle had sinister implications for the French crown. For it strengthened links of vassalship between the Midi and the house of Albret, the only great feudal house in that corner of France. As Monluc shrewdly noted, Jeanne encouraged Condé to fight, but only in the south. He suspected that she hoped to create a large and independent southern state for her son. Monluc's fears may well have been justified, for early in 1569 towns in the south controlled by the Huguenots received orders signed by Louis de Condé and Henri de Navarre instructing them to levy taxes from all their inhabitants to help pay for the war. Thus Montauban was asked to contribute 9,411 livres out of a total sum of 150,000 livres. The parlement denounced these levies as outright theft and as oppression of the people, but they took place none the less. Later, in 1571, Coligny paid homage to Henri de Navarre, receiving in return the helm and golden spurs. Charles IX retaliated by reviving the old right of seisin: he confiscated Jeanne d'Albret's French domains. But he could not exercise this right in Béarn and Lower Navarre, which lay outside his kingdom. He admitted as much, but declared that both states needed protection while their ruler, Jeanne, and her son were being held captive at La Rochelle. On 4 January 1569 Monluc authorized the authorities in Guyenne to act against Jeanne's subjects wherever they might be. The parlement of Bordeaux promptly rounded up transhumant livestock which had come to the *landes* from the mountains of Béarn. Monluc's men carried out the task, which netted spoils valued at 600,000 livres.[45]

Monluc believed that Béarn might easily be conquered in the absence of its ruler. Anjou backed the idea, but did not think Monluc could be spared from Guyenne. He appointed instead Antoine de Lomagne, seigneur de

44 J. W. Thompson, *The Wars of Religion in France, 1559–1576* (New York, 1909), pp. 394–6.
45 Garrisson, *Protestants du Midi*, pp. 171–2.

Terride, whom he detached from his army. Monluc blamed Montmorency-Damville for this decision and never forgave him. At first, Terride's campaign went well. Town after town, including Pau, surrendered to him, while the countryside was laid waste. Jeanne d'Albret's lieutenant had to take refuge in the castle of Navarrenx, which Terride besieged on 27 April 1569. On 21 June Montgomery arrived in Castres bearing a commission from Condé and Navarre. Within four weeks he reached the Toulouse area at the head of the viscounts' combined armies. By forced marches he reached Navarrenx, forcing Terride to abandon the siege. Pursued by the viscounts, he surrendered on 13 August and died soon afterwards. His captains were killed almost to a man.[46] Béarn had been saved by Montgomery. Monluc was appalled by this turn of events, which he saw as a threat to Guyenne and even to the kingdom. He blamed everyone: Francis I for having allowed Navarrenx to be fortified, Terride for his failure to follow up his success, and, above all, Montmorency-Damville for betraying the king of France.[47] But he could not hide his admiration for Montgomery's generalship. 'One has to admit,' he wrote, 'that in all our wars there has not been a finer action than this one.'[48]

Admiral Coligny, meanwhile, withdrew across the Charente and marched south where the Huguenots remained strong thanks to the military successes in that area of Montgomery and his fellow 'viscounts'. Within a short time Coligny was joined by thousands of troops. By the time he reached Montpellier he had between 10,000 and 12,000 men. On 3 January 1570 he and Montgomery joined forces. A serious dispute between the royal governors, Monluc and Damville, gave them an almost clear run in Upper Guyenne and Languedoc. They grew rich on the spoils of war, carrying their depredations to the walls of Toulouse, which they besieged from 22 January to 20 February 1570. A chain of fortresses reaching from the Atlantic coast to the heart of France gave the Huguenots control of the Loire. Provence and Lower Languedoc were in their hands while Montauban, Albi and Castres formed a line of defence in the west. In Upper Languedoc, they were less strong, yet they held a number of towns. When they conquered Tarbes in January, the Huguenots had a chain of fortresses stretching directly north from Béarn to Bergerac and Angoulême.

Coligny's original plan was to spend the rest of the winter in Gascony and Guyenne with Port-Sainte-Marie as his base. He hoped to bring up heavy artillery from Béarn in order to take all the towns on the river

46 Thompson, *The Wars of Religion in France*, pp. 397–401.
47 Garrisson, *Protestants du Midi*, p. 173.
48 P. Courteault (ed.), *Commentaires de Blaise de Monluc* (Paris, 1925), vol. 3, p. 202.

Garonne. He even hoped to blockade Bordeaux, but soon changed his mind. He believed that the crown would not think seriously about peace as long as the war remained confined to provinces remote from Paris. So as the new fighting season began, he decided to put pressure on the government by taking the war nearer to the capital. After besieging Toulouse unsuccessfully, his army moved towards Carcassonne and Montréal. Then it marched up the Rhône as far as Chalon-sur-Saône.

The Peace of Saint-Germain (8 August 1570)

The crown watched helplessly as local governors and commanders failed to stop the Admiral's march north. The governor of Languedoc, Marshal Henri de Montmorency-Damville, showed little inclination to pursue the Huguenots. It seems that he was already dissociating himself from the hard line favoured by the Guises and other Catholic extremists. Two other marshals, François de Montmorency, Damville's elder brother, and François de Vieilleville, were equally lethargic.Their attitude reflected divisions among the nobility. Even within the king's council opinion was sharply divided. As Coligny drew nearer to Paris, moderate voices grew louder. The crown nevertheless tried to make a stand on the Loire. After enough money had been collected, a new force was raised at Orléans. Led by Marshal Cossé, it engaged Coligny inconclusively at Arnay-le-Duc (Burgundy) in June 1570. Picking up guns and reinforcements at Sancerre and La Charité, the Admiral then marched on Paris.

Peace talks had taken place intermittently during the war, but the Huguenots, having learnt the lesson of Longjumeau, wanted solid guarantees that a new peace treaty would be honoured. As late as 24 December Coligny remained sceptical about the crown's sincerity. Writing to Jeanne d'Albret, he said: 'I know well that the King wants to sign the peace, which he wants to give us, with the tip of his sword. Such "peace" is nothing but cheating.'[49] From December 1569 to March 1570 the negotiations were deadlocked over the issue of public worship. In March Coligny and the queen of Navarre sent representatives to the king to press their demands. Other sticking points concerned the choice of security towns and payment of the *reiters*. In July the Huguenots agreed to discuss the right of worship on the basis of the edict of January 1562. A settlement soon followed. The Peace of

49 Shimizu, *Conflict of Loyalties*, p. 135.

Saint-Germain which was signed in August marked for the Huguenots a definite advance on earlier settlements, for they were granted four security towns – La Rochelle, Montauban, La Charité and Cognac – for two years. In addition, they were allowed freedom of conscience throughout France and freedom of worship where it had taken place before the war, in two towns per *gouvernement* and in the homes of nobles with superior rights of justice. But Protestant worship was still banned in Paris and at court. Coligny, it seems, was prepared to compromise on public worship for three reasons: first, he believed that the civil war, if it continued, would ruin both France and his party; secondly, he was keen to transfer the fighting from France to the Netherlands; and thirdly, he wished to be reconciled with the king by means of a foreign war.[50] Under the new edict Huguenots were also to be admitted to all universities, schools and hospitals; they were to have their own cemeteries and were given certain privileges to protect them from biased judgments by the parlements. All confiscated property and offices were to be returned. The king's 'dear and well beloved cousins', the prince of Orange and Louis of Nassau, recovered their possessions in France.[51]

50 Ibid., pp. 137–8.
51 Stegmann (ed.), *Édits des guerres de religion*, pp. 67–81; Sutherland, *The Huguenot Struggle for Recognition*, pp. 358–60.

CHAPTER EIGHT

St Bartholomew's Day and after (1572–1575)

The Peace of Saint-Germain lasted only two years. Yet historians generally believe that it represented a genuine effort by the French crown to heal the religious division of France. The withdrawal of the cardinal of Lorraine following a quarrel over a love affair between his brother, the duc de Guise, and King Charles IX is said to have cleared the way for more moderate members of the king's council to influence policy. They included François de Montmorency, the governor of Paris and the Île-de-France, Jean de Morvillier, the Keeper of the Seals, and Paul de Foix, archbishop of Toulouse.[1] As for the queen-mother, it seems that she rested her hopes for a lasting peace on a plan to marry her daughter, Marguerite, to Henri de Navarre, the young leader of the Huguenot party. The historian, Denis Crouzet, firmly believes that Charles IX, acting under the neo-platonic influence of his tutor, Jacques Amyot, tried to persuade his courtiers to rid the kingdom of evil by setting their sights on the harmony that rules the cosmos.[2] This was allegedly the purpose of his creation on 10 November 1570 of the Academy and Company of Poetry and Music. Court festivals in which music, dancing, painting and poetry all played a role and which Catherine de' Medici zealously promoted had the same objective, so it is claimed.[3]

In the absence of minutes of the king's council for this period it is difficult to know exactly what the king and his ministers had in mind. La Noue

1 A. Jouanna, *La France du XVIe siècle, 1483–1598* (Paris, 1996), pp. 461–2; S. Carroll, *Noble Power during the French Wars of Religion* (Cambridge, 1998), pp. 134–5.

2 D. Crouzet, *La nuit de la Saint-Barthélemy: un rêve perdu de la Renaissance* (Paris: Fayard, 1994), pp. 213–40.

3 F. A. Yates, *The French Academies of the Sixteenth Century* (London, 1988), pp. 19–27; R. J. Knecht, *Catherine de' Medici* (London, 1998), pp. 236–41.

suggests that Charles IX had grown tired of war, which 'deprived him of his pleasures, undermined the obedience and love that were his due, spoiled the kingdom, emptied his coffers and consumed his forces'.[4] What is certain is that the peace opened up new possibilities of action in two areas: matrimonial diplomacy and the Netherlands. On 26 November 1570 Charles IX married Elizabeth, the second daughter of the Emperor. His sister married Philip II of Spain. Thus the dynastic link between the houses of Valois and Habsburg which had been forged in 1529 with the marriage of Charles V's sister, Eleonor, to Francis I was revived. Meanwhile, Catherine de' Medici sought two other marriages for her children: the first, between her daughter, Marguerite, and Henri de Navarre, and the second between her son, Henri, duc d'Anjou and Queen Elizabeth I of England. Both marriages had important religious implications and, partly for this reason, encountered opposition. Huguenots generally were not keen on the Valois–Navarre marriage. Jeanne d'Albret, Henri's austerely Protestant mother, viewed it with suspicion. Admiral Coligny was equally unenthusiastic. He would have preferred a marriage between Navarre and the English queen.[5] As for the duc d'Anjou, he refused to marry a Protestant queen, who was almost twice his age and was still regarded as a bastard by the Catholic world. His place as suitor was consequently taken by his younger brother François, duc d'Alençon.[6]

In 1571, while Catherine promoted her matrimonial schemes, the idea of a French military intervention on the side of the Dutch rebels in the Netherlands began to be actively canvassed in France. Their leader, William of Orange, had left France to prepare an invasion of the Netherlands from Germany, but his brother, Louis of Nassau, and many other Dutch exiles had stayed behind. While harassing Spanish shipping from their base at La Rochelle, they also planned to invade the Netherlands from the south at the same time as Orange did so from the east. But this required the co-operation of Charles IX, who had so far shown little interest in state affairs. It seems, however, that he had become jealous of the military successes scored by his brother, Anjou, in the last civil war. He was thus not averse to meddling in the Netherlands on his own account, particularly as Philip II was at that moment occupied by a serious revolt in southern Spain. The talks for an Anglo–French marriage also opened up the possibility of English co-operation in a Dutch enterprise. On 19 July 1571 Charles IX attended a secret meeting at the château of Lumigny and another soon afterwards at Fontainebleau.

4 F. de La Noue, *Discours politiques et militaires*, ed. F. E. Sutcliffe (Geneva, 1967), p. 783.

5 J. Shimizu, *Conflict of Loyalties: Politics and Religion in the Career of Gaspard de Coligny, Admiral of France, 1519–1572* (Geneva, 1970), pp. 150–52.

6 P. Chevallier, *Henri III* (Paris, 1985), pp. 143–5; M. P. Holt, *The Duke of Anjou and the Politique Struggle during the Wars of Religion* (Cambridge, 1986), pp. 22, 24.

Nassau attended at least the second of these meetings, during which a plan for the partition of the Netherlands between France, England and the Empire was considered. However, English co-operation depended on a matrimonial alliance between England and France which failed to materialize.[7]

In September 1571 Admiral Coligny returned to court. He was warmly received by Charles IX at Blois, admitted to his council and given a large sum of money and a rich abbey.[8] But Catherine de' Medici continued to distrust him. She opposed his warlike designs against Spain, yet needed his support for the marriage between her daughter, Marguerite, and Henri de Navarre. At first, Coligny opposed the match because he feared that it might lead to Henri's abjuration, but eventually he came to accept it as the essential prerequisite to a war with Spain. Catherine's distrust was not the only problem facing the Admiral at this time. Most French Catholics regarded him not only as a heretic but as a rebel. And the Guises continued to look for an opportunity to bring about his ruin. In November it was reported that they were gathering funds and followers in Paris. Huguenots gathered at Châtillon in order to protect him. France seemed on the verge of another civil war but the danger was narrowly averted. In March 1572 Charles IX again formally cleared Coligny of any guilt for the murder of the second duc de Guise, but this did nothing to end the vendetta. Only the Admiral's blood could satisfy the Guises.[9]

Charles IX was, it seems, anxious to rid himself of his mother's tutelage. By 8 October 1571 he had given his approval to an armed intervention by France in the Netherlands, but his mother, who was most anxious to avoid a war with Spain, got the decision rescinded. Even so, Nassau and other Dutch exiles in France stepped up their preparations for an attack on the Netherlands. On 1 April 1572 the Dutch 'Sea Beggars' opened a decisive new chapter in their struggle against Spain by capturing the port of Brill, and on 14 April William of Orange declared war on her. Nassau pressed Charles IX to support the rebels, but he felt unable to go against the wishes of his mother and of his councillors, save Coligny. So Nassau acted alone. In late May he and some Huguenot confederates seized the towns of Valenciennes and Mons. Coligny again pressed the king to enter the war, but in vain. On 7 June Charles forbade his subjects to cross the Dutch border in support of Nassau. In July, however, he allowed a small Huguenot army led by Jean de Hangest, seigneur de Genlis, to march to the relief of Mons, which was being besieged by the duke of Alba. Charles claimed that the expedition had been mounted in defiance of his ban, but the duke treated the Huguenot raid as an act of aggression by France.

7 N. M. Sutherland, *The Massacre of St Bartholomew and the European Conflict, 1559–1572* (London, 1973), p. 175.

8 M. Simonin, *Charles IX* (Paris, 1995), p. 265.

9 Shimizu, *Conflict of Loyalties*, pp. 147–9; Knecht, *Catherine de' Medici*, pp. 143–4.

Unfortunately for Charles, the Genlis expedition was intercepted on 17 July before it could reach Mons and decisively crushed. Genlis was taken prisoner and on him was found a written promise from Charles IX to aid the rebels.[10]

The Genlis affair made it all the more necessary for Coligny to aid William of Orange in the Netherlands. After a brief visit to his home at Châtillon, the Admiral returned to Paris to promote his war plan at court. He pointed to the dangers France would face in the event of Orange being defeated and to restlessness among his Huguenot followers. According to Tavannes, Coligny said that he could not restrain them and that the choice facing the king was between war with Spain and civil war in France.[11] But Catherine de' Medici not only dreaded a conflict with Spain; she also resented the influence which Coligny was exerting on her son. She was afraid that if he got his way, nothing would stand in his way of achieving supreme authority at her expense. The papal legate, Salviati, shared this view. France, he believed would fall prey to the Huguenots if she went to war with Spain. On 10 August the king's council opted for peace, but this did not stop another Huguenot army from gathering near Mons. Coligny also gathered a force of 12,000 arquebusiers and 2,000 horsemen. Catherine, alarmed by these developments, may well have decided that the time had come to get rid of Coligny.

In the meantime, the negotiations for the marriage between the king's sister, Marguerite, and Henri de Navarre moved towards a happy conclusion. The prince's mother, Jeanne d'Albret, was finally persuaded to come to the French court. On 11 March the marriage contract was signed, but Jeanne did not live to witness the nuptials. She died, probably of pleurisy, on 9 June.[12] Preparations for the wedding were not suspended, however. As the day approached, Huguenot nobles converged on the capital as did their Catholic rivals. The Guises with their large clientèle took up residence at the Hôtel de Guise and in houses belonging to the clergy. The concentration within the capital of men who had only recently been fighting each other was evidently fraught with risk of renewed violence, particularly as the atmosphere in Paris was feverishly hostile to the Huguenots.

Catholic anger

Whatever the government may have expected from the Peace of Saint-Germain, it did not heal the divisions among the king's subjects. Two years

10 Shimizu, *Conflict of Loyalties*, pp. 165–8; D. Crouzet, *La nuit de la Saint-Barthélemy*, pp. 338–48.
11 Shimizu, *Conflict of Loyalties*, p. 173.
12 N. L. Roelker, *Queen of Navarre: Jeanne d'Albret, 1528–1572* (Cambridge, Mass., 1968), pp. 387–90.

of formal peace were marred by frequent acts of violence committed by Huguenots and Catholics in various parts of France. In Rouen the new edict proved as difficult to enforce as its predecessor. A bloody affray occurred on 18 March 1571 as a party of some 500 Huguenots made their way to a Sunday service at Bondeville. As they passed a priest carrying the Blessed Sacrament to a dying man, some Catholic bystanders, who fell upon their knees, called out to the Huguenots to uncover themselves. The reply was a volley of insults and stones, whereupon fighting broke out. Forty Huguenots were allegedly killed. Five men, who were arrested for their part in the massacre, were set free by an angry mob. The town council complained to the king, who sent a commission led by Montmorency and a large force of soldiers. The repression was savage: 66 death sentences were passed and fines totalling 4,000 livres levied. Rouen's militia was reorganized so as to make it more effective, but the violence continued.[13]

Elsewhere in France it was the same story. In the Midi the apparent change of direction adopted by the crown since the peace was itself a cause of violence. In Orange, on 3 February 1570, the Huguenots tried to expel the Catholic garrison and to seize the castle, but were beaten back by the Catholic population. Some were besieged inside houses where they had taken shelter. Fugitives complained of their treatment to their leaders, including the prince of Orange and Admiral Coligny. Charles IX entrusted the city to a governor chosen by Orange. The result was a new outbreak of violence in reverse. This time several Catholics were executed and others hanged in effigy. Among them were the superiors of the mendicant orders.[14]

Nowhere did feelings run as high as in Paris. The Edict of Saint-Germain had ordered the demolition of any monument likely to incite religious unrest. Such a monument was the Cross of Gastines, which had been erected on the site of a house, once used for Huguenot services, which had been razed to the ground. The cross soon became a symbol of Parisian opposition to religious toleration. Its removal by an armed guard to the Cemetery of the Innocents set off violent disturbances. The king ordered justice to be done but to little avail: some minor trouble-makers were punished, but the main culprits evaded arrest. Charles IX, it seems, misjudged the mood of the capital. The removal of the Cross of Gastines was only one Catholic grievance among many. There was much economic hardship in the capital as a consequence of the last war, bad harvests and high prices. To make matters worse the king tried to tax the Parisians to the tune of 600,000

13 P. Benedict, *Rouen during the Wars of Religion* (Cambridge, 1981), p. 121.

14 M. Venard, *Réforme protestante, Réforme catholique dans la province d'Avignon au XVIe siècle* (Paris, 1993), p. 542.

livres in order to buy off the foreign mercenaries who had come to the aid of the Huguenots. The Parisians said that they could not afford this sum; they also resented having to pay for the Protestant war effort. Eventually, Charles IX had to be content with less, but even this was hard to collect. The king also resorted to unpopular fiscal expedients. Wealthy Parisians, for example, were coerced into buying annuities or *rentes*. As public confidence in them collapsed, Charles turned to private financiers, mostly Italians, who acquired the *rentes* for cash and drew the interest until they decided to dispose of them. The king, meanwhile, continued to borrow, while even more tenuous sources of income were assigned to the payment of *rentes*. Offices were another source of grievance. Under the Peace of Saint-Germain those which had been taken from Huguenots and given to Catholics were to be handed back to their former owners. Since the crown had virtually no money, dispossessed Catholics could not hope for adequate compensation. Similarly people who had taken over houses vacated by Huguenots during the war had to return them. They were promised compensation from the proceeds of a tax on Huguenots returning to the capital, but probably got nothing. Catholics were promised first call on new leases as they became available but this was not enough to quell their resentment. They felt that rebels were being favoured at the expense of the king's loyal subjects.[15]

Parisians viewed with dismay Coligny's return to the French court. Some historians have cast doubt on the degree of influence which he was able to exert on the king. They may be right, but the perception of contemporary observers was different. Noting that the Admiral's return coincided with the withdrawal from court of the Guises and that Charles IX was insisting on the strict enforcement of the recent peace edict, they drew their own conclusion. It was also Coligny who had asked for the removal of the Cross of Gastines. The news that the king's sister was about to marry the Huguenot prince of Navarre increased suspicion that Protestants were now controlling the court. So did rumours of a possible French invasion of the Netherlands. Charles IX, it was said, had secretly backed the enterprise and had been promised Flanders in return for a Protestant victory.

The wedding of Henri de Navarre and Marguerite de Valois was celebrated at the cathedral of Notre-Dame on 18 August 1572. It was followed by four days of glittering festivities in the form of tournaments, banquets, balls and ballets, all of them in sharp contrast to the poverty afflicting many Parisians. On 22 August Admiral Coligny was shot as he walked back to his residence from the Louvre. He was only wounded, but the attempt on his

15 B. Diefendorf, *Beneath the Cross: Catholics and Huguenots in Sixteenth-Century Paris* (Oxford, 1991), pp. 85–92.

life was a hugely important event politically, signalling a return to civil war. The assailant, who managed to evade capture by the Admiral's escort, was probably Charles de Louviers, seigneur de Maurevert, who had tried to kill him before. He may have been acting on his own account, but was more probably employed by the Guises in pursuit of their old vendetta against the Admiral. Historians are still debating the issue.[16] As news of the attempted assassination spread through Paris, Coligny's colleagues gathered at his bedside. They were joined by the king, his mother and other courtiers. Charles IX promised to punish those responsible for the crime. A judicial enquiry, held on 23 August, implicated Henri duc de Guise. Meanwhile, steps were taken by the municipal authorities to restrain Parisians from venting their hatred of the Huguenots. In spite of the tense atmosphere in the capital, the Admiral decided to stay there, but he asked the king for protection and was given a bodyguard of 50 arquebusiers.[17]

The massacre of St Bartholomew's Day (24 August 1572)

The attempt on the Admiral's life set off a chain of events of unprecedented violence. Catholics feared a Huguenot uprising as rumours circulated among them of a plot to murder the king and his family. Such reports may have reached the king, who had not forgotten the *Surprise de Meaux*. A pre-emptive strike may have commended itself to him. According to Tavannes, whose evidence is subject to caution, the king and his council, meeting on 23 August, decided that 'it was better to win a battle in Paris, where all the leaders were, than to risk it in the field and fall into a dangerous and uncertain war'.[18] Prime responsibility for the slaughter was entrusted to the king's Swiss and French guards and to those of the duc d'Anjou serving under the dukes of Guise and Aumale.

Early on the morning of 24 August soldiers of the king's guard led by Guise and other Catholic noblemen broke into Coligny's residence and murdered him in cold blood, throwing his body out of an upstairs window. While the head was cut off and embalmed for dispatch to Rome, the rest of

---

16 Sutherland, *The Massacre of St Bartholomew*, pp. 295–6; J.-L. Bourgeon, *L'Assassinat de Coligny* (Geneva, 1992), *passim*; Diefendorf, *Beneath the Cross*, p. 93; J. Estèbe, *Tocsin pour un massacre: la saison des Saint-Barthélemy* (Paris, 1968), pp. 107–110; M. Venard, 'Arrêtez le massacre!', *R.H.M.C.*, 39 (1992), pp. 645–61.

17 Estèbe, *Tocsin pour un massacre*, pp. 113–15.

18 J.-L. Bourgeon, *Charles IX devant la Saint-Barthélemy* (Geneva, 1995), pp. 19–20; D. Crouzet, *La nuit de la Saint-Barthélemy*, pp. 390–2.

the body was mutilated by a mob and dragged through the streets for three days before it was hanged from the gibbet at Montfaucon like that of a common criminal. The Admiral's cruel fate became the centrepiece of many Protestant pamphlets which claimed that he had been martyred for his faith.[19] The attack on the Admiral's lodging was followed by a general massacre of Huguenots in Paris by Catholic mobs. There is no evidence that this had been planned by the government, though words spoken in the heat of the moment by Guise may have given that impression. Many Parisians were only too willing to believe that Charles IX had at last thrown his authority on the side of cleansing the kingdom of heresy. Despite a royal command that the killing should cease, it continued for nearly a week and jealousy as much as religious fanaticism may have fuelled the violence, aided by alcohol. The role played by the Parisian militia in the massacre remains controversial. Relatively few of the captains, it seems, played an active role. Significantly, they were the same men who had committed acts of violence earlier in the religious wars. One boasted that he had killed 400 Huguenots single-handed. Not all Parisian Catholics, however, turned into murderers. While many remained quietly in their homes, some tried to protect Huguenots. Thus Philippe Duplessis-Mornay was sheltered first by an innkeeper, then by his family's notary. His future wife was protected by various Catholics until she fled from the capital. Yet Catholics in general approved of the massacre. The sudden springing to life of an old hawthorn bush in the Cemetery of the Innocents was interpreted as a sign of divine approval.[20]

In Rome, news of the massacre caused rejoicing. Pope Gregory XIII held a *Te Deum* and a commemorative medal was struck showing an angel overseeing the slaughter of Coligny and his friends. The painter Vasari was commissioned to paint frescoes in the Vatican palace commemorating the massacre. At the same time the pope instructed his nuncio in France to arrange for surviving Protestants to be brought back into the church.[21]

Protestant polemicists, writing after the massacre, were convinced that it had been planned long in advance. Simon Goulart, for instance, traced its origin to the Peace of Saint-Germain, alleging that the treaty's purpose had been to lull the Protestants into a false sense of security. The French government, he claimed, had encouraged the Dutch rebels in order to lure Coligny and the other Huguenot leaders to Paris ostensibly to discuss final preparations for war with Spain, but in reality to have them all wiped out.[22]

19 R. M. Kingdon, *Myths about the St Bartholomew's Day Massacres, 1572–1576* (Cambridge, Mass., 1958), pp. 5, 28–50.

20 Diefendorf, *Beneath the Cross*, pp. 93–106.

21 Kingdon, *Myths about the St Bartholomew's Day Massacres*, pp. 42, 46.

22 Ibid., pp. 42–3.

A papal courtier, Camillo Capilupi, claimed to know of documents proving that it had been premeditated, but none has so far come to light.[23] A present-day historian, Jean-Louis Bourgeon, has suggested that Spain and probably the Holy See were behind the plot to kill the Admiral. He interprets the eagerness with which the Spanish ambassador accused the French government of the crime as significant. 'Despite its unfolding in two stages (23 and 24 August),' writes Bourgeon, 'nothing, it seems, was less improvised than the St Bartholomew['s Day massacre]: which does not mean that it was intended to be as brutal and traumatic.'[24] In his judgment, the elimination of the Huguenot leadership was to be the first step in a campaign to force the government to change its policies. The perpetrators wanted the annulment of the Navarre marriage, the abrogation of the Edict of Saint-Germain, the return to power of the Guises, the exclusion of Huguenots from the king's council, the Parlement and other bodies, a curb on taxation, the abandonment of French interference in the Netherlands and a realignment of French foreign policy in line with the objectives of Philip II and Pope Gregory XIII. Bourgeon points to powerful pressure groups which were preparing to force Charles IX to give up his policies. As supporting evidence, he points to a judicial strike by the Parlement on 19 August and to a huge propaganda campaign mounted by parish priests and preachers.[25] The truth will probably never come to light. Nor are we ever likely to know who advised Charles IX to destroy the Huguenot leaders. Catherine de' Medici, the duc d'Anjou, the comte de Retz and the duc de Guise have all been named. Denis Crouzet believes that the decision to kill the Huguenot leaders could not have been premeditated. He sees it as an impetuous move by the king and his ministers aimed at salvaging the neo-platonic dream of a harmonious kingdom which the attempt on Coligny's life had seriously imperilled.[26]

The St Bartholomew's Day massacre was not confined to Paris. The killing was repeated in other towns, including La Charité, Meaux, Bourges, Saumur, Angers, Lyon, Troyes, Rouen, Bordeaux, Toulouse and Gaillac. In most of these towns violence erupted as soon as news of the Parisian massacre was received. In some the authorities rounded up Huguenots and killed them systematically; in others, mobs were responsible. It seems that everywhere the murderers imagined that they were carrying out the king's wishes, yet evidence exists that Charles IX ordered his lieutenants to stop the carnage. He admitted that he had ordered the execution of the Protestant

---

23 Ibid., pp. 43–5.

24 Bourgeon, *L'Assassinat de Coligny*, p. 62.

25 Bourgeon, *L'Assassinat de Coligny*, pp. 62–3.

26 Crouzet, *La nuit de la Saint-Barthélemy*, p. 183.

leaders in order to nip in the bud a plot they had been preparing against him, but he condemned the mass violence which had broken out since. However, it seems that the king also dispatched verbal instructions to at least a few provincial officials ordering them to deal sternly with Huguenots in their areas, only to countermand them. His hesitation may have cost Protestant lives. Charles was undoubtedly under pressure from Catholic extremists in his entourage. A letter from his brother, the duc d'Anjou, to the governor of Saumur proves that he for one wanted the massacre to spread. In nearly all the towns where killings took place anti-Protestant feeling had been fanned by events in the first decade of civil war. In all, except perhaps Bordeaux and Rouen, there was considerable mob involvement. However, in many towns no massacres took place: Huguenots were briefly imprisoned, mainly for their own protection.[27]

Effects of the massacres

The massacre of St Bartholomew in Paris and other towns seriously weakened the Protestant cause. Many Huguenots, who could not believe that God would have allowed such a slaughter of His own children, abjured their faith. Even the two young princes of Navarre and Condé, the nominal leaders of the Huguenot movement, who had survived the massacre at court, were received into the Catholic faith. But unlike many of their co-religionists, they acted under compulsion, having been given one of three choices by Charles IX: abjuration, death or life imprisonment. On 3 October Navarre had to beg forgiveness from the pope and on the 16 October he ordered Catholicism to be re-established in Béarn. Thereafter he behaved as if the massacre had never taken place, fraternizing with Guise and others.[28]

A contemporary reported that 5,000 Huguenots lapsed following the massacre. Ten years later, Jean de L'Espine said that the French Protestant churches had lost two-thirds of their members, an estimate confirmed by findings from Rouen. The Catholic parish registers reveal a flood of re-baptisms of Calvinist children making their reintegration into the Catholic fold. Many adult Huguenots formally abjured in the cathedral. At least 3,000 Protestants in Rouen became reconciled to the Catholic church. Others preferred to emigrate, mainly to England. Charles IX tried to spur further conversions by banning all Calvinists from royal offices, but Catholic hopes that the massacre had destroyed the Protestant church in France were soon

27 P. Benedict, 'The St Bartholomew's massacres in the provinces', *H.J.*, 2 (1978), pp. 211–34.
28 Kingdon, *Myths about the St Bartholomew's Day Massacres*, pp. 47–50.

dashed. The chain of Protestant strongholds across southern France and up the west coast to Poitou ensured its survival as well as the continuation of the civil wars. Yet the Huguenots had suffered a crippling blow from which they never fully recovered. When the Reformed church in Rouen resumed its regular meetings in 1578 it was only a fraction of its size in the 1560s; from a community of 16,000 souls it had sunk to one of around 3,000 and the decline was to prove permanent.[29]

The massacre also had a devastating effect on the relationship between the Huguenots and the crown. During the first three wars their leaders repeatedly voiced their loyalty to the king. They blamed only his evil advisers for the kingdom's misfortunes, but this distinction was not easily sustained once the king had himself admitted responsibility for the murder of Coligny and his friends. Huguenots who had so far adhered to the doctrine of non-resistance which Calvin and other Protestant reformers had preached were now forced to look for a new justification of armed opposition to the crown.[30]

All Huguenot writers believed that the Catholics had planned the massacre of St Bartholomew ever since that of Vassy. Catherine de' Medici, they alleged, had been a party to the plot, at least since her meeting with the duke of Alba at Bayonne in 1565. The recent slaughter was seen as an expression of Italian duplicity derived ultimately from the writings of Machiavelli. The duc d'Anjou, it was said, always carried a copy of *The Prince* in his pocket. Innocent Gentillet, a Huguenot who fled to Geneva after the massacre, published in 1576 a furious tirade, called *Anti-Machiavel* in which he blamed Machiavelli directly for the French government's 'infamous vices'. By so doing he helped the Huguenots to present their resistance as a legitimate act of self-defence. Many Huguenot pamphlets which appeared after the massacre continued to be straightforward diatribes, but instead of limiting their attacks to the Guises they extended them to the royal family. *Le reveille-matin des Français et de leurs voisins* is addressed not only to Frenchmen but also to their neighbours. In it the prophet Daniel offers a daring solution to France's problems. In addition to an armed alliance of Protestant powers, he lays down 40 laws for the government of France which strongly resemble the network of political assemblies set up by the Huguenots in Languedoc in 1574 (see below pp. 185–7). The pamphlet ends with an appeal to all Frenchmen, whatever their religion, to overthrow tyranny and to reassert their ancient rights.

Another Huguenot treatise, the *Politique*, suggests that unjust laws cannot be obeyed but denies the right of individuals to resist. This belongs to the

29 Benedict, *Rouen during the Wars of Religion*, pp. 125–50.

30 Q. Skinner, *Foundations of Modern Political Thought* (Cambridge, 1978), vol. 2, pp. 302–38.

'inferior powers'; that is to say, to people who by virtue of their office have elected the prince and may therefore depose him. But the *Politique* goes beyond this classic Calvinist argument by affirming that inferior agents have the right to lead resistance in the interest of the true faith. The argument is supported by numerous examples drawn from history of rulers who have been lawfully overthrown. Another political treatise, the *Discours politiques des diverses puissances establies de Dieu au monde* (Political discourses on different powers set up by God in this world), makes a strong and uncompromising case for resistance to a tyrant, leading if necessary to his murder. No one, it declares, deserves a more glorious reputation than a tyrant's assassin.[31]

Even after 1572 some Huguenot thinkers were anxious to repudiate as far as possible the more populist elements in Calvinist polemical writings. Although their main concern was to call their membership to arms, they also needed to look outside their own ranks for support, possibly among moderate Catholics who disapproved of the brutal methods used by the Valois government. To appeal to such people or at least not to offend them, the Huguenots needed to find a non-sectarian justification for rebellion. In 1573 François Hotman published his *Francogallia*. On the surface this was a work of antiquarianism dealing with Gauls, Romans and Franks, but it was clearly relevant to the contemporary scene. All France's current problems, Hotman claims, are due to an attack by Louis XI on her ancient constitution; the crown had usurped functions which had originally been exercised by the people acting through their representatives in the estates. These representatives, according to Hotman, had originally elected the king and retained the power to control his actions. They could make and unmake him. Here was a historically based theory of popular sovereignty which could be used by the Huguenots to discredit the government and to gain wide support for their movement.[32]

Du droit des magistrats sur leurs sujets (On the rights of magistrates over their subjects) was written by Théodore de Bèze, Calvin's principal lieutenant.[33] He published it anonymously in 1574 in Germany where he joined the prince of Condé after he had escaped from the French court and reverted to Protestantism. In his treatise de Bèze indicates that a ruler should only be obeyed if his commands are consonant with those of God; otherwise resistance is obligatory. A ruler who has usurped power can be opposed by every means, including assassination, even by private persons; but a lawful ruler can

31 Kingdon, *Myths about the St Bartholomew's Day Massacres*, pp. 70–1, 161–8, 173–82, 202.

32 Ibid., pp. 140–9; F. Hotman, *Francogallia*, Latin text by R. E. Giesey, trans. J. H. M. Salmon (Cambridge, 1972).

33 T. de Bèze, *Du droit des magistrats*, ed. R. M. Kingdon (Geneva, 1971).

only be resisted by 'inferior magistrates' who are of two kinds: noblemen or elected municipal officials. Power, de Bèze maintains, comes ultimately from the people and those who have elected the sovereign must ensure that it is used properly; if not, they must depose the sovereign. De Bèze shared Hotman's belief that the Estates-General was the best source of relief from tyranny.

Another highly influential Calvinist work was the *Vindiciae contra tyrannos* (Defence of liberty against tyrants) which is commonly attributed to Philippe Duplessis-Mornay.[34] It was published in 1579. The treatise is organized around four questions relating to obedience to a ruler who issues commands opposed to God's law. The author develops a theory of two contracts: one between God and the people; the other between the ruler and his subjects. Each carries mutual obligations. A king who breaks the law of God loses divine support as expressed by the leaders of His church, and one who breaks his promises to his subjects loses their obedience. Royal power, the author asserts, rests on popular consent and, being conditional, can be revoked. A usurping tyrant may be resisted by anyone, but a lawful one can only be resisted by the officers of the kingdom. These are of two kinds: those with local or regional responsibility, like provincial governors or town mayors, and those with national responsibilities, like peers of the realm or Marshals of France.

The massacre of St Bartholomew's Day dealt an almost fatal blow at the Huguenot movement. It wiped out its principal leaders and many of their followers, and demoralized the rest, inducing some to abjure and others to go into foreign exile. But the massacre did not destroy the movement, which survived in the west and south where it controlled a number of fortified towns. The peace of Saint-Germain could not be revived, of course, after an act of such seeming betrayal by the crown. As the massacre had destroyed any trust that had existed between the Huguenots and the Valois government, they could no longer blame the king's ministers rather than the king himself for their misfortunes. They had to find new justifications for armed resistance. At the same time they set out to underpin their military effort by means of a new political organization. This has sometimes been interpreted by historians as an attempt to reproduce on French soil the republican institutions which the Dutch rebels were setting up; yet for all their disenchantment with the Valois government, the Huguenots remained basically loyal to the ideal of monarchy. Henri de Navarre, whose enforced abjuration was only temporary, had, after all, a strong claim to the throne and might eventually prove to be their saviour.

34 Kingdon, *Myths about the St Bartholomew's Day Massacres*, pp. 218–19; *Vindiciae contra tyrannos*, ed. G. Garnett (Cambridge, 1994).

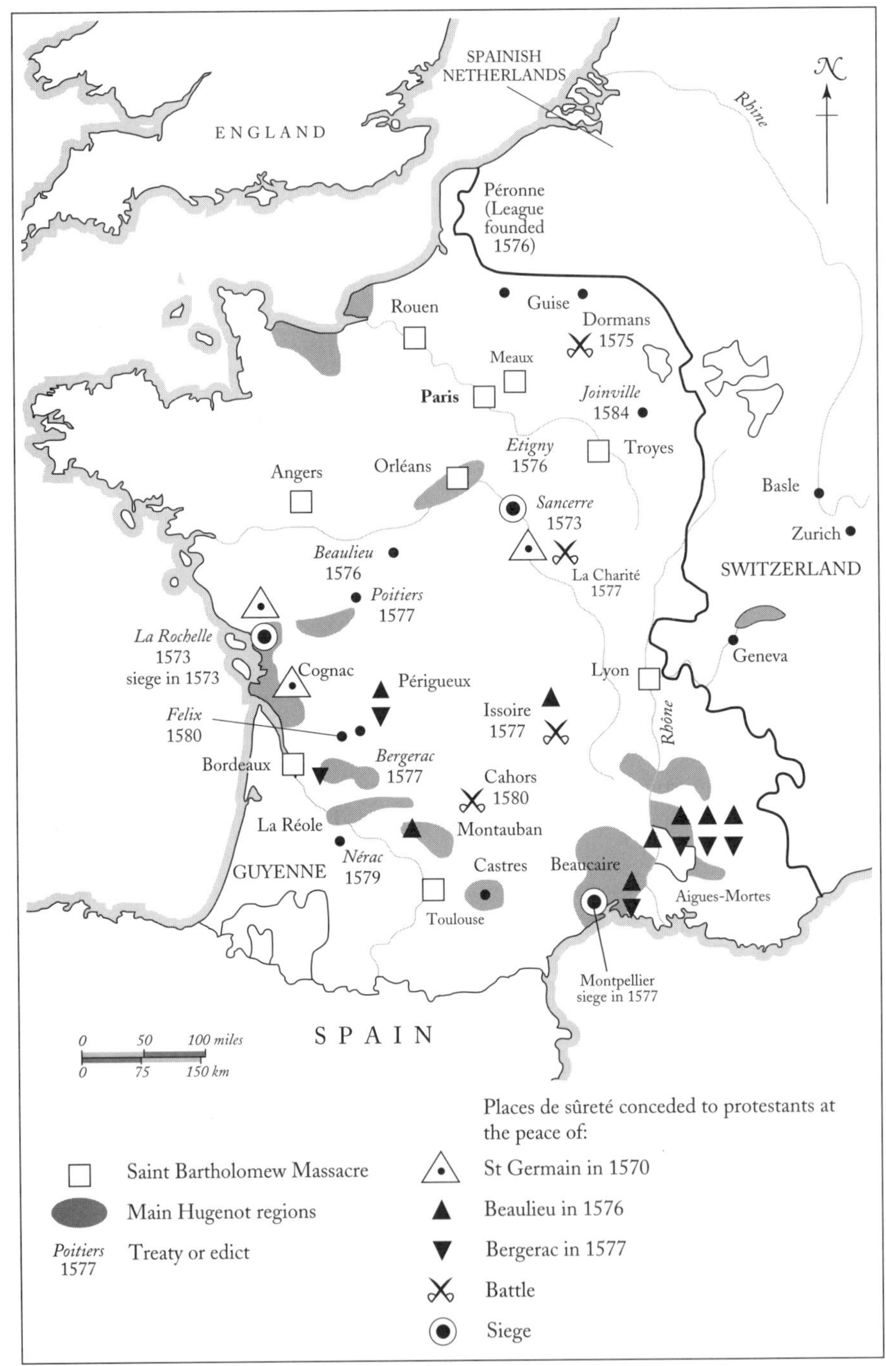

Map 5 The wars from 1572 to 1585

Source: Based on Michel Péronnet, *Le XVIe siècle, 1492–1620* (Paris, 1995), map 10. Adapted from D. Potter, *The French Wars of Religion* (London, 1997).

CHAPTER NINE

From La Rochelle to Beaulieu (1572–1576)

The chief military result of the massacre of St Bartholomew's Day was to shift the main area of operations to south of the Loire where the Huguenots retained control of a number of fortified towns, and conflict took the form of sieges rather than pitched battles. This worked to the disadvantage of the crown, which kept its artillery mainly in Paris or along the northern and eastern frontiers of the kingdom. Transporting it beyond the Loire proved difficult as communications were poor. The most important Huguenot stronghold was La Rochelle on the Atlantic coast which, as a port, had the advantage of being able to communicate directly with the Huguenots' foreign allies in England and the Netherlands. Shipwrights and sailors maintained links with the Dutch Sea Beggars and supplied the inhabitants with prizes seized on Spanish ships.[1] Charles IX would have liked to receive the submission of La Rochelle peacefully for the siege of Saint-Jean d'Angély had demonstrated the difficulties attendant on such an operation. La Rochelle was much stronger, so besieging it was likely to prove more costly still in men and money. The crown opened negotiations with the Rochelais soon after the massacre of St Bartholomew, but, having lost all faith in the government, they refused to submit and closed their gates to Armand de Biron, whom the king had appointed as their governor. They set about mobilizing a defence force, recruitment being preceded by a census of the available manpower. Rochelais as well as refugees from other parts of France

1 J. de Pablo, 'Contribution à l'étude de l'histoire des institutions militaires huguenotes: L'armée de mer huguenote pendant la troisième guerre de religion', *A.R.*, 47 (1956), pp. 64–76. This gives a brief account of the activities of Huguenot corsairs under Jacques de Sores in 1570, but offers no indication of how they might have been affected by La Rochelle's blockade in 1573.

were ordered to appear before special commissioners, anyone who refused being threatened with expulsion from the town. On this basis, the town's defence council was able to levy a *cornette* of light horse to defend the hinterland and 16 companies of infantry to guard the town itself.[2] Protestant pastors helped to stiffen the resistance. Believing that the Almighty would ensure the triumph of their cause, they drew comfort from the miraculous deliverance of Samaria, as told in the Bible.[3]

By November 1572 it had become clear that force would have to be used against La Rochelle. On 4 November Henri, duc d'Anjou wrote to the comte du Lude, governor of Poitou: 'Since the Rochelais wish to be stubborn and to disobey his [the king's] wishes, and believing that the peace of the kingdom, which I keenly desire, rests on the reduction of the said town and on the punishment of such rebels, I have prayed the king to put me in charge of the enterprise. I am ready to assemble all the necessary forces in order to go soon; and although the season is unsuited to such an enterprise, yet if it is pursued energetically, as it should be, we will overcome all difficulties.' But a whole month elapsed before Anjou was given his command. Meanwhile, Charles IX sent François de La Noue to La Rochelle, still hoping for a peaceful accord with the inhabitants. La Noue was empowered to offer the Rochelais freedom of conscience and the maintenance of their privileges in return for their accepting Biron as governor, but they refused to negotiate without consulting the other Protestant churches.[4]

Gathering an army with which to besiege La Rochelle was, as always, a slow and difficult process. Almost every part of the kingdom was made to contribute in some way. A huge effort – perhaps the greatest effort of the entire civil war period – was put into marshalling the artillery. This comprised 42 cannon and great culverins, 354 personnel from the Paris Arsenal, 220 teamsters and 4,850 pioneers. Transporting such a train from Paris to La Rochelle proved arduous, as it had to go overland for much of the way.[5] Supplying the army with food and drink was also complicated. Under a contract signed with the merchants of Niort at the end of 1572, they were to supply the army each day with 30,000 loaves, 10,800 pints of wine and 20,000 lb. of beef.[6] In January 1573 the cumulative cost of preparations for the siege amounted to 534,000 livres, of which only 287,000 had actually

2 J. de Pablo, 'Contribution à l'étude de l'histoire des institutions militaires huguenotes: L'armée huguenote entre 1562 et 1573', *A.R.*, 48 (1957), pp. 196–7.

3 2 Kings 6:24–7:20.

4 F. de La Noue, *Discours politiques et militaires*, ed. F. E. Sutcliffe (Geneva, 1967), p. 11.

5 J. Wood, *The King's Army: Warfare, Soldiers and Society during the Wars of Religion in France, 1562–1576* (Cambridge, 1996), pp. 161, 173.

6 A. Jouanna, *La France du XVIe siècle 1483–1598* (Paris, 1996), p. 475.

been paid with money raised from Parisian money-lenders or from the sale of offices. The crown hoped to fund the deficit and continuing expenses of half a million livres per month by a forced sale of *rentes* spread across 42 towns and by further loans.[7] Pending Anjou's coming, Biron organized a blockade on land and by sea. Throughout the winter a stream of men and munitions flowed in his direction, but siege operations were hampered by bad weather, unpaid and mutinous troops and by sorties by the Rochelais. They, for their part, invited La Noue to become their governor. He accepted with the king's consent, thereby finding himself in the curious position of serving Charles IX while opposing his army. He soon came to realize, however, that his position was untenable, and on 12 March joined Anjou's army.

La Rochelle was protected on the landward side by a dry moat and walls which were reinforced at intervals by bastions, the most famous being the *bastion de l'Évangile* which lay directly opposite Anjou's camp. On the seaward side the approaches to the harbour were commanded by forts. By the time Anjou joined Biron outside La Rochelle on 11 February with his army, the town's investment on land had been completed but no approach trenches had been dug and the harbour's entrance had only been partially closed by the sinking of ships.[8] The shore batteries were also incomplete. Anjou's army numbered about 25,000 men, not counting the crews of the ships offshore. He soon completed the harbour's closure, reconnoitred the defences and consulted his council of officers. Distributing commands, however, proved contentious, and agreement was not easily secured on how best to approach the town walls. Anjou was accompanied by Navarre, Condé, the dukes of Aumale and Guise, Guillaume de Thoré, the youngest of the Montmorency brothers, and his young nephew, Henri de Turenne. The presence of La Noue and of the princes, who had abjured their faith at the time of the massacre, served to dilute the army's denominational character. When François d'Alençon arrived at the camp, a number of noblemen, who had been angered by the Parisian massacre, gathered around him. It was said that he had openly regretted Coligny's death. This marked the beginning of a rapprochement between moderate nobles on both sides who believed in the urgency of opposing tyranny. The gathering of so many important lords in one spot was seized upon by many young nobles as a wonderful opportunity of gaining military renown. Among them was Brantôme, who went to La Rochelle unpaid and accompanied by six or

7 Wood, *The King's Army*, p. 294.

8 P. Rambeaud, 'Le siège de La Rochelle (1572–1573), un exemple de poliorcétique à la fin du XVIe siècle', *Revue de Saintonge et d'Aunis*, 17 (1991), 49–60. Nevers' and Anjou's reports on the siege are in B.N. Fr. 4765, fos. 15–53, 57–77 respectively. I owe these references to the kindness of Dr Alan James.

seven well-equipped nobles. He wore a fine suit of Milanese armour and rode a beautiful mare. Later, he remembered the siege as an almost festive occasion during which he had been befriended by the duc de Guise.[9]

On 26 February work began on trenches leading to the town's moat and on gun batteries, but it was hampered by lack of materials, bad weather, heavy casualties among the pioneers and by frequent sorties from the town. On 20 April the trenches finally reached the counterscarp and moat near the *bastion de l'Évangile*, which Anjou chose as his point of attack. But as the work progressed new hazards were discovered, notably pillboxes concealed in the moat from which sharpshooters might fire on troops attacking the wall. New gun batteries capable of pounding the bastion were established on the moat's shoulder. In the meantime the Rochelais strengthened their inner defences.[10]

From February until June 1573 Anjou launched eight major assaults against La Rochelle. The first, on 7 April, was preceded by a furious bombardment. The *bastion de l'Évangile* was badly damaged as well as sections of the curtain wall. About 200 nobles armed with cuirasses and small shields were given the task of scaling a breach, but many were roasted alive as incendiary devices thrown by the defenders rained down upon them. After two hours the assault was called off. It had only achieved a toehold at the base of the bastion. Anjou wanted to renew it next day, but finding that he had only 100 cannon-balls left, more had to be fetched from the fleet. On 8 April the townsmen laid down a smokescreen so thick that 'you would have thought it was a pit of Hell'. On 10 April another royal assault was repulsed. Anjou blamed his own men for this. They 'began to frighten themselves and be greatly vexed, and even openly to disband so that I expected in the end to find myself someday left all alone'.[11] Work on the approaches was almost at a standstill as only 400 pioneers remained of the several hundred at the start of the siege. On 14 April a mine exploded, bringing down part of the bastion, but at the same time it threw tons of rock and earth on to Anjou's troops, causing numerous casualties. Before a new assault could be launched, troops and guns had to be diverted to counter a new threat. On 19 April a Huguenot relief fleet, commanded by the comte de Montgomery, arrived off La Rochelle from England, but withdrew next day rather than face the harbour defences.

According to an English observer, supplies in Anjou's camp soon ran out and dysentery became rife. The Tuscan, Cavriana, reported that the troops

9 M. Lazard, *Pierre de Bourdeille, seigneur de Brantôme* (Paris, 1995), pp. 135–6.

10 Wood, *The King's Army*, pp. 255–8.

11 Ibid., p. 260.

were dying in large numbers. Filthy and in rags, many were no longer obeying orders. In early May the camp's suppliers raised their fee by 20 per cent. *Gendarmes*, who could no longer feed their horses, had to be sent home. Only 200 pioneers were left and attempts to recruit more proved fruitless. The French infantry units were below half strength. Survivors refused to man the trenches and some fled whenever the enemy launched a sortie. A lack of powder virtually silenced the artillery. Yet Anjou still hoped to capture the bastion. On 23 May he received 6,000 Swiss reinforcements, but they were armed only with pikes. Taking advantage of the confusion that attended their coming, the Rochelais attacked the trenches, spiking four guns and capturing a number of standards. On 30 May, after he had launched another unsuccessful assault, Anjou disbanded 60 companies of infantry. He wrote to the king: 'My anger is boundless that the assault should have failed on account of the cowardice [*méchanceté de coeur*] of the soldiers, for the captains did well . . . After seeing what I saw that day, I am almost ashamed to be French. If you had seen that, you too would have been angry.'[12] Later that day, panic swept through Anjou's camp for no apparent reason. His tent was trampled upon and he described himself as half-dead. Nevers was too exhausted to leave his quarters. Nobles were ordered to man the trenches in the absence of soldiers. The Rochelais taunted the besiegers by displaying flags they had captured and by playing at cards and dice. During the next few days, Anjou tried to restore the army's morale, but soon came to realize that it was no longer effective. An Englishman reported that there were only 2,000 French troops left. Two more attacks launched against La Rochelle failed to breach inner defences which the Rochelais had erected.[13] In a final report to the king, written in July, Anjou blamed his defeat on insufficient artillery, manpower and food: 'the artillery equipment limped in piece by piece and at a snail's pace,' he wrote, 'and I lacked good soldiers, so that I could not totally invest the city or have the means to prepare three batteries and three breaches . . . As for powder, I was never able to learn for certain how much there really was. Besides, it came only in such small amounts that at times I ran out completely, and when I had powder, I lacked cannon-balls. All this did I endure.'[14]

On 29 May Anjou learnt that he had been elected as King of Poland. This gave him an excuse for bringing the siege to an honourable conclusion. A truce was arranged, then a peace: under the Edict of Boulogne

12 Ibid., p. 265.

13 Ibid., pp. 259–67.

14 B.N. mss fr. 4765, f. 75v–77r. Cited in ibid., p. 154.

Protestant worship was to be allowed in the town, but only in private houses. Attendance at Protestant baptisms or weddings was to be limited to ten people. Marshal Biron made a brief ceremonial entry into La Rochelle. Meanwhile Anjou's camp was broken up. As the troops were disbanded, the artillery was removed to Paris and to various provincial depots. Anjou returned to Paris.

The siege of La Rochelle has been rightly described as 'the most important and decisive military episode of the entire period of the early wars of religion'.[15] While it demonstrated the growing military difficulties faced by the crown, it also undermined the army's morale and effectiveness. Royal losses incurred during the siege were out of all proportion to the results obtained. Brantôme estimated them at 22,000. According to Cavriana, 'deadly fevers and other maladies had reduced our army to such a state that out of ten combatants it would be hard to find one who was not suffering from wounds or hideous sores. The backbone of the operation, the nobility, had suffered particularly. The harsh weather encountered during the siege had weakened our bodies, and far from being able to fight the enemy, we could hardly draw breath.'[16] Precise casualty figures are not available. Wood's 'very conservative guess' is that 'the army suffered at least 6,000 combat casualties over the course of the siege', a figure which sickness and desertion would surely have doubled.[17] Near the end many infantry companies could muster no more than 25 men and the few companies of cavalry were but a shadow of their former selves. It seems that only 7,400 French troops survived; in other words, half the original strength. A handful of pioneers remained and by mid-May the artillery personnel had been reduced to only 27 per cent of its original strength.

The rate of casualties was especially high among the officers. A list kept by Filippo Strozzi, colonel-general of the infantry, contained the names of 266 officers killed. Another Catholic account named 132. Eighty came from three veteran regiments which originally had 100 officers. Another contemporary list names 155 French captains and gives the fate of each one. Only 42 escaped injury. Sixty-six (42.6 per cent) were killed and 47 (30.3 per cent) wounded. Thus the casualty rate among captains at the siege was 73 per cent. Even allowing for France's relatively buoyant population, it would have been difficult for the crown rapidly to make up such losses with adequately trained officers.[18] Likewise the siege emptied the kingdom of guns and munitions faster than they could be stockpiled. The royal

15 Wood, *The King's Army*, p. 246.
16 P. Cavriana, *Histoire du siège de La Rochelle en 1573* (La Rochelle, 1856), p. 147.
17 Wood, *The King's Army*, p. 269.
18 Ibid., pp. 270–71.

treasury was also seriously depleted. An *état par estimation* for 1574 tells a grim story. The crown expected a nominal gross revenue of 14.8 million livres from taxes, the royal domain and miscellaneous extraordinary revenues, but the amount which it regarded as collectable was only 9.2 million (63 per cent of the total) and about half this sum was earmarked for administrative costs. Another half a million livres had to be allowed for non-productive revenues, called *non-valeurs*. So, all in all, the crown could only expect 4.5 million livres. Its anticipated expenditure for 1574 was 19.9 million livres. This comprised operating costs of 10.8 million and unpaid debts of 9.1 million. The crown also planned to spend 4.4 million on arrears of pay; 3.5 million on the administration and the court, and 3.2 million on the repayment of loans. Thus altogether it expected to disburse 11.9 million livres. Nearly all of its debts were the direct result of a decade of civil war. The result was a deficit of 15.3 million livres. 'With more than a third of royal revenues alienated or uncollectable, and another third consumed by fixed local charges, the crown had barely enough money to pay a skeleton peacetime force, and no money at all to pay additional anticipated obligations of three times that magnitude.'[19] From the mid-1570s onwards the crown could no longer afford large-scale military operations. A year was about as long as the king could afford to fight; hence the brevity of the later civil wars. Pitched battles were now abandoned in favour of sieges. 'In this process,' writes Wood, 'the resistance of La Rochelle was more than a beacon of hope and a sign from the heavens for the Protestants . . . It was a harbinger of the type of military stalemate that was to characterize the final decade and a half of the civil wars.'[20]

Although the siege of La Rochelle was the main event of the fourth civil war, the crown also faced resistance elsewhere, notably at Sancerre in Berry. This too came under attack from royal forces after it had refused to submit to royal demands. The siege of Sancerre is more famous than that of La Rochelle thanks to a remarkable account written by Jean de Léry, a Calvinist minister. In addition to providing an almost day-by-day account, he offers an extraordinary description of the famine which befell the inhabitants. Sancerre never lacked wine, but ran out of meat and bread, and Léry describes how the inhabitants fed themselves, first on horses, asses and mules, then on cats, dogs, rats and mice, and lastly on leather and parchment. Instead of wheat, the people ate grasses and roots, some of which turned out to be poisonous. He instances one case of cannibalism, a vine-dresser and his wife who ate their infant daughter. Léry's account was designed to

19 Ibid., pp. 295–300.
20 Ibid., pp. 271–2.

encourage similar heroism elsewhere: it showed that Protestants were prepared to accept extreme deprivation and to risk agonizing deaths in defence of their faith.[21]

The war in the south

News of the massacre of St Bartholomew reached Montpellier on 30 August 1572. Although the local Huguenots were naturally alarmed, they were reassured by the provincial governor, Joyeuse, who chose to obey royal letters of 24 August, calling on all provincial governors and lieutenants-general to observe the Peace of Saint-Germain and to punish only those Protestants who contravened it. But Charles IX's public admission on 28 August of responsibility for the massacre prompted rejoicing among Catholics in the Midi and the massacre, early in October, of Huguenots in Toulouse, Gaillac and Rabastens. Their co-religionists accordingly took steps to defend themselves 'until it pleased God, who holds the king's heart in His hand, to change' that of Charles IX, whom they henceforth saw as their tyrant. Articles of association were drawn up at Nîmes for all the towns held by the Protestants now and in the future. Jean de Saint-Romain, seigneur de Saint-Chamond, was elected chief and general of the Protestants of Nîmes, Uzès, the Cévennes and the Vivarais. On 1 November the dioceses of Albi, Castres and Saint-Pons entrusted their defence to the marquis de Paulin.[22]

Soon after the massacre Charles IX added to the powers of Henri de Montmorency-Damville, governor of Languedoc, by appointing him lieutenant-general in the Lyonnais, Dauphiné and Provence. He was given the dual task of ensuring the security of towns loyal to the king and of reconquering the rebellious ones. On 30 October he regulated the defence of towns. Each one was to appoint a captain with complete authority in military matters. Damville also provided garrisons of regular troops. Their command was organized within the existing network of financial and administrative areas, called civil dioceses. Each became a military zone under a governor appointed by Damville. But he was desperately short of men. In November 1572 he informed Anjou that he had found only five companies of infantry in Languedoc, each reduced to 60 men. He formed new ones,

---

21 G. Nakam, *Au lendemain de la Saint-Barthélemy: histoire mémorable du siège de Sancerre (1573)* (Paris, 1975).

22 C. Thievant, *Le gouverneur de Languedoc pendant les premières guerres de religion (1559–1574) Henri de Montmorency-Damville* (Paris, 1993), pp. 184–5.

recalled a company from Guyenne and summoned some Corsican companies from neighbouring provinces. By 29 November he disposed of 18 companies of cavalry and infantry with which to guard Toulouse, the Lauraguais, Castres and Albi, but he needed more and appealed to the crown for reinforcements. Charles IX promised him ten companies and 2,000 Corsicans, but Damville only received a total of 1,200 Corsicans in dribs and drabs.[23]

In February 1573 Damville systematically besieged rebellious towns in Lower Languedoc, his ultimate objective being Nîmes, the main Huguenot stronghold of his *gouvernement.* He laid siege to Sommières but, lacking supplies and munitions, accepted the town's surrender on generous terms in April. He soon informed the king that the Huguenots wanted a general peace. Charles IX urged him to moderate his campaign, but not to concede freedom of worship. Damville's task, however, became more difficult after Anjou's peace treaty with the Rochelais. This had conceded freedom of worship not only to the inhabitants of La Rochelle but also to those of Montauban and Nîmes, who had played no part in the talks. Damville was ordered to enforce the pacification Edict of Boulogne in Languedoc, but the defenders of Nîmes wanted far more concessions from the crown than was offered by the edict. Damville allowed them to confer with their co-religionists in Montauban even as he besieged them. They submitted demands which the king dismissed as 'very impertinent and unreasonable', including freedom of worship, free access to offices, special tribunals, the rehabilitation of Coligny, and a complete change of French foreign policy. The king was asked to ally with the Protestant powers in order to guarantee the 'union' which he had allegedly entered upon with all his subjects, both Catholic and Protestant. Such demands were obviously unacceptable, but instead of rejecting them outright, Charles IX sent commissioners to assist Damville in finding a peace settlement on his own far more restricted terms. Meanwhile, a truce was declared in the south, but this merely played into the hands of the rebels, for discipline among Damville's troops was undermined by inactivity. The Huguenots also took advantage of the truce to capture and sack a number of small towns. On 24 November they occupied Pomerols and Florensac, whereupon Damville put his forces on a war footing. He offered the Huguenots a new truce, but continued to distrust them. Charles IX wanted him to bring them to accept the Edict of Boulogne, but failed to give him either money or enough troops to impose

23 Ibid., pp. 186–90. See also M. Greengrass, 'Henri de Montmorency-Damville et l'administration des armées provinciales de Languedoc', in *Avènement d'Henri IV. Quatrième centenaire.* Colloque: Bayonne, 1988, pp. 103–23.

a settlement. In February royal commissioners were sent to the Midi in another bid to find peace. Meanwhile another truce, due to expire on 15 April, was repeatedly ignored as towns came under attack from both sides. It was still in being when a plot was discovered at court implicating Damville. He was replaced as lieutenant-general in Languedoc, Dauphiné and Provence by the Prince-dauphin, the son of the duc de Montpensier, yet he remained officially governor of Languedoc. The military situation in the Midi was consequently overturned, as Damville found himself obliged to ally with the Huguenots and moderate Catholics in defence of what he now saw as the interests of the kingdom.[24]

Fraternal discord

On 10 September Henri d'Anjou took a solemn oath as King of Poland in the cathedral of Notre-Dame and on 2 December took leave of his mother and of members of the court of Lorraine at Blamont at the start of his Polish odyssey.[25] His departure left the way clear for his younger brother, François d'Alençon, to assert himself. He hoped to succeed Henri as lieutenant-general of the kingdom, but was opposed by the Guises, who linked him with the house of Montmorency. Alençon was, in fact, close to Marshal Montmorency. He also tried to win the support of the marshal's brother, Henri de Montmorency-Damville. Rumours also circulated at court of a possible alliance between Alençon and William of Orange, the leader of the Dutch rebels. In November 1573 a former agent of Alençon, who had joined Orange's service, asked Charles IX to send an army under his brother to assist the rebels. Charles had no wish to antagonize Spain by accepting this demand, but he did give the Dutch covert assistance in the form of a subsidy. The first instalment was paid to Louis of Nassau at Blamont when the French court was there.

In January 1574 Charles IX promised to appoint Alençon as lieutenant-general, but the Guises immediately set about discrediting him. On 16 February the sieur de Ventabren, one of Alençon's men, was attacked in the Louvre by Henri de Guise, who accused him of having been hired by Marshal Montmorency to assassinate him. Although the charge was never substantiated, Montmorency had to leave the court. Furthermore, the king broke his promise to Alençon by appointing Charles, duke of Lorraine as

24 Thievant, *Le gouverneur de Languedoc*, pp. 293–307.
25 P. Chevallier, *Henri III* (Paris, 1985), pp. 202–7.

Lieutenant-general of the kingdom. Catherine de' Medici has been blamed for this move. She apparently feared that Alençon might use the position of lieutenant-general to seize the throne in the event of Charles IX dying while his brother, Henri, was in Poland.

Montmorency's banishment deprived moderate Protestants and Catholics of their leader, and young noblemen now turned for patronage to Alençon, whose status as a prince of the blood made up for his youth and lack of political experience. They included Condé and Navarre, Méru, Thoré, Marshal Cossé, the seigneur de Montaigu, the comte de Coconas and the seigneur de La Mole. This group has often been described as *Politiques,* but as yet they were too inexperienced and disorganized to constitute a party. Although many favoured religious co-existence, religion interested them less than their own private ambitions. The word *politique* was, in any case, seldom used before 1584 and then pejoratively.[26]

On 27 February the court fled in confusion from Saint-Germain-en-Laye to Paris after Protestant troops had been seen in the château's vicinity. Their purpose, it was alleged, was to set free the princes of Condé and Navarre, who had been held at court since the massacre of St Bartholomew and to enable them to join the rebels in the Netherlands. The plot, however, misfired. The sieur de Guitry, who was in charge of the troops, was captured and disclosed that the plot had been aimed not at the king but at the Guises. This was confirmed by Alençon. The chancellor, René de Birague, wanted Alençon and Navarre to be executed as traitors, but Charles IX refused to take such a step. Instead, the two princes were put under a heavy guard and made to sign an oath of loyalty. As for Condé, he was able to leave the court in the spring of 1574. Reverting to the Calvinist faith, he went to the Palatinate to raise troops.[27]

The fifth civil war (November 1574–May 1576)

The failed coup at Saint-Germain coincided with a well-planned Huguenot uprising in many parts of France. Towns were seized in Lower Normandy, Poitou and the Rhône valley. Although desperately short of money, Charles IX had to issue a call to arms. Three armies were assembled: one

26 M. P. Holt, *The Duke of Anjou and the Politique Struggle during the Wars of Religion* (Cambridge, 1986), pp. 34–8.
27 Ibid., pp. 38–9.

in Normandy under Matignon, another in Poitou under Montpensier and the third in Dauphiné under the Prince-dauphin. Their purpose was to retake towns which had fallen to the Huguenots: Saint-Lô and Carentan in Normandy, Fontenay and Lusignan in Poitou and Pouzin and Livron in Dauphiné. In May Matignon besieged the fortress of Domfront held by the comte de Montgomery, who had recently come to Normandy from Jersey with an expeditionary force. Catherine de' Medici was keenly interested in the outcome of this siege as Montgomery was the man who had accidentally killed her husband in 1559. After he had surrendered, Matignon sent him to Paris where he was promptly tried and executed, to the queen-mother's evident satisfaction. On 10 June Matignon's army recaptured, first Saint-Lô, then Carentan, before being disbanded without payment. The infantry and artillery were sent to assist Montpensier in Poitou. He captured Fontenay on 22 September after a siege lasting three weeks and then moved to Lusignan, where the siege lasted four months. Though heavily bombarded, the garrison succeeded in repelling several assaults. Meanwhile the royal troops, still unpaid, deserted in droves, causing widespread damage to the countryside. Lusignan capitulated on 26 January 1575 whereupon Montpensier dismissed part of his army. The rest of the troops were sent to garrisons in the west where their conduct was again the subject of loud complaints.[28]

The defection of Montmorency-Damville (13 November 1574)

In April 1574, as Marshal Montmorency returned to court, another plot was uncovered. This time it was intended that Alençon and Navarre should escape to Sedan where they were to be joined by 300 cavalry under Turenne. The king immediately placed the princes and Montmorency under close guard and ordered the arrest of some 50 alleged plotters, including Coconas and La Mole. Under questioning, La Mole denied all knowledge of the plot, but Coconas indicated that its scope was much larger than had been suspected. When Alençon was questioned, he said that he had only wanted to go to the Netherlands. As for Navarre, he admitted that he and Alençon had feared a new massacre. Birague again called for the princes to be executed, but Charles IX chose to spare them. La Mole and Coconas, however, were put to death. On 4 May Montmorency and his kinsman

28 Wood, *The King's Army*, pp. 33–4.

Artus de Cossé, both of them Marshals of France, were arrested although they had distanced themselves from the plot. They were to remain in prison for 18 months. The government may have been responding to diplomatic pressure from Spain following a disastrous defeat suffered by the Dutch rebels on 14 April when both Louis of Nassau and Christopher of the Palatinate were killed. On 18 June, as we have seen, the queen-mother relieved Montmorency-Damville, Marshal Montmorency's brother, of his command in the Midi in spite of the fact that he seems not to have been a party to the plot. Damville's anger is understandable. It was prompted not only by his brother's arrest, but also by the crown's evident distrust of him and by the hostility shown to him by the parlement of Toulouse. He consequently drew closer to the Huguenots of Languedoc, while remaining a devout Catholic. He felt the need to defend his 'house' and honour against his unjust treatment by the crown; and he also had learnt from experience that the only alternative to eliminating the Huguenots by force was to reach an understanding with them.[29]

On 30 May 1574 Charles IX died. His mother, Catherine de' Medici declared herself regent pending the return from Poland of her son, Henri, who now succeeded to the French throne as Henry III. Alençon and Navarre were made to sign another oath of loyalty. As the heir presumptive, Alençon was no longer so keen to leave the court, but his relations with the Huguenots continued to be a source of worry to Catholic extremists. The political situation in France and the threat of intervention by Elizabeth I of England, William of Orange and the German princes called for Henry III's speedy return, but he refused to be rushed. After deserting his Polish subjects, he allowed himself to be entertained by various princes on his way home, nowhere more lavishly than in Venice. He did not reach Lyon till 6 September where the court remained for several months. One of the new king's first acts was a public show of amity towards Alençon and Navarre. They were allowed to come and go as they pleased, yet continued to be closely watched.[30]

The most urgent problem facing Henry III was the situation in the Midi which had taken a dangerous turn as a result of Damville's defection. Some of the king's councillors urged him to seek a settlement with the Huguenots, while others, including his mother, pressed him to use force. Damville was ordered to disband his army and either join the king in Lyon or retire to Savoy without prejudice to his property in France. His reply, however, was a manifesto, issued on 13 November in which he blamed foreigners in the king's council for France's troubles. They stood accused of preventing the

29 Jouanna, *La France du XVIe siècle*, p. 501.
30 Chevallier, *Henri III*, pp. 233–47.

nobility from gaining access to offices and dignities. Two royal armies, Damville complained, were being sent to Provence: the one under Retz, a foreigner, and the other under Uzès, an ex-iconoclast. Denying that fear of assassination had caused him to take up arms, Damville explained that he had done so in response to appeals from 'the princes of the blood, officers of the crown and peers of the realm' as well as from the French provinces. As an officer of the crown, a native Frenchman and the descendant of 'Christians and barons of France', he had felt impelled to seek a remedy for the current disorders.[31]

Damville's manifesto was only one of several similar declarations issued by leaders of a group of noblemen, known as the Malcontents, who constituted an important new force in the French civil wars, which had hitherto been, in the main, denominational. With the advent of the Malcontents the wars assumed a less religious and more political character. Religion was not forgotten, but following the massacre of St Bartholomew many nobles came to believe that a reform of the state was an essential precondition to any religious settlement. A deep malaise among them, which the fifth war revealed, did not stem from a global political or economic collapse of their class, but from a crisis in their relations with the crown. Royal patronage, on which so many of them had come to depend, worked well as long as it was fair, but recent developments (the youth of the king and factional strife provoked by the religious schism) had created a climate of favouritism from which many nobles felt excluded. They also resented the place increasingly occupied in the civil service by men of the robe. Although some nobles of the sword were well educated, most of them had no desire to devote years to study in the universities. They believed that they deserved offices at least as much as men who had never fought and frequently tried to show their distinctiveness by acts of often senseless bravado. Lastly, many noble families, like that of Montmorency, were split by religion in ways contradicted by traditional ties of kinship, friendship and solidarity, especially in the Midi. It was not unknown for a Protestant nobleman to assist a Catholic kinsman or vice versa during the wars. By the mid-1570s many nobles had grown tired of fighting their friends and relations. The bloody siege of La Rochelle may have served to convince them that religious conflict was playing into the hands of sinister elements at the heart of government which were seeking the destruction of France's ancient liberties.[32]

The rationale for rebellion advanced by Damville and other disgruntled noblemen was more elaborately enunciated in a number of treatises published

31 Ibid., p. 271; Thievant, *Le gouverneur de Languedoc*, pp. 312–14.

32 Jouanna, *La France du XVIe siècle*, pp. 495–8.

around the same time. They included the *Briève remonstrance à la noblesse de France* (Brief remonstrance to the nobility of France), which has been ascribed to the Huguenot jurist, Innocent Gentillet; the *Discours merveilleux*, which combines a serious political argument with a lengthy indictment of Catherine de' Medici; and *France-Turquie*, which tries to show that France has become a Turkish tyranny. Common to all these texts is the theme that foreigners, mainly Italians, have taken charge of the government with a view to destroying the kingdom's ancient laws. In order to achieve this purpose, however, they have to destroy the great noble houses of France, which are the traditional defenders of those laws. That rather than the extermination of the Huguenots, so it is claimed, was the real purpose of such bloody events as the massacre of St Bartholomew and the siege of La Rochelle.[33]

The provinces of the Union

From Lyon, Henry III and his mother travelled to Avignon, where she tried to negotiate with Damville, but he suspected that she only wanted to detach him from his Huguenot allies. He consolidated his position, called a meeting of the provincial estates and bombarded Saint-Gilles. In the meantime, representatives of the Protestant churches signed a 'treaty of association' with Catholics at Nîmes in which the need for religious toleration was accepted. 'Until such time as God through His grace unites us in religion,' the treaty declared, we must 'each and everyone of us live so that the conscience of each is left at peace . . . each in this respect will have complete freedom of conscience so that no one will be debarred from the traditional exercise of his faith . . . peacefully and in mutual charity, without incidents or insults.'[34]

While these developments were taking place, the Huguenots of the Midi set up a federal state. Its foundations had been laid by a series of political assemblies, held in various towns (Nîmes, Bagnols, Montpellier, Anduze) since November 1562, but it only began seriously to take shape after the massacre of St Bartholomew. At Millau in December 1573 a kind of constitution was drawn up and in July 1574, also at Millau, Condé was chosen as 'governor general and protector' and Damville as governor and the king's

33 Ibid., pp. 502–3; Q. Skinner, *The Foundations of Modern Political Thought* (Cambridge, 1978), vol. 2, pp. 304–9.
34 Jouanna, *La France du XVIe siècle*, p. 508.

lieutenant-general in Languedoc with responsibility, in Condé's absence, for 'ensuring the crown's conservation'. An assembly, meeting at Nîmes in January and February 1575, called itself 'the Estates-General of the Provinces of the said Union'. The name 'United Provinces of the Midi', chosen by some historians to describe the new federation, is seriously misleading since it implies an analogy with the republican constitution adopted by the Dutch rebels, whereas the Huguenots remained consistently loyal to the idea of monarchy.[35] They described the aim of the constitution of December 1573 as 'the glory of God, the advancement of Christ's reign, the good and service of this crown, and the common repose of this kingdom'. The delegates at Millau in July 1574 vehemently denied that they had ever thought of deserting their natural lord, the king. There was never any question of the 'Provinces of the Union' breaking away from the kingdom. The aim of its founders was not the creation of a separate state, but the reform of the existing one. The federation enjoyed a high degree of autonomy, albeit under the king. As Greengrass has shown, the reluctance to alienate permanently the property rights of the Catholic church even during periods of open warfare 'reflects an underlying conservative royalism within the Huguenot cause'.[36]

The constitution laid down at Nîmes was as follows. Supreme authority was vested in a general assembly, meeting every six months, made up of representatives from each of the five provinces in the Union. It passed laws, decided peace or war and voted taxes. An executive officer, called the Protector, had charge of military affairs and was assisted by a permanent council appointed by the general assembly. Each province or *généralité* was allowed a considerable measure of autonomy: an assembly, meeting every three months, was elected by the towns. This assembly appointed a permanent council and a general responsible for 'the administration and conduct of the war'. A similar degree of independence was accorded to the towns and villages: municipal officers were empowered to administer local affairs, enforce law and order and control taxation. Justice was left to magistrates of the *bailliages* and *présidiaux*. Cases on appeal were judged by special courts, one for each province with an equal number of Protestant and Catholic

35 Jean Delumeau first coined the phrase in *Naissance et affirmation de la Réforme* (Paris, 1965), p. 181 and Janine Garrisson adopted it in *Protestants du Midi 1559–1598* (Toulouse, 1980), p. 185. The analogy with the Dutch rebels is refuted by M. Péronnet, 'La république des Provinces-Unies du Midi: les enjeux de l'historiographie' in *Protestantisme et révolution* (Actes du 6e colloque Jean Boisset, Montpellier, 1989), pp. 5–26.

36 M. Greengrass, 'Financing the cause: Protestant mobilization and accountability in France', in P. Benedict, G. Marnef, H. van Nierop and M. Venard (eds.), *Reformation, Revolt and Civil War in France and the Netherlands, 1555–1585* (Amsterdam, 1999), pp. 236–7.

judges. The federation was funded out of the taxes normally paid to the crown, the salt tax, confiscated ecclesiastical revenues and extraordinary levies on Huguenot churches. Revenues were administered by a federal controller, federal receivers and provincial controllers. The larger towns had their own fiscal officials.[37]

The federation was not as revolutionary as one might think, for the towns and villages of the Midi had a long tradition of self-government. Its provincial assemblies were also comparable with the old provincial estates and *états particuliers*. It is likely that, except for increased taxes, the local people saw little change between the old regime and the new, especially as the personnel remained largely unchanged. The effectiveness of the new state was restricted by geographical factors and internal divisions. Huguenots living north of a line drawn roughly from Grenoble in the east to Saint-Jean d'Angély in the west were excluded although they sometimes sent representatives to the southern assemblies. Many large towns (Toulouse, Bordeaux, Marseille, Avignon, Aix and Agen) also lay outside the Union's control. Constant friction disturbed the relations between the great nobles who led the military operations and members of the assemblies and councils. The Protector was, first, the prince de Condé, then Damville and finally, Henri de Navarre, who escaped from the French court in February 1576. These strong men did not take kindly to being controlled by an assembly dominated by Calvinist pastors and men of the robe. They were even less submissive to a permanent council whose *raison d'être* was to control their actions.

Funding the Huguenot war effort

Devotion to the Protestant cause was not enough to sustain the Huguenot war-machine. The troops needed to be fed and equipped, while the German mercenaries were notoriously avaricious. They went on strike or even returned *en masse* to Germany if their pay was not forthcoming. To some extent, the Huguenot leaders were able to help themselves to royal taxes in areas under their control, but, as Mark Greengrass has shown, the Huguenot war effort was not funded from 'pre-determined revenues, carefully constructed credit-lines and well-stocked war-chests'.[38] The Protestant assemblies raised limited funds in the areas under their control; even so,

37 Garrisson, *Protestants du Midi*, pp. 185–93.
38 Greengrass, 'Financing the cause', p. 253.

desperate measures and hand-to-mouth expedients were the order of the day. 'The Huguenot war-chest was always precariously sustained, and often empty – it had no grip on the regular revenues of the realm.'[39]

The Huguenots tried to spread the tax burden as widely as possible within the areas under their control. This meant initially seizing the movable goods of churches and confraternities and selling them. This was an important feature of the first civil war, when a large number of towns fell under Huguenot control. Thereafter the Huguenots needed to broaden the basis of their funding. Protestant assemblies sanctioned the confiscation of the wealth of the Catholic laity at large, but this was more easily decreed than done. The property had to be carefully listed and valued by commissioners, in itself a long process. Huguenot noblemen sometimes seized property before commissioners could intervene. Elsewhere local resistance had to be overcome. Nor were the returns always rewarding. Renting out ecclesiastical property was even more complicated. Benefices had to be carefully collated before their revenues could be auctioned and the prices they fetched were often very small. Nor were alienations straightforward. Much ecclesiastical revenue was already farmed out, sometimes to Protestants. Some benefices might be assigned by a local governor or war council to a particular individual. In theory, the receipts from ecclesiastical rentals should have been considerable, but, in practice, they were slow in coming and often disappointing.

Privateering became an important resource after La Rochelle had become Protestant. Ships captured as prize were sold and letters of marque stipulated that goods seized as prize should serve as a contribution to the Huguenot cause. According to the English ambassador, privateering was vital early in 1570 for keeping the German *reiters* in the field. Even so, the collection of prize-dues was often difficult. Another means of spreading the tax burden open to the Huguenots was to expropriate royal taxation. They did not try to build up a new tax system, preferring instead to batten on the existing one. The alienation of all forms of royal taxation was sanctioned by successive Protestant assemblies, but the brevity of the wars in the 1560s limited the amount of recoverable revenues. After 1563 the Huguenots tended to control areas where the yield from royal taxation was small. Various 'forced loans' were also imposed on Huguenot towns. In 1567, 100,000 livres were raised in this way and more in 1573–4. Such loans, however, created indebtedness and, in some cases, notably at La Rochelle, they were resisted. Deputies at the Protestant assemblies continually deplored the 'great, foolish and extreme costs' of the wars and were fearful of the rough justice

39 C. Oman, *A History of the Art of War in the XVIth Century* (New York, 1937), p. 403.

which unpaid troops would mete out to the Protestant community. Protestant ministers often found themselves competing with the demands of war for their salaries. The assemblies were also faced with charitable demands arising out of the wars.

The Huguenots, like the crown, were driven to borrow. Thus in the first civil war the German princes lent 100,000 florins for an army to be sent to Condé at Orléans and in 1586 John Casimir's intervention was backed by an English loan of 100,000 écus. Such loans required collateral and needed to be repaid. Huguenot nobles often gave their jewels by way of security. Thus Condé pledged jewels worth 50,000 écus for the levy of 8,000 *reiters* and 3,000 *landsknechts.* Jeanne d'Albret sent the crown jewels of Navarre to London as security for a loan in 1569 and never saw them again. Salt also served as collateral. For example, an English loan of £20,000 in 1569 was secured by mortgaging the returns from salt production around Brouage. The salt-pans near Peccais were similarly used. The compulsory purchase of salt was sometimes used as a kind of forced loan on the well-to-do in Protestant areas.

Hard bargaining over the payment of German mercenaries figured prominently in peace talks between the Huguenots and the Crown. The latter often assumed most of the debt, but, as Greengrass observes, this was 'like asking a convicted bankrupt to guarantee a mortgage'. Such engagements became part of the public debt and many outlived the civil wars. Negotiations for the hiring of mercenaries became more difficult in the 1570s and 1580s as the German princes stiffened their demands. The Huguenot leaders looked to the Protestant congregations for support. Commissioners were required to assess how much each congregation was worth.

While it is clear that funding the war effort was a struggle for both sides, it is less clear what effect this had on the duration of the wars. According to a Venetian ambassador, writing in 1575, the ability of Huguenots to divert royal revenues into their coffers helped to prolong the wars. 'How can there ever be peace in the realm,' he asked, 'since it is the plain truth that for its own gain [each faction] stands ready to foment war? Thus where the king spends thousands in the fighting, they spend nothing – at least nothing of their own, but rather of others and of the king. And while the king destroys himself, they, on the contrary, pile up their holdings, holdings which they would lose if peace were to come, as they would lose their power and following, with the danger that these might never return again.'[40] But, taking a diametrically different view, Greengrass argues that financial necessity

40 E. Albèri, *Relazioni*, ser. 1, 4; 358–9. Cited by M. Wolfe, *The Fiscal System of Renaissance France* (New Haven, Conn., 1972), pp. 151–2.

drove the Huguenots 'inevitably and repeatedly' to seek peace with the crown. In his view, it was because each civil war was so brief that 'the construction of a Huguenot finance-state became such a sisyphean task'. Huguenot resourcing was 'on a hand-to-mouth, short-term and fundamentally unstable basis'; it was 'highly localized, impossible to predict and difficult to collect and control'.[41] In other words, the problem was cyclical: the wars were too short to allow the setting up an efficient funding system without which the Huguenots could not fight longer ones.

Alençon's flight from court (15 September 1575)

On 10 January 1575 Henry III left Avignon for northern France. Having failed to impose his authority on the Midi, he suffered a further humiliation outside Livron, a town which Bellegarde was besieging for him, when a crowd of women hurled abuse at his party from the top of the town walls. On 13 February Henry was crowned at Reims and, on the following day, married Louise de Vaudémont, a kinswoman of the Guises. Meanwhile, in the west, Montpensier managed to capture a number of small towns commanding the approaches to La Rochelle, but he failed to seize the Île de Ré. As the war seemed to be getting him nowhere, Henry tried to negotiate. On 11 April, he received a deputation sent by Damville. The king began by explaining that he had returned from Poland with the intention of embracing all his subjects without discrimination, but turned angry when the deputies presented sweeping demands. They asked for freedom of Protestant worship throughout the kingdom, bipartisan law courts in all the parlements, surety towns, the release of Marshals Montmorency and Cossé, a meeting of the Estates-General, rehabilitation of the victims of the St Bartholomew's Day massacre and punishment of their murderers. Henry was prepared to offer only freedom of worship in the *places de sûreté* and in two towns per *gouvernement*. Catherine de' Medici informed the deputies that her son would never go back to the Edict of January. An assembly of the Union was then called by Damville to consider the king's response. This resulted in another deputation being sent to him which laid down two essential preconditions for further talks: freedom of Protestant worship throughout France and the release from prison of the two marshals.

41 Greengrass, 'Financing the cause', pp. 240, 253.

In the meantime, fighting continued in many parts of France, but its character was changing. Instead of large armies being involved, forces of a few thousand men, each under a captain, carried out raids against towns and villages, sprang ambushes and generally caused mayhem in the countryside. Pillage, rape and exacting ransoms were the order of the day. Religion seemed to matter less than settling old scores or satisfying private ambitions and lust. Among the bolder captains was Montbrun who, after plundering Henry III's baggage on his way to Avignon, routed a large force of Swiss mercenaries. But fate eventually caught up with him: he was captured, tried by the parlement of Grenoble and executed.

On 13 September 1575 François d'Alençon fled from the court in Paris and, on reaching Dreux, issued a manifesto which repeated Damville's earlier demands. He asked for the removal from court of all foreigners, for a religious settlement pending a church council, and for the Estates-General to be called. The war now took on a more serious character, since the Malcontents could claim legitimacy by virtue of their association with a prince of the blood who claimed the title of 'protector of the liberty and public good of France'. Their movement also grew in strength as perhaps as many as 1,000 noblemen rallied to Alençon's standard, knowing that they had little to lose by such a move: if he won, all would be well; if not, the king would have to pardon him as his brother. Henry III suddenly seemed terribly alone.[42]

Early in October an army of 2,000 German *reiters* under John Casimir of the Palatinate invaded Champagne. The alarming prospect of a possible link-up between them and the rebels in the west and south of France prompted the king to send his mother on a peace errand. She met Alençon at Chambord in late September. The duke asked for the release of the two marshals, which Henry III reluctantly conceded, but peace depended on Catherine agreeing to more demands. Eventually, on 21 November, a truce of seven months was signed at Champigny. Alençon was promised five towns (Angoulême, Niort, Saumur, Bourges and La Charité) as security for the truce, while Condé was promised Mézières. Freedom of worship was granted to the Huguenots in towns already in their hands and in two others per *gouvernement*. The *reiters* were promised 500,000 livres provided they remained east of the Rhine. Catherine hoped that the truce would lead to a lasting peace, but this was not to be.[43] The governors of Angoulême and Bourges refused to hand over their offices to Alençon. Nor could he control

42 Holt, *Duke of Anjou*, pp. 50–54; Chevallier, *Henri III*, pp. 302–5.
43 Holt, *Duke of Anjou*, p. 59; Chevallier, *Henri III*, pp. 305–18.

the actions of Condé and John Casimir. On 10 October part of John Casimir's forces had been defeated by the duc de Guise at Dormans but this had been only a minor setback. On 9 January the Germans, numbering more than 25,000 men, crossed the Meuse into France, taking Henry III completely by surprise. The defences of Paris were strengthened and a royal army was assembled at Gien under the king's command. The rest under Guise's brother, the duc de Mayenne, stood by at Vitry-le-François. But the royal troops were unpaid, unfed and in rags. They could only shadow John Casimir's army as it advanced south, reaching Dijon on 31 January 1576 and Moulins, on 4 March.

Catherine hoped that Alençon would stay neutral, but he saw advantages to be gained by siding with the invaders. The truce of Champigny was not being observed. Most of the towns which he had been promised were refusing to admit his men. In December he accused the chancellor, Birague, of trying to poison him and made this a pretext to break the truce. He went to Villefranche where Turenne joined him with 3,000 arquebusiers and 400 horse. Henry III's predicament could hardly have been worse. Montpensier's sudden departure from Normandy to assist him had been the signal for a new Huguenot revolt, and in the Midi Damville remained unchallenged. On 5 February Navarre fled from the court. He promptly reverted to his Calvinist faith and, retiring to his lands in the south-west, began raising an army.[44]

The Peace of Monsieur (6 May 1576)

On 9 April Alençon issued another declaration: 'We have decided,' he said, 'to exploit the means given to us by God to win by force the peace and tranquillity that we could not achieve by way of reason.'[45] Left with no choice but to make peace, Henry III once again called on his mother to treat on his behalf. She met Alençon and his fellow Malcontents at Chastenoy, near Sens, and virtually conceded all their demands. The result was the Edict of Beaulieu, which was proclaimed on 6 May. It became known as 'the Peace of Monsieur' (the title given to the king's younger brother) because everyone believed that it had been forced on Henry III by Alençon.

44 Wood, *The King's Army*, p. 36.

45 Holt, *Duke of Anjou*, pp. 63–5.

For the first time the Huguenots were given freedom of worship throughout the kingdom except within two leagues of Paris or the court, wherever that might be. They were allowed to build churches or *temples* almost anywhere and admitted to all professions, schools and hospitals.[46] Also for the first time bipartisan courts, comprising judges of both religions, were to be set up in every parlement. The massacre of St Bartholomew was condemned as a crime and its victims, including Coligny, were rehabilitated. Eight surety towns were ceded to the Huguenots, two each in Languedoc, Guyenne, Dauphiné and Provence. A meeting of the Estates-General was to be called within six months. Traditionally, this was a step taken by the king on his authority alone; this time, however, it arose from a treaty between him and his subjects. Secret articles rewarded the Malcontents. Alençon added Anjou, Touraine and Berry to his apanage and assumed the title of duc d'Anjou. Henri de Condé and Damville resumed their governorships of Picardy and Languedoc respectively. John Casimir, who had asked the Huguenots for the three bishoprics of Metz, Toul and Verdun, was given the duchy of Étampes instead. Navarre's governorship of Guyenne was confirmed and extended to cover Poitou and Angoumois.[47]

The edict did not automatically rid France of foreign troops. John Casimir laid down exorbitant terms for the removal from French soil of his *reiters*. He asked for payment of 1.7 million livres by 7 June and for old debts to be settled. Henry III's finance minister, Bellièvre, made frantic efforts to raise the necessary cash. He even had to pawn jewels and plate. Caught between John Casimir's rapacity and the greed of money-lenders, Henry was reduced to despair. 'I can assure you,' he wrote, 'that if I could extricate myself at the cost of my own blood, I would not spare myself.' On 5 July Bellièvre reached an agreement with John Casimir. The *reiters* would leave on receipt of two months' wages. Six French noblemen were sent as hostages to the court of Lorraine as part of the deal.[48]

The Peace of Monsieur provoked widespread indignation among Catholics, who viewed it as a 'sell-out' to the Protestants. Placards denouncing it appeared all over Paris and the king had to hold a *lit de justice* to ensure its

46 By proclaiming a genuine religious pluralism, unlike earlier edicts which stipulated categories of privilege, the Edict of Beaulieu removed the need for commissioners to oversee its execution and avoided the legal chicanery which had bedevilled the implementation of earlier edicts. See M. Greengrass, 'Pluralism and equality: the Peace of Monsieur, May 1576' (forthcoming).

47 A. Stegmann (ed.), *Édits des guerres de religion* (Paris, 1979), pp. 97–120; N. M. Sutherland, *The Huguenot Struggle for Recognition* (New Haven, Conn., 1980), pp. 228–31, 361–2.

48 O. Poncet, *Pomponne de Bellièvre (1529–1607). Un homme d'état au temps des guerres de religion* (Paris: École des chartes, 1998), p. 88.

registration by the Parlement. Acutely conscious of the shame which he had incurred as a result of the peace, he even refused to see his mother for two months afterwards. He also ordered the bells of Notre-Dame to be silenced as a *Te Deum* celebrated the end of hostilities. Writing to Pope Gregory XIII on 20 May, the king admitted his distress and powerlessness. The price of peace had been the crown's humiliation.

CHAPTER TEN

The sixth war (December 1576–September 1577)

The League of Péronne (1576)

The almost complete freedom of worship conceded to the Huguenots by the Peace of Monsieur scandalized militant Catholics. Defensive associations which earlier Protestant successes had prompted in 1562 and 1568 suddenly reappeared. In Paris a perfume-maker, called La Bruyère, and his son, who was a councillor of the Châtelet, led resistance to the edict. Secret meetings were held each day and a list of supporters circulated. However, the movement was allegedly nipped in the bud by De Thou, first president of the Parlement.[1] Outside Paris, Picardy took the lead in opposing the settlement. This is not surprising given the province's crucial strategic importance. On learning that Condé was to become governor of the province, Jacques d'Humières, the governor of Péronne, begged the king on 5 May not to allow it to fall into Protestant hands. One hundred and fifty noblemen, led by Jacques d'Applaincourt and Michel d'Estourmel, rallied to his support. Secret talks involving representatives of the three orders in the town led to the setting up of an organization with an elected council. According to the Venetian ambassador, Spanish agents encouraged these moves because they did not want to see a Protestant garrison so close to the Netherlands.[2] On 8 June Henry III wrote to d'Humières deploring the disobedience of the inhabitants of Péronne and the support they were getting from the Picard nobility. He ordered the governor to expel d'Applaincourt

1 De Thou, *Histoire universelle* (The Hague, 1740), vol. 7, pp. 423–4.
2 N. M. Sutherland, *The Huguenot Struggle for Recognition* (New Haven, Conn., 1980), p. 239.

and d'Estourmel from the town. Henry also ordered other nobles to desist from opposing the edict of pacification. In the weeks that followed, d'Humières was joined by the governors of Ham and Doullens. Finally, on 9 July, Henry III decided not to hand over Péronne to Condé, who was compensated with Saint-Jean d'Angély.[3]

Two documents, both called *Manifeste de Péronne*, have been linked to the League of Péronne. The first, in the name of 'the prelates, lords, nobles, captains, soldiers and inhabitants of the towns and countryside of Picardy', expresses their fear that Péronne, under Condé, might become a centre for the diffusion of Protestantism. They have accordingly pledged their property and lives, even to the last drop of their blood, to ensure that the town and province remain within the king's obedience and Catholic faith. With this end in mind, they have set up a 'holy and Christian union' of all the king's subjects to fight the 'ministers of Satan' and Huguenot rebels. They swear to obey the church, the king and 'the principal leader of the said confederacy'. They envisage a militia, a council, and noblemen with links to others in the neighbourhood. They also wish to make contact with France's neighbours, to have a nobleman to represent them at court and to employ a secretary alongside their leader. Finally, they aim to draw up a list of supporters, to recruit as many as possible and to maintain a small garrison in each *place forte* and château of the region. The second text is much shorter. In addition to pledging themselves to defend the Catholic church and the king's authority, the authors call for the restoration of the 'rights, privileges, franchises and liberties' which had existed in the time of Clovis and of better, more profitable, ones if such could be devised. In pursuit of these ends, they pledge their lives and goods, and promise to obey 'the leader who will be appointed'. The text also foresees a convention with other provinces of the kingdom. The first document was published as two pamphlets in 1576 by opponents of the League, who may have been Protestants. Both documents were subsequently published by Protestant historians. No manuscript or signed version of either has ever been found. Either or both may be taken as the founding documents of the League of Péronne, but this has yet to be proved.[4]

3 Henry III, *Lettres*, vol. 2, pp. 443–4; M. Orléa, *La noblesse aux États généraux de 1576 et de 1588* (Paris 1980), pp. 36–7.

4 Orléa, *La noblesse aux États généraux*, pp. 37–8; Sutherland, *The Huguenot Struggle for Recognition*, pp. 239–40. In 1583 Gabriel du Préau, a canon of Péronne cathedral, published a history of the church in two volumes. This contains a detailed account of events at Péronne in May and June 1576 which suggests that articles of association were indeed drawn up. See M. Greengrass, 'Pluralism and equality: the Peace of Monsieur, May 1576' (forthcoming).

How far was the League of Péronne instigated by the house of Guise? It has long been assumed that the unnamed leader of the manifesto was intended to be Henri de Guise. According to Maimbourg, the seventeeth-century historian of the League, it was Guise who wrote the manifesto and sent it to d'Humières for circulation. But Jean-Marie Constant believes that historians have confused the Leagues of 1576 and 1585. They were quite different, he argues. In 1576 the League was similar to the Catholic associations which had been formed in the 1560s and the Guises were, as yet, relatively powerless in Picardy.[5] This opinion is not shared by Carroll, who claims that 'Guise clients were deeply involved' in promoting the League. Jacques d'Applaincourt, who played a leading part in the movement, was the *enseigne* in the company of the duc d'Aumale. Carroll also demonstrates that important social changes had been taking place in Picardy. The Bourbons had lost support following Condé's adherence to Protestantism, and the Guises were well placed to exploit the resulting vacuum. They were, in any case, closely related by marriage to the Bourbons and could count on the support of the cardinal de Bourbon, who, as archbishop of Rouen, opposed the Edict of Beaulieu.[6]

The case against Guise rests to a large extent on a document of doubtful authenticity which was found on the body of Jean David, a barrister in the Parlement of Paris, who died in Lyon while returning from a mission to Rome in June 1576. It has been taken as proof that the Guises were plotting to depose Henry III. It describes the Capetians as a degenerate race living under a divine curse and praises the descendants of Charlemagne (that is to say, the house of Lorraine) as 'flourishing and full of spiritual and bodily vigour'. Their rights, it argues, should de recognized by the appointment of the duc de Guise, first, as Lieutenant-general of the kingdom, then, with papal permission, as king of France after Henry III's banishment to a monastery. Meanwhile, the duke would lead a popular uprising and organize Catholic militias in the parishes. The Estates-General would swear fealty and obedience to the pope, adopt the Tridentine decrees, ensure the strict application of their decisions and declare their wish to live as Catholics. Anyone opposing the estates would be deprived of his rights and executed. The document circulated in Paris in September 1576 and was shown to Henry III. He showed no interest in it until he received another copy sent by his ambassador in Spain who had been given it by Philip II. It found its way into the royal library after Guise's assassination

5 J.-M. Constant, *La Ligue* (Paris, 1996), pp. 70–76.

6 S. Carroll, *Noble Power during the French Wars of Religion: The Guise Affinity and the Catholic Cause in Normandy* (Cambridge, 1998), pp. 161–6.

in 1588 and might prove useful to the king as he tried to justify that crime. The document was also avidly taken up by Protestants in the 1580s in order to bring the Guises into discredit as rebels.[7] Whatever its status may have been, the David document is likely to have caused Henry III serious worry, for he was intensely suspicious by nature.

The League of 1576 was not restricted to Péronne. Apart from Paris, Angoulême and Bourges, it reached Brittany, Normandy and Poitou, but not Burgundy. In June Huguenots were warned that Amiens, Abbeville, Saint-Quentin, Beauvais, Corbie and other towns in Picardy and even in the Netherlands had joined Péronne in opposing the peace. In July Henry III asked the municipal authorities in Amiens to urge the people to abide by the settlement. A league of Picard nobles was seeking to win over towns in support of Péronne and Doullens; they were also assembling troops and raising funds. In August the king urged the *échevins* of Montdidier not to join the Picard 'league and associations'. The duc de Montpensier, governor of Brittany, was instructed by the king to suppress 'secret moves and practices' involving 'arms and horses' in his *gouvernement*. In mid-September, Louis de La Trémoïlle, duc de Thouars, and 60 nobles formed a league for the defence of Catholicism at Sainte-Hermine in Poitou. In October the local *bailli* was ordered to use every means at his disposal to resist 'leagues and associations' with leaders in common. In the same month the *bailli* of Rouen was alarmed by a gathering of troops around the city. He suspected either a Huguenot rising or 'another league which the people call a Holy league'. Thus, it seems that within a short time the League of Péronne had become almost nationwide.[8]

If the role of Henri de Guise in the League of Péronne remains controversial, it seems that he did assist its diffusion to the rest of the kingdom. 'Without any possible doubt,' writes Manfred Orléa, 'the leader of the League in 1576 is the duc de Guise.'[9] In June the king was warned of a secret association of noblemen and towns dedicated to resisting the edict of pacification by armed force if need be. The dukes of Guise, Mayenne and Nemours, who were suspected of being its leaders, were required by the king to swear on oath that they would respect the edict. But Constant does not think that, as yet, the Guises were powerful enough to challenge the crown. L'Estoile in his *Journal* refers to the 'limited means which the House

7 J.-M. Constant, *Les Guise* (Paris, 1984), pp. 193–6; Sutherland, *The Huguenot Struggle for Recognition*, pp. 240–44.

8 M. Orléa, *La noblesse aux États généraux*, pp. 38–9.

9 Ibid., p. 39.

of Lorraine had at that time [February 1577] to agitate'.[10] Constant points to the contrast between their area of military recruitment as compared with that of other nobles. The companies of Henri de Guise were drawn mainly from Champagne, Brie, Lorraine and Burgundy. His cousin, Elbeuf, raised his troops mainly in Normandy and Picardy, and his brother, Mayenne, in *gouvernements* entrusted to the Guises. By contrast the king's brother, Anjou, recruited troops from a much wider area (Champagne, Brie, the Loire valley, Berry, Île-de-France, Lorraine, Vermandois and Normandy). The Guises did not normally go in for secrecy, according to Constant. When they acted, they did so openly, even brazenly; he surmises that if they did not do so in 1576, it was because they fundamentally agreed with the king.[11]

Henry III was in a very difficult situation. He had always been a die-hard Catholic: having defeated the Huguenots at Jarnac and Moncontour, he had a heavy responsibility for the massacre of St Bartholomew. He had since besieged the Huguenots in La Rochelle and had only reluctantly accepted religious toleration in Poland as part of the price for becoming its king. On his return to France, he remained committed to restoring religious unity among his subjects and viewed the concessions made to the Huguenots in the Edict of Beaulieu as a personal defeat and humiliation. He longed to expunge this but needed money and troops to do so. The difficulties which he faced over the payment of John Casimir and his *reiters* revealed the extent of his poverty.[12] He hoped that the forthcoming meeting of the Estates-General would assist him.

The Estates-General of Blois (1576)

Under the Peace of Monsieur, the king had undertaken to call the Estates-General within six months, but the Huguenots, who had pressed for this, were almost completely excluded from the election of deputies. Intimidation of voters by Leaguers was reported from many areas. The time and place of the elections were often announced only during Mass. Huguenots were consequently excluded. Even where they were allowed a voice in the choice of deputies and the drafting of *cahiers de doléance*, they were almost

10 Pierre de L'Estoile, *Registre-journal du règne de Henri III*, ed. M. Lazard and G. Schrenck (Geneva, 1996), vol. 2, p. 102.

11 Constant, *La Ligue*, pp. 75–6.

12 O. Poncet, *Pomponne de Bellièvre (1529–1607). Un homme d'état au temps des guerres de religion* (Paris, 1998), pp. 136–7.

always in a minority. Here and there violence broke out, notably at Provins where a group of men were forcibly evicted from a meeting to elect deputies for the nobility.[13] Only a handful of Huguenots were elected for the whole kingdom, three of them nobles. One of them was prevented from attending the estates by other business.[14]

The deputies began to arrive in Blois in mid-November and soon got down to business. They numbered 383: 110 clergy, 86 nobles and 187 third estate.[15] The three estates – clergy, nobility and third estate – met separately to draw up their *cahiers de doléances* based on the local petitions which each deputy had brought with him. At the end of the session each order was to submit a general *cahier* to the king. In addition to an extensive programme of reform which the deputies aimed to promote in their *cahiers*, they had to face three major problems: how to restore religious peace to the kingdom; how to bring order to the king's finances; and how to ensure the effective participation of the estates in government. With respect to the first problem, a majority of the deputies opposed the recent edict of pacification. Many believed that the best way to restore religious peace was to eradicate heresy. The clergy did not hesitate to call for religion in France to be restricted to the Catholic faith. It has traditionally been assumed that the nobility also wanted to overturn the recent edict of pacification, but, as Mack Holt has shown, a significant minority shared the more tolerant attitude advocated in the third estate by a group led by Jean Bodin.

None of the few local *cahiers* that survive for the second estate advocates a renewal of the war to enforce religious uniformity. The *cahier* that was drawn up in Nivernais merely notes that Frenchmen would be better off if they remembered that there is only 'one God to serve'. Otherwise it focuses on issues of direct concern to the nobility, such as the sale of judicial offices or the cost of providing arms. While recognizing that they owe the king military service, the nobles argue that the cost of providing him with troops should not be borne by them alone. They urge the king to raise an army of 50,000 men by means of the *taillon*, a special tax from which they are exempt. They feel that their traditional role in government is being undermined by false nobles who buy offices, by taxes and by foreigners at court.

The issue of religious uniformity and of the renewal of the war surfaced by the end of the first week of the estates as several prelates began to lobby noble deputies. One of these, Pierre de Blanchefort, the noble deputy for

13 F. Bourquelot (ed.), *Mémoires de Claude Haton* (Paris, 1857), vol. 2, pp. 863–5.

14 On the close links between the deputies of the first and second estates of Upper Normandy, see Carroll, *Noble Power during the French Wars of Religion*, pp. 166–7.

15 J. R. Major, *The Deputies to the Estates General in Renaissance France* (Madison, 1960), pp. 163–5.

Saintonge, kept a diary. 'To-day [29 November],' he writes, 'I was called to a particular conference at the residence of one of the prelates of this kingdom, along with many others of his rank and some other deputies from the nobility, where a certain formula of association was proposed; whose purpose was to break the last edict of pacification and to place the king at war against those of the so-called religion . . . I remarked that it seemed to me that the king ought not to be counselled to go to war, because of the recent injuries the kingdom has suffered, and that anyone who favours civil war is ungodly and deserves our prayers.'[16] Blanchefort tried to persuade the clerics not to support the formula of association. While stating that he wished to see only one religion in the kingdom, he affirmed his belief in the peaceful co-existence of two religions, as demonstrated in Germany and Switzerland. Persecution, he indicated, did not work; after 30 years of persecution, the Huguenots remained strong. Blanchefort refused to sign the formula, arguing that a war that was not ordered and led by the king was unjust. He noted, however, that other nobles did sign the formula.

The move by prelates and nobles to form associations aimed at overturning the peace constituted a serious threat to the king's authority. The Edict of Beaulieu, unpalatable as it was to Henry, was nonetheless a piece of royal legislation which had to be upheld as long as he did not rescind it himself. Henry could not allow his subjects to take the law into their own hands by forming armed leagues. If, on the other hand, he could contrive to lead the opposition, he might at least safeguard his authority until the estates gave him the resources needed to enforce it. Hence Henry's decision to set up a league of his own. On 2 December he sent out to all the provincial governors a deed of association which he wanted everyone to sign.[17] In each province a force of armed and mounted men was to be set up and funds raised for its upkeep. The governors were to be assisted by six chief men of their province and, in each *bailliage,* one or two noblemen, or others of sufficient substance and loyalty, were to be chosen as advisors. Catholics who refused to join an association were to be regarded as enemies of God, king and country. Finally, peaceful Protestants were assured that their freedom of conscience (but not, by implication, of worship) would be respected as well as their lives and property 'provided that they do not violate whatever His Majesty might ordain after the conclusion of the Estates-General'. By making himself head of the Catholic League with his own formula of association, Henry hoped to reaffirm his authority and to dissuade other

16 B. M. Blois, Mss. 89 fol 25r. Cited by M. P. Holt in 'Attitudes of the French nobility at the Estates-General of 1576', *S.C.J.*, 18 (1987), p. 494.

17 Henry III, *Lettres*, vol. 3, pp. 85–8.

Catholic extremists from acting independently. By this move he became, in effect, the leader of the Catholic party. Historians generally have interpreted it as a cunning ploy designed to circumvent Guise ambitions. But, as Constant has indicated, such an explanation seems unnecessary in 1576. The Guise plot remains unproven and the king's action was consistent with his present beliefs and past behaviour.[18]

The third estate were more divided than the clergy or the nobility on the question of religious unity. During the separate session of the *gouvernement* of the Île-de-France, the deputies drew up a *cahier* demanding that only the Catholic religion should be recognized. Pierre le Tourneur, alias Versoris, a Parisian lawyer, presented the *cahier* to the general assembly of the third estate for acceptance, but Jean Bodin, author of the *Six Books of the Republic* and the deputy for Vermandois, put forward a counter-proposal calling on the king to preserve peace among his subjects and to summon a council within two years to decide the religious question. A few days later, Versoris put forward a revised proposal which demanded the restoration of religious unity 'by the most gentle and holy ways that His Majesty shall devise'. Six *gouvernements* (Normandy, Champagne, Languedoc, Orléannais, Picardy and Provence) supported this motion and five (Burgundy, Brittany, Guyenne, Lyonnais and Dauphiné) specified that religious union should be secured 'without war'. The majority, however, refused to accept this qualification, insisting on the complete suppression of the Protestant faith and the banishment of all Huguenot ministers, deacons, elders and schoolmasters. In effect, the third estate declared war on the Huguenots.[19]

On 19 December the second estate discussed and voted on the issue of religious uniformity. A majority backed the motion supporting the maintenance of one religion in their general *cahier*. Henry III hoped that the Estates-General would enable him to reverse the humiliation of the Edict of Beaulieu. Having publicly undertaken to give it effect, he secretly wanted an excuse to abrogate it. If possible, he wanted his subjects to bear the responsibility for this volte-face. He, therefore, welcomed the estates' demand that only the Catholic religion should be recognized in his kingdom. Indeed, he largely engineered that decision by the pressure which he had exerted on the elections to the estates. The diary of the duc de Nevers provides evidence of continuing pressure on members not only of the nobility but also of the third estate. However, the king's policy carried

18 Constant, *La Ligue*, pp. 71–2.

19 M. Greengrass, 'A day in the life of the third estate: Blois, 26th December, 1576' in A. E. Bakos (ed.), *Politics, Ideology and the Law in Early Modern Europe* (University of Rochester Press), pp. 73–90.

grave risks. It needed to be secretive for fear of unleashing a new massacre of St Bartholomew. Already a rumour circulated that a massacre was being planned for 15 December. Henry had to issue a formal denial: 'I have no greater wish or desire,' he said, 'than to ensure that my subjects live in mutual friendship, unity and concord.'[20]

By 22 December Henry III was apparently confident of success. He informed his mother's council that he could no longer accept two religions in his kingdom or break his coronation oath. On 3 January he made his decision public. Meanwhile, his privy councillors urged him to join the Estates-General in showing to the Protestants that the kingdom wanted Catholicism to be its only religion. Henry was also pressed to guarantee the safety of loyal Huguenots while preparing to fight the rest. Before coming to blows with them, the king and the estates sent representatives to Condé, Navarre, and Damville with an invitation to come to Blois and discuss the religious situation with Henry. Condé refused to receive the deputation while denouncing the Estates-General as a puppet body, set up and corrupted by the king's agents. Navarre's response was more polite: he asked the estates to reconsider their demand for religious unity.[21]

Henry III had hoped that the estates, having voted for religious unity, would give him the necessary resources to bring this about, but he had seriously misjudged their mood: they were willing enough to play his game as long as it cost them nothing. As soon as he requested money, they recoiled. The king wanted, if not a subsidy, at least permission to alienate parts of the royal domain; in the event, he got neither. On 31 December M. de Nicolai, first president of the *Chambre des comptes* reported to the estates on the royal finances. He attributed their deplorable state to debts Henry III had inherited from his predecessors and urged the deputies to find a remedy. At his request, an audit commission was set up by the estates. Hoping to avert new demands, the noble deputies decided on 7 January that the king could form an adequate army for three months by raising the *taillon*. Next day, several noble deputies called on the other estates to explain their proposal. The clergy condoned it while disclaiming all responsibility. The third estate responded by demanding a reduction of the *taille* and the abolition of the *taillon*.[22] They insisted that the nobles should share the costs of war and supply the *arrière-ban* at their own expense. On 9 January the audit commissioners produced their report. Instead of

20 Henry III, *Lettres*, vol. 3, p. 99.
21 Greengrass, 'A day in the life of the third estate', pp. 88–9.
22 On the *taillon*, see M. Wolfe, *The Fiscal System of Renaissance France* (New Haven, Conn., 1972), p. 350.

suggesting ways of raising new funds, they blamed the current fiscal crisis on royal extravagance and on alienations of crown lands.[23] On 30 January Henry III sent Anjou and Guise to beg the nobles to provide him with six months' military service at their expense. Blanchefort's diary shows that, as the meeting wore on, more noble deputies began to question the decision to renew the war. The deputy for Brittany warned of the danger which the king's demand presented to his people, while the deputy for Chartres argued that it was more important to establish a firm peace than to replenish the king's coffers.

The estates submitted their final *cahiers* to the king on 9 February. He asked them to await his replies in Blois, but many went home regardless. The nobility's *cahier* did not call for a renewal of the war against the Huguenots, nor did it endorse any Catholic formula of association. Only one article out of 246 called for uniformity of religion. Some articles called for the reform of abuses in the church but, in the main, the *cahier* focused on noble privileges and the administration of justice. False and foreign nobles were accused of undermining the traditional role of the *noblesse de race* in both government and society. The *cahier* also complained that the nobility's traditional exemption from taxation had been gradually eroded since the start of the civil wars. It demanded a ban on anyone taking up arms without the king's permission and that membership of the *gendarmerie* be limited to nobles of at least four years' military experience. The *cahier* also complained of venality of office, of fiscal abuses and of new and excessive subsidies and taxes. It asked for a reduction in the number of offices and sovereign courts to the levels that had existed under Louis XII, for a ban on the 'villainous and detestable traffic and sale . . . of judicial offices', for the chancellor to be 'a true and native Frenchman' (the existing chancellor, René de Birague, was an Italian), for the abolition of the *élus* and their *élections*.[24] The *cahiers* of the other estates were equally disgruntled. The deputies of the third estate explained that they had been instructed by their constituents to ask for lower taxes, not to levy new ones. Pleading poverty, they called for a reduction of the *taille* to its level under Louis XII. Only the clergy offered any financial assistance to the king. Under pressure from the cardinals of Bourbon and Guise, they granted him the paltry sum of 450,000 livres. When Henry III tried to raise an additional 300,000 by alienating crown lands, he was foiled by the third estate, including Bodin, who vigorously defended the law of inalienability. 'They won't help me with their

23 O. Ulph, 'Jean Bodin and the Estates-General of 1576', *Journal of Modern History*, xix (1947), p. 291.

24 Holt, 'Attitudes of the French nobility at the Estates-General of 1576', pp. 497–500.

[money],' Henry complained, 'and they won't let me help myself with mine; it's too cruel.'[25]

On 28 February the duc de Montpensier, who had once been a zealous persecutor of Huguenots, spoke movingly to the estates about the distress he had witnessed on returning from his mission to the king of Navarre. 'When I consider the evils which the recent wars have brought us,' he said, 'and how much this division is leading to the ruin and desolation of this poor kingdom . . . and the calamities such as those which I saw on my journey here, of poor people immersed in poverty without hope of ever being able to raise themselves from that state except by means of peace . . . I am constrained to advise their Majesties to make peace . . . being the only remedy and best cure that I know of for the evil that has spread all over France.'[26] The duke indicated that he still believed in a single Catholic religion for the kingdom, but advised toleration of the Huguenots until they could be reconciled by some peaceful means. Soon afterwards, he presented a remonstrance to the king signed by 24 nobles protesting at their estate's decision to renew the war. Henry III received it graciously but indicated that he had to follow the advice of the majority of the second estate and of his council.[27]

The king's predicament was compounded by the League's distrust. The Picard nobles would only swear his oath of association on condition that their franchises and privileges were respected. When d'Humières tried to gain control of Amiens, he was refused entry and the king had to exempt the inhabitants from the League in return for a payment of 8,000 livres. Henry had every reason to feel discouraged. He had opted for war, not out of religious fanaticism, but in order to efface the humiliation of the Edict of Beaulieu. As war stared him in the face, he could not count on the League's support and was virtually penniless. On 1 March Henry was forced to revise his policy. 'Gentlemen,' he told his council, 'each of you has seen how hard I have tried to honour God and how much I have wanted only one religion in my kingdom. Needless to say, I have even solicited the deputies of the three estates and asked them to vote for religious uniformity in the belief that they would help me carry out this holy resolution. But seeing what little money they have given me, I have little hope of executing my intentions . . . and do not consider myself a failure if, for the present, I do not speak out in favour of permitting just one religion in my kingdom,

25 P. Chevallier, *Henri III* (Paris, 1985), p. 353.

26 Mack P. Holt, *The French Wars of Religion 1562–1629* (Cambridge, 1995), p. 108.

27 Mack P. Holt, *The Duke of Anjou and the Politique Struggle during the Wars of Religion* (Cambridge, 1986), pp. 85–6.

because I simply do not have the means to do it.'[28] The king was supported in the council by his mother. She argued that religious unity would be achieved only if the kingdom were preserved, not destroyed by civil war. According to Bodin, the peace party in the council included Biron, Cossé, Montpensier, Jean de Morvillier and Pomponne de Bellièvre. They were opposed by Guise, Mayenne, Nevers and the cardinal de Guise.[29] Henry now hoped that if there was to be war, it would be short. The only bright spot for him was his reconciliation with Damville in March. Henry offered him the marquisate of Saluzzo and its dependencies if he would hand over the towns he was holding without prejudice to his governorship of Languedoc.[30] After accepting the deal, Damville renewed his allegiance to the king and deserted his Huguenot allies.

The sixth war (December 1576–September 1577)

The Huguenots had never pinned any hopes on the Estates-General. By the end of December 1576 they had taken up arms in Poitou and Guyenne. But, without the *reiters* and following the defection of Anjou and Damville, they were necessarily weaker, except in the south of France. Henry III appointed Anjou as the commander of his army to secure his loyalty, but the duke had only the appearance of leadership. The real command of the king's forces was given to the duc de Nevers, seconded by the dukes of Guise and Mayenne. But Henry still had to find the means of paying his army. He reckoned that he needed at least two million livres. He hoped to get 1.2 million from forced loans on the walled towns and the rest from the *taille*. He also hoped for an additional million from a clerical tenth.[31] The towns begged to be exempt, or they were slow to pay or simply refused to do so, yet the king did manage to raise 20 companies of *gendarmerie*, 60 of infantry, 18 cannon and 6 smaller guns, and powder and shot for 10,000 discharges.[32] However, he had only enough money to keep them in the field

28 *Mémoires de Nevers*, vol. 1, pp. 176–7. Cited by Holt in 'Attitudes of the French nobility at the Estates-General of 1576', p. 503.

29 Lalourcé and Duval, *Recueil des pièces originales*, vol. 3, p. 370. Cited by Holt, 'Attitudes of the French nobility at the Estates-General of 1576', p. 503 n. 48.

30 Henry III, *Lettres*, vol. 3, pp. 177–8.

31 Henry III, *Lettres*, vol. 3, p. 215; Holt, *The Duke of Anjou*, p. 88.

32 B.N., ms. fr. 3337, fols. 13–17. Cited by Holt, *The Duke of Anjou*, p. 88 n. 76.

for a month. 'Please do the best you can to ensure that our deniers are used sparingly,' he wrote to Nevers, 'for as you know they are hard to come by, especially as the infantry must be paid in cash.'[33]

As the court moved from Blois to Chenonceaux in the spring, the army gathered at La Chapelle-d'Anguillon, north of Bourges, with a view to besieging La Charité-sur-Loire, which the Huguenots had recently taken by surprise. As it waited for the duc de Guise and other noblemen to arrive, it began to run short of food and provisions. On 21 April Anjou informed the king that neither the money intended for the infantry nor the food and wine, which had been promised by the town of Orléans, had arrived. He begged for an immediate delivery of wheat to feed his men. The king replied that the local inhabitants would have to meet his need. But the army had enough shot and powder to besiege La Charité. Henry was most anxious that his brother should not expose himself to danger. 'I am very distressed,' he wrote to Nevers on 26 April, 'to hear that my brother and some of the princes and chief noblemen who are with him are regularly exposing themselves to every sort of danger like common soldiers. I fear some sinister or irreparable accident, so please tell my brother from now on to be more careful . . . It is not proper for the head of the army, especially a person of such quality and respect, to expose himself to such hazards.'[34]

The siege of La Charité began on 25 April. The town, after being bombarded for seven days, surrendered on 2 May, whereupon it was sacked by the royal troops. Anjou was given a hero's welcome when he returned to the court at Chenonceaux. On 28 May he rejoined the army as it laid siege to Issoire in Auvergne. By now the king's army numbered only about 5,000 men. The town's governor, Chavignac, was warned four times of the dire consequences of resistance, but he stood firm after invoking the Edict of Beaulieu. Henry instructed Anjou to punish the town severely for its disobedience.[35] This was done after the town had capitulated on 12 June. 'Most of the town,' writes de Thou, 'and all its riches were reduced to cinders.'[36] Countless women were raped. On 19 July Anjou was given another hero's welcome at court, this time at Poitiers. Meanwhile, as Nevers complained that he no longer had any ammunition, his troops dragged themselves through the Limousin. On 21 July Henry urged the duke to accept 30,000 livres which the town of Limoges had offered him in place of billets for his troops.[37] After more complaints from Nevers, the king had to admit that his

33 Henry III, *Lettres*, vol. 3, p. 215.
34 Henry III, *Lettres*, vol. 3, p. 226. Cited by Holt, *The Duke of Anjou*, p. 89.
35 Henry III, *Lettres*, vol. 3, p. 277.
36 De Thou, *Histoire universelle*, vol. 5, p. 373.
37 Henry III, *Lettres*, vol. 3, p. 326.

treasury was empty and that his troops could not be paid. Eventually, Nevers was recalled along with the rest of the army.

Although the Huguenots had lost La Charité and Issoire, they retained many strongholds in the south. Moreover, Navarre and Condé were still at large with their forces. When they captured Brouage on the Atlantic coast and began receiving aid from England, Henry III decided to come to terms. He gave Montpensier full powers to negotiate in his name. Peace was signed at Bergerac on 14 September and confirmed in the Edict of Poitiers of 17 September.[38] This allowed Protestant worship in the suburbs of one town per *bailliage* and in places held by the Huguenots on 17 September. Bipartisan courts were retained only in the parlements of Aix, Bordeaux, Grenoble and Toulouse, the proportion of Protestant judges being reduced to one-third. The Huguenots were allowed eight surety towns but only for six years. Finally, all leagues and associations were banned. Thus, the freedom of Protestant worship which had been conceded in 1576 was considerably curtailed. The new situation represented a compromise between the extremes represented by the Edict of Boulogne of 1573 and that of Beaulieu of 1576. It provided the kingdom with a peaceful respite which lasted eight years save for a brief lapse in 1579–80. Henry III was to use it to shore up his authority after the severe knocks which it had suffered since 1574.

---

38 Sutherland, *The Huguenot Struggle for Recognition*, pp. 271–3, 362–8.

CHAPTER ELEVEN

The Catholic League (1578–1589)

A study of the French civil wars, even one that is primarily concerned with military matters, cannot leave out of account the economic background, for this produced new grievances capable of erupting into violence. Furthermore, it is important to realize that the wars, however damaging to the lives of ordinary French people, were not solely to blame for their misfortunes.[1]

The Price Revolution contributed significantly to the distress which occurred in much of France during the reign of Henry III. Prices had been rising for a variety of reasons since the last two decades of the fifteenth century, but in the 1570s they achieved new peaks.[2] A major reason for this was a sequence of bad harvests. A drought in the summer of 1583 caused many deaths among the poor of Lyon during the ensuing winter. Crops varied from province to province: in 1578 grain was scarce in Brittany yet plentiful in Guyenne; in 1580 the reverse was true. But lack of transport prevented a surplus in one area being moved to another in need. War added to the difficulties. The frequent passage of troops disrupted arable farming. Claude Haton has left vivid descriptions of the effects of famine and war. In 1573 there were bread riots in Provins.[3] Three years later, John Casimir's army and the *reiters* retreating through Champagne, followed by local war bands and the king's army, inflicted terrible suffering on the local peasantry.[4]

1 A. Jouanna, *La France du XVIe siècle 1483–1598* (Paris, 1996), pp. 541–54; J. H. M. Salmon, *Society in Crisis: France in the Sixteenth Century* (London, 1975), pp. 206–16.

2 M. Baulant and J. Meuvret, *Prix des céréales extraits de la Mercuriale de Paris (1520–1698)* (Paris, 1960), vol. 1.

3 F. Bourquelot (ed.), *Mémoires de Claude Haton* (Paris, 1857), vol. 2, pp. 716–32.

4 Ibid., pp. 850–51.

Industry was at first boosted by the rise in prices, but in time it began to suffer, as the higher cost of food left people with less money to spend on manufactured goods. In certain industries, like silk or printing, journeymen were fed by the master. As a result, the cost of labour increased and the goods became more expensive and, therefore, less competitive internationally. The main threat to the French cloth industry came from cheap English imports. Several cloth-making regions, notably Paris, Troyes, Poitou and, to a lesser extent, Languedoc, were badly hit. French merchants also lost a traditional outlet, as English manufactured goods, like hats and shoes, flooded into Spain. Imports from Italy did terrible damage to the French silk industry. Whereas in the mid-century Lyon had 3,000 looms employing between 12,000 and 15,000 workers, by 1573 only 200 were still functioning.[5] The crown tried to protect the home industries by legislation, but the effects were nullified by numerous exemptions conceded by the king to foreign merchants.

International commerce was less seriously affected by the wars. Breton merchants complained of the activities of corsairs based in La Rochelle and the wine trade was hit by a reduced demand from the Netherlands in the wake of the revolt. But in general, the ports along the Atlantic and Channel coasts – Bordeaux, Nantes and Rouen – continued to prosper until the eighth civil war. In the Mediterranean, Marseille took advantage of the Cyprus war of 1570–73 to wrest part of the Levantine spice trade from the Venetians. Within France, trade was hit by banditry on the roads and by a proliferation of river-tolls imposed by greedy land-owners. The fairs of Lyon were seriously affected in 1576 by the sack of Antwerp, Europe's leading money-market. Monetary chaos caused by wild fluctuations of the bi-metallic ratio and by the free circulation of foreign coinage was another harmful factor. Yet banking, albeit of a dangerously speculative kind, continued in Lyon till 1585.[6]

The rise in agricultural prices hit all workers who were paid wholly or partly in cash. Small peasant proprietors with little surplus to sell were pauperized. Furthermore, royal taxation increased. The *taille* and its *crues* rose from around 6 million livres in 1561–5 to 7.12 million in 1575. In real terms the level was lower than under Henry II. Even so, a wage-earner had to work longer to meet his fiscal obligations. Peasants also had to pay seigneurial dues, the *dîme* and occasional taxes imposed by the various warlords. If they were hit by famine or plague, they had no option but to

---

5 R. Gascon, *Grand commerce et vie urbaine au XVIe siècle: Lyon et ses marchands* (Paris, 1971), vol. 1, pp. 59–65; vol. 2, pp. 668–72, 716–18.

6 Ibid., vol. 2, pp. 645–9.

sell their holdings. This process began long before the civil wars which merely accelerated it. Some social groups benefited from inflation, particularly if their rents rose more slowly than prices.

A marked feature of the late sixteenth century in France was a widening gap between rich and poor. Some people managed to feather their own nests quite well during the civil wars. Two forms of investment commended themselves: royal offices and land. The sale of offices (venality) continued to flourish in spite of much contemporary criticism of the practice and calls for its abolition from the Estates-General. What is more, the king created many new offices as a means of replenishing his coffers. Even so, he was never able to satisfy the demand.[7] Many merchants bought offices mainly in order to enhance their social position. Some offices, of course, carried nobility with them. The salaries paid to office-holders were sizeable, but more lucrative still were the gratuities (*épices*) which office-holders could expect in return for their judicial or administrative services. The highest offices offered access to such profitable activities as farming the revenues of the royal domain. Many families of the Parisian robe became extremely rich. Offices were also very attractive because the crown allowed their hereditary transmission. Thus many offices were monopolized by certain families, much to the disgust of outsiders who wanted to acquire them.

Land was another popular form of investment at this time. The revenues from land were not especially high, but its ownership was essential to social respectability. In order to rise in the world a bourgeois or merchant needed to acquire a *seigneurie*. One consequence of the civil wars was to put more land on the market, some of it alienated church property. The majority of purchasers were bourgeois and merchants. Peasants, except for a few big *laboureurs*, could not begin to compete.

The civil wars cannot be said to have caused the economic crisis which hit France in the reign of Henry III, but they added to the sufferings of various social groups, particularly those who were on the bread-line. They also offered some people opportunities of exploiting their neighbours. Many impoverished noblemen (*hobereaux*) began to exact ransoms from travellers in addition to plundering the countryside. Thus Montaigne was once robbed by 15 to 20 noblemen who also demanded a big ransom from him.[8] Many small captains, leaders of armed bands or custodians of fortresses tried, sometimes successfully, to become accepted as noblemen by boasting of their fighting experience.

---

7 R. Mousnier, *La vénalité des offices sous Henri IV et Louis XIII* (Paris, 1971), pp. 35–92.

8 M. de Montaigne, *Essais*, bk III, ch. 12.

Henry III: a controversial monarch

Henry III is not highly rated among French monarchs. Much of the unpopularity which he incurred in his own day has rubbed off on his historical reputation.[9] He is often presented as an irresolute king who surrounded himself with young favourites, called *mignons*.[10] The word *mignon* in the sixteenth century did not carry any pejorative meaning: it meant simply a 'favourite'. Despite their extravagant fashions and affected ways, the *mignons* were brave men quick to take offence and to draw their swords. In 1578 the king created a new, more select, order of chivalry – the Order of the Holy Spirit – to replace that of St Michael, which had become debased in his estimation.[11] Henry's own fastidiousness was mocked by contemporaries who identified personal hygiene with effeminacy. He was also derided for his extravagant displays of religiosity. The king expressed the wish to relieve his subjects of the misery and calamities which afflicted them by doing penance for his own sins and vices. In 1583 he set up a confraternity of White Penitents and took part in their public processions, wearing a robe of white sackcloth with a knotted girdle and a hood over his head and face. The king also established a confraternity of Hieronymites. This consisted initially of 12 members of the court, who retired to cells in the forest of Vincennes.[12] However, Henry's efforts to promote Catholic piety did little to remove public suspicion of the court. It was widely perceived as immoral and as the basic cause of political, economic and social instability.[13]

In recent years historians have tried to reach a more balanced view of Henry III.[14] They recognize in him an intelligent man, who genuinely wanted to reform his kingdom. He invited scholars to discuss philosophical matters in his presence at the Louvre. These meetings, which became known as the Palace Academy, were intended to equip Henry intellectually and morally for the responsibilities of kingship. They brought together most of

9 K. Cameron, *Henry III: A Maligned or Malignant King?* (Exeter, 1978), *passim*; D. Potter, 'Kingship in the Wars of Religion: the reputation of Henri III of France', *E.H.Q.*, 25 (1995), 485–528. For a contemporary assessment, see E. Pasquier, *Lettres historiques*, ed. D. Thickett (Geneva, 1966), pp. 306–13, 436–48.

10 J. Boucher, *La cour de Henri III* (Rennes, 1986), pp. 23–6; P. Champion, 'La légende des mignons', *Bibliothèque d'humanisme et Renaissance*, vol. VI (1939).

11 R. de Lucinge, *Lettres sur la cour d'Henri III en 1586*, ed. A. Dufour (Geneva, 1966), pp. 15–16; L. Bourquin, *Noblesse seconde et pouvoir en Champagne aux XVIe et XVIIe siècles* (Paris, 1994), p. 122.

12 F. Yates, *The French Academies of the Sixteenth Century* (London, 1988), pp. 152–76.

13 S. Carroll, *Noble Power during the French Wars of Religion: The Guise Affinity and the Catholic Cause in Normandy* (Cambridge, 1998), p. 194.

14 P. Chevallier, *Henri III* (Paris, 1985); Boucher, *La cour de Henri III*.

the French literary personalities of the day, including the poet Ronsard. Speech at the Academy appears to have been free, as Henry wanted instruction, not flattery.[15] Although devoted to his mother, he nevertheless wanted to be his own master and tried as far as possible to rely on noblemen wholly devoted to himself. He chose men of his own generation unattached to powerful family clans. This inevitably alienated noblemen who felt excluded from royal favour. In time two of Henry's *mignons*, Anne de Joyeuse and Jean-Louis de Nogaret, duc d'Épernon, became immensely powerful at court. The king first noticed Joyeuse in 1577, created him duke in 1581, and married him off to his sister-in-law, Marguerite de Vaudémont. The lavish festivities or 'magnificences', which accompanied the wedding and lasted about a fortnight, were seized upon by critics of the government as proof of its extravagance at a time when the kingdom was experiencing social distress.[16] Having become the king's brother-in-law, Joyeuse was appointed governor of Normandy, the richest province in France, and, in June 1582, Admiral of France in place of the duc de Mayenne, who received 120,000 écus by way of compensation.[17] His appointment has been interpreted as a bold move by Henry III to impose his authority on Normandy, a province where the Guises commanded a powerful clientèle.[18] Joyeuse was given precedence over all the other noblemen at court, except those belonging to sovereign houses.

Jean-Louis de Nogaret, duc d'Épernon, became a sort of prime minister, anticipating to some extent the roles played by Richelieu and Mazarin in the next century. The fact that his family background was fairly modest made him eminently acceptable to the king, who wanted a reliable servant wholly devoted to himself. By heaping on Épernon offices and governorships, Henry was, in effect, denying them to the Guises and placing them in hands which he considered safer. Being optimistic and energetic by nature, Épernon made up for king's nervous and irresolute disposition. But, knowing that his fate depended on Henry's favour, he tried to buttress his position by acquiring strategic governorships. They comprised Provence, Metz, Boulogne, and, after October 1587, Normandy, Aunis, Saintonge and Angoulême. As colonel-general of the infantry and Admiral (an office taken over from Joyeuse after his death) Épernon effectively controlled the king's forces.[19]

Henry III upset many nobles by his household reforms, which came in three stages. In September 1574 he introduced some changes to its daily

---

15 R. J. Sealy, *The Palace Academy of Henry III* (Geneva, 1981), *passim*.

16 F. A. Yates, *Astraea: The Imperial Theme in the Sixteenth Century* (London, 1975), pp. 149–72.

17 Carroll, *Noble power during the French Wars of Religion*, p. 187.

18 Ibid., pp. 195–6.

19 Pasquier, *Lettres historiques*, pp. 413–19.

routine. Great nobles were excluded from his *lever*, and, instead of meeting his council in the morning, the king shut himself up with his mother and chancellor. At dinner, he insisted on the gentlemen of his chamber being hatless as they served him. He had a barrier erected around his table in order to keep the public at a distance. Some noblemen left the court in disgust, while others derided the innovations. Such was the rumpus that the king was forced to backtrack: he readmitted the *grands* to his *lever*, removed the barriers from his table (temporarily) and granted after-dinner audiences. But he had repudiated the familiarity which many nobles had come to regard as theirs of right. In August 1578 Henry III again tried to regulate his household in writing. Two features were quite new: first, never before had the king's timetable been fixed with such clock-like precision; secondly, never had admissions to his chamber been given a strict order of precedence. In 1582 new rules were added. A dozen courtiers were invited to share a round table with the king informally every Sunday, and the chief steward was instructed to lay two places at the end of the king's table. One was permanently reserved for Joyeuse or Épernon. Never before had such favouritism been written into a household book. In 1585 Henry issued another regulation which revolutionized protocol at court by reshaping his lodging and controlling the movement of courtiers within it.[20]

Anjou and the Netherlands

The Peace of Bergerac was soon threatened by events in the Low Countries. After the Spanish capture of Namur on 24 July 1577, the Dutch rebels redoubled their efforts to gain the duc d'Anjou's support. But Henry III, who did not wish to be dragged into a foreign war by his brother, forbade his subjects to take any part in the Dutch revolt. In the meantime, Anjou's position at the French court became intolerable, as his followers, led by Bussy d'Amboise, exchanged verbal abuse and blows with the king's *mignons*. On 10 January 1578 Bussy challenged one of them to a duel involving 300 men on either side. The king banned the fight, but not a day passed without brawls between his and Anjou's servants. On 14 February the duke fled from the court and began raising troops at Angers. Henry III feared that his

20 D. Potter and P. R. Roberts, 'An Englishman's view of the court of Henri III, 1584–1585: Richard Cook's "Description of the Court of France"', *F.H.*, 2 (1988), 312–44.

move would be widely interpreted as the start of a new civil war. Anjou, however, assured the Parlement, Damville, Navarre and Condé that he remained loyal to the crown and upheld the Peace of Bergerac. Henry, in the meantime, tried to restore harmony at court, but tensions remained. On 27 April three *mignons* fought a duel with three of Guise's followers. Two were killed on each side. Heartbroken, Henry III gave his favourites a magnificent tomb which, according to L'Estoile, further damaged his reputation.[21]

Anjou, meanwhile, offered to lead an army into Hainault in exchange for some border towns, but his troops were little better than a rabble. 'They were all vagabonds, thieves, and murderers,' wrote Haton, 'men who renounced God along with the worldly debts they owed. These slaughtermen were the flotsam of war, riddled with the pox and fit for the gibbet. Dying of hunger, they took to the roads and fields to pillage, assault, and ruin the people of the towns and villages, who fell into their clutches in the places where they lodged.'[22] Henry III tried to stop their march, while Catherine de' Medici lectured Anjou on the dangers facing the kingdom should he persist in his enterprise. He retorted that he could not ignore cries for help reaching him from the Low Countries. On 12 July he arrived at Mons and informed William of Orange that he had come to assist the States-General in their just quarrel. A month later, he signed a treaty with them. In exchange for his military assistance over three months, the States appointed him 'Defender of the liberty of the Netherlands against the tyranny of the Spaniards and their allies', but this title conveyed no authority. The States also promised to consider Anjou as Philip II's possible successor. The duke, for his part, swore to protect the rights of Dutch Protestants and not to attempt to separate the Catholic provinces from the rest. Such hopes as the Dutch had placed in Anjou's help soon evaporated, as his unpaid troops began to desert, ravaging the countryside as they went home. In the autumn of 1578 Anjou reopened his matrimonial talks with Elizabeth I of England. She indicated that she would never marry someone she had not met, and Henry III and Catherine de' Medici encouraged Anjou to visit England if only to remove him from the Low Countries. On 5 January 1579 he wrote to the secretary of state, Villeroy, justifying his Dutch expedition. He explained that he could not return to the French court where he was seen by everyone as a 'common criminal'.

---

21 F. Billacois, *Le duel dans la société française des XVIe et XVIIe siècles* (Paris: EHESS, 1986), p. 147.

22 Bourquelot (ed.), *Mémoires de Claude Haton*, vol. 2, p. 937.

Provincial anarchy

Although France was now officially at peace, the real situation, especially in the south, was closer to anarchy. The pattern of the independent nobleman recruiting his own band and waging war in his private interest became clearly established under Henry III. Such a man was Captain Merle who terrorized the hill towns of Gévaudan and Auvergne over ten years. He would only surrender his conquests in return for compensation and frequently ignored the peace treaties signed by his superiors. Such conduct could provoke peasant risings. Thus in 1578 peasants of Provence, called *Razats*, who were made up of Catholics and Protestants, took up arms. Though their main purpose was self-defence, their movement seemed at times aimed at the nobility. In 1579 they massacred a group of nobles at Cuers, and, about the same time, the peasants of Callas sacked the château of their seigneur. Large-scale peasant revolts also broke out in Vivarais and Dauphiné. In 1579 Marshal Bellegarde warned Lesdiguières, the Protestant commander in Dauphiné, that arming peasants threatened seigneurial authority, an opinion shared by Catherine de' Medici. In July 1579 she warned the king that to license 'the armed communes and *menu peuple*' in the name of religion was to invite social unrest. She was aware of bitter hostility between the nobility and the underprivileged.[23]

Among the towns visited by Catherine in 1579 was Romans, a textile centre in Dauphiné. She was greeted by a large crowd of craftsmen led by a draper, Jean Serve, alias Paumier, who had recently wrested control of the town's gates and walls from the local patriciate. Romans was in the grip of serious civil unrest, as was the surrounding countryside. In 1580 the patriciate used the carnival celebrations to stage a comeback: Paumier was murdered and several of his followers executed. These tragic events revealed the rich complexity of French provincial life in the late sixteenth century and underlined the peril of generalizing about the motives behind the Wars of Religion: each town, each community had its own distinctive reasons for resorting to arms. According to Le Roy Ladurie, the uprising in Romans was 'a nearly perfect example of the class struggle', but he also believes that the popular unrest was essentially 'a rejection of the burgeoning of government'. The nobility was attacked in 1579–80 primarily because of its anomalous privilege of tax-exemption.[24]

---

23 Salmon, *Society in Crisis*, pp. 208–10.

24 E. Le Roy Ladurie, *Carnival: A People's Uprising at Romans, 1579–80* (London, 1980), *passim*.

Leading nobles also squabbled among themselves. In Provence, the comte de Carcès, the king's lieutenant, opposed the comte de Suze, whom the king had appointed as provincial governor. In Guyenne, the governor, Henri de Navarre, was opposed by his lieutenant, Marshal Biron. In Languedoc, Coligny, the governor of Montpellier, resisted the provincial governor, Damville. Meanwhile, Huguenot soldiers attacked castles and churches as well as merchants and travellers. Henry III delegated to his mother the task of imposing order in the south. She met Navarre and Damville, signed a treaty at Nérac with the Huguenots on 28 February 1579, and presided over the estates of Languedoc.[25] Wherever she went, Catherine urged mutual understanding while stressing the need to obey the king. She prevailed on the comte de Suze to resign, but the situation in the Midi remained precarious.

Yet it was in the north that the seventh of the Wars of Religion began. It has been called 'the Lovers' War' following a contemporary suggestion that it sprang from Marguerite de Valois' amorous intrigues, but the conflict was really started by Condé, who, angered by Catholic resistance to his becoming governor of Picardy, seized the town of La Fère in November 1579. The prince accused the duc d'Aumale of seeking to revive the Picard League. The confrontation between the houses of Lorraine and Bourbon at La Fère epitomized their struggle to control Picardy.[26]

Fighting also broke out in the Midi, and, in May, Navarre stormed Cahors.[27] Elsewhere, however, the Huguenots suffered setbacks. The duc de Mayenne captured from them the fortress of La Mure in Dauphiné; Marshal Biron prevented Navarre from advancing into Guyenne and, in September 1580, Marshal Matignon recaptured La Fère. Many Protestants, however, kept a low profile. Except for a few places in Languedoc which were stirred up by Coligny's son, François de Châtillon, the province as a whole remained peaceful. The duc d'Anjou also opposed the war, which threatened his plans in the Netherlands. In November 1580 he negotiated the Peace of Fleix, which confirmed the Treaty of Nérac and allowed the Huguenots to retain their surety towns for six more years.[28]

Anjou now hoped that Henry III would support his enterprise by adequate funding, but the king, who was most anxious to avoid a conflict with

25 J.-H. Mariéjol, *Catherine de Médicis* (Paris, 1920), p. 290; H. de la Ferrière and B. de Puchesse (eds.), *Lettres de Catherine de Médicis*, 10 vols (Paris, 1880–1909), vol. 6, pp. 260, 282; vol. 7, p. 446.

26 Carroll, *Noble Power during the French Wars of Religion*, p. 183.

27 J.-P. Babelon, *Henri IV* (Paris, 1982), pp. 273–5.

28 Salmon, *Society in Crisis*, p. 204.

Spain, gave his brother minimal support. After seizing Cambrai in August, Anjou was driven back to the Channel coast. In October he visited England and made a pact with Elizabeth, who nevertheless indicated that she had no intention of marrying him. After returning to the Low Countries, he assumed the title of 'Duke of Brabant', but his fortunes did not improve. By October 1582 he had become desperate. 'Everything is falling apart in ruin,' he wrote, 'and the worst part of it is that I was given hopes which had led me too far to back down now.'[29] An attempt by him to seize Antwerp in January 1583 failed miserably. In October he returned to France for good. However, in March 1584 his health began to deteriorate and he died on 10 June.

The death of Anjou was a momentous event as it raised acutely the problem of the succession to the French throne. For Henry III had no son and seemed unlikely ever to have one. This left the Huguenot leader, Henri de Navarre, as heir presumptive to the throne under the Salic law, a prospect which filled most Catholics with alarm. Henry III sent Épernon to Pau to discuss the succession with Navarre. In talks which lasted nearly a month the duke urged Navarre to abjure his faith in the interest of preserving the king's authority and ensuring the kingdom's welfare. Henry III even threatened to declare Navarre guilty of lèse majesté unless he complied, but the Protestant leader was unmoved.[30] He tried to reassure Catholics by promising them toleration should he become king, but past experience and the persecution of their English co-religionists by Elizabeth I made them fear the worst of a Protestant succession.

The Catholic League

The prospect of a Huguenot becoming the next king of France plunged France into a political crisis more dangerous than any since 1559.[31] In September 1584 Guise, his brothers, the duc de Mayenne and cardinal de Guise, and two other nobles founded an association at Nancy aimed at excluding Navarre from the throne.[32] They looked for support from outside

29 M. P. Holt, *The Duke of Anjou and the Politique Struggle during the Wars of Religion* (Cambridge, 1986), p. 179.

30 M. Wolfe, *The Conversion of Henry IV: Politics, Power and Religious Belief in Early Modern France* (Cambridge, Mass., 1993), pp. 40–41.

31 Ibid., pp. 44–50.

32 Early in the 1580s the Guises became involved in a plot to help their cousin, Mary Stuart, who was a prisoner in England. The duke spent much time in Normandy in 1581 and 1582 preparing an expedition, but it had to be dropped for lack of adequate funding. See Carroll, *Noble Power during the French Wars of Religion*, pp. 188–92.

the kingdom. Philip II had been prepared to support anyone likely to cause trouble in France regardless of religion. In 1577 and 1578 he had made offers to Henri de Navarre; he had even given money to the Huguenots of Guyenne – anything to distract the French from the Netherlands. But Anjou's death changed everything. It caused both rejoicing and concern in Spain: the duke of Parma could now besiege Antwerp without further interference from France, but the prospect of Navarre's succession to the French throne raised the spectre of an openly hostile regime in Paris. Philip's minister, Don Juan de Zúñiga, suggested three possible courses of action: open military intervention, an alliance with Henry III, or a secret alliance with French Catholics. Since the first option was likely to prove ruinous and Henry III had proved unreliable, Zúñiga recommended the third. Noting, however, that the Catholics had no credible candidate for the throne should Henry III die childless, he proposed a marriage between one of Philip's daughters by Elizabeth de Valois and the duke of Savoy. Philip acted accordingly. His envoys signed the secret treaty of Joinville with the Guises on 31 December 1584 and in the following year the duke of Savoy married Philip's daughter, Catalina.[33] Under the Joinville treaty, the parties undertook to defend the Catholic faith and to extirpate Protestantism from France and the Netherlands. They recognized Navarre's aged uncle, cardinal de Bourbon, who was the only Catholic prince of the blood, as the lawful heir to the throne, and promised to see the decrees of the Council of Trent accepted as part of France's 'fundamental laws'. The future king was to renounce France's alliance with the Turks and stop privateering against Spanish shipping. Philip II for his part agreed to subsidize an armed rising by the League to the tune of 600,000 écus.[34]

Many nobles joined the new movement, including the duc de Nevers, the comte de Brissac, the baron de Sennecey, disgraced *mignons* and most of Anjou's former followers. Military operations began simultaneously. After raising troops in Champagne during March 1585, Guise captured Chalon. Meanwhile, Mayenne took Dijon, Mâcon and Auxerre. As governors of Champagne and Burgundy respectively, they rallied their supporters and set about recruiting more. In Brittany, Normandy and Picardy, other members of the Guise family – Mercoeur, Elbeuf and Aumale – stirred up agitation.[35] Soon much of northern and central France passed under Guise control and cardinal de Bourbon was taken to Reims in anticipation of his crowning. On 30 March 1585 the Leaguers published at Péronne a manifesto

33 G. Parker, *The Grand Strategy of Philip II* (New Haven, 1998), p. 172.

34 J.-M. Constant, *La Ligue* (Paris, 1996), p. 115.

35 Carroll, *Noble Power during the French Wars of Religion*, pp. 198–201.

explaining why 'de cardinal of Bourbon, the princes, peers and lords of the cities and communities' were opposing those who threatened to subvert the Catholic religion and the state. The manifesto stressed the risk of persecution which faced Catholics in the event of a Huguenot becoming king. It denounced the warlike acts by Protestants and urged Catholics to prepare for a new civil war. The king's ministers, Joyeuse and Épernon, were accused, without being named, of paving the way to the throne for a heretic and of depriving other nobles of powers and titles in order to secure for themselves complete control of the armed forces. The manifesto also called for the abolition of all taxes and extraordinary subsidies introduced since the reign of Charles IX and for triennial meetings of the Estates-General.[36]

Historians are divided in their interpretation of the Péronne manifesto. While Denis Crouzet has stressed its religious aspect, seeing it as the expression of a mystical urge among Catholic nobles to share in the task of saving society, Arlette Jouanna argues that the defence of material interests, such as 'house' and honour, was at least as important to the Leaguers as spiritual concerns.[37] For they had reason to fear that the exclusion from royal favour, which they had already experienced at the hands of the *mignons*, would become that much worse in the event of a Protestant becoming king. The path to honours would be closed to them, thereby reducing the size of their clientèles by which the greatness of their lineages was measured. Seen from this angle, the Péronne manifesto was a malcontents' charter. In Pasquier's opinion, the princes 'all wanted to share the cake rather than it should be distributed to two or three'.[38] And they had a point: the *mignons* were monopolizing governorships and other offices at their expense. Thus Joyeuse was appointed Admiral instead of Mayenne, and Épernon became colonel-general of the infantry in place of Filippo Strozzi.

Henry III was strangely fatalistic about the crisis which was building up. Writing to Villeroy on 14 August 1584, he admitted feeling like a man who seems content to drown rather than save himself. He set up a new bodyguard, called the Forty-five, made up of young bloods from Gascony and Languedoc, but he lacked the resources necessary to oppose the League by force. Once again, he looked to his mother to extricate him from his predicament. On 9 April she began talking to the duc de Guise and cardinal de Bourbon at Épernay. It is sometimes alleged that her dislike of Épernon made her lean towards the Guises, but the evidence does not bear this out.

---

36 Ibid., pp. 122–5.

37 B. Diefendorf, 'The Catholic League: social crisis or apocalypse now?', *F.H.S.*, 15 (1987), 332–44; D. Crouzet, *Les Guerriers de Dieu*, 2 vols. (Paris, 1990), vol. 2, p. 290; Jouanna, *La France du XVIe siècle*, p. 580.

38 Pasquier, *Lettres historiques*, p. 253.

She did all in her power to defend her son's interests against overwhelming odds.[39] The Guises treated her badly, playing for time as they built up their forces, their aim being not only to destroy Protestantism in France, but also to secure for themselves governorships and surety towns. Writing to the duc de Nevers on 28 May, Guise announced: 'I shall be leaving soon to receive my *reiters* and rapidly to assemble forces everywhere in order to be ready to conclude things as they should be stick in hand, then to fall on the Protestants.' 'All of this,' Catherine, wrote, 'makes me understand that he [Guise] is playing with words.' She 'could see very well, as did everyone else, that it was not religion which motivated them [the Guises], but the wish to surprise towns and to seize money'. Early in June, Catherine reported that Aumale's troops had occupied all the villages around Reims. The people had fled before them as if from devils, leaving villages utterly void of animals, people or goods. 'If this goes on,' wrote Catherine, 'all is lost, everyone is in despair.' She estimated that Guise disposed of 25,000 men and 2,000 horses, excluding the forces of Elbeuf, Brissac and others. On 10 June Schomberg warned the secretary of state, Brulart: 'If the king stands firm, we shall soon see these people at the gates of Paris.'[40] On 7 July the royal negotiators effectively surrendered. Under the treaty of Nemours Henry III promised to pay the troops which had been raised against him and conceded a number of surety towns to the Leaguers, the lion's share going to Guise, whose clients also received favours, pensions and governorships.[41] An edict arising out of the treaty banned Protestant worship and ordered all pastors to leave the kingdom at once. Their flocks were given six months in which to abjure or go into exile. Huguenots were debarred from all public offices and were to hand over the surety towns which they held. Setting aside the Salic law, the edict also deprived Henri de Navarre of his rights to the throne. On 18 July Henry III held a *lit de justice* to get the edict registered. Privately, however, he confided that the edict would bring only ruin to the kingdom.[42]

Navarre, in the meantime, was establishing himself as the military and political leader of the Huguenot party. Since 1575 he had been Protector of the Reformed churches and at their assembly of Montauban (April–May 1581) he had shown political skill. But the Peace of Nemours presented him

39 De la Ferrière and de Puchesse, *Lettres de Catherine de Médicis*, vol. 8, p. 245.

40 Édouard de Barthélemy, 'Catherine de Médicis, le duc de Guise et le traité de Nemours d'après des documents inédits', *R.Q.H.*, xxvii (1880), pp. 465–95. I owe this reference to the kindness of Professor Mark Greengrass.

41 E. Haag, *La France Protestante* (Paris, 1846–59), vol. 10, pp. 184–7; N. M. Sutherland, *The Huguenot Struggle for Recognition* (New Haven, Conn., 1980), p. 364.

42 P. Chevallier, *Henri III roi shakespearien* (Paris, 1985), p. 577.

with his biggest challenge to date. He claimed later that half his moustache had turned white on hearing about the treaty.[43] Writing to Catherine de' Medici, he refused to accept a settlement to which he had not been a party. 'I am bound to oppose with all my strength,' he said, 'those who wish to cause the ruin of the crown and house of France.' On 10 August 1585 Navarre and Condé met Damville near Lavaur and renewed the alliance between Protestants and 'United Catholics'. In a joint manifesto, they accused the house of Lorraine of seeking 'to extinguish the house of France and to take its place'. While affirming their belief in the indestructibility of Protestantism, Navarre and Condé promised to respect Catholics and their faith. The Protestant leaders and Damville reaffirmed their loyalty to the crown and explained that they had no alternative but to fight the Leaguers who were its real enemies.[44]

Henry III may have hoped to get round the treaty of Nemours in the same way as he had evaded the Peace of Monsieur, but the situation was different now. Guise had the support of the majority of Catholic nobles and also of a number of towns. The support gathered by the League is easily explained. The prospect of a Protestant reaching the throne alarmed many town-dwellers. In the League they found the realization of a Christian ideal whose triumph would ensure their salvation. It also held out the hope of a change of regime. The reforms which had been promulgated by the Ordinance of Blois (1579) had so far been largely ineffective: justice was as badly administered as ever, civil war was endemic, pillaging by soldiers was rife, taxation was heavier and the venality of offices continued to flourish.[45] Furthermore, the price of bread had doubled between 1578 and 1586, causing much hardship among the urban poor. All this in addition to the personal unpopularity of Henry III and his *mignons* played into the hands of Guise and his followers.

Among the towns supporting the League, Paris was the most radical.[46] It set up its own organization, which became known as the Sixteen, after the number of districts in the capital from which members of the central committee were elected. The Parisian League was set up late in 1584 by Charles Hotman, sieur de La Rocheblond, and by three clerics: Jean Prévost, Jean Boucher and Matthieu de Launoy. They nominated other Catholic zealots and respectable Parisians to join them. Each new member was required to take an oath of secrecy and loyalty. Even so, a royal agent, Nicolas Poulain,

43 Babelon, *Henri IV*, p. 349.

44 Ibid., p. 355.

45 Mark Greengrass, *France in the Age of Henri IV* (London, 2nd edn, 1995), p. 25.

46 Jouanna, *La France du XVIe siècle*, pp. 581–3.

managed to infiltrate the movement and kept the king informed of its activities. Historians have given close attention to the social composition of the Parisian League. Of its 51 members, 66.5 per cent were lawyers or merchants of middling status; 19.5 per cent were senior civil servants, but they tended to be younger sons. The only nobleman was the sieur d'Effiat, but his membership was short-lived. The clergy was represented by parish priests, monks and Jesuits. A smaller body than the council of the Sixteen co-ordinated the League's activities. It met at the Sorbonne or in the Jesuit house behind the church of Saint-Paul or in the homes of the various members. The Sieur de Mayneville acted as the link between the League and the duc de Guise.

Historical opinion is divided regarding the aims of the Parisian League. According to Élie Barnavi, it was a movement of protest by urban notables of middling rank against the monopoly of major offices enjoyed by relatively few noble families as a consequence of venality.[47] Robert Descimon disagrees. For him, the Parisian League was an attempt by urban officials to restore traditional institutions of local government which had suffered as a result of the crown's excessive promotion of the Robe.[48] Denis Crouzet dismisses these materialistic considerations. For him, the League was an attempt to establish a mystical union with God – the only true king – at a time when many people believed that the world was coming to an end. If its members were to be saved, they needed to rid the kingdom of the pollution of heresy. This was the message disseminated by the League's many preachers and pamphleteers. They warned the people that the Huguenots were planning a massacre as well as Navarre's accession to the throne.[49]

Our knowledge of the early years of the League rests largely on Parisian sources; comparatively little is known about the League in provincial towns, for many of the records have been destroyed. The Parisian Sixteen certainly wanted to set up a network of similar bodies across the kingdom and sent out agents to bring this about. One of them, a lawyer, was sent to Rouen, but we do not know if he succeeded in his mission. What is certain is that pro-League sentiment was widespread in the city. Memories of the bitter conflicts in the 1560s and 1570s remained vivid and people feared that Huguenots might avenge the local massacre of 1572. Furthermore, the citizens were made aware of the persecution of Catholics in England by refugees fleeing across the Channel. A memorandum sent to Henry III by

47 Élie Barnavi, *Le Parti de Dieu. Étude sociale et politique des chefs de la Ligue parisienne, 1585–1594* (Louvain, n.d.).

48 R. Descimon, *Qui étaient les Seize? Mythes et réalités de la Ligue parisienne, 1585–1594* (Paris, 1983).

49 Crouzet, *Les Guerriers de Dieu*, vol. 2, pp. 361–461.

the lieutenant-general, Carrouges, showed that pro-League sentiment was strong among the clergy and the *parlementaires*; less so in the city council. Carrouges took appropriate security measures, but Henry III decided to tighten his hold on Rouen by sending an armed garrison under his favourite, Joyeuse, the new provincial governor. This proved counter-productive. The population pleaded with the king to remove the garrison, which he duly did, causing foreign observers to see this as a defeat for the king.[50] Leagues were certainly set up in towns of the Île-de-France, Champagne, and Burgundy, as well as in Lyon. In April 1585 an anti-Huguenot coup by a small group of Leaguers in Marseille was foiled.[51]

Henry III looked to the Catholics to pay for the war which they were forcing on him. On 11 August 1585 he asked the municipality of Paris for 200,000 écus. At the same tme, he informed the Parlement that he would no longer pay its judges. Henry explained that if he had kept the peace so far, it was not out of disloyalty to the Catholic faith, but because he realized how difficult it would be to break it. He made it clear that he was not prepared to face ruin alone and warned the cardinal de Guise that he would not hesitate to help himself to church revenues.[52] On 9 September Pope Sixtus V issued a bull depriving Navarre and Condé of their rights to the French throne. Henry III refused to publish it, as it contradicted the Salic law, but copies circulated among the general public. While Gallicans were shocked at this papal intrusion into France's domestic affairs, the Leaguers rejoiced. Protestants were naturally furious. On 11 October Navarre, using the pen of Duplessis-Mornay, protested formally to the Parlement. Meanwhile, on 1 October Damville issued a manifesto. His policy, he declared, was to keep the peace, to place his trust in a future church council, to uphold the laws of the kingdom and the rights of princes of the blood.[53]

On 7 October Henry III issued an edict even harsher for the Huguenots than that of 18 July. They were now branded as traitors whose goods were to be sold for the king's benefit, and were allowed only six months in which to abjure or leave the kingdom. All Condé's followers were to be hunted down and their property seized. Navarre responded on 30 November by ordering the confiscation of property belonging to noblemen and churchmen who had joined 'the enemies of the state'. Writing to Catherine de' Medici, he warned that the papacy was using religion to dispose of the

50 P. Benedict, *Rouen during the Wars of Religion* (Cambridge, 1981), pp. 168–71.
51 W. Kaiser, *Marseille au temps des troubles, 1559–1596* (Paris, 1991), pp. 263–9.
52 Chevallier, *Henri III*, p. 578.
53 Ibid., pp. 581–2.

French crown as it wished and that Henry III himself might find himself deposed.[54] Both sides appealed to public opinion before coming to blows. On 1 January 1586 Navarre wrote to the three estates. He reminded the clergy of their Christian duty to keep the peace. Turning to the nobles, he showed that the honour of the kingdom was at stake. How could they allow its fate to be decided from outside by the pope? He deplored in advance the shedding of noble blood which France needed to defend herself against foreign aggressors. Navarre's letter to the third estate was also compassionate. 'I am complaining,' he wrote, 'that I cannot defend myself without causing innocent people to suffer. I am born a Frenchman. I sympathize with your woes. I have tried to exempt you from civil wars and I will never spare my life to cut them short.' Such persuasive pleading had to be countered by the League. One of its founders, Louis Dorléans, in a work entitled *Avertissement des catholiques anglais aux Français catholiques* (Warning by the English Catholics to the French Catholics), warned his co-religionists of the fate they could expect if they allowed a heretic to become king: they would endure the same persecution as English Catholics were suffering under Elizabeth.[55]

Propaganda alone could not win a war; money was needed to pay for arms. When the clergy met in October, Henry III required his finance minister, Bellièvre, to show that four armies were needed to fight the Huguenots and that their upkeep would cost two million livres per month. The clergy reluctantly agreed to the sale of church lands worth 50,000 écus per annum. The bishop of Paris was sent to Rome in order to get papal permission for a more substantial sale of church property. Sixtus V agreed to an alienation of 100,000 écus in two instalments. This angered the clergy, who felt that their traditional exemption from taxation was being impugned. Henry III threatened to hold a *lit de justice* to enforce publication of the bull, but before any proceeds of the sale could reach his coffers, war with the Huguenots got under way.

Thanks to their alliance with Damville, the Huguenots had managed to strengthen their position in Guyenne and Languedoc. In Dauphiné Lesdiguières had recaptured several towns; in Poitou Condé had repulsed an invasion by Mercoeur, but had then laid siege to Brouage. After being defeated, he had fled to Guernsey. If the military situation in south-west France was confused early in 1586, along the north-east border it was clear enough. Measures had to be taken to stop an invasion by German *reiters*. Early in March 1586 the king gave Henri de Guise command of

54 Ibid., p. 582.
55 Ibid., pp. 583–4.

50 companies of infantry and between 5,000 and 6,000 cavalry. Another royal army under Marshal d'Aumont was sent to Auvergne and Languedoc, while Biron fought Condé. Within two months, the latter seized Saint Jean d'Angély. However, Henry III showed no inclination to fight seriously. According to de Thou, he had given secret instructions to certain trustworthy governors to fight only half-heartedly. It seems that Henry, underestimating the League's fanaticism, still hoped for peace. On 26 April, he pandered to it by publishing another harsh edict against the Huguenots, yet as Holy Week approached, he set off on a religious retreat to Chartres.[56] Meanwhile, fighting continued. Mayenne and Biron captured Monségur and Lusignan respectively for the king, but his generals were criticized at court for being lethargic. Henry III tried to silence criticism by giving commands to his two favourites, Joyeuse and Épernon. The former was sent to Auvergne and Languedoc, and the latter to Dauphiné and Provence.

Both sides in the war were desperately poor. On 16 June Henry went to the Parlement to obtain registration of 27 fiscal edicts, a legislative avalanche which infuriated Parisians. Placards insulting the king and his mother soon appeared all over the capital.[57] Meanwhile, Navarre managed to get English help. Elizabeth I offered him 50,000 crowns, then doubled the amount after learning of Parma's victories in the Netherlands. The money was paid to John Casimir, regent of the Palatinate, who also received a subsidy from the king of Denmark. He promised in return to raise an army of 8,000 *reiters* to assist the Huguenots. As the threat of a German invasion grew, Catherine de' Medici again offered her diplomatic services. She was hampered on all sides, notably by the pope, who warned her that Henry III would never reign in peace unless heresy were extirpated from his kingdom. The League, too, opposed a settlement. Its preachers in Paris accused the king of dealing in secret with Navarre and of deliberately impeding the war effort. In September Henri de Guise and the cardinals of Guise and Bourbon met near Noyon. They decided to reject any peace, to stand by the last anti-Huguenot edict and to act independently of the king. Meanwhile, Catherine tried to persuade Navarre to negotiate. Despite her age and poor health, she travelled south along dangerous roads in winter. Navarre agreed to meet her at Saint-Brice, near Cognac, but he was playing for time pending the arrival of John Casimir's *reiters*.[58] He said he needed first to consult the Protestant churches. On 13 March Catherine returned to Chenonceaux empty-handed.

56 *Journal de l'Estoile pour le règne de Henri III*, ed. L.-R. Lefèvre (Paris, 1943), p. 446.

57 Ibid., pp. 449–50.

58 Babelon, *Henri IV*, p. 370; Pasquier, *Lettres historiques*, pp. 263–4.

In the meantime, Catholic opinion in France was outraged by the execution in England of Mary Queen of Scots. She was instantly elevated to the rank of Catholic martyr, and a torrent of abuse directed at Elizabeth I and her Huguenot allies poured from the League's pulpits and presses. Henry III was accused of having betrayed her. A rumour circulated in Paris that 10,000 Huguenots were concealed in the suburbs, waiting for a signal to avenge the massacre of St Bartholomew's Day. In February Henry III had shut himself up in the Louvre after learning of a plot by the League to kidnap him and force him to hand over power. On 15 March another plot to remove him came to light.[59] Guise, who was defending the border of Champagne, was not to blame. In fact, he warned the Sixteen not to act without him and they duly complied. Meanwhile, they offered Henry an army of 24,000 men, paid for by the Leaguer towns and under their own commanders, to defend the kingdom against the *reiters*. At the same time a new oath was proposed for members of the League whereby their obedience to the king was made conditional on his acting as a true Catholic.

Henry III had, in effect, lost control of the kingdom. The Guises were doing as they pleased: Guise besieged Sedan and Jametz, towns belonging to the duc de Bouillon, while Aumale seized towns in Picardy. In May Catherine de' Medici had talks in Reims with Guise and the cardinal de Bourbon. They agreed to extend a truce recently signed at Bouillon, but refused to hand over the towns of Doullens and Le Crotoy to the duc de Nevers, whom the king had appointed as governor of Picardy. Early in July, Henry met Guise at Meaux and tried unsuccessfully to persuade him to make concessions to the Huguenots. Although the duke made a great show of his obedience to the king, his real master, as he admitted to the Spanish ambassador, Bernardino de Mendoza, in June, was Philip II of Spain.[60]

The War of the Three Henrys (1587–1589)

The relief army which John Casimir, regent of the Palatinate, had raised with money from Elizabeth I, the king of Denmark and the German princes invaded the duchy of Lorraine in August 1587. It consisted of 4,000 *reiters*, 3,000 *landsknechts*, 12,000 Swiss and 2,300 men under the young duc de Bouillon. John Casimir having declined the overall command, this was

59 *Journal de l'Estoile*, pp. 486–8.

60 De Lamar Jensen, *Diplomacy and Dogmatism: Bernardino de Mendoza and the French Catholic League* (Cambridge, Mass., 1964), pp. 51–5, 70–71, 73, 87–8.

entrusted to baron Fabian von Dohna, whose general staff comprised a number of French nobles, notably Condé's secretary, La Huguerie, who wrote an account of the expedition. In the absence of a prince of the blood, Navarre had asked that Bouillon be given supreme authority. But the commanders disagreed from the start about objectives. Bouillon wanted to relieve his own fortresses which the Guises were besieging; Navarre had ordered Lorraine to be sacked so as to punish its duke for his support of the Guises and of the League; John Casimir wanted the war to be taken into France. As for the German troops themselves, they were keen to remain as near as possible to the northern border of France. From Lorraine, the relief army entered Champagne where it was joined by François de Châtillon and troops from Languedoc. Navarre wanted the army to wait at Roanne until he could join it.

Meanwhile, the king sent Joyeuse to fight Navarre in the west. The duke knew that Épernon had displaced him in the king's favour, and hoped that a victory would help him regain lost ground. As he was now related by marriage to the Guises, a victory might also qualify him to head the League. His army comprised 6,000 foot (i.e. four regiments of arquebusiers) and 2,000 horse (i.e. 24 companies of *gens d'armes*, six of *chevau-légers* and two of Albanians). After gathering his forces at Saumur, he moved into Poitou at the end of July. As Navarre's army was too small relatively to risk a battle, he withdrew to the safety of La Rochelle after evacuating a number of towns of lesser importance and strengthening others with supplies and munitions. Joyeuse, in the meantime, overran Poitou, putting to the sword entire garrisons; but disease and desertion soon weakened his army.[61] On 15 August he returned to Paris after ordering his camp master, Lavardin, to seek refreshment for his army in Touraine. Emerging from La Rochelle, Navarre with a force of only 200 horse and 300 arquebusiers pursued Lavardin as far as Chinon but lacked the artillery needed to dislodge him from the town. He did, however, recover Poitou in less than a fortnight and almost reached the Loire.

Following the lavish celebrations in Paris for Épernon's marriage to Marguerite de Foix-Candale, Henry III left Paris on 12 September.[62] He went first to Étampes, where the duke was to take up his command of the 24,000 strong army of the Midi, then to the river Loire where he took up a position aimed at preventing a link-up between Navarre and the relief army from Germany. As for Joyeuse, he raised a new army at Tours before resuming operations in Poitou. Navarre, in the meantime, allied with two

---

61 *Journal de l'Estoile*, p. 495.
62 Ibid., pp. 501, 503.

Catholic members of the house of Bourbon: François de Bourbon, prince de Conti, and Charles de Bourbon, comte de Soissons. He also recruited nobles in Maine, Anjou and Normandy. A small force, led by Turenne, crossed the Loire from the south and attacked a force which Mercoeur was bringing to Joyeuse from Brittany. Joyeuse tried unsuccessfully to prevent Turenne from retreating across the Loire. At Saumur he learnt that the enemy had crossed the river and was heading for Loudun.

Exactly what Navarre was planning at this stage is unclear. It seems that the renewed royal offensive took him by surprise and that he longed for John Casimir's *reiters* to take some of the pressure off him; but they were not keen to go further south into France. They were tired after their long marches, their supplies were running short and they were all too aware of the hatred which they aroused among the local population. On finding Henry III encamped at Gien, they decided to follow the right bank of the river and push westward towards Tours and Saumur. Navarre's own army was too small to risk a confrontation with Henry III's army. Seeing that winter was approaching, his only practical option was to fall back on Guyenne, to raise more troops and to join forces with Damville. Joyeuse set off in pursuit. He tried to prevent Navarre from crossing the river Isle near Coutras, but Navarre managed to slip past him. On 20 October 1587 Joyeuse decided to attack. Though not particularly well placed, Navarre accepted the challenge. The two opposing armies faced each other on a plain east of Coutras. They were of roughly equal size: each had between 4,000 and 5,000 infantry; the Huguenots had 1,200 to 1,500 horse, and Joyeuse 1,500 to 1,800 horse. But they were soberly dressed, hardened veterans, whereas Joyeuse's cavalry was made up of inexperienced young noblemen anxious to show off their valour. They wore velvet doublets, silk sashes and multicoloured plumes. Before battle was joined, the Huguenots offered up prayers to the Almighty and sang the 118th psalm. Their guns then opened fire, wreaking havoc among Joyeuse's infantry. His cavalry then charged only to give way at several points to a counter-charge by Navarre's cavalry. While some of Joyeuse's men fled, others, including the duke himself and his younger brother Claude, were cut down. The battle lasted only two hours. Two thousand royalist dead remained on the field, including 300 noblemen. According to Mornay, the Huguenots lost only two nobles 'of mediocre condition' and barely 30 men. Navarre ordered the wounded to be cared for, the dead to be honoured and many prisoners to be released without ransom.[63]

63 D. Buisseret, *Henry IV* (London, 1984), pp. 21–5; *Journal de l'Estoile*, pp. 505–6; Pasquier, *Lettres historiques*, pp. 268–70.

Coutras was Navarre's first real battle. Previously he had fought only in skirmishes or surprise attacks on towns. His latest biographer has summed up his martial qualities as follows:

> Henry did not think in terms of a 'campaign'; he reacted on the spur of the moment to a given situation: it was in the field that his faculties lit up. When he thought it necessary to fight, all his senses – faultless observation, perspicacious judgement – were aroused. His mind excelled and his eye ruled supreme when he needed to assess a site, select a position, seize a favorable opportunity, and to spring a surprise. His youthful determination and personal bravery allowed him to lead his cavalry squadrons by force of example, then to turn a situation into a victory. He was a fighter par excellence.[64]

But Navarre was no strategist. Instead of following up his victory by joining the German relief army north of the Loire, he allowed his army to break up and went to Béarn to lay captured Catholic standards at the feet of his mistress, Corisande d'Andoins. As Sully put it: 'after eight days all the hoped for fruits of so great and signal a victory floated away like smoke on the wind'.[65]

Meanwhile, the relief army advanced westward towards the Beauce, but it soon began to fall apart. The *reiters* set off on their own only to be defeated twice by Guise, first at Vimory on 26 October, then at Auneau on 24 November. The Swiss, in the meantime, came to terms with Henry III: they agreed to go home in return for four months' pay, supplies and equipment worth 50,000 écus.[66] On 8 December the Germans surrendered to Henry III: they agreed to depart in return for cash and under a strong escort. Guise, who had hoped to annihilate the Germans on their return through Lorraine, felt cheated of the fruits of victory; Catholic zealots, infuriated by the settlement, blamed Épernon.[67] On 23 December Henry III returned to Paris in triumph. He attended a *Te Deum* at Notre-Dame and ordered a magnificent funeral for Joyeuse; but the plaudits of the crowd could not hide the fact that the only victorious commanders of the war had been the king's enemies: Guise and Navarre. The League's preachers in Paris praised Guise's bravery without which 'the ark would have fallen to the Philistines'. The Sorbonne decreed that a ruler whose conduct was not acceptable could be lawfully deposed.[68] The pope, for his part, complained

64 Babelon, *Henry IV*, pp. 383–4.
65 D. Buisseret and B. Barbiche (eds.), *Les oeconomies royales de Sully* (Paris, 1970), p. 196.
66 *Journal de l'Estoile*, p. 507; Pasquier, *Lettres historiques*, pp. 273–7.
67 R. Bonney, *The King's Debts* (Oxford, 1981), p. 25.
68 *Journal de l'Estoile*, p. 508.

that money which he had allowed the king to raise had been used to subsidize the kingdom's destroyers.

Henry III now provoked the League's fury by giving Épernon offices previously held by Joyeuse. He became governor of Normandy and Admiral of France. He was also appointed governor of Angoumois, Aunis and Saintonge in place of Bellegarde, who had been killed at Coutras. Guise had wanted the governorship of Normandy as a reward for defeating the Germans. The appointment of Épernon, as Pasquier noted, lost Henry III more nobles than had been killed at Coutras.[69] The duke was accused by the League of robbing the kingdom. His personal wealth may not have been as large as the League imagined, but it had been built up within a decade. A flood of pamphlets and woodcuts portrayed him as the Devil incarnate. One pamphlet, called *The tragic and memorable history of Piers Gaveston, Gascon nobleman, formerly the favourite of Edward II king of England*, was but a thinly disguised incitement to murder Épernon.[70] On 4 and 9 March Henry III gave splendid funerals to Anne and Claude de Joyeuse. A commemorative medal was struck bearing the inscription, *Victima pro salvo domino, fit in aethere sidus*: Having given his life to save the king, Joyeuse had become a star in the firmament. In the meantime, news reached Paris of Condé's death at Saint-Jean d'Angély following a brief illness, and the League lit bonfires in celebration.

The Day of the Barricades (12 May 1588)

The duc de Guise needed to topple Épernon before gaining the king's favour, without which his clientèle was likely to fall away. For he was far from wealthy. Cavriana, the Tuscan agent, estimated his income in 1588 at 100,000 écus and his debts as 700,000 écus. By the end of Henry III's reign these had risen to one million livres.[71] One means of putting pressure on the king was for Guise to ally with the Parisian League. But he needed to look beyond the toppling of Épernon to the royal succession, no less. For who would succeed Henry III, should he die childless? The candidate most acceptable to Catholics was cardinal de Bourbon, but, being in his sixties, he was unlikely to rule for long. Did Guise think of seeking the throne for himself or for one of his relatives? No one knows; but a pamphlet attributed

---

69 Pasquier, *Lettres historiques*, p. 270; Bonney, *The King's Debts*, p. 25.

70 Chevallier, *Henri III*, p. 436; *Journal de l'Estoile*, p. 569.

71 Boucher, *La cour de Henri III*, pp. 91–2.

to Pierre d'Épinac, archbishop of Lyon, is suggestive. After advising the duke on the best ways of getting round the king, he suggests that he should first seek to become Constable. This might enable him to create a new royal dynasty as the mayor of the palace, Charles Martel, had done in the eighth century.[72]

Early in 1588 Guise and the other main Leaguers met at Nancy and addressed a number of demands to the king. They asked for Épernon's dismissal, the acceptance of Guise tutelage in the fight against heresy, and publication of the decrees of the Council of Trent. Guise then overran the territory of the duc de Bouillon, who had just died, and blockaded Sedan. Aumale, in the meantime, tried to stir up trouble for Épernon in Normandy. He could count on the backing of Spain, as Philip II instructed his ambassador, Mendoza, to harm the favourite by every possible means. 'The people of France,' wrote L'Estoile, 'poisoned by the false words of the League, hated this man to death, and called him the chief of the Navarrists and politiques.'[73] During the spring of 1588 several attempts were made to murder him, causing the king to tighten security at the Louvre.

Political tension in Paris was aggravated by economic factors. Since 1586 the cost of food had risen steadily and beggars were flocking into the capital from the countryside. In August, 'the poor people of the countryside, dying of hunger went about in gangs and cut the half-ripe grain in the fields, then ate it on the spot . . . in spite of the measures taken by the owners of the fields. Sometimes they threatened to eat them too, if they would not allow them to eat the grain.'[74] The crisis lasted through the winter of 1586–7. Parisians were each asked to contribute 7 livres 16 sols per annum for the upkeep of the poor. On 3 June 1587 a *setier* of corn cost 30 livres at the Halles. On 22 July there was a popular rising against bakers.[75] In the spring of 1588 the fiscal demands of the government fuelled popular unrest in the capital, but similar troubles also occurred elsewhere. A royal attempt to regulate guilds caused a popular revolt at Troyes and the plundering of houses owned by Italian merchants. In December 1586 some 20 Norman villages refused to pay the *taille* and other taxes.

Tension between the king and Guise exploded in May. The duke, who had been forbidden by the king to enter the capital, chose to defy the ban in response to an invitation from the Sixteen. Guise tried to justify his conduct to the king, who decided not to arrest him. During the night of

72 J.-M. Constant, *Les Guise* (Paris, 1984), pp. 205–7.
73 *Journal de l'Estoile*, p. 545.
74 Ibid., p. 456.
75 Ibid., pp. 493, 499.

11 May, however, Henry introduced troops into the capital and posted them in various strategic places. His aim, so it was said, was to round up Guise's supporters and execute them. The Parisians, however, shocked by the king's infringement of their traditional right of self-defence, poured into the streets and erected barricades.[76] The royal troops came under attack from the mob, while royal ministers sent out to help them ran into trouble. At first, Guise did nothing to appease the Parisians, but eventually he rode through the streets in response to an appeal from Henry. Such was the duke's popularity that he was able to bring the troops to safety, but the Parisians remained under arms. On 13 May Henry slipped away from the capital and went to Chartres.[77]

As Paris fell under the control of the Sixteen, Guise occupied various towns around the capital in order to safeguard its supplies pending a confrontation with the king. This, however, did not happen, largely as a result of Catherine de' Medici's mediation. Eventually Henry III accepted nearly all the League's demands in a new Edict of Union: he dismissed Épernon, reaffirmed the Treaty of Nemours, recognized the cardinal de Bourbon as heir-presumptive to the throne, bestowed more governorships on the Guises, and appointed the duke himself as Lieutenant-general of the kingdom. But the Parisian League took no chances: measures were taken to defend the capital against a possible royal attack and the militia was purged to ensure its loyalty.

The Estates-General of Blois (1588)

While resisting all attempts to lure him back to Paris, Henry III prepared to avenge his recent humiliation. On 8 September, he surprised everyone by sacking all his ministers, replacing them by hard-working young men.[78] Henry also called a meeting of the Estates-General. He tried to influence the elections, but most of the deputies supported the League, which was able to exploit the king's failure to pay the salaries of office-holders and the interest due to *rentiers*. Revenues normally used to pay them had been diverted by Henry towards paying for the war. By 1585 office-holders were owed more than a year's pay and arrears of *rentes* amounted to over 4 million livres. On 12 August 1588 the *Chambre des Comptes* asked for the appointment of new ministers who would run the king's finances efficiently and honestly. It asked for contractual obligations to be honoured before

76 Ibid., p. 551; Pasquier, *Lettres historiques*, pp. 286–301.
77 Constant, *Les Guise*, pp. 166–79; Pasquier, *Lettres historiques*, pp. 302–3.
78 Pasquier, *Lettres historiques*, pp. 329–32.

revenues were assigned to other expenses, and complained that existing financial ordinances were not being applied. On 19 December the king agreed to the creation of a *chambre de justice* or extraordinary financial tribunal, whose members were to be chosen by the estates. Despite Henry III's acceptance of some of their fiscal demands, they remained truculent. Claiming that monarchs owed their authority to the estates, they asked to know why their decisions needed to be ratified by the king's council. Henry suspected that members of the third estate were being manipulated by the aristocratic League. He also felt sure that Guise had encouraged the duke of Savoy's invasion of Saluzzo in October.[79]

Although Henry had often seemed feeble in the past, he now acted ruthlessly. On 23 December the duc de Guise was lured to the king's chamber in the château of Blois and brutally murdered by the Forty-five, Henry's bodyguard. Next day, the duke's brother, the cardinal de Guise, was also murdered, while other prominent Leaguers and members of the Guise family were imprisoned. They included the cardinal de Bourbon, the League's candidate for the royal succession. Henry claimed that the Guises had been plotting his deposition and death, but the murder of the Guises, far from bringing him security, proved an unmitigated disaster. What little credit he had left among many Catholics disappeared. Even his most loyal supporters expressed revulsion at the crime.[80] The Estates wound up their business quietly, but in parts of France controlled by the League news of the murders set off an explosion of grief and anger. Henry III's crime gave a tremendous boost to the League in towns all over France. Whereas in May 1588 it had only controlled a few towns outside Paris (Sens, Troyes and Auxerre), early in 1589 it gained control of many more, including Agen, Amiens, Bourges, Dijon, Le Mans, Nantes, Poitiers, Rouen and Toulouse. Only Lyon held out for a short time. In all these towns moderate councillors were replaced by radical Leaguers, who were for the most part merchants, lawyers and lesser office-holders. Being mainly concerned to promote and defend their own private interests, they viewed the leaders of the aristocratic League with suspicion, even hostility. A system of provincial councils was soon set up to co-ordinate their actions. In some towns, like Marseille and Arles, Leaguer dictatorships were set up which lay outside the control of the Guises, the Sixteen and the provincial councils.[81] If the towns north of the Loire supported the League, some in the south, including

79 Chevallier, *Henri III*, pp. 656–62; Pasquier, *Lettres historiques*, pp. 337–50.

80 Wolfe, *The Conversion of Henry IV* (Cambridge, Mass., 1993), p. 42; Bonney, *The King's Debts*, pp. 28–9.

81 M. P. Holt, *The French Wars of Religion* (Cambridge, 1995), pp. 134–5.

Toulouse and Marseille, also did so. A number of provincial governors did likewise. Among them was Guise's younger brother, Charles, duc de Mayenne, who now became the effective leader of the aristocratic League.[82]

Nowhere was the reaction to the murders in Blois stronger than in Paris, where preachers called for vengeance on 'the new Herod'. In Crouzet's opinion, the assassination of the Guises was seen by many people as an eschatological premonition. Henry III was identified with Antichrist and the capital swept by a veritable wave of expiatory processions. Some were official and linked to religious services, but others were popular and seemingly spontaneous. Huge crowds of nude penitents and of children clad in white walked through the streets, sometimes at night. Historians have assumed that the participants had been mobilized by fanatical preachers, but Denis Richet has suggested that the processions may have been an outward manifestation of an underlying spirit of Catholic regeneration which was to outlast the civil wars.[83] Within hours of the news from Blois reaching Paris, pamphlets circulated, exalting the Guises as martyrs. Their cousin, the duc d'Aumale, was appointed governor by the town assembly. A new revolutionary body, the Council of Forty, was added to the municipal council. Its members – 9 clergymen, 7 noblemen and 24 of the third estate – repudiated their allegiance to the blood-soaked tyrant of Blois, a measure ratified by the Faculty of Theology of the university. On 7 January 1589 the council released Frenchmen from their obedience to the king and called on them to take up arms. In May Pope Sixtus V summoned Henry III to Rome to explain his conduct, under threat of excommunication.

Meanwhile, a new administration was set up in Paris. Special committees of nine members in each district elected representatives to a council of the Sixteen. The homes of 'politiques' were searched, taxes imposed on the rich 'for the defence of the Catholic religion'. At the same time, the mob attacked royal images. A picture of the king and the Order of the Holy Spirit in the Augustinian church was destroyed, as were the tombs of the *mignons* in the church of Saint-Paul. On 16 January a group of Leaguers broke into the Parlement and carried off the first president, Achille de Harlay, and two of his colleagues. Brisson was appointed in his place and other vacancies filled by Leaguers. The Châtelet, too, was purged. Packed as it now was, the Parlement unanimously recognized cardinal de Bourbon

---

82 *Journal de l'Estoile*, pp. 580–4; Pasquier, *Lettres historiques*, pp. 351–76; Constant, *Les Guise*, pp. 9–19, 226–8; Chevallier, *Henri III*, pp. 662–77.

83 Crouzet, *Les Guerriers de Dieu*, vol. 2, p. 379; D. Richet, 'Politique et religion: les processions à Paris en 1589', in *De la réforme à la Révolution* (Paris, 1991), pp. 69–82. On the preachers, see A. Lebigre, *La révolution des curés* (Paris, 1980). Richet argues that their influence has been exaggerated by historians.

as King Charles X of France, but as he was Henry III's prisoner, decisions had to be taken in his name.[84]

On 12 February Mayenne entered the capital at the head of an army. Although lacking the charm and charisma of his murdered brother, he was politically astute and had built up a strong clientèle in his *gouvernement* of Burgundy.[85] The capital acclaimed him as a saviour and the Sixteen appointed him Lieutenant-general of the kingdom. But Mayenne, who was no democrat, promptly added 14 of his friends to the General Council of the Union and the Council of Forty. He also reserved to himself all political decisions. He set up his own administration, comprising a council of state, a keeper of the seals and secretaries of state. In exchange for large ransoms, he secured the release of the *parlementaires* from the Bastille.

The assassination of Henry III (1 August 1589)

Following the death of Catherine de' Medici on 5 January 1589, Henry III found himself alone.[86] He was caught between the forces of the League to the north and east and those of the Huguenots in the south. The king controlled three towns on the Loire (Tours, Blois, and Beaugency), Bordeaux and the provinces of Berry and Dauphiné. He badly needed an ally as well as money. He was reduced to pawning the crown jewels to help pay for the war. On 17 February he secured a loan of 1.2 million livres, but his credit rating was too low to attract larger amounts. He also borrowed quite small sums from members of his entourage. Only by allying with Henri de Navarre could he hope to fight on. The king may have assumed that the financial help Navarre was getting from abroad was more substantial and his troops more numerous and better paid than was the case.[87] On 26 April the two Henrys signed a truce. Four days later, at Pléssis-lès-Tours, they sealed their accord. Taking this as further confirmation of Henry III's secret atheism, the Leaguers called on all true Catholics to resist the 'vilain Hérode'.[88] Combining their armies, the two Henrys marched on

84 Constant, *La Ligue*, pp. 213–41; E. Barnavi and R. Descimon, *La Sainte Ligue, le juge et la potence* (Paris, 1985), pp. 46–71; Pasquier, *Lettres historiques*, pp. 316–24.

85 H. Drouot, *Mayenne et la Bourgogne. Étude sur la Ligue (1587–96)* (Paris, 1937), vol. 1, pp. 173–83; *Journal de l'Estoile*, p. 614.

86 Pasquier, *Lettres historiques*, pp. 386–90.

87 Bonney, *The King's Debts*, p. 29.

88 Wolfe, *The Conversion of Henry IV*, p. 43.

Paris, capturing Senlis and Pontoise on the way. As they laid siege to the capital – Henry III at Saint-Cloud and Navarre at Meudon – a frenzy of anti-Valois sentiment exploded among the inhabitants. Processions invoked the Almighty's assistance, preachers clamoured for Henry III's extermination as Satan's agent. Among those who heard the message was a young Dominican friar, Jacques Clément. On 1 August he went from Paris to the king's camp. On being admitted to Henry III's presence, he stabbed him fatally. Henry was the first king of France to die by the hand of one of his own subjects. His assassination demonstrated how far the mystique of monarchy had sunk since 1572. Before dying, Henry recognized Navarre as his heir, but warned him that he would only gain the throne by becoming a Catholic.[89]

It was with jubilation that Parisians greeted the news of the king's death. It was seen by many Catholics as the completion of the sacred mission which the massacre of St Bartholomew had only partially fulfilled. Henry's demise seemed to remove the last obstacle in the path of a Catholic triumph in France. Clément was 'canonized' by the League's propagandists. 'A new David has killed Goliath,' wrote Boucher, 'a new Judith has killed Holofernes.'

89 Pasquier, *Lettres historiques*, pp. 431–4; Chevallier, *Henri III*, pp. 696–704.

CHAPTER TWELVE

The conquest of the kingdom (1589–1592)

Before he died, Henry III recognized Henri de Navarre as his heir.[1] This ensured him much support among members of the late king's entourage, but Navarre's Protestantism was unacceptable to many Catholics. Following heated arguments between commanders of the Catholic army at Saint-Cloud, François d'O conveyed their terms to Henri: he was to abjure his faith, banish all Protestant worship in France and reserve all offices to Catholics. Henri refused, but on 4 August he declared that he would uphold the Catholic faith 'without changing anything' and his fervent desire was to be instructed in it by 'a good, legitimate and free general national council'.[2] He promised to call such a body within six months. Protestant rights would be guaranteed pending a peace settlement. Towns and fortresses captured from the rebels would be placed under Catholic control. Henri also promised to punish those who had plotted Henry III's assassination and to protect his servants.[3] Having accepted these terms, the Catholic captains recognized Henri as King Henry IV. They asked him to call a meeting of his followers within two months to discuss state affairs pending a meeting of the Estates-General. The League, of course, remained resolutely hostile to the new king. On 7 August the Parlement of Paris recognized cardinal de Bourbon as King Charles X even though he was still a prisoner, and even among Catholic servants of the late king there were many defections, notably Montholon, the Keeper of the Seals, the dukes of Épernon and Nevers.

1 For reactions to the regicide see M. Wolfe, *The Conversion of Henry IV* (Cambridge, Mass., 1993), pp. 50–8.

2 R. Bonney, *The King's Debts* (Oxford, 1981), p. 30.

3 D. Buisseret, *Henry IV* (London, 1984), p. 28; J.-P. Babelon, *Henri IV* (Paris, 1982), pp. 456–7; Wolfe, *The Conversion of Henry IV*, pp. 56–7.

Henry IV tried to stem the disintegration of his army by addressing his captains on the evening of 4 August. Repeating his promises in the Saint-Cloud Declaration, he criticized deserters as men devoid of virtue and honour and those who stayed by his side as '*gens de bien*' whom God always protects.[4] But his words failed to convince many. As soldiers deserted rather than serve a heretic, the royal army besieging Paris dwindled in size from 40,000 to 18,000.[5] With so few men at his disposal Henry had to lift the siege.

The new king was pitifully weak. He described himself as a king without a kingdom, a husband without a wife, and a warrior without money. He sold off his patrimonial lands in Béarn and Navarre or mortgaged them to creditors. He might have helped himself by renouncing Henry III's debts, but such a course would have been politically risky. On 14 August 1589 Henry signed an agreement with a mercenary captain, called Dompmartin. He was to levy 1500 *reiters* by 25 October and received an advance payment of 27,000 livres. In return, Henry undertook to pay the troops in monthly instalments with no more than a fortnight's delay. All arrears of pay were to be settled before the troops were disbanded or immediately after a royal victory, but the promise could not be fulfilled, as the king's revenues were neither regular nor predictable. Everything rested on his retaining the trust of the mercenary captains. A declaration of bankruptcy would have lost him his army.[6]

Outside the Protestant areas of the Midi, only seven large towns (Caen, Châlons-sur-Marne, Clermont, Compiègne, Dieppe, Langres and Tours) supported Henry IV. Although urged by several of his advisers to retire south of the Loire, the king preferred to go to Normandy. He had been told that more towns might declare for him if he visited them in person; he also wanted to be closer to potential assistance from England. In the meantime he appealed to the various authorities in provincial France to declare their loyalty and confirmed the administration which Henry III had set up at Tours following his flight from the Parisian League. The duc de Mayenne followed Henry into Normandy declaring that he would either throw him into the sea or bring him back to Paris in chains.[7]

The battle of Arques (21 September 1589)

On reaching Dieppe on 26 August, Henry began to fortify the town and its suburb of Le Pollet. Mayenne, moving slowly as usual, reached it on

4 Wolfe, *The Conversion of Henry IV*, p. 57.

5 Buisseret, *Henry IV*, p. 28.

6 Bonney, *The King's Debts*, pp. 34–5.

7 J.-M. Constant, *La Ligue* (Paris, 1996), p. 349.

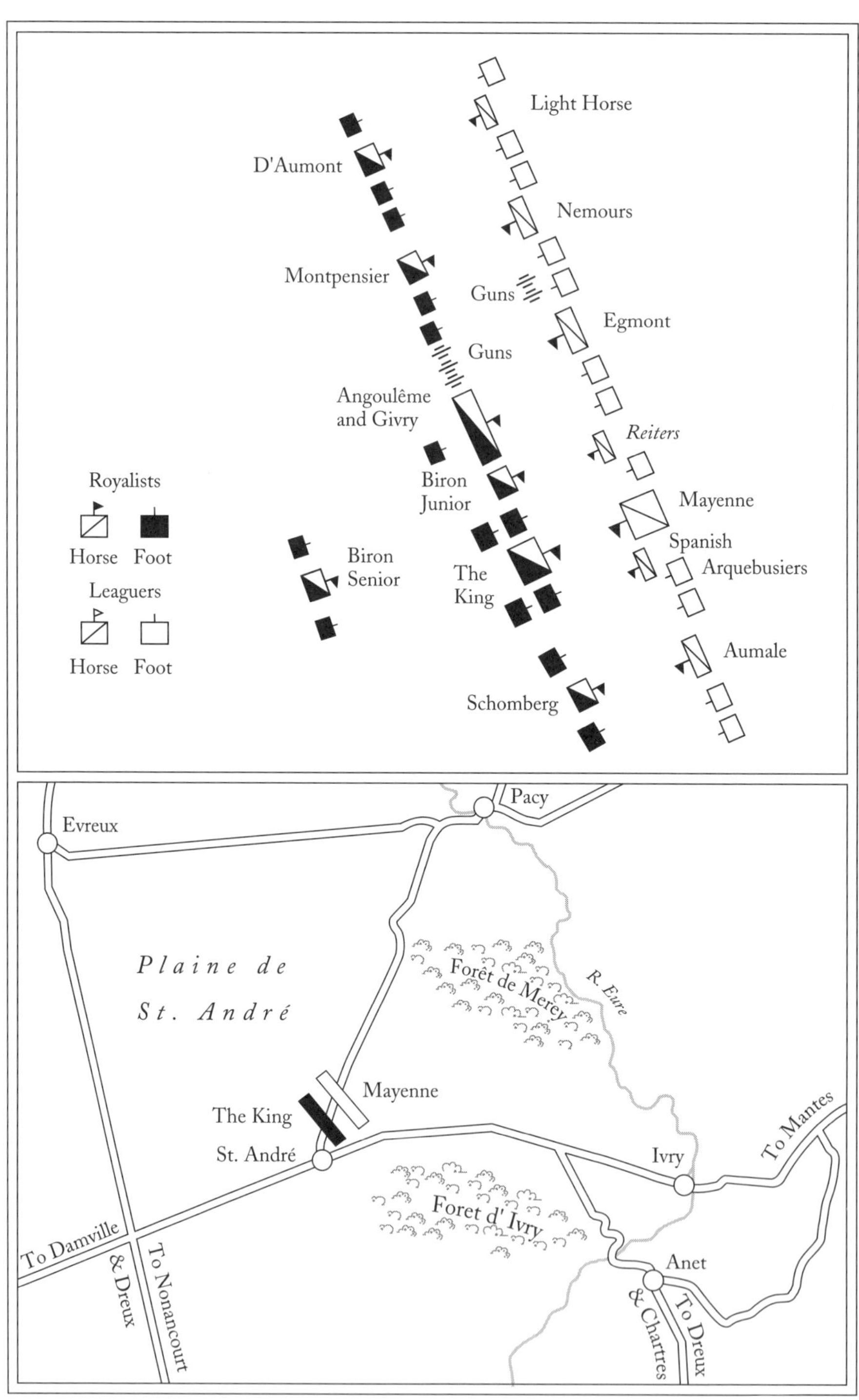

Map 6 Battle of Arques, 21 September 1589 and topography of the Dieppe–Arques country

Source: Sir Charles Oman, *A History of the Art of War in the Sixteenth Century* (London, 1937).

13 September. After testing Henry's defences for three days, he withdrew to the south-east, hoping to force a crossing at Arques, which Henry had fortified with two parallel trenches, one of which was covered by the guns of the local castle. The two armies were very unevenly matched. As against Mayenne's 4,000 cavalry and 20,000 infantry, Henry IV had only 1,000 cavalry and 4,000 infantry, but his defensive position was strong, particularly since the topography at Arques only allowed Mayenne to bring part of his force to bear at any one time.

Battle was joined on 21 September 1589. Henry and his cavalry stood between the two trenches waiting to give support wherever necessary. Mayenne ordered his German foot to outflank Henry's first trench. As the infantry holding it fell back in confusion, Mayenne's cavalry charged through the middle. A furious battle ensued. The Swiss defending Henry's second trench stood firm. Then the morning fog lifted, enabling the guns of Arques castle to open fire. Mayenne had to withdraw after suffering heavy casualties. Dividing his forces, he tried to capture Dieppe harbour, then Arques castle, only to be twice rebuffed.[8] Henry had won the battle despite the last-minute defection of his Catholic Swiss pikemen. They quit, not for religious reasons, but as a protest against their wage arrears. The king had the ringleaders executed in front of the entire army.[9]

Henry IV now received urgently needed reinforcements. On 23 September 13 ships arrived from England bringing money (£20,000 in gold), munitions and victuals as well as 50 noblemen. They were soon followed by 1,200 Scots and by 4,000 English troops. On 1 October Henry met the duc de Longueville, Marshal d'Aumont and the comte de Soissons, who brought further reinforcements of French noblemen whom they had recruited in the provinces. With an army now 18,000 strong, Henry decided to march on Paris. He reached Mantes on 28 October and Saint-Cloud and Meudon on the next day. Parisians, who had been brainwashed by the League's propaganda into believing that Henry had been defeated (some thought even killed) at Arques, were dismayed to see his troops closing in on the capital's suburbs. After occupying Saint-Germain-en-Laye, Henry divided his army into three corps under Biron, d'Aumont and Châtillon respectively. Each was followed by two cannon, two culverins, a troop of noblemen on foot and a squadron of cavalry. The king, Soissons and Longueville led the cavalry. Attacking on 1 November, they encountered stiff resistance from the Parisian militia. As one suburb after another fell, the royalists plundered

8 The best account of the battle of Arques remains that in C. Oman, *A History of the Art of War in the XVIth Century* (New York, 1937), pp. 485–92.

9 Wolfe, *The Conversion of Henry IV*, p. 90.

with impunity; and Henry, who had not been able to pay them, felt unable to intervene. As Châtillon's troops approached the walls, they shouted 'St Bartholomew!' According to L'Estoile, the king looked at his capital from the top of the tower of Saint-Germain-des-Prés.[10] But the Parisians stayed within their walls rather than seek a confrontation. When Mayenne returned to the capital from Picardy he was greeted like a saviour and immediately set about fortifying the Porte Saint-Jacques.

Henry, who had no artillery, could only fall back. After two months in the field, he lacked the funds to maintain his army at full strength. He disbanded the nobles, retaining only the paid troops. On his way south, at Châteaudun, he met representatives of the Swiss cantons, who acknowledged him officially as King of France. They were the first foreign power to do so. After storming Vendôme on 20 November and executing its governor, Henry reached Tours, where Henry III had set up a sort of government 'in exile' comprising a parlement and other sovereign courts. Their members had fled from the Parisian League. The king's council was chaired by two prelates: the cardinal de Vendôme, who was Keeper of the Seals, and the cardinal de Lenoncourt. Henry IV retained the secretaries of state who had served his predecessor. The royal finances were still administered by the marquis d'O. Tours also became the centre of propaganda in support of Henry's cause. From its presses many pamphlets poured scorn on the League.

Mayenne and the League

Arques proved a turning-point for the League. Provincial leaders, who earlier had ignored Mayenne's call for Catholic solidarity, became even less inclined to follow him after his defeat. The duke consequently was more than ever dependent on Spain and the papacy for funds and arms. His isolation within the League made it difficult for him to negotiate with Henry IV. Peace terms which he received from the king after the battle of Arques made no mention of the king's conversion, which all Catholics saw as a *sine qua non* of any settlement. Indeed, the king now seemed less inclined to abjure than he had been before his victory: he was even attending Calvinist services each week. Catholic loyalists urged Mayenne formally to demand Henry's conversion in exchange for recognizing his right to the throne; a move fiercely resisted by some of Mayenne's advisers, who urged

10 *Journal de l'Estoile pour le règne de Henri IV*, ed. L.-R. Lefèvre (Paris, 1948), vol. 1, p. 27.

him not to treat directly with the loyalists without first consulting the pope, the duke's foreign allies and the Catholic estates. While accepting Mayenne as leader, the Leaguers did not want him to take any major decision without first consulting them. Seeing how weak he was, the duke acted with caution. Early in October, he explained to the loyalists that peace could only be achieved once the safety of the kingdom had been assured by Henry's conversion to the Catholic faith. Conversion, in other words, had to come before recognition, not the other way round.

Both Leaguers and loyalist Catholics looked to the papacy for support. News of Henry IV's victory at Arques seems to have convinced Pope Sixtus V that some kind of accommodation had to be reached with Henry. Reversing years of bitter hostility towards him, he accepted in principle the king's readmission to the Church. As a major concession, Sixtus invalidated Henry's 1572 conversion to Catholicism so that he could no longer be seen as a 'relapsed heretic'. In September 1589 he sent Cardinal Caetani to France as legate with instructions to seek a reconciliation of the warring factions, but Caetani was no peace-maker. From the start he refused to meet Henry or his Catholic allies. Citing the dangers facing Catholicism should the League collapse, he urged the pope to send more subsidies to Mayenne and to work for more military assistance from Spain. The legate's bellicosity convinced Catholic loyalists that they had no alternative but to support Henry. Some warned Caetani that he threatened to provoke a schism between France and the Holy See. The legate did his utmost to galvanize the Parisian League: he used the Parlement and Sorbonne to lend an official cast to his policies; he persuaded League prelates to boycott an assembly of the clergy at Tours which was to discuss the king's religious instruction; and he threatened to excommunicate anyone who contacted Henry or his agents.[11]

France, at this stage, was a bewildering patchwork of allegiances. While certain regions adhered to the League, others were more responsive to royalist propaganda. Everywhere, however, the final decision rested essentially with the provincial governors and parlements. The governors of Berry, Bourbonnais, Marche and Limousin declared for the king, and, in Dauphiné, Lesdiguières came to terms with Alphonse d'Ornano, who had been appointed governor by Henry III. The parlements varied widely in their attitude to the new king. Rennes came out in his favour in spite of Mercoeur, the province's governor, who was a Leaguer. Bordeaux hesitated for a time despite pressure from Matignon and the *Bureau de la Ville*. Grenoble followed the League, as did Toulouse in spite of governor Damville's support

---

11 Ibid., pp. 92–7.

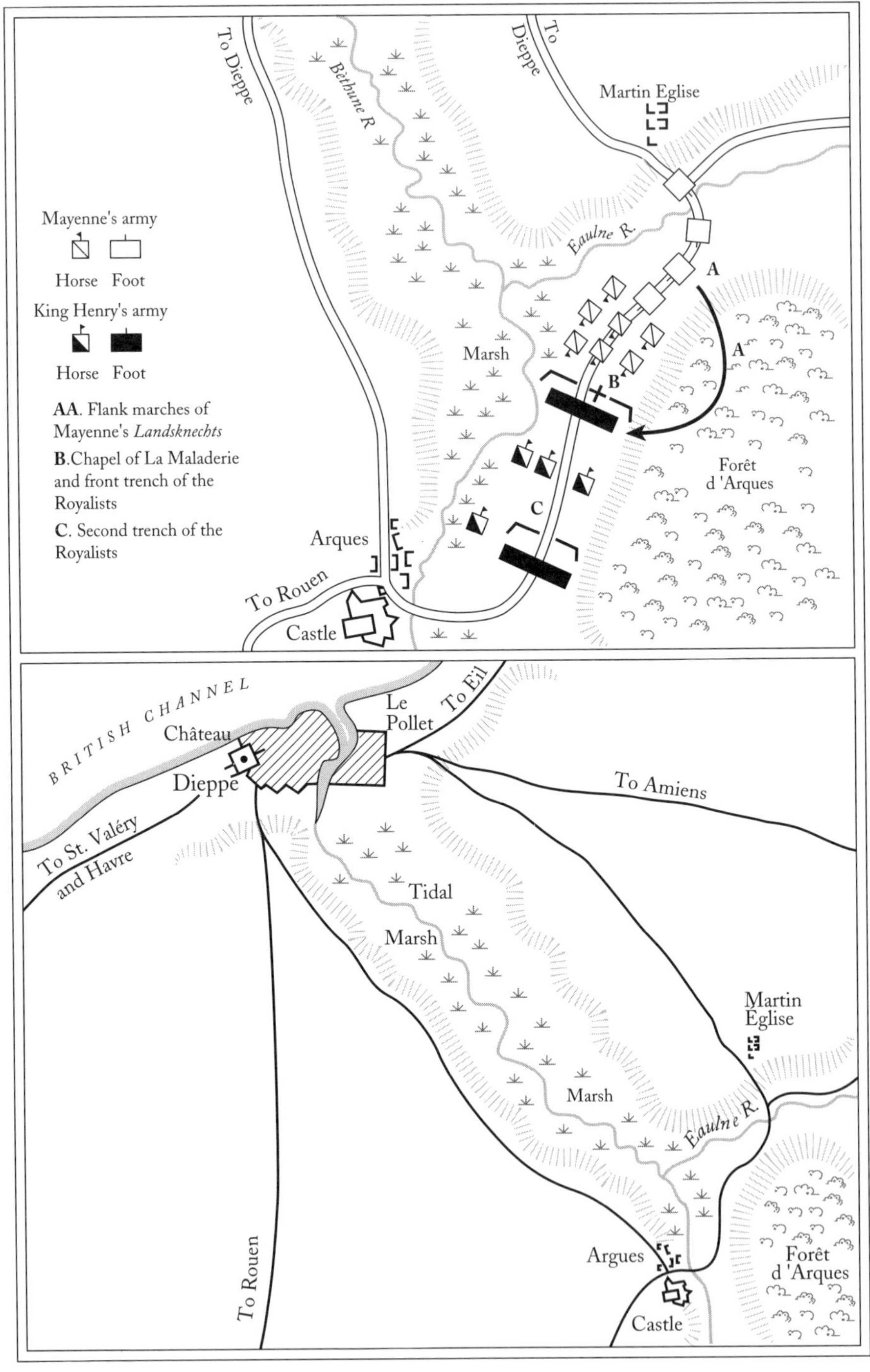

Map 7 Battle of Ivry, 14 March 1590
Source: Sir Charles Oman, *A History of the Art of War in the Sixteenth Century* (London, 1937).

for Henry. Here and there, notably at Senlis, violence erupted between Leaguers and royalists. So general was the confusion that there could be no question of calling the Estates-General for the time being. The meeting which had been promised for October was accordingly put off until March. All that Henry IV could do for the present was to remain in the public eye, keep up the pressure of his own propaganda and seek to raise more help from the nobility and from friends abroad.[12]

The battle of Ivry (14 March 1590)

After spending only eight days in Tours, Henry IV resumed his military campaign. Given the evident hostility of the Seine region, he decided to establish his power base further south in Touraine, Anjou and Maine. He seized Le Mans on 2 December and Laval on 10 December. Here, he was joined by the prince de Dombes, the son of the duc de Montpensier, who came with a fair number of Breton nobles alienated by Mercoeur's tyranny.[13] With his army thus strengthened, Henry caught up with Biron at Alençon. The king now aimed to resume the campaign in Normandy, a province which attracted him not only on account of its proximity to England but also because it was the richest province in France and could, therefore, provide him with badly needed funds. As he marched on Rouen, Henry seized many important towns. Writing to his mistress, he boasted that he had captured Lisieux without firing a shot and looked forward to raising 60,000 écus from the inhabitants. His army was almost free of disease and growing by the day.[14] The only towns in Normandy still controlled by the League were Rouen and Le Havre.

Mayenne, meanwhile, had also been building up his forces. He summoned the feudal levy for 15 January 1590 and Philip II sent him 500 arquebusiers and 1,200 cavalry under the count of Egmont. Soon towns near Paris which had fallen to the king were recaptured by the League. This prompted a change of plan by Henry IV. On learning that Mayenne was besieging Meulan, he decided once again to interrupt his Norman campaign. While Montpensier pushed ahead with part of the royal army, Henry himself made a U-turn and laid siege to Dreux. Mayenne went to the town's relief, whereupon Henry lifted the siege and retreated along the Eure valley. On 13 March he drew up his army on the Plaine de

12 Babelon, *Henri IV*, pp. 478–9.
13 Ibid., p. 480.
14 Ibid., p. 481.

Saint-André, south-east of Évreux: six cavalry squadrons in line, with some infantry screening them in front and other groups of infantry in between the squadrons. The guns were roughly in the centre of the line behind which Marshal Biron commanded a small reserve. Opposite the king's army, that of the League was arrayed in much the same way.[15]

At daybreak on 14 March the king, who had spent part of the night overseeing preparations, ensured that his troops had their backs to the sun and the wind. He disposed of 3,000 horse and 8,000 foot; Mayenne had 5,000 horse and 12,000 foot.[16] Before battle was joined, Henry harangued his men. He urged them to rally to his white hat plume (*panache blanc*) if they should lose sight of their standards (*cornettes*). 'You will find it,' he said, 'on the path to victory and honour.'[17] His plan was to smash the left of the enemy's line with his own squadron, supported by Swiss infantry. As the artillery on both sides opened fire, the opposing squadrons manoeuvred a little before colliding. For a time, it was difficult to tell who was winning. While d'Aumont's squadron routed the League's light horse, Egmont did likewise to the royal one. Between the squadrons of Montpensier and Nemours the struggle was about equal, but, on the right, the king crashed through Mayenne's arquebusiers and cavalry, completely breaking them up. A flanking charge by Biron's reserve scattered Egmont's squadron and soon the Leaguers were in full flight. Their cavalry had been severely mauled, and their infantry almost annihilated.

Ivry was essentially a cavalry action. Neither the infantry nor the artillery had taken much part. Henry's captains had once again shown that they were virtually invincible when faced by opponents who still favoured the cumbersome lance.[18] The king's cavalry preferred the *pistolade*, a tactic invented by the king. His men would close in on the enemy before discharging their pistols, then charge with their swords. Ivry was a great victory for Henry: 6,000 Leaguers were left dead on the field, thousands taken prisoner, about 40 standards captured along with guns and a huge amount of baggage.[19] Several medals were struck to commemorate the event. One showed Henry as an emperor crowned with laurels, and, on the reverse, a ploughman driving his team of oxen with the motto *Discutit ut coelo phoebus*

15 Oman, *A History of the Art of War*, pp. 496–505. See also Buisseret, *Henry IV*, p. 33 and Babelon, *Henri IV*, pp. 481–4.

16 Buisseret's figures. Babelon's are slightly different.

17 A. d'Aubigné, *Histoire universelle*, ed. A. Thierry (Geneva, 1981–95), vol. 8, pp. 168–70.

18 Buisseret, *Henry IV*, p. 33.

19 The Leaguer, Nicolas Brulart, in his *Journal* gives the cavalry losses as 300 on either side. Of the 4,000 Swiss who fought for Mayenne, only 26 survived the battle. See *Journal d'un Ligueur Parisien (1588–1590)*, ed. X. Le Person (Geneva, 1999), p. 170.

pax nubila terris (Peace disperses the clouds on earth as the sun does in the sky).[20] The humiliation for Mayenne was correspondingly deep: his reputation as a general in both France and Spain never recovered. Nor was Ivry Henry IV's only victory. On the same day, at Issoire in Auvergne, Monsieur de Curton, Henry's lieutenant, routed the local Leaguers, killing their commander. At Libourne, the people lit bonfires in celebration and the parlement of Bordeaux decided at last to recognize the king.

The siege of Paris (7 April–30 August 1590)

No one knows exactly what plan of action, if any, Henry had in mind after Ivry. Mayenne's army was no more and Paris lay only 36 miles away without a garrison and panic-stricken; yet for some unknown reason Henry was content to spend a fortnight at Mantes after the town had opened its gates to him. Maybe he was detained by another amorous intrigue, as he had been after Coutras.[21] Or perhaps Henry had to sort out troubles with his captains, who claimed rewards for their contribution to the recent victory, or with the Swiss, who threatened mutiny unless they were paid. Heavy rain had also churned up the roads, making them impassable for artillery. But, for whatever reason, Henry stayed put, and when eventually he did move, he embarked on a leisurely curve of conquest through Corbeil, Melun, Provins, Bray-sur-Seine and Montereau, coming to a halt at Sens.[22] According to Babelon, the king had decided to blockade Paris, seeing that his army was too small to surround it or to risk an assault.[23] The curve of conquest was designed to cut off the capital's supplies. The towns he occupied commanded traffic along the upper Seine. The king also seized a number of bridges and erected a pontoon at Charrières as a further obstacle to traffic while easing the passage of his troops.

Experience had taught Henry IV that it was a mistake to attack Paris from the south, as this allowed the defenders to receive assistance from the northern provinces where the League was strongest. So this time he planted his headquarters on the north side, on the hill of Montmartre.[24] At the same

20 Babelon, *Henri IV*, p. 486.

21 Oman, *A History of the Art of War*, p. 506. According to Constant, La Ligue, p. 250, Henry awaited the arrival of munitions and artillery which he needed to besiege Paris.

22 *Journal d'un Ligueur Parisien*, pp. 171–4.

23 Babelon, *Henri IV*, p. 489.

24 *Journal d'un Ligueur Parisien*, p. 178.

time, he stationed his troops at Saint-Ouen, La Chapelle, Aubervilliers, Pantin, Le Bourget, Louvres and Gonesse. The artillery was positioned facing the Porte Montmartre and at Montfaucon whence it could bombard the city and strike terror among the inhabitants. Mayenne's response to all this activity was to call a council of war at Saint-Denis. It was attended by the Spanish ambassador, the papal legate and the Guises. He invited them to remain in Paris while he himself tried to rebuild his forces by calling on foreign aid and by a new recruiting drive in Leaguer areas. Mayenne's young brother, the duc de Nemours, was appointed governor of Paris, and immediately took steps to replenish its food stocks. On 2 June the municipal authorities tried to relieve pressure on the city's food stocks by ordering all peasants who had come with their produce and all vagabonds to leave within 24 hours, but the order was not enforced. As a result, 30,000 'useless mouths' remained at the charge of the community. To defend Paris Nemours disposed of 1,500 *landsknechts* and as many Swiss and arquebusiers. He also had the urban militia totalling 48,000 men (3,000 for each of the capital's 16 districts). By comparison the royal army was very small, no more than 20,000 men.[25]

The siege of Paris, which began on 7 May, inflicted terrible hardships on the poorer inhabitants. The governor and municipal authorities believed that they had enough stocks of corn, wine, oats and vegetables to feed the population, estimated at 200,000, for one month. But the siege lasted till 30 August and shortages became apparent as early as 15 June.[26] The duchesse de Montpensier allegedly thought of one way of feeding the poor. This was to dig up the bodies in the Cimetière des Innocents, grind the bones into a powder, mix this with water, and turn it into loaves. These were duly distributed, but not for long, as those who ate them died at once. Safer by far were various kinds of broth, some made of oats, others of dog or cat meat. The Spanish ambassador, apart from distributing largesse to the poor, set up soup kitchens at street corners, dispensing donkey or mule soup.[27] On 27 June the Sixteen ordered the clergy to ensure that the poor received one meal a day, but the clergy showed no great enthusiasm in obeying the command. An inspection of religious houses revealed that they had enough supplies for six months. L'Estoile describes how the poor fought

25 Buisseret's figure (*Henry IV*, p. 35); Babelon says 13,000 (*Henri IV*, p. 492). Wolfe's suggestion (*The Conversion of Henry IV*, p. 99) that Henry IV was dissuaded from launching an attack on Paris by his Catholic allies assumes that he had an 'overwhelming military advantage'. In fact, an assault by him even early in the siege would have been suicidal.

26 *Journal d'un Ligueur Parisien*, pp. 175, 177–8.

27 De Lamar Jensen, *Diplomacy and Dogmatism: Bernardino de Mendoza and the French Catholic League* (Cambridge, Mass., 1964), p. 207; Constant, *La Ligue*, p. 252.

each other for food and even cites a few instances of cannibalism. Some young children were chased like animals for their meat.[28] Some of these stories may have been overblown, but the fact remains that bodies of famine victims became an everyday sight in the streets of Paris. Altogether 13,000 of the 30,000 victims of the siege are said to have died of hunger.[29] Henry IV was not untouched by the plight of the Parisians. On 23 July he allowed 3,000 to leave the capital. Some tried to seize the opportunity to gather corn in the fields outside the walls, but were prevented from doing so.[30]

Davila, the contemporary Italian historian of the French civil wars, suggested that the Parisians viewed their sufferings as an expiation. 'In such dire extremities,' he writes, 'wherein death was ever present, the common folk [*menu peuple*] took pleasure in suffering, having long become convinced that the persecution they were enduring was a glorious martyrdom to save souls and uphold the faith.' Even so, the morale of Parisians began to falter as their sufferings grew worse. The League tried to stop the rot by calling on preachers to deliver rousing sermons. They exhorted the people to face death rather than peace at the hands of a heretic and promised them salvation if they died upholding the Catholic faith. Huge processions were also organized as demonstrations of religious zeal and solidarity. One such on 14 May was particularly remarkable. It consisted of monks and friars, armed with arquebuses, halberds and daggers, and led by the bishop of Senlis and the prior of the Carthusians. They marched in ranks, four deep, behind banners representing Christ and the Virgin. Their cassocks were pulled up and their cowls lowered on to their shoulders; some wore a breastplate or a helmet. The papal legate, who blessed them, called them 'the new Maccabeans'. But their skill in the use of firearms did not always match their zeal. A salute fired in honour of the legate killed his almoner.[31] One of the biggest processions took place on 31 May when the relics of Saint-Denis were carried to Notre-Dame. The duc de Nemours and other nobles solemnly swore to dedicate their lives to saving Paris for the Catholic faith and to die rather than swear obedience to the king of Navarre (this was how Henry IV was officially referred to by the League; he was also known, more popularly, as *le Béarnais*). Everyone present joined in one great act of communion. A letter written by Mayenne from Péronne was also read out in which he announced that he had gathered a fine army and would soon march on Paris. This greatly cheered the Parisians.[32]

---

28 *Journal de l'Estoile*, vol. 1, p. 67; Constant, *La Ligue*, pp. 250–51.
29 Constant, *La Ligue*, p. 252.
30 *Journal de l'Estoile*, vol. 1, p. 57.
31 Ibid., pp. 46–7.
32 Ibid., p. 48.

Not everyone in Paris supported the League. The diarist, Pierre de L'Estoile, to whom we are indebted for much of our information about events in the capital during the siege, was a Politique. As such, he and his friends were spied upon by the Sixteen. The siege was accompanied by a wave of searches, arrests, fines, imprisonments and summary executions. On 4 June some bourgeois who dared to wish openly for peace with Henry IV were thrown into the Seine. Eleven days later the Parlement forbade under pain of death any move to negotiate with the king. On 23 June a town crier was hanged for taking letters to the king from Parisian sympathizers. On 30 June a lawyer, who had been in touch with the enemy, was executed publicly.[33] On 1 August an assembly of the main governing bodies in Paris, meeting in the Salle Saint-Louis of the Palais, decided to send Pierre de Gondi, bishop of Paris, and Pierre d'Épinac, archbishop of Lyon, to Henry IV and to the duc de Mayenne in order to beg them to bring peace to the kingdom. They were explicitly forbidden by Nemours to raise the subject of the king's conversion for fear that he might take them at their word. When the prelates met Henry at the abbey of Saint-Martin-des-Champs, they addressed him as 'king of Navarre', whereupon he pointed out that if that was his title, he could not see why he was expected to pacify Paris and France. However, he said that he was not going to quibble over a mere formality, and was prepared to treat his subjects with clemency provided he, not a third party (viz. Mayenne), was given the credit for this. Whether the talks were intended seriously or not is uncertain; they may have been simply intended to allow time for a relief army to reach Paris. The Sixteen, however, took the move seriously and protested at talks being held with a heretic. Public opinion within Paris was sharply divided.[34] On 8 August, a group of armed Politiques staged a demonstration inside the Palais. A mob invaded the Parlement, calling for 'bread and peace'. The authorities, having been forewarned by a preacher, easily put down the unrest. A number of arrests and punishments ensued, but the governor, Nemours, did not carry the repression as far as the Leaguers wanted.[35]

The prospect of Paris falling into the hands of a heretical monarch was altogether too much for Philip II, who had barely recovered from the Armada disaster, to accept. Already, on receiving the news of Henry's victory at Ivry, he had informed Alexander Farnese, duke of Parma and captain-general of the army of Flanders, that the strategy which he had hitherto followed to aid the French Catholics would no longer serve.[36] He

33 *Journal d'un Ligueur Parisien*, p. 179.

34 Ibid., pp. 184–7; Babelon, *Henri IV*, pp. 495–6; Wolfe, *The Conversion of Henry IV*, pp. 99–100.

35 *Journal de l'Estoile*, vol. 1, pp. 49, 51–2, 64–5; Constant, *La Ligue*, pp. 254–5.

36 G. Parker, *The Grand Strategy of Philip II* (New Haven, 1998), p. 274.

commanded the duke to invade France at once with a large army. Parma reluctantly obeyed. Leaving a minimum force to contain Maurice of Nassau in the Netherlands, he invaded France with 14,000 Spanish veterans. On 23 August he was joined at Meaux by Mayenne, who brought with him 10,000 foot and 2,000 horse which he had recently raised in northern France. Henry IV's army was roughly equal in size, as he had received sizeable reinforcements from the south, but he was faced by a dilemma. If he gathered up the army which was besieging Paris in order to face Parma, the capital's supply routes would once again be open. On the other hand, if he defeated Parma quickly, he would be able to resume the siege before too much food had entered the city. After weighing the options, he decided to force a battle, if possible. Drawing all his troops from west and south of Paris, he took post at Chelles with 7,000 horse and nearly 20,000 foot. But Parma chose not to be drawn. He made full use of entrenchments against which cavalry was useless. However, while the two armies stood facing each other for five days, a Spanish detachment sneaked across the Marne and took Lagny by surprise, thereby unblocking one supply route to Paris.[37]

On 9 September Henry IV retreated. As he moved towards Saint-Denis, he made one last attempt to capture Paris. He detached some infantry under Châtillon to try to enter the capital by clambering over its rampart, but they were foiled by a vigilant patrol of armed Jesuits.[38] On 12 September Parisians were delighted to learn that Henry had split up his army into several parts and sent them to Touraine, Champagne, Normandy and Burgundy respectively, leaving only some troops near Paris. By 17 September corn was being sold in the capital for only 5 écus per *setier*, whereas it had cost 24 écus as recently as 13 September. On the following day, Mayenne arrived with his lieutenants and his council but they were not fêted by the Parisians, who had still not recovered from their recent sufferings. On 22 September Parma laid siege to Corbeil, while he himself visited Paris incognito with a few horsemen. He then returned to Corbeil which was taken by storm on 16 October.[39] Towards the end of November the duke returned to the Netherlands leaving Mayenne in charge of the League's forces. Henry IV pursued him at a safe distance.

A major problem facing Henry IV was lack of money. In July 1592 Sublet d'Heudicourt, an *intendant des finances*, acting on the king's orders, recognized debts of over 800,000 livres and over 3.2 million livres respectively to two mercenary captains, Dompmartin and Christian von Anhalt.

37 Oman, *A History of the Art of War*, p. 510; Buisseret, *Henry IV*, pp. 36–7.

38 *Journal de l'Estoile*, vol. 1, pp. 73–4.

39 Ibid., pp. 74–6, 78.

They had to accept *rentes* and written promises as security for the arrears of pay. The solemn contracts which had been entered upon when their troops had been raised had not been honoured. Consequently, Henry had to accept the decision of the *reiters* and *landsknechts* to return home. He did, however, manage to keep the Swiss in return for a new recognition of the debts he owed them and solemn assurances to assign repayment on secure revenues. But Henry was again to default on his promise. In March 1593 the Swiss complained to the *Chambre des Comptes* of debts they were owed amounting to between 9 and 12 million livres. All they were offered was 1.5 million from the sale of crown lands. As Bonney writes: 'in view of his difficulties in paying the mercenary troops, it is difficult to see how any coherent military strategy could have been put into effect'.[40]

An important factor which Henry IV could try to exploit was the division of the Catholic League into two movements with quite divergent aims. The Parisian League, led by the Sixteen, was a radical movement which put religion before the state in its order of priorities and viewed the latter as a kind of federation of urban 'republics' rather than as a centralized monarchy. Mayenne's League, on the other hand, was made up of great and lesser nobles and high-ranking churchmen, who were committed to the traditional institutions of monarchy. The duke had his own council of state which followed him on his travels like that of the king. The Sixteen felt excluded from Mayenne's dealings with the provincial Leagues. In September 1590 they submitted six demands to the duke: they asked him to press on with the war against the Protestants without thought of peace; to invoke help from the pope and the king of Spain without worrying about the consequences; to purge his council of profiteers and 'Politiques' who put state before religion; to assume responsibility for all actions taken by 'the Catholics of Paris'; to set up a special tribunal made up of elected judges to try all those who 'contravene the union of Catholics'; lastly, to restore the sovereign powers of the Council of the Union. These demands were rejected by Mayenne and his councillors on the grounds that their implementation would 'reduce the State of France to a republic in which they [the Parisian Leaguers] saw themselves as holding sovereign power and by this means ruining the nobility'.[41]

The blockade of Paris continued into 1592 after Henry IV's withdrawal, albeit more slackly. The atmosphere within the capital remained highly charged as Leaguer zealots accused so-called Politiques – Catholics who were prepared to consider peace with Henry IV – of treason. Exasperated

40 Bonney, *The King's Debts*, p. 35.
41 Constant, *La Ligue*, pp. 365–70.

by Mayenne's political conservatism, the Sixteen tried to impose their views by mounting a series of coups. On 6 November 1591 a new council, known as the Council of Ten, was set up consisting of fanatical members of the Sixteen. At the same time, committees in each district of the capital hunted down suspects. On 15 November two *parlementaires* – the first president, Barnabé Brisson, and a councillor, Claude Larcher – and Jean Tardif, a councillor of the Châtelet, were summarily executed for having shown leniency to a man charged with contacting the enemy. Whether the crime was prompted simply by religious fervour or by social resentment does not concern us here. The fact remains that it was an act of terror, nor was it the only one. According to L'Estoile, a list circulated of names of Politiques followed by the letters 'P', 'D' or 'C', standing for *pendu* (hanged), *dagué* (stabbed) and *chassé* (expelled). Altogether the number of victims of the terror may not have been large: the Sixteen are said to have tried and executed about a dozen 'traitors'. Others, like the potter Bernard Palissy, died in prison. Alarmed by this turn of events, Mayenne decided to intervene. On 28 November 1591 he entered Paris in force. Some of the Sixteen were arrested, and the four responsible for the hangings on 15 November were themselves sent to the gallows.[42] Next day, Mayenne took charge of the bourgeois militia and appointed new captains who were made to take an oath of loyalty to himself. All men who were not qualified by their social status to bear arms were disarmed. By his firm action Mayenne effectively destroyed the Sixteen as a political force. Henceforth only the aristocratic League headed by Mayenne and his friends mattered.[43]

The problem of the succession

The Leaguers had reason to feel grateful to the king of Spain for his timely intervention during the siege of Paris, but, in fact, many viewed him with suspicion on account of his designs on the French throne. For their king, Charles X, the old cardinal de Bourbon, had died in his prison at Fontenay on 9 May. It was said that on his death-bed he had recognized Henri de Navarre as his heir. Be that as it may, his death opened up the way to new claimants to the throne. Under the Salic law, Henry was the rightful king, but he was unacceptable to many Catholics as long as he remained a Protestant. Among possible Catholic claimants was the cardinal de Vendôme,

42 E. Barnavi and R. Descimon, *La Sainte Ligue, le juge et la potence* (Paris, 1985), *passim*; Constant, *La Ligue*, pp. 370–83.

43 Constant, *La Ligue*, pp. 379–83.

the fourth son of the first prince de Condé, but no one seemed to take him seriously. Another was the marquis de Pons, Henry III's nephew, whom Catherine de' Medici had once regarded as a possible substitute for the king of Navarre. Yet another was Philip II's half-French daughter, Isabella Clara Eugenia, but she was ruled out by the Salic law. The upshot of this genealogical tangle was that the Leaguers had no generally recognized candidate for the throne during the last four years of the war. Some could see important advantages in supporting the Infanta's claim, but most hated the idea. Of these, many were prepared to accept Henry, if he would only give up his Protestant faith. They begged him to be 'instructed', but for more than two years he wavered between gaining the throne by force and sacrificing his religion. His final decision depended on how the war would proceed.[44]

Henry IV owed much of his success so far to the support of Catholic loyalists. His problem was how to retain it without antagonizing his Protestant co-religionists. While putting off his conversion for as long as possible, he tried to balance the parties. As Catholics continued to dominate the court, Henry continued to rely for advice on an inner circle of Huguenots. The result, however, was 'a debilitating dualism in the royal government'.[45] After the siege of Paris, Henry had to make further concessions to Catholics in order to retain their allegiance. The shift in the confessional balance was exemplified by the appointment in September 1590 of Philippe Hurault, comte de Cheverny, as Keeper of the Seals. He reshaped the court, enhancing its Catholic character. From late in 1590 Catholic churchmen assumed a more visible presence. While Henry IV remained a Protestant, control of the Gallican church fell largely to Renaud de Beaune, archbishop of Bourges, who supervised the distribution of benefices. The royal chapel celebrated Mass each day, offering prayers for the king's conversion. Royal entries into towns publicized the court's orthodoxy.

But Catholic loyalists grew restless as the king failed to honour his pledge to be instructed in the Catholic faith. Their impatience underlay the formation of the so-called *Tiers Parti* (Third Party), a plot aimed at deposing Henry in favour of a Catholic Bourbon. Rumours surfaced as early as 1589 that Henry's cousin, Charles, cardinal de Vendôme, aspired to the throne. As he had never taken major orders, he could envisage marriage as a layman and having children. It seems that members of the *Tiers Parti* were in the main loyalist prelates and former servants of Henry III. But secrecy proved impossible to maintain, as Henry IV had informants close to the cardinal. A rash attempt by Vendôme, in March 1591, to enlist the support

44 Oman, *A History of the Art of War*, pp. 511–13.
45 Wolfe, *The Conversion of Henry IV*, p. 101.

of Pope Gregory XIV misfired badly, when the pope excommunicated Henry and all his Catholic supporters. Loyalist Catholics led by Nevers were so offended by the pope's meddling in France's domestic affairs that they reaffirmed their support for Henry. 'The force of the Tiers Parti,' writes Wolfe, 'lay in the potential, rather than the actual, realization of uniting Catholics behind a resolution which excluded Henry IV.'[46] On 6 July 1591 Henry continued his balancing act by issuing the Edict of Mantes which was intended to retain the support of both loyalist Catholics and Huguenots. The edict was in two parts: the first restated the king's willingness to undergo instruction once he had enough leisure to do so; and the second revoked the Edict of Union of 1588, replacing it by earlier edicts of pacification which had granted concessions to Huguenots. Loyalist pressure on the king to convert gathered momentum in the autumn as an assembly of the clergy met at Chartres. In November it asked for a mission to be sent to the new pope, Innocent IX, to inform him of Henry's intention to begin Catholic instruction as soon as possible. Henry accepted the move in the hope of assuaging his critics' impatience. He still feared that the *Tiers Parti* might turn its grievances into open opposition. Meanwhile, he continued to hold out for a military resolution of his quandary.[47]

The siege of Rouen (November 1591–March 1592)

Following Henry IV's failure to take Paris, his advisers urged him to attack Rouen, the League's main stronghold in northern France after the capital. The city was said to be poorly defended and its capture would again disrupt traffic to Paris along the Seine. But Henry had other things on his mind. Once more he allowed an affair of the heart to dictate his movements. As he was shadowing Parma across Picardy in November 1590, he met Gabrielle d'Estrées for the first time at the château of Coeuvres and from this moment seemed concerned only to satisfy her and her rapacious relatives. They had an interest in Chartres. So this was where Henry decided to go. He laid siege to the town in February and, after capturing it, reinstated Gabrielle's uncle, François de Sourdis, as governor, a position which he had held until 1588.[48]

46 Ibid., p. 106.

47 Ibid., pp. 100–8; Babelon, *Henri IV*, pp. 523–7.

48 Buisseret, *Henry IV*, pp. 37–8; Babelon, *Henri IV*, pp. 511–16.

A feature of the final phase of the French civil wars was a significant increase of foreign involvement. The rival parties in France had always relied on hiring foreign mercenaries, mainly German or Swiss, and this process continued. In the summer of 1589 Henry III had sent an envoy to England to obtain a loan from Elizabeth I with which to raise troops in Germany, but the queen was unenthusiastic. The German expedition to France in 1587, which had cost her 100,000 écus, had achieved nothing beyond pillage; but her attitude changed after Henry III's assassination. French envoys received a loan of £20,000, then another of £15,000. In the meantime, Henry IV's agents in the Netherlands had negotiated a loan of 30,000 écus. One of them, Incarville, came to England to negotiate a loan from the City of London to be repaid from the customs duties of Bordeaux and La Rochelle. By June 1590, however, he had been able only to raise £2,000. Meanwhile, Horatio Palavicino was sent by Elizabeth to Germany to assess the prospects of hiring a new army for Henry IV. Then, as Parma's intervention obliged Henry to lift his siege of Paris, Elizabeth and the United Provinces rallied round. She sent him £10,000, and they provided him with powder, wheat and warships. At this juncture Henry sent the vicomte de Turenne to England to find money with which to hire an army in Germany, but Elizabeth was only prepared to assist on her own terms. After experiencing the Armada, her main concern was to ensure that Spain could not gain a foothold on the French side of the Channel from which to spring another invasion attempt. In other words, she expected Henry to guard Dieppe and, if possible, recapture Rouen. In the end, Turenne was disappointed. Elizabeth had no objection to Henry IV raising an army in Germany, but believed that it should be funded by German contributions. She was prepared to contribute £10,000 on condition that the German army marched westward towards the coast of Flanders rather through Lorraine. From England, Turenne went to Germany, where he succeeded in raising 6,000 cavalry and 9,000 infantry. He mustered them on 1 August near Frankfurt and marched them across the Rhine under their commander, Christian von Anhalt.[49]

While Henry IV was pursuing his own agenda, a struggle for the control of Brittany was taking place between the duc de Mercoeur, representing the League, and the prince de Dombes, who supported Henry. In the absence of any active involvement by the king himself, both parties looked abroad for assistance. In November 1590 Dombes sent an envoy to England with a request for 2,000 foot soldiers, powder, shot and pikes, but Elizabeth I excused herself. Later, however, she considered withdrawing 3,000 English

49 H. A. Lloyd, *The Rouen Campaign, 1590–1592* (Oxford, 1972), pp. 31–48.

troops from the Netherlands for service in Brittany. Before taking a final decision, however, she needed to know Henry's intentions. She sent him an envoy to find out and, in a personal message, urged him to watch out for Parma. 'Prevent his coming,' she warned, 'do not wait for him to come.'[50] Meanwhile, Mercoeur reminded Philip II that Brittany was a convenient base for 'the enterprise of England'. Philip duly responded by sending an expeditionary force 4,000 strong, which captured Blavet, then Hennebont. Seriously alarmed, Elizabeth's council gave orders on 27 March for 3,000 troops to be raised. Some were to go to Flushing, the rest to Brittany. But there was also serious concern in England about the fate of Dieppe, which was being threatened by Tavannes at Rouen and Villars at Le Havre. The English merchant, Otwell Smyth, asked for 3,000 Englishmen to defend Dieppe. Elizabeth promptly sent 600 under Sir Roger Williams.[51] Henry IV, for his part, knew nothing of all this, and, far from considering an incursion into Normandy, summoned Montpensier and his forces out of that province to join him. Even with Chartres taken, the king was reported to be thinking of engaging Mayenne in battle.

From Chartres, Henry IV seized Noyon and installed Gabrielle d'Estrées' father as governor, and his brother as bishop. Quoting Buisseret, 'not for the first or last time, Henry showed that when Venus was in the ascendant his judgment was defective'.[52] Not every historian agrees, however. Howell Lloyd thinks that the seizure of Noyon was 'wholly consistent with his [Henry's] strategic priorities: to gain control over his kingdom by dominating its capital, and to prepare to resist the greatest single challenge to that control, in the shape of Parma'.[53] Noyon lay between Compiègne and Saint-Quentin, on the direct route from Paris to Brussels. Its capture strengthened not only the king's partial blockade of Paris but also his control of other strongpoints in the region. Furthermore, the terms of Noyon's surrender included an indemnity of 40,000 écus which would go some way towards paying his soldiers. The situation, Lloyd argues, was far too fluid and complex to allow Henry to fling himself into Normandy at Elizabeth I's bidding. Mayenne still held court at Ham, unwilling to do battle, yet within 13 miles of Saint-Quentin. The king's own loose federation of supporters was restive. Already that summer he had had to issue three proclamations: one giving fresh concessions to Protestants, another reaffirming his concern for Gallican Catholicism, and a third protesting against recent

50 Ibid., p. 59.
51 Ibid., pp. 50–65.
52 Buisseret, *Henry IV*, p. 38.
53 Lloyd, *The Rouen Campaign*, p. 110.

papal bulls against him. 'Rarely can the balance of political opinion within France have seemed more delicately poised.'[54]

Once Noyon had been taken, Henry might have been expected to go to Normandy, but he preferred to visit the duc de Nevers in the Ardennes. On 29 September, at Vandy near Verdun, he inspected the army which Turenne had raised in Germany. In the meantime, Elizabeth I wrote to Henry, offering him 3,000 or 4,000 troops if he would try to recover Rouen. Her offer seems to have made an impact. Henry, who had been hovering between Paris and Chartres, suddenly swung westwards, sending Biron ahead. Louviers fell to the king and it was reported that he was heading for Dieppe. On 25 June his envoy, De Réau, presented to Elizabeth a message from Henry in which he expressed his gratitude and explained why he had not taken her valuable advice sooner. Circumstances had stood in the way, but now he was ready to act. However, he needed 5,000 or 6,000 infantry, 200 or 300 horse, 30 or 40 pioneers, 12 pieces of artillery with enough ammunition to fire 5,000 shots, 3 sizeable ships and 3 *pataches* to guard the Seine estuary during the siege. He also required licences to transport supplies out of England and permission to borrow 200,000 écus in the City of London. Elizabeth agreed to send 4,000 soldiers, but would pay for them only for two months; thereafter Henry would have to do so or they would be withdrawn. As security for the expedition, for Norris' force in Brittany and for other advances to Henry since September 1589, Elizabeth required a written document under the Great Seal of France and that her commissioners should receive all the revenues from tolls, taxes, customs and duties payable within and around the towns of Rouen and Le Havre until she was fully reimbursed.[55] Henry accepted these terms, and, in August, the English expeditionary force, led by the Earl of Essex, crossed the Channel to Dieppe.

The two months passed after Essex had landed in France without any action on Henry IV's part. Feeling that she had been duped, Elizabeth urged the earl to come home. Henry, in the meantime, was being pressed from all sides. Apart from Elizabeth, there was Turenne with his Germans at Metz awaiting his orders, and Nevers who had threatened to quit his command unless Henry came to Champagne. Another problem was the inheritance of the duc de Bouillon, who had died leaving only an unmarried sister as his heir. Without the king's presence, the situation in north-eastern France seemed likely to fall apart.[56] But another reason for Henry's reluctance to respond to Elizabeth may have been his dislike of sieges. He

54 Ibid., p. 111.
55 Ibid., pp. 73–7.
56 Ibid., pp. 104–6.

far preferred operations, like cavalry reconnaissances, calling for more dash. So he sent Marshal Biron to besiege Rouen without waiting for him. In the king's absence, Biron and Essex besieged Gournay, whose capitulation reassured Elizabeth. She agreed to extend Essex's stay in France and even granted another request from Henry IV for more aid.[57]

On 11 November 1591 Biron laid siege to Rouen. The town was defended by its new governor, André de Brancas, sieur de Villars, who was also governor of Le Havre. Three urgent tasks faced him: to strengthen Rouen's fortifications, to raise money for munitions and soldiers' pay, and to conserve food supplies. In all three he encountered reluctance, criticism and outright opposition from the municipal authorities, but he was skilful enough to enlist the co-operation of the urban militia. Villars took steps to repair the city's fortifications, which had been poorly maintained. He ordered certain buildings, mainly in the suburbs, to be demolished, and had the town walls reinforced with earth. At selected points, especially next to the gates, artillery platforms were erected. But these improvements were confined to the walls; they did not project beyond them as bulwarks or bastions. The ditches were deepened but remained for the most part dry. In addition to the fortifications, Villars relied on guns and professional soldiers. He had brought from Le Havre 40 pieces of artillery with shot and powder. He reinforced the garrison with 500 light horse, 200 *hargulutiers* (mounted arquebusiers) 1,200 French infantry and 300 German infantry. Altogether the governor disposed of about 6,000 men. But these troops, of course, had to be paid. They required 14,000 écus per month. Villars asked the Rouennais for ever larger sums: 5,000 écus in early August and 30,000 by the end of the month. Such demands encountered resistance from the municipal authorities, but eventually a system was set up to assess each parish for contributions. An uneasy *modus vivendi* was achieved between the garrison and the townspeople. In March 1592, however, there was no longer enough coin in the city to pay the army. Soon unpaid troops were raiding Rouen's bakeries. Villars decided to mark up the face value of available coins for the duration of the siege. Finding enough victuals was another headache for the governor. In October 1591, on the eve of the siege, he had called on all bourgeois to store enough food for six months, and on the peasants in the countryside around to bring as much grain, wine and cider as possible into the city. As the siege began, an elaborate system of control was set up regarding the grinding of corn. Bakers objected, of course, and complaints of profiteering soon arose. On 13 December the parlement issued a decree stipulating maximum prices. In

57 Babelon, *Henri IV*, pp. 518–19.

mid-January 1592, as complaints of hoarding mounted, a search of houses was ordered.[58]

Outside Rouen, the besiegers began to organize themselves. Henry IV joined Biron and Essex there on 23 November, after his army had pillaged its way through Picardy. He stationed himself at Darnétal. The king's army was never sufficiently large to blockade Rouen completely. Its encampments were not linked so that the townspeople were able to continue foraging, and even to tend gardens, beyond the city's walls. Failing a blockade, the besiegers could attack either the fort of Sainte-Catherine or the city itself. The king chose the first option. After he had brought batteries to bear on the curtain and bulwark, the fort's garrison made a powerful sortie aimed at spiking the guns, but the attempt failed. A week later, English pioneers were put to work on the approaches to the fort. The besiegers gradually brought artillery into play, but their marksmanship was poor. The English trenches lacked depth and were so badly sited that the enemy guns were able to fire along them with devastating effect. On 3 January a joint attack by Henry and Essex on the enemy counterscarp was thrown back. Discouraged, Essex wrote to Burghley: 'I desire for private respects to be rid of this French action.'[59] After his pioneers had been driven back by a sortie on 13 January, the earl returned to England. The French besiegers then launched an attack on Rouen only to be repulsed once more.

During the siege the city's morale was diligently sustained by processions, by sermons and by incessant reminders of God's proven support. The Rouennais nevertheless rested their hopes on Parma and Mayenne. The duke of Parma was known to be planning a new invasion of France, but, lacking soldiers, reserves and supplies, he was in no hurry to obey Philip II. His Spanish army, which had dwindled in size, was unpaid and demoralized. Nor was the duke the commanding figure who had recaptured Antwerp in 1585. He was stricken with gout and afraid of losing control of the Netherlands by removing part of his army to France. In answer to his request for more troops, Philip II had only sent money and then not enough. It was not until November that he left Brussels for Valenciennes to review 16,000 men. On 28 December, he met Mayenne at Guise. In the meantime, Henry had left Noyon and returned to Rouen, leaving the way clear for Parma to dominate Picardy. Once in France, the duke sent infantry to garrison the town of La Fère which he hoped to use as a base of operations and a place of retreat. But Mayenne demurred. In negotiations over the

58 Lloyd, *The Rouen Campaign*, pp. 136–46.

59 Ibid., p. 157; P. Benedict, *Rouen during the Wars of Religion* (Cambridge, 1981), pp. 217–18.

succession to the French throne with the duke and other Leaguers, Parma put the Infanta's case, but met with a blank response. Evidence was emerging that Mayenne was ready to treat with Henry IV if he was disappointed by Spain. Meanwhile, Parma moved westward through Picardy. At Nesle, he held a council of war which decided to go to Rouen's relief, but intelligence indicated that fresh forces had been joining Henry IV while Parma's were dwindling in size. According to a muster held at Nesle on 16 January, the duke disposed of 13,546 infantry and 4,061 cavalry, but in reality his forces were fewer. Their arrears of pay amounted to 157,392 écus. Parma needed to move fast, but his waggons and artillery were bogged down. As the duke pressed on towards Rouen, he marshalled his army in a close and protective formation.[60]

As Parma drew near, Henry seemed threatened with a repetition of the siege of Paris in 1590, but this time he reacted differently. About 26 January he left all his infantry with Biron outside Rouen, and set off himself with 7,000 cavalry, his intention being to harass Parma's progress wherever possible. The campaign that followed is not easy to unravel. Parma was extremely cautious. His troops marched in a compact formation. The infantry had the heavy cavalry in the middle and the light cavalry on both flanks and in front. The rival armies came face to face on 3 February on the Bresle, a small river dividing Picardy from Normandy. Henry had come to Aumale, where he had left the dukes of Nevers and Longueville with the bulk of his troops. He then crossed the Bresle with 1,000 horse, and on 5 February rashly led a charge against Parma's cavalry screen, only to be cut off from his base. In an ensuing skirmish, the king was wounded, albeit lightly. Some 60 of his nobles, however, were allegedly killed, and only a timely intervention by Nevers averted a catastrophe.[61]

While Henry recovered from his wound at Dieppe, Parma seized Neufchâtel (12 February). He then resumed his orderly march on Rouen. On 24 February, Villars, taking advantage of Henry IV's absence, launched a violent attack on Biron's entrenchments. Taking them completely by surprise, he overran them, blew up the royalists' stores and captured many pieces of artillery. Biron, coming up with his reserves too late, was repulsed and wounded. He retired to Darnétal. On 26 February the siege of Rouen seemed almost over, yet Parma merely sent a token force into the city. He was allegedly dissuaded from going there by Mayenne, who feared that the city might become a Spanish stronghold outside the League's control. A great opportunity of crushing Henry IV decisively was accordingly

60 Lloyd, *The Rouen Campaign*, pp. 175–7.

61 Ibid., pp. 178–9; Buisseret, *Henry IV*, p. 39; Oman, *A History of the Art of War*, p. 516.

missed. Parma now posted part of his army at Neufchâtel, before returning to Picardy with a large force and besieging Rue at the mouth of the Somme.

By now Villars' resources were becoming strained and as his losses grew, so did complaints within Rouen. On 16 April, thousands of Rouennais rioted at the town hall and in the courtyard of the Palais de Justice. They demanded 'peace or bread'. Villars and his cavalry had to disperse them. The governor accused fifth-columnists of fomenting the disturbances, but there was no denying that the uneasy combination of municipal council, parlement and governor was now facing mass popular opposition within the city. For five winter months the city's resources had sufficed to stave off serious scarcity, but with the onset of dearth the city's morale collapsed. Meanwhile, outside the walls, Henry IV took advantage of Parma's withdrawal, to join Biron at Darnétal with some 5,000 horse. They then resumed the siege of Rouen. A Dutch fleet landed 3,000 men at Quilleboeuf, thereby cutting the city's line of communication with the sea. The royalists opened up their old trenches and brought up artillery. Hard-pressed, Villars warned Parma that, unless help was forthcoming, he would not be able to hold out beyond 20 April. This time Parma responded quickly. He rushed to Rouen with 5,000 horse and 12,000 foot, forcing Henry to draw his army back to positions south of the city. On 21 April, Parma and Mayenne entered the city in triumph.[62]

The liberation of Rouen did not mark the end of its sufferings: famine and disease persisted. The surrounding countryside had been stripped bare by the besiegers, who had also brought with them infectious diseases. The parish registers reveal a serious mortality crisis which lasted until 1592. By early in 1593 nearly three times as many people had been buried as in a normal year. Nearly all were victims of famine and disease provoked by the fighting. The crisis followed upon four years of economic hardship. The war saw a sharp decline in Rouen's trade. Imports and exports were only 15 to 35 per cent of the pre-1588 levels. Unprecedented cuts had to be made in the taxes levied on the city's products 'given the necessities and calamities of the time'. The economic crisis also caused shifts of population. Peasants flocked into Rouen seeking the safety of its walls. Thus, the 5,000 inhabitants of Darnétal moved to Rouen when Henry IV occupied the *bourg*. Yet the number of baptisms recorded in parish registers fell by 15 per cent between 1579 and 1594. This was probably due to the flight from the city of many foreign merchants, royal officials, apprentices and artisans.[63]

62 Lloyd, *The Rouen Campaign*, pp. 179–82.

63 Benedict, *Rouen during the Wars of Religion*, pp. 221–4.

The economic crisis in the countryside was even worse than in Rouen, for the continual fighting had prevented peasants from cultivating the land. Tenants had to sue for a reduction of their rent, and villages for a diminution of the *taille*, on account of their crops and livestock having been requisitioned, their houses burnt down and money extorted from them by armed bands. The English intervention in the Rouen campaign had been especially disastrous as the troops had come without supplies and had been encouraged by their officers to feed off the countryside. The crisis in agricultural production also affected Rouen, for its ecclesiastical institutions had extensive rural holdings from which they drew most of their income. Many bourgeois also owned lands outside the city. So the destruction of the countryside seriously affected their income.[64]

Parma's Spanish officers urged him to attack Henry, but Mayenne did not feel strong enough to risk a battle. He persuaded the duke to turn his attention to Caudebec, a Leaguer town blocking the road to Le Havre. This was a grave miscalculation since it allowed Henry to rebuild his army which had dwindled in size over the winter. Many nobles, who had drifted home saying they were exhausted, now returned refreshed and in considerable numbers. The king soon disposed of 8,000 cavalry and 18,000 infantry. He then tried to trap Parma in the Pays de Caux between the Seine and the sea. Meanwhile, on 27 April, the duke captured Caudebec, but he was wounded in the action so that Mayenne had to take over his command for a time. He moved to Yvetot. After some skirmishing on 1 and 2 May, the two armies faced each other for a week. After leading several attacks, Henry eventually succeeded in driving Mayenne's troops into Yvetot. At this juncture, Parma resumed his command. While holding on to Yvetot, he sent a force to fortify the approaches to Caudebec and ordered Villars to send to Caudebec boats and pontoons downstream from Rouen. Then, on the night of 17 May, he marched his army out of Yvetot and brought it secretly to Caudebec. On the night of 21 May, after the bridges and pontoons had been lashed together, Parma's army – 15,000 men in all – crossed the Lower Seine at a point where the river was deemed impassable. The pontoons were dragged to the south bank and set alight. By the time Henry arrived at the scene, the enemy had flown. After crossing the Seine, Parma's army marched at speed, reaching Saint-Cloud in only five days. The duke threw 1,500 infantry into Paris to reinforce the Spanish garrison, then returned to the Netherlands by way of Champagne. On 2 December, however, the duke, who had never fully recovered from his

64 Ibid., pp. 224–6.

wound, died at Arras, depriving the League of one of history's outstanding commanders.[65]

Parma's rapid withdrawal from Normandy left Henry IV with a problem. He could try to pursue the duke, or resume the siege of Rouen, or he might attempt to seize Paris; but none of these options seemed feasible for various reasons. Parma was far ahead and no one knew where he was going; Rouen evoked bitter memories among the royal troops; and the garrison of Paris had been reinforced by Mayenne. The king's army, moreover, having been scraped together from many quarters, was in no fit state to undertake any major operation. The nobles wanted to go home and the foreign auxiliaries were coming to the end of their term of service. So Henry decided to give up serious campaigning for the moment. He allowed his army to break up and set off with a *camp volant*, or flying force, of 3,000 horse and 6,000 foot. By-passing Paris, he turned up in Champagne, hoping, it seems, to relieve Épernay, the only town in that region which he could call his own. It capitulated, however, before he could arrive and Henry spent several weeks trying to regain it. During the siege, Marshal Biron, the king's chief lieutenant, was killed. Épernay fell on 8 August and was soon followed by Provins. After failing before Meaux, Henry returned to Normandy. As the year 1592 ended, Henry was no closer to capturing Paris. He had shown the superiority of his cavalry, but horses were useless for street-fighting.[66]

The provincial stalemate (1592)

In the meantime, royalists and Leaguers fought each other in other parts of France. In the west, the Leaguer duc de Mercoeur, who was firmly entrenched in Brittany, and the seigneur de Boisdauphin, launched an offensive aimed at regaining Maine and Anjou from Henry IV.[67] A royal army, consisting of 6,700 men and 800 horses, tried to seize Craon, but was beaten off, on 23 May, by the League's superior Spanish infantry. Laval, Mayenne and Château-Gontier soon fell. Elsewhere, however, the League was less successful. In Languedoc the duc de Joyeuse, aided by the Spaniards, threatened Montauban after occupying Carcassonne. He planned to enter Guyenne and besiege Villemur, but was defeated on 20 October by a royal army led by Épernon and a force of nobles from Upper Auvergne. In

65 Lloyd, *The Rouen Campaign*, pp. 183–9; Oman, *A History of the Art of War*, pp. 520–25.
66 Buisseret, *Henry IV*, pp. 39–40.
67 Babelon, *Henri IV*, p. 521.

south-east France, the Protestant leader, Lesdiguières, sought to prevent the duke of Savoy from occupying Provence. The latter was helped by the duc de Nemours, leader of the League in the Lyonnais. He planned to turn the region into a principality for himself. It seems that a process was under way whereby a number of provinces would be lopped off and turned into peripheral duchies, like Lorraine and Savoy. While Brittany had, in effect, regained its independence under Mercoeur with Spain's blessing, Provence, Dauphiné and the Lyonnais seemed likely to fall under Savoy's influence. This threat to the integrity of the French kingdom was resolutely opposed by Lesdiguières in Dauphiné, who even managed to carry the war into Piedmont. Meanwhile, Épernon managed to hold on to Provence. Despite these successes, however, Henry IV seemed unable to conquer the kingdom. As the year 1592 ended in a military impasse, many people began to think that only a peaceful compromise would revive the kingdom.[68]

68 Constant, *La Ligue*, pp. 397–8; Buisseret, *Henry IV*, pp. 40–41.

CHAPTER THIRTEEN

Conversion and peace (1592–1598)

After 30 years of almost continuous and destructive warfare, the French people in the 1590s had every reason fervently to desire peace. War was not wholly to blame for their troubles, as we have seen (pp. 209–11). A change of climate was partly to blame for poor harvests and rising prices. In Languedoc, grain prices between 1585 and 1600 sextupled, wages lagged behind prices, and textile production fell. As prices reached their highest levels of the century in the 1580s, taxes also rose. In 1586–7 nearly the whole of France underwent a subsistence crisis; in the north, wheat prices rose by almost 700 per cent. And famine struck again in 1590. In Aix, corn prices soared in 1591–2. As people became undernourished, they fell prey to epidemic diseases which the armies also helped to spread. Everywhere in Europe bubonic plague was rife. But there were many other diseases as well, including influenza, smallpox and typhus. In Marseille, in 1580, thousands died of plague, and other towns – Beaune, Dijon, Chalon-sur-Saône – were also badly hit. All major towns in the Midi suffered at least one outbreak between 1585 and 1598, as did those in Picardy in 1596–7. The countryside was also gravely affected. Wherever plague struck, people fled. These tended to be the better-off so that many urban activities, notably markets and fairs, were suspended. Lawlessness was given free rein as municipal officials fled.

But if not wholly to blame for the wretched state of France at the end of the sixteenth century, war certainly made it far worse. Between 1589 and 1592 military engagements were most intense north of the Loire and particularly around Paris. Towns ran into debt as they bolstered their defences, paid for troops and gave supplies to passing armies in the hope of averting pillage. Troop movements disrupted production, exacerbated food shortages and boosted food prices, while sieges decimated urban populations. The death rate in Rouen rose dramatically, as we have seen, during the siege in 1591–2 (see p. 262). The ravaging of the countryside by troops of either side contributed to the abysmally poor agricultural yields in the 1590s.[1]

A graphic account of the sufferings caused in part by war is contained in the private diary of Eustache Piémond, notary and secretary of the small town of Saint-Antoine in Dauphiné. Piémond despised the Huguenots' methods of warfare: their use of woodland for cover, their living off the countryside, their seizure of granaries and haystacks, and the forts which they used 'to eat the people'. He accused them of attacking towns on feast days, of robbing prisoners and of using new weapons to settle old scores. Huguenots were to him indistinguishable from brigands who infested the roads, particularly after pacifications, when unpaid troops became a menace. But the notary was also critical of the royal armies, especially in the wars of the League between 1586 and 1595. Their campaigns, in his opinion, were a farce; they achieved nothing other than ruining the people. Piémond complained of tax levies by the provincial governor without the consent of the local estates. Large amounts of bread, grain, wine and fodder for the military were demanded from the people at short notice, especially in the harvest season, while military commissioners distrained cattle, sheep and produce. By March 1590 sowing and tilling had become impossible around Saint-Antoine. Billeting, sometimes for regiments larger than the town, placed an enormous strain on food reserves. It also led to various forms of extortion: pillage, imprisonment of peasants, ransoms, protection rackets and the seizure of food supplies. If a town closed its gates, the soldiery was likely to ravage the surrounding countryside. A military company might also seek revenge later on by imprisoning the town's consuls and forcing them to pay for a past wrong.[2]

The hardships suffered by the peasantry as a result of the activities of unruly soldiers were bound sooner or later to provoke unrest. Sometimes, this expressed itself in violence against its social superiors. Thus in Brittany, in September 1590, a wedding party, including some 60 nobles, was completely wiped out by armed peasants. The most important peasant rising was that of the *Croquants*, which began in 1593 and soon spread to a large

---

1 S. A. Finley-Croswhite, *Henry IV and the Towns: The Pursuit of Legitimacy in French Urban Society, 1589–1610* (Cambridge, 1999), pp. 14–17; J. Jacquart, 'Bilan économique des guerres de religion' in *Avènement d'Henri IV. Quatrième centenaire*, vol. 1 Coutras (Pau, 1989), pp. 133–48.

2 M. Greengrass, 'The later Wars of Religion in the Midi', in P. Clark (ed.), *The European Crisis of the 1590s* (London, 1985), pp. 106–9.

part of western France.[3] Some of the peasant gatherings were frighteningly large. At La Boule, near Bergerac, between 20,000 and 40,000 peasants assembled in May 1594. Most contemporary observers saw the main cause of the movement as the cruelties and illegal extortions of the nobility, but in the opinion of one historian 'it was not the normal administration of the seigneurial regime, but rather its gross abuse in circumstances of civil anarchy, that provoked the risings. The plight of the peasantry was the result of three decades of civil war.'[4] The poet Agrippa d'Aubigné despised the *Croquants* but was not indifferent to their suffering. In *Les Tragiques* he describes the plight of a wounded and starving peasant of Périgord who had been left to die by soldiers after witnessing their slaughter of his wife and children. Henry IV showed sympathy for the cause of the peasants. He allegedly said that if he had not been born to inherit the crown, he would have been a *Croquant.*[5] 'There can be no doubt,' writes Holt, 'that the peasant risings of 1593–94 helped to convince Henry IV that a peace settlement and an end to the civil wars was urgently needed.'[6]

Henry IV's conversion (25 July 1593)

On 26 January 1593 the Estates-General of the League, comprising only 128 deputies, met in Paris to decide who should succeed Charles X on the throne. The opening speech was made by Mayenne, as Lieutenant-general. Meanwhile, Henry IV promulgated two acts: the first denied the validity of the assembly and the second suggested that it might be useful to have a series of conferences between representatives of the estates and his own. Though bitterly resisted by Cardinal Pellevé and the more extreme Leaguers, this proposal was accepted on 9 March by a majority of the estates. Twelve deputies of the estates were accordingly picked to meet eight royal representatives. They began their talks on 29 April at Suresnes, near Paris. A ten-day truce was agreed, allowing negotiations to proceed. The main protagonists were Renaud de Beaune, archbishop of Bourges, for the

3 Y. M. Bercé, *Histoire des Croquants*, 2 vols. (Paris and Geneva, 1974), vol. 1, pp. 257–93; H. Heller, *Iron and Blood: Civil Wars in Sixteenth-Century France* (Montreal, 1991), pp. 120–36.

4 J. H. M. Salmon, *Society in Crisis: France in the Sixteenth Century* (London, 1975), p. 282.

5 Ibid., p. 285; D. Buisseret, *Henry IV* (London, 1984), pp. 54–5.

6 M. P. Holt, *The French Wars of Religion, 1562–1629* (Cambridge, 1995), p. 157.

king, and Pierre d'Épinac, archbishop of Lyon, for the League.[7] It soon emerged that Épinac and his colleagues would not challenge Henry IV's constitutional right, only his religion. On 17 May Beaune announced that Henry had decided to become a Catholic. This caused consternation among Leaguer extremists. On 2 April the duke of Feria came to the Estates with various proposals from Philip II in support of his daughter's claim to the French throne, but the majority of deputies resented the pressure being exerted by Spain. Feria's presence and that of Spanish troops in the capital proved counter-productive to the Infanta's cause. The estates declared that 'our laws and customs prevent us from calling forward as king any prince not of our nation', and on 28 June the Parlement reaffirmed this position. Meanwhile, the delegates at Suresnes extended the truce several times. On 8 August most of the deputies to the Estates-General went home.[8]

Henry IV, meanwhile, was being instructed in the Catholic religion. On 16 May he announced his decision to abandon the Protestant faith, and on 25 July he solemnly abjured in the abbey of Saint-Denis.[9] His conversion removed the League's main reason for excluding him from the throne, but doubts remained as to his sincerity. An outspoken sceptic was Jean Boucher, who, in August, preached a series of sermons under the title *Sermons de la simulée conversion* (Sermons on the simulated conversion). France, he argued, as a Christian state must have a Christian ruler. Henry IV, as an excommunicate, could not qualify. Since no bishop could absolve someone who had been excommunicated by the pope, Henry remained a heretic. The Estates-General were bound, therefore, to elect a genuine Catholic as ruler.[10]

Normally, a king of France was crowned at Reims, but as that town was still in the hands of the League, Henry used Chartres, where some medieval *sacres* had taken place. In place of the oil in the Holy Ampulla, which was also kept at Reims, he used a more accessible oil said to have been given by the Virgin to St Martin of Tours. Henry's coronation took place among the usual pomp on 27 February 1594. During the ceremony, he promised *inter alia* to 'expel from all lands under my jurisdiction all heretics denounced by the church'.[11] Many large towns now rallied to him, but in Paris he continued

---

7 M. Wolfe, *The Conversion of Henry IV: Politics, Power and Religious Belief in Early Modern France* (Cambridge, Mass., 1993), pp. 125–31.

8 Buisseret, *Henry IV*, p. 43.

9 Wolfe, *The Conversion of Henry IV*, pp. 146–55; M. Greengrass, 'The public context of the abjuration of Henry IV', in K. Cameron (ed.), *From Valois to Bourbon: Dynasty, State and Society in Early Modern France* (Exeter, 1989), pp. 107–26.

10 Wolfe, *The Conversion of Henry IV*, pp. 159–60.

11 R. A. Jackson, *Vive le Roi! A History of the French Coronation from Charles V to Charles X* (Chapel Hill, N.C., 1984), p. 45; Wolfe, *The Conversion of Henry IV*, p. 174; J.-P. Babelon, *Henri IV* (Paris, 1982), pp. 575–82.

to be opposed by radical elements until March 1594. Mayenne, however, had left the capital, and the governor, Charles de Cossé-Brissac, had been won over to the king. Early in March a plan was worked out to capture the city. On 19 March Brissac held a secret meeting at the Arsenal, doubtless to discuss final arrangements. Meanwhile, Henry IV gathered his forces at Senlis. On 22 March they converged on the capital from all sides except the south. Two gates were opened from within and a chain across the Seine was lifted. Meeting with little resistance, the royal troops converged on the city centre. At 6 a.m. Henry entered Paris by the Porte Neuve and attended mass at Notre-Dame. In the meantime, his heralds and troops distributed pamphlets designed to reassure the inhabitants as to the king's intentions. Some Leaguers tried to whip up resistance, but were soon suppressed. From Notre-Dame the king went to the Louvre for lunch. He then toured the streets as watching crowds cried out 'Vive le Roi!' About 2 p.m. he watched the departure from the capital of 3,000 foreign troops: Neapolitans, Spaniards and Walloons. As they left, Henry allegedly called out to their commander, the duke of Feria, and his fellow captains: 'My compliments to your master, but do not come back!'[12]

Only about 120 Leaguers in Paris refused to submit to the new regime and were accordingly banished from the capital. Brissac became a marshal of France and François d'O succeeded him as the capital's governor. On 28 March the Parlement and the other sovereign courts were formally re-established, and on 30 March a decree cancelled all legislation passed since 29 December 1588 'to the prejudice of the authority of our kings and royal laws'. Over Easter, Henry IV went out of his way to demonstrate his orthodoxy: he washed the feet of the poor on Maundy Thursday, visited the sick at l'Hôtel Dieu, freed some prisoners on Good Friday and touched 600 victims of scrofula on Easter Sunday. Soon afterwards he won over the Faculty of Theology. In September 1595 he reached an agreement with Pope Clement VIII. In return for his absolution, Henry promised to recognize the insufficiency of his abjuration, to publish the decrees of the Council of Trent, to restore Catholicism in Béarn and to appoint only Catholics to high office.[13]

The submission of Paris persuaded many other towns to do likewise. Municipal magistrates, who had originally supported the League for religious reasons, advocated accepting Henry IV now that he had become a Catholic. Their feelings were well expressed in a manifesto issued by the authorities in Riom. They had joined the League because of his Calvinist

12 P.-V. Palma-Cayet, *Chronologie novenaire* and *Chronologie septenaire*, ed. J. A. Buchon (Paris, 1836), p. 629. Cited by Buisseret, *Henry IV*, p. 53. See also Babelon, *Henri IV*, pp. 583–91.

13 Buisseret, *Henry IV*, pp. 53–4.

faith, but now they could see no reason to continue doing so. Henry IV was also able to exploit urban disenchantment with the League for failing to deliver on its promises. A carpenter of Reims, Jean Pussot, who had been a Leaguer, denounced the duc de Guise in his journal for profiteering from the war. In Dijon, Hennequin, the parlement's first president, argued that the inhabitants wanted to accept Henry IV, but he was opposed by a few powerful Leaguers. Some urban authorities found themselves under popular pressure to renounce the League. This was demanded, for example, by weavers in Amiens, wine-growers in Dijon and by militia captains in Lyon. On 8 February 1594 the Lyonnais threw away their green Leaguer scarves for white royalist ones. A militia captain put up a large portrait of Henry IV outside the town hall and, next day, Alphonse d'Ornano marched into the city and accepted its surrender. Not every town submitted to Henry IV without a struggle. Laon, for example, only capitulated in July 1594 after he had besieged it. Other towns in Picardy and Île-de-France followed suit rather than undergo the same fate.[14]

The towns may have been won over by Henry IV but they made him pay heavily for their submission. Town governors who aided the surrender were handsomely rewarded. Thus the sieur de Saisseval, governor of Beauvais, received a share of 2,600 écus for helping to bring about the town's capitulation. Claude de La Châtre, governor and lieutenant-general of Berry, received 250,000 écus for bringing Orléans and Bourges into the king's camp. 'Treaties of capitulation' contained clauses which excluded Protestants from worship within a town and confirmed the office-holders whom Mayenne had appointed. Henry's followers, whose offices had been taken over by Leaguers, were promised compensation. Sometimes, too, Henry agreed to settle a town's debts, to remit arrears of *taille* and to exempt it from tax for some years. Huge sums were also paid to noblemen. As Sir George Carew remarked: 'those, who hazarded their lives and fortunes for settling the crown upon his head, [the king] neither rewardeth nor payeth; those who were of the League against him, he hath bought to be his friends and giveth them preferments'.[15] According to Sully, Henry spent between 30 and 32 million livres in treaties 'for the recovery of the kingdom'. He was accused of demeaning the monarchy by paying out such bribes, but, as he told Sully, he would have had to pay ten times as much to achieve the same result by the sword.[16]

---

14 Finley-Croswhite, *Henry IV and the Towns*, pp. 17–22.

15 Sir George Carew, 'A relation of the state of France', in T. Birch (ed.), *An Historical View of the Relations between the Courts of England, France and Brussels, 1592–1617* (1749), p. 478. Cited by R. Bonney, *The King's Debts* (Oxford, 1981), p. 43.

16 Bonney, *The King's Debts*, p. 44.

The war against Spain

Towards the end of 1594 Henry had to face several threats. In Burgundy, Mayenne was relying on the support of Spanish forces in Franche-Comté; in the Lyonnais, Nemours had introduced troops from Savoy; in Provence, Épernon had joined the opposition; in Languedoc, Joyeuse was resisting Montmorency after breaking off talks; and in the west, Mercoeur was threatening Anjou and Maine. But Henry knew that, without the active support of Spain, the League would almost certainly crumble. On 17 January 1595, therefore, he declared war on Spain. His move, according to Villeroy, had three objectives: first, to 'lift the mask of religion' which his opponents were using as a cover for their resistance; secondly, to give himself the option of taking the war on to Spanish soil; and thirdly, to reassure the Protestant powers that his conversion had not turned him into a puppet of Spain. Henry IV, on the contrary, intended to show how Philip II's ambition was destroying Christendom's unity. By declaring war on Spain, he transformed the civil war into a foreign war aimed at liberating French soil, and turned the Leaguers into traitors.[17]

Anxious as Henry IV was to defend the northern border of France, he was also aware of the risk that the Spanish forces in north Italy posed for Burgundy. This danger materialized in May when an army, 10,000 strong, under Velasco, the Constable of Castile, marched on Dijon to assist Mayenne. He, having lost the town to the royalists, was still holding the citadel. Responding to calls for help from Marshal Biron, Henry left Paris on 24 May, gathered an army at Troyes, and marched swiftly to Dijon. On 5 June, a small cavalry force under Biron encountered the Spaniards near the village of Fontaine-Française. Biron thought they were only outriders, only to discover that the whole of the Spanish vanguard was upon him. Even after the king had joined the fray, the royal forces were heavily outnumbered, yet by leading furious cavalry charges Henry forced Velasco to withdraw. He was the last king of France to lead the cavalry into battle and did so sometimes on the spur of the moment without being fully prepared. At Fontaine-Française he had discharged his pistol and needed another, whereupon the seigneur de La Varenne, who watched over him, handed him one of his own, fully loaded and ready to be fired. Two days after the battle, Henry knighted La Varenne in recognition of his timely intervention.[18]

17 Babelon, *Henri IV*, p. 608.

18 D. Buisseret, 'Henri IV et l'art militaire', in *Henri IV, le roi et la reconstruction du royaume* (Pau: Association Henri IV, 1989), pp. 334–6.

Fontaine-Française may not have been a major battle, but its consequences proved very important; for Velasco, after falling out with Mayenne over tactics, refused to have anything more to do with him. Without Spanish help, the duke could not hope to regain Dijon. While he retired to Chalon, Henry mopped up various castles in Burgundy. Tavannes surrendered Dijon's citadel on 13 June in return for the promise of a marshal's baton and 12,000 écus. Having tightened his hold on Burgundy, Henry carried out a destructive raid into Franche-Comté, but Velasco failed to react. Nor was he prepared to assist the League. On 22 September under the Treaty of Lyon, which reaffirmed the neutrality of the 'two Burgundies', Henry IV effectively removed the Spanish threat from his eastern border. Mayenne was thus reduced to the status of an isolated rebel. Meanwhile, wherever Henry went in Burgundy he was acclaimed by the people. He endeared himself to them by his simple attire, his torn doublet and by word and gesture. In June and July several Leaguer nobles went over to his side. Among them was the elderly comte de Charny, lieutenant-general of Burgundy, who was soon followed by lesser fry. While some submitted in the hope of being rewarded by the king, others offered him supplies and munitions.[19]

Finding himself virtually alone, Mayenne began talks with royal agents. Clement VIII's absolution of Henry IV helped him to save face in respect of what remained of the League. His main concern was to retain the governorship of Burgundy which had been his for 22 years, but on this Henry IV stood firm: he gave the post to Marshal Biron. Eventually, under the Peace Edict of Folembray (31 January 1596) Mayenne received the governorship of Île-de-France and three security towns: Chalon-sur-Saône, Seurre and Soissons. His son was appointed governor of the *bailliage* of Chalon for six years. Henry IV took upon himself the payment of Mayenne's war debts. The duke was declared innocent of Henry III's murder and all decrees which had been issued against him were annulled. He was cleared of all liability in respect of appointments to offices, acts of war and financial measures. Burgundian Leaguers who had been appointed to offices by Mayenne were allowed to keep them. A few weeks after this treaty was signed, Mayenne made his submission to the king at Montceaux.[20] The dukes of Épernon and Joyeuse soon followed suit. As Guise had already joined the king in January, only the duc de Mercoeur among the great nobles remained obdurate.

Having more or less gained control of Burgundy (there was still a certain amount of local disorder by petty nobles), Henry needed urgently to direct

19 H. Drouot, *Mayenne et la Bourgogne: Étude sur la Ligue (1587–1596)* (Paris, 1937), vol. 2, pp. 417–40.

20 Ibid., pp. 450–63.

his efforts to defending the northern frontier of his kingdom from another Spanish offensive, this time led by the count of Fuentes, the new governor of the Low Countries, who was an able but cruel general. After capturing Le Catelet on 25 June 1595, Fuentes marched on Doullens, an important stronghold north of the Somme, and seized it after inflicting heavy losses on the French garrison. 'Them of Abbeville and Amiens do demand garrisons, they fear so for the Spaniards,' wrote Otwell Smyth to Essex on 24 July. 'The taking of Dorland [Doullens] so furiously maketh them all to tremble, it is to be feared that if the King come not into Picardy all stands in great danger to be lost. The enemy is 16,000 men strong and yet looketh for more forces daily.'[21] From Doullens, Fuentes moved against Cambrai. Henry was still in Lyon at the time, but saw the danger. Writing to Boisdauphin on 12 September, he said that he would save Cambrai or die in the attempt.

Henry IV, however, was again desperately short of money. His appeals for help from abroad fell largely on deaf ears. Except for the duchy of Tuscany, none of the Italian states was prepared to free itself from Spanish tutelage. The Protestant powers no longer trusted Henry after his conversion. The German princes and England offered Henry virtually nothing; only the Dutch and the Swiss provided loans and some troops. So the king was forced to raise money at home, but this encountered stiff opposition. Royal tax collectors came under attack from the people; an attempt to reduce the amount of interest paid to *rentiers* in Paris was fiercely opposed by the Parlement; a proposed tax on walled towns was blocked by the *Cour des aides*; and sales of royal domain were resisted by the sovereign courts.[22]

The war, meanwhile, was going badly for Henry. Early in October the inhabitants of Cambrai, who had been subjected to a fierce bombardment by Spanish guns, opened one of their gates to the enemy. The unpopular French governor, Balagny, retired to the citadel, but surrendered on 7 September. After gathering a large army, Henry laid siege to La Fère, the last remaining Spanish outpost south of the Somme. He had at his disposal 2,000 cavalry, 3,000 Swiss, 2,500 *landsknechts*, 4,000 French 'skirmishers' who were 'ill paid and daily disbanding', and 1,800 French infantry under La Noue, besides more than 2,000 under Justin of Nassau. But the siege proved difficult and costly. The king bombarded his council of finance with letters of complaint. His exasperation is reflected in a letter to Sully: 'My shirts are torn, my trousers are worn out, my larder is often bare, and, for two days, I have had to dine and eat out with others. My purveyors say that

21 Cal.MSS.Salisbury, vol. V, p. 189. Cited by Buisseret, *Henry IV*, pp. 58–9.

22 M. Greengrass, *France in the Age of Henry IV* (London, 2nd edn 1995), p. 127.

they can no longer feed me because they have received no money for the past six months. By this you may judge whether I should be thus treated and whether I ought any longer to permit financiers and treasurers to let me die of hunger while they sit at well-laden and stocked tables.'[23]

The siege of Amiens (April–September 1597)

In the spring of 1596 the Spaniards launched a new offensive. They captured Calais in April, then Ardres. In May, things began to look up for Henry when La Fère at last capitulated, but his need for money remained acute. He called an Assembly of Notables but a proposal for a sales tax (the *pancarte*) was only registered by the Parlement after prolonged resistance. Meanwhile, Marshal Biron gathered munitions and supplies in various Picard towns, including Amiens, in preparation for an attack on Arras in the spring. Unfortunately, the citizens of Amiens claimed the privilege of self-defence and refused to admit a royal garrison. On 11 March 1597 a force of Spaniards disguised as peasants entered the town in broad daylight and captured it. Henry IV, who was in Paris at the time, was shattered by the news. He gathered his councillors in haste and told them that Amiens had to be recaptured although this was likely to prove difficult. Once again, Henry looked to Rosny to come to the rescue, but the urgency of the situation called for expedients, not reforms. The crisis was worsened by the refusal of Huguenot commanders, Bouillon and La Trémoïlle, to assist the king with their 6,000 troops. They also began to seize his revenues in areas under their control. It was even possible that they would make common cause with Catholic 'Malcontents'.[24] Writing to Schomberg, Henry IV said: 'I am not only unwell, but also assailed by so many problems and burdens that I hardly know which saint to invoke in order to lead me out of this unfortunate situation.' While the *Chambre des Comptes* refused to register new fiscal edicts, the municipality of Paris proved equally uncooperative. The mayor protested at the king's failure to pay the *rentes* and complained of corruption in the fiscal administration. Parisians were prepared to grant 360,000 livres to pay for 3,000 Swiss troops for six months, but Henry needed 3.6 million to raise an army and 450,000 livres each month thereafter to pay for its upkeep. The Parisians pointed out that 27 million livres,

23 Henri IV, *Lettres*, iv, 567. Cited by Greengrass, *France in the Age of Henry IV*, p. 128.
24 Greengrass, *France in the Age of Henry IV*, p. 101.

which had been raised in taxes in 1596 had been misused on royal largesse. They saw the fall of Amiens as symptomatic of fiscal maladministration.[25]

While Henry IV set off on 12 March for Picardy where he reinforced the garrisons, gathered troops and munitions, and summoned the *ban et l'arrière ban,* his council of finance took urgent steps to fund the campaign: offices were created, a loan raised from the 'better off', certain debt repayments deferred, and a *crue* on salt levied. On 8 May a special tribunal (*Chambre royale*) was set up ostensibly to prosecute corrupt or lazy fiscal officials, but in reality to frighten them into buying themselves off by making non-refundable advances to the king. Once this purpose had been achieved, the court was disbanded and a general amnesty declared for the interested parties. At the same time, two edicts in June and July created a third holder for each office in the fiscal administration, so that a rota was established, each officer serving one year in three instead of one in every two. Enforcing these measures did not prove easy as they had to be registered first by the sovereign courts. The Parlement's obstructionism angered Henry IV so much that he came to the court on 21 May and sharply rebuked its members, accusing them of disloyalty at a time of national emergency.[26]

Biron had been besieging Amiens with only 3,000 men since April. He was joined on 8 June by Henry IV with sizeable reinforcements, including artillery. The king was accompanied by the Secretary of State, Villeroy, who had the duty, in wartime, of keeping the lists of troops and transmitting the king's orders to the field commanders. In the meantime, the Council of finance remained in Paris under Sully's direction. Throughout the summer, he corresponded actively with the king and Villeroy. At the same time, he sold newly created offices, oversaw the manufacture of cannon at the Arsenal, supervised purchases of victuals and munitions, sent urgently needed cash to pay the troops, and kept a close watch on the activities of the *Chambre des comptes.* The king, for his part, kept up the pressure on the minister. On 8 July, for example, he asked for 4,000 écus needed to pay his artillery: that very day, eight artillerymen had deserted for lack of pay. Henry also needed money for his stables and even for his own clothes. 'For I am stark naked,' he wrote, 'and it seems to me unreasonable that I should be treated thus considering all that I am doing for the salvation of France.'[27]

By June 1597 Henry IV had thrown a series of forts linked by trenches around Amiens. The works, which were directed by a Frenchman, Jean

25 Bonney, *The King's Debts*, pp. 50–53.

26 Ibid., p. 53; B. Barbiche and S. de Dainville-Barbiche, *Sully: l'homme et ses fidèles* (Paris, 1997), pp. 74–5.

27 Ibid., pp. 75–6.

Errard, were so substantial that traces of them are still visible today in aerial photographs. By the end of August the king disposed of some 20,000 infantry, 3,000 cavalry and 45 cannon. Supplying such a huge army was not easy. Royal officials working with merchants engaged for the occasion provided the victuals. As from 1 July, 29,000 loaves of bread were needed each day. Other provisions were doubtless bought from the sutlers' tents visible on contemporary plans of the French camp. These also show a fortified pontoon bridge which the king threw across the Somme. The army's supplies came by boat from Abbeville. Near the bridgehead Villeroy had set up a field hospital, the first of its kind in France. It could cater for 250 wounded soldiers, mostly infantrymen.[28] The Spanish garrison defending Amiens was numerically inferior to the king's army: 4,000 infantry and 1,000 cavalry. The king could also count on support of royalists within the city where the League had become unpopular.[29] On 3 September the commander of the Spanish garrison was killed. Later that month, a relieving army 21,000 strong and led by Cardinal-Archduke Albert marched south from Brussels. It arrived outside Amiens on 15 September. While Henry IV was away hunting, Biron and Mayenne (now fighting for the king) beat off two successive attacks, inflicting heavy losses. As the cardinal withdrew, the citizens of Amiens surrendered. On 20 September Henry IV sent his most famous letter: 'Brave Crillon, hang yourself for not having been here last Monday on the finest of all occasions and one that may never be seen again. You may be sure that I missed you greatly. The cardinal who called on us with much fury, has gone home with much shame. I hope to be in Amiens next Thursday, where I shall not tarry before undertaking another enterprise, for I now have one of the finest armies imaginable. Only brave Crillon, who will always be welcome and well regarded by me, is missing. Adieu!'[30] On 25 September the king did indeed make his entry into Amiens. Sitting on his horse, sceptre in hand and surrounded by dukes and princes of the blood, he witnessed the departure of the Spanish garrison. As the troops marched past, they lowered their standards and the captains genuflected. The marquis de Montenegro is even said to have kissed the king's boot. The terms of the Spanish surrender were extremely generous. They were allowed to carry away their dead and wounded in hundreds of carts.[31] But Henry had not forgiven the Amiénois for their refusal to admit his troops.

---

28 Buisseret, 'Henri IV et l'art militaire', pp. 336–40.

29 For an interesting account of divisions within Amiens' ruling élite see Finley-Croswhite, *Henry IV and the Towns*, pp. 23–46, but she confuses the date of the town's surrender. This was in September 1597, not August.

30 Cited by Babelon, *Henri IV*, pp. 621–2.

31 I owe this information to the kindness of Prof. Mark Greengrass.

Before leaving the town he ordered the erection of a citadel so that the inhabitants should no longer speak of 'our town'.[32]

'We have recovered Amiens,' Henry IV wrote to Duplessis-Mornay, 'we must now recover Brittany. Our wishes, forces and means must be turned in that direction.' Mercoeur, who continued to hold out for the League in Brittany, felt isolated following the fall of Amiens; he was also being harassed by Marshal Brissac. The time had come for Henry IV to act, especially as the Bretons were complaining of his slowness in liberating them. So early in 1598 the king set off westward with an army 14,000 strong. As he approached, the towns expelled their Leaguer garrisons. Dinan was followed by Fougères, Vannes, and Hennebont. The king also received the submissions of the governors of Craon and Rochefort in Anjou and of Mirebeau in Poitou. Mercoeur judged the time ripe to give in. Henry received his emissaries at Angers and an accord was reached on 20 March. The duke gave up the governorship of Brittany in return for the enormous sum of 4,295,000 livres. He also agreed to the marriage of his only daughter to the king's illegitimate son, César de Vendôme.[33]

The Edict of Nantes (13 April 1598)

From the time of his abjuration, Henry's relations with his former co-religionists had deteriorated. They knew that he had sworn at his coronation to extirpate all heresy from his kingdom and were dismayed by his efforts to appease the League. Protestant assemblies at Sainte-Foy (1594), Saumur (1595) and Loudun (1596) had seen the development of an increasingly intransigent group. They sought a legal settlement guaranteeing their 'state within the state'. The militancy of the Huguenots was reflected in the noble domination of the assembly at Châtellerault (1597).[34] By this time, as we have seen, they had become so alienated from the king as to refuse him assistance to recapture Amiens. By the spring of 1598, however, Henry's situation had much improved: he had recaptured Amiens and was negotiating peace terms with Spain. Mercoeur had abandoned his lone resistance in Brittany. So the Huguenots were induced, after much hard bargaining, to accept the Edict of Nantes.[35] This consisted of four documents: 92 general

32 Agrippa d'Aubigné, *Histoire universelle,* ed. A. Thierry, vol. IX (Geneva, 1995), pp. 128–9.

33 Babelon, *Henri IV*, pp. 622–3.

34 Holt, *The French Wars of Religion*, p. 162.

35 R. Mousnier, *The Assassination of Henry IV: The Tyrannicide Problem and the Consolidation of the French Absolute Monarchy in the Early Seventeenth Century* (London, 1973), pp. 144–51, 316–63; N. M. Sutherland, *The Huguenot Struggle for Recognition* (New Haven, 1980), pp. 328–32.

articles, 56 secret articles and two royal *brevets*. The 92 articles generally reaffirmed the provisions of earlier edicts. Liberty of conscience was conceded and Protestant worship under three headings: first, on the estates of Huguenot nobles; secondly, at two places in each *bailliage* to be decided by royal commissioners; and thirdly, wherever Huguenots could prove that it had been openly practised in 1596 and 1597. Article 27 removed the religious qualification from the right to acquire or inherit any office. Bipartisan courts (*chambres mi-parties*) were to be set up in the parlements to judge lawsuits involving Protestants. However, Huguenots were not allowed to impose taxes, to build fortifications, to levy troops or to hold political assemblies. The so-called 'secret' articles were not really secret: they attempted to harmonize the general articles with specific promises which had been made to certain towns, such as Paris or Toulouse, exempting them from heretical services within their walls and immediate suburbs. Some clauses dealt with the establishment of Protestant universities and the training of ministers. The two *brevets* were in some ways the most important feature of the edict, as they granted Protestants a limited degree of military and political independence. One *brevet* provided for the payment of stipends to Protestant pastors from public funds; the other allowed the Huguenots to hold for eight years all the towns which they occupied in August 1597. It also arranged for annual royal payments to their garrisons.[36]

The Edict of Nantes has often been mistakenly interpreted as an attempt to establish a permanent regime of religious toleration in France. By describing the edict as 'perpetual and irrevocable', Henry meant that it could only be countermanded by another edict registered by the parlements. Nor was the edict aimed at establishing a lasting regime of religious toleration. Its purpose was to create the conditions which in time would allow the kingdom to regain its traditional Catholic unity. Henry IV clearly wanted this. The preamble to the edict's public articles states: 'now that it has pleased God to give us a beginning of enjoying some Rest, we think we cannot imploy ourself better [than] to apply to that which may tend to the glory and service of his holy name, and to provide that he may be adored and prayed unto by all our Subjects: and if it hath not yet pleased him to permit it to be in one and the same form of Religion, that it may at the least be with one and the same intention.'[37] By deliberately avoiding any mention of belief or doctrine the edict focused on the need to integrate the Huguenots socially into a Catholic state. Even within its own limitations, the edict was far from even-handed. While the Huguenots were given important

36 Greengrass, *France in the Age of Henry IV*, pp. 100–6.
37 Mousnier, *The Assassination of Henry IV*, p. 317.

concessions, they were denied equality of status with Catholics. Whereas the latter enjoyed freedom of conscience and worship everywhere in France, the Huguenots' right to worship was severely restricted. What is more, the edict called for a restoration of Catholic worship where it had been banned by the Huguenots. The latter were also obliged to observe Catholic feast days by abstaining from work. They were forbidden to sell books outside areas under their control and had to submit any printed matter to official censors. Finally, they had to obey Catholic laws on marriage and contracts, and were expected, like Catholics, to pay the tithe. Huguenot extremists disliked the edict, but the majority appear to have realized that Henry IV could not have secured a fairer settlement for churches that included barely 6 or 7 per cent of his subjects.[38]

In spite of the restrictions imposed on the Huguenots by the edict, Catholic resistance was fierce. In Paris the clergy organized street demonstrations and processions against it. The Parlement refused at first to register it, forcing the king to administer a fatherly rebuke. His speech to a group of *parlementaires* who came to see him at the Louvre was remarkable for its directness:

> You see me here in my study, where I have come to speak to you, not in royal attire like my predecessors, nor with cloak and sword, nor as a prince who has come to speak with foreign ambassadors, but dressed like the father of a family, in a doublet, to speak freely to his children . . . What I have done is in the cause of peace. I have secured peace abroad and I desire peace at home. You are obliged to obey me, if for no other consideration than my rank and the duty of all my subjects have towards me, particularly all of you, members of my Parlement . . . I am aware that there have been intrigues in the Parlement, and preachers urged to talk sedition, but I shall take care of such people without expecting any help from you . . . I shall nip in the bud all factions and attempts at seditious preaching; and I shall behead all those who encourage it. I have leapt on to the walls of towns; surely I can leap over barricades, which are not so high.[39]

Two weeks later the Parlement registered the edict, albeit with an important modification. Article 2 was altered in such a way as effectively to deny Huguenots the right to have churches outside their own secure towns. In time the provincial parlements grudgingly followed suit: Grenoble did so in September 1599, Dijon and Toulouse in January 1600, Aix and Rennes

38 E. Labrousse, 'Calvinism in France, 1598–1685', in M. Prestwich (ed.), *International Calvinism, 1541–1715* (Oxford, 1985), p. 285.

39 Mousnier, *The Assassination of Henry IV*, pp. 364–5.

in August 1600 and Rouen only in August 1609.[40] Thus in many parts of France the edict did not become law for some considerable time.

Even when the Edict of Nantes had become legally binding, it needed to be enforced. Commissioners were sent out to the provinces, usually in pairs – one Catholic and one Protestant. They were chosen from men experienced in public affairs. An idea of the difficulties they experienced may be gathered from the minutes of visitations in Dauphiné. Villages with a Catholic population or a seigneur intent on resistance could frustrate the commissioners for years. They had to cope with disputes over such matters as confessional numbers, the ancestry of Huguenot churches, and the return of refugees. In the Oulx valley the commissioners were not able to enforce Protestant worship until 1614. A major difficulty they had to overcome was the siting of Huguenot churches. More often than not, Protestant services had been held in confiscated Catholic churches. As these were returned under the edict, new Protestant temples had to be built. The commissioners had to decide where to put them and how to pay for them. Sometimes, they had to sort out the confessional balance on town councils or deal with ecclesiastical benefices. They encouraged local communities to assemble and swear to live as good neighbours under the king's authority. Local notables were sometimes persuaded to embrace each other and swear to put aside their differences. 'In this way,' writes Greengrass, 'stability was nurtured gradually and from below, from the roots of local sociability which the civil wars had only temporarily trampled on.'[41] Outside Dauphiné commissioners also encountered opposition. In the north and east, the siting of sites of Protestant worship proved especially difficult. Only two were set up initially in Picardy although there were many Huguenots in the province. In Champagne the commissioners had to adjudicate between Huguenot communities competing to be chosen as sites for worship. The siting of churches in the suburbs of main towns was especially contentious.[42]

There is no doubt that Henry's ultimate objective was religious unity. Speaking to the cardinal of Florence in September 1598, he said that the garrison towns given to the Huguenots were only temporary, as he hoped that all Protestants would have abjured by 1606. In 1607 Jean Hotman de Villiers told Pierre de l'Estoile that the king was backing his efforts and those of others to reunify the churches. The king realized that religious concord was only achievable within the framework of the Gallican church and for this reason he tried, seldom successfully, to persuade Huguenot

40 Greengrass, *France in the Age of Henry IV*, p. 108.
41 Greengrass, *France in the Age of Henry IV*, p. 110.
42 Ibid., pp. 108–111.

nobles to abjure their faith. One of his successes was Jacques d'Hilaire, seigneur de Jovyac, who dedicated a book to the king entitled *The Happy Conversion of Huguenots*. But Henry was careful not to offend the Huguenots by giving special favours to those who abjured: as Mack Holt writes, 'Henry was very faithful to the Huguenots and never sold them out.' He worked hard in defence of their rights, thereby fuelling speculation among Catholics that he was a Nicodemite, in other words, a Catholic in public and a Calvinist in private. In the interest of keeping the peace, he maintained visible ties with the Huguenot community. There were many Huguenot nobles at his court and a number served in his council. Foremost among these was the baron de Rosny, who became duc de Sully in 1606.[43]

The Edict of Nantes was not fundamentally new: it formed part of the long series of religious edicts reaching back into the sixteenth century and incorporated some of their provisions, but unlike them it lasted longer, largely on account of war-weariness on both sides. The edict, in fact, was only a truce which enabled Protestants and Catholics to live side by side within the state pending religious reunification. Neither side regarded it as permanent. It fell short of what many Huguenots wanted: equality with Catholics. It did not create 'a state within the state', as is sometimes claimed, for the two *brevets* on which this claim rests were personal promises made by Henry IV which did not bind his successors. By paying the Huguenots for their churches and garrisons, he bought their loyalty and bound them more closely to the monarchy. At best the edict made them a privileged group within the kingdom, but one that remained heavily dependent on royal favour.

The Peace of Vervins (2 May 1598)

While Henry IV was fighting Mercoeur in Brittany, two of his agents, Bellièvre and Brûlart de Sillery, negotiated a peace treaty with Spain, which was signed at Vervins on 2 May 1598. It laid down that all towns captured by either side since the peace of Cateau-Cambrésis in 1559 should be returned. Thus France had to give back Cambrai, but recovered Ardres, Calais, Doullens and other places. The fate of the marquisate of Saluzzo, which the duke of Savoy had seized in 1588, was referred to papal arbitration, but Clement VIII, after some feeble efforts on his part, abandoned the responsibility. In 1599 the duke, Charles-Emmanuel, decided to negotiate

43 Holt, *The French Wars of Religion*, pp. 169–71.

directly with Henry IV. On visiting Fontainebleau, he denied that he had come to surrender the marquisate. The matter was then submitted to a committee chaired by the Patriarch of Constantinople. On 27 February an agreement was reached. The duke promised to surrender Saluzzo by 1 June or to cede other territories. Soon afterwards, however, he sought Spanish aid to defend Saluzzo. By July Henry realized that he had been duped. On 11 August he declared war on Savoy. As French troops invaded the duchy, capturing Chambéry and other towns, the pope intervened. On 17 January 1601 a new treaty was signed. Henry gave up Saluzzo, but received in return Bresse, Bugey, Valromey and Gex. The loss of Saluzzo deprived France of the power to counterbalance Spanish influence in northern Italy. On the other hand, Henry acquired the pont de Grésin, part of the vital 'Spanish road' used by Spanish armies marching to the Low Countries from the Milanese. Henceforth, France was able to cut it at will, thereby forcing the Spaniards to look for an alternative route to the north through the Grisons.

The assassination of Henry IV (14 May 1610)

Although Henry IV is remembered as one of France's most popular kings, no less than 20 attempts were made on his life during his reign. In August 1593 Pierre Barrière tried to kill him in Melun, allegedly with the encouragement of the Jesuits. The king, who had not yet been absolved by the pope, was still regarded by many Catholics as a lapsed Catholic. In December 1594 he was stabbed by Jean Chastel, a law student, and slightly injured. Chastel was executed and the Jesuits banished from the kingdom after the Parlement had wrongly implicated them in the crime. In 1596 a Flemish Dominican, called Ridicauwe, came to France intent on killing Henry. So the king was never out of danger. Extreme Catholics continued to cast doubt on the sincerity of his conversion and to see him as an agent of Satan. On 14 May 1610 Henry was fatally stabbed through the open window of his coach as he was travelling across Paris. The assailant, Ravaillac, claimed under torture that he had acted alone. He believed that the king had failed in his Christian duty by not forcing the Huguenots to become Catholics. Unhinged as he almost certainly was, Ravaillac was not alone in regarding Henry as a tyrant whom a private person could lawfully kill. His action was backed by a body of political theory which had been evolved during the religious wars.

The king's assassination plunged France into a crisis similar to that of 1559, when Henry II had been accidentally killed. Both monarchs were in their prime at the time and left only children to succeed them. Henry's son, Louis XIII, was eight years old in 1610, so that his mother, Marie de' Medici, became regent. She had been brought up as a Catholic in Italy and soon upset the Huguenots by alienating the duc de Sully, who, as a Protestant himself, was best able to defend their interests in the royal council. He resigned early in 1611, leaving the government in the hands of three so-called 'greybeards' – Jeannin, Villeroy and Brûlart – all of them ex-Leaguers, albeit moderate ones. The Huguenots had good reason to wonder if the Edict of Nantes would be honoured. Inevitably, they looked to their own nobility to defend them. Condé having already abjured, only two Huguenot noblemen were capable of wielding sufficient influence: Bouillon and Rohan. The former urged his co-religionists to trust the regent as they had trusted her husband, but his advice fell on deaf ears. The Huguenots wanted a more militant champion. In 1611 at their assembly in Saumur, they appointed Rohan as their political and military leader. He was supported by several other nobles, including La Force, Soubise and Châtillon. The 'Saumur assembly', writes Holt, 'underscored the total repoliticization of the Huguenot movement led by the grandees, something the Edict of Nantes had been designed explicitly to prevent.'[44]

The last religious war (1610–1629)

The Edict of Nantes is traditionally regarded as marking the end of the French Wars of Religion. 'Its peculiarity,' writes E. Labrousse, 'is that it was to remain in force – at least on paper – for eighty-seven years.'[45] However, it would be wrong to imagine that relations between Catholics and Protestants in France remained peaceful for the whole of that time. The situation that existed in the diocese of Luçon where Armand du Plessis, the future cardinal Richelieu, became bishop in 1609 may not have been untypical. While the Huguenots complained that he was harassing them in various ways, Catholics alleged that they were not always allowed to worship in peace by their Huguenot neighbours. The bishop and his clergy complained several times to the king about damage being done to churches by Huguenots. Another Catholic grievance was the refusal of Huguenots to pay certain taxes.[46]

---

44 Ibid., p. 175.

45 E. Labrousse, 'Calvinism in France', p. 285.

46 R. J. Knecht, *Richelieu* (London: Longman, 1991), p. 68.

In May 1611 the regent, Marie de' Medici, ordered the deputies attending a Protestant assembly at Saumur to disperse after they had appointed six spokesmen to defend their interests at court; but they would not listen. Instead they declared their assembly to be permanent and sent various extreme demands to Marie. Talks between them lasted four months. In the end, the delegates dispersed but on terms which were deemed harmful to the kingdom's political unity. According to Richelieu, they were bent on 'disturbing the peace of the state and on fishing in troubled waters'. The bishop stated his position in his closing address to the Estates-General of 1614. Huguenots who resorted to violence, he said, should be severely punished; the rest should be left in peace. 'We desire only their conversion,' he declared, 'and we wish to promote it by our example, teaching and prayers. These are the only weapons with which we want to fight them.'[47]

The deputies of the clergy at the Estates-General of 1614 were more militant: while they were prepared to accept the Edict of Nantes as a temporary political necessity, they believed that Protestantism should be banned in France. They also held that the Edict of Nantes should be enforced in Protestant areas and were horrified to learn that the small independent *comté* of Béarn was not covered by it. Here, Catholic property remained in Protestant hands and the Mass was banned. The estates accordingly demanded not only the restoration of Catholicism in Béarn, but also the annexation of the territory to France. When the king's council, on 25 June, ordered Catholic worship and all church property to be restored in Béarn, the local estates protested, whereupon Louis XIII marched south with an army intent on imposing his will. On 15 October, at Pau, the council of Béarn asked for a royal pardon, but Louis responded by dismissing the town's Protestant governor and replacing him by a Catholic. On 19 October he formally annexed Béarn and Navarre to France, and ordered the restoration of Catholic worship and the restitution of church property in both territories. Next day, a *Te Deum* was celebrated in the churches of Pau.[48]

The French annexation of Béarn was not the only calamity suffered by Protestants at this time; another was the defeat at the White Mountain by the Habsburgs of the Calvinist ruler Frederick V, Elector Palatine and King of Bohemia. The two events, happening so close together, struck fear into the hearts of Huguenots, who had been feeling increasingly vulnerable since the death of Henry IV. In December 1620, at an illegal assembly at

47 J. M. Hayden, *France and the Estates General of 1614* (Cambridge, 1974), pp. 15–16.

48 A. D. Lublinskaya, *French Absolutism: the Crucial Phase, 1620–1629* (Cambridge, 1968), p. 172; Knecht, *Richelieu*, pp. 70–71.

La Rochelle, they decided to resist the government by force, if necessary. Not all the Huguenot nobility were a party to this decision. Lesdiguières, Sully and Bouillon stayed away from the assembly, leaving the responsibility for action to die-hards, such as La Force, Soubise, and La Trémoïlle. The assembly ordered troops to be raised at public expense. Protestant France was divided into eight military regions or *cercles* under the supreme command of Henri de Rohan. The security towns were put on a war footing and provincial assemblies were instructed to organize resistance. In short, the independent Huguenot state in the Midi, often mistakenly referred to as a 'republic', was revived. The Chancellor, Brûlart de Sillery, expressed his dismay to Venetian ambassadors:

> I tell you in confidence, Messieurs, I do not know what will become of us. The disease is in our blood and in our entrails. The Huguenots have set up a body which damages the king's authority and wrests the sceptre from his hand. At La Rochelle they hold an assembly without permission, they draw up statutes, they decide on taxes, they collect money, they arraign militias, they build fortifications as if the king did not exist and as if they were absolute masters.[49]

Not all members of the government relished the prospect of renewed conflict with the Huguenots, but Louis XIII did not hesitate. Indeed, he may be said to have fired the first shot. For he decided to march against the Huguenots of the south almost one month before the decisions taken at La Rochelle. Before setting off from Saumur he took communion and prayed as if he was launching a crusade. After capturing Saint-Jean d'Angély on 24 June, his confidence grew apace. 'He is so determined to come to the end of his enterprise,' wrote the Venetian ambassador, 'that he treats with contempt those who assure him of the contrary. He says in effect that he is on the way to becoming truly king of France and that anyone who seeks to sidetrack him will never be his friend.'[50] In August 1621 the assembly of the Gallican clergy, meeting at Bordeaux, was invited by the king's commissioner to grant Louis one million livres towards the fulfilment of his sacred mission. While the clergy looked for ways of raising this sum, the royal crusade gathered momentum. On 4 August Clairac surrendered after a ten-day siege. At Montauban, however, Louis encountered stiff resistance. The siege dragged on from 21 August until 18 November and the king's army

49 J. Garrisson, *L'Édit de Nantes et sa révocation* (Paris, 1985), p. 65.
50 Ibid., p. 66.

melted away under the combined impact of desertion, treason and plague. Out of a force of 20,000 men only 4,000 remained. Louis was forced to retreat while his minister, Luynes, negotiated with Rohan.

Following his humiliation, Louis returned to Paris and ordered peace talks with the Huguenots, but winter passed without a decision. In April 1622 the king gathered an army at Nantes, whence he advanced westwards and confronted a large Huguenot army led by Soubise that had been ravaging Brittany and Poitou. On 15 April the royal forces defeated him on the Île de Riez. The king then erected a fortress, called Fort-Louis, commanding the landward approaches to La Rochelle. By midsummer, 8,000 royal troops were encamped outside the town. But instead of attacking La Rochelle immediately, Louis XIII preferred to lay siege to Montpellier, another major Huguenot stronghold. The defenders looked to Rohan for help, but he had trouble raising troops and money. When he advanced in October, he found his way barred by the king's army and decided not to risk a battle. Louis XIII, for his part, was becoming anxious about the situation in Italy, where the Habsburgs had gained control of the Valtelline, a strategically important Alpine pass. Thus both sides had sound reasons for signing the Peace of Montpellier (18 October 1622). While confirming the Edict of Nantes, this provided for the destruction of Huguenot fortifications, except at La Rochelle and Montauban.

The Huguenots emerged seriously weakened from the war of 1622. Except for five towns and the Cévennes, they had lost control of Languedoc. La Rochelle was being systematically isolated, but the government knew that its capture would be difficult and costly. It also needed to consolidate its position in the south, as the Peace of Montpellier was not easily enforced. Being extremely reluctant to demolish their walls, the Huguenots offered all kinds of excuses to defer the process.[51] But the crown, while attending to other problems, did not lose sight of its ultimate objective of conquering La Rochelle. It maintained a strong garrison at Fort-Louis and set about weakening Rohan's position by encouraging Protestant nobles to become Catholics.

Richelieu by now had become the king's chief minister. He was much concerned with foreign affairs. French troops occupied the Grisons and laid siege to Genoa, but, after a promising start, the French military effort slowed down, largely through lack of money. The cardinal's position in the government was also threatened. This seemed a good moment for the Huguenots to try to regain lost ground. Soubise started a revolt and called

51 Lublinskaya, *French Absolutism*, pp. 211–12.

on the people of La Rochelle to join him, but they were sharply divided. The ruling oligarchy assured the crown of its loyalty, but was overruled by the rest of the citizens. In May 1625 La Rochelle joined Soubise's rebellion.[52] With so many French troops committed elsewhere, Richelieu bided his time by exploiting the divisions among the Rochelais. He was still negotiating with them when a large royal fleet under the duc de Montmorency approached La Rochelle, cutting off its communications with Soubise whose fleet lay off the Île de Ré. After a running battle lasting two days, Soubise was defeated and fled to England. On 5 February 1626 a peace treaty was signed: the Rochelais were forbidden to own any warships and required to demolish a fort. The king, for his part, kept Fort-Louis and garrisoned the offshore islands of Ré and Oléron. The Rochelais were unhappy with the settlement. Despite reassurances from Richelieu, they believed that the crown was intent on destroying them as a first step towards ruining the Protestant religion in France as a whole. They turned to England for help, but an expedition to the Île de Ré mounted by the duke of Buckingham in July 1627 proved a total fiasco.

Buckingham's ignominious defeat and withdrawal enabled Louis XIII to blockade La Rochelle. A line of fortifications was built on the landward side and a dry-stone dyke across the harbour. The Rochelais still looked mainly to England for assistance, but they also turned to their co-religionists in the Midi. On 11 September 1627 a Protestant assembly at Uzès confirmed Rohan as commander-in-chief of all the Huguenot churches and accepted an alliance with England. Many Huguenot towns, however, refused to join the revolt and made it difficult for Rohan to raise enough money to support an army. He fought quite well against Condé and Montmorency, the royal commanders in the south, but was gradually cornered in the Cévennes.[53] Thus he was unable to answer La Rochelle's cry for help. On 10 February 1628 Louis XIII returned to Paris, leaving Richelieu in charge of military operations. In August the king began to grow weary of the siege which was absorbing a huge amount of money. So peace-feelers were extended to the Rochelais. The mayor was keen to fight on, but opinion within the town was sharply divided. After another English relief effort had failed, the citizens asked for Louis' pardon. Although some of his councillors wanted La Rochelle to be severely punished, Richelieu successfully pressed for clemency. The Rochelais were allowed to keep their lives, property and faith, but not their fortifications or privileges. On 1 November Richelieu celebrated

52 D. Parker, *La Rochelle and the French monarchy* (London, 1980), pp. 42–3.
53 Lublinskaya, *French Absolutism*, p. 218.

Mass in the church of St Margaret. Later that day, Louis XIII entered La Rochelle surrounded by his troops. Two days later he took part in a religious procession. On 18 November he left after laying down rules for the town's administration. This was now given to royal officials and La Rochelle's ancient privileges were annulled, exposing its inhabitants to the full rigour of royal fiscality.

As far as religion was concerned, the Rochelais had to accept a revival of Catholicism in their midst. The crown provided for the reorganization of parishes, the maintenance of priests and Catholic control of hospitals. The Protestant *temple* in the city centre was turned into a Catholic church, though Huguenots were promised a new church on a site to be chosen by the king. Papal permission was sought to turn La Rochelle into a bishopric. Between 1628 and 1637 a large number of religious orders set up houses in the town. Huguenots were forbidden to settle if they had not resided in the town before 1629. As Catholics were not similarly restricted, they soon came to outnumber Protestants. By the mid-1630s they numbered 10,000 as against 8,000 Huguenots.

The fall of La Rochelle was followed by the surrender of the Huguenots in the Midi. This did not happen immediately, as the king's army was moved to Italy for a time. Rohan was also encouraged to continue resisting by promises of aid from England, but these never materialized. Eventually Richelieu brought the army back to Languedoc. In May 1629 Privas was mercilessly sacked after a siege lasting ten days. Other Huguenot towns preferred to submit without a struggle. On 28 June Louis XIII issued the Edict of Alès. Though often called a peace, this was not a treaty but an act of remission or pardon. While confirming the basic text of the Edict of Nantes, it cancelled the additional clauses guaranteeing the Huguenots' political and military rights. All their fortifications and fortresses were now to be demolished. After Louis XIII's return to northern France, Richelieu stayed in Languedoc to oversee personally the destruction of the walls in 20 towns. When Montauban asked for a reprieve, he threatened to besiege the town. The citizens promptly gave way; even so, Richelieu took 12 hostages before lifting his threat of reprisals. He then entered the town under arms and after celebrating a *Te Deum* at the church of St Jacques, watched the removal of the first stone from the town's ramparts.

If the Huguenots had ceased to be a political force, they remained a significant religious minority. Their right of worship was recognized in theory by the state, but they were the victims of much intolerance between 1629 and 1685. Official harassment of Huguenots was backed up by the *Compagnie du Saint-Sacrement*, a Catholic secret society dedicated to converting heretics and keeping them out of the professions and trades. Yet, in spite of continued persecution, the total number of Huguenots did not decline between 1630 and 1656; it may even have risen.[54] Thus, the so-called Peace of Alès did not destroy them; it simply destroyed their semi-independent political status. Henceforth, they also ceased to pose a military threat to the French crown.

The French Wars of Religion may be said to have had two endings: the first, in 1598 when the Edict of Nantes produced a peace more lasting than any of the previous pacifications since 1562; and the second, in 1629, when the so-called 'peace' of Alès destroyed the Huguenots' political and military power. Thereafter, France reverted to being a Catholic state containing a relatively small Protestant minority living under an increasingly intolerant regime, especially after 1661, until it lost all of its rights with the revocation of the Edict of Nantes by Louis XIV in 1685. But if France's religious wars may be said to have ended, her civil wars did not. Aristocratic discontent, which had served to fuel religious dissent in the sixteenth century to the extent of sometimes being confused with it, survived the Edict of Nantes. This may be said to have removed religion from politics. There is evidence that Marshal Biron's revolt during the reign of Henry IV was part of a Spanish-inspired plot to overturn the Edict of Nantes, but its true nature remains controversial.[55] In essence, it strongly resembles the kind of aristocratic uprising which became a regular feature of French political life in the early seventeenth century, culminating in the so-called Fronde of the princes. Religion played no significant part in this unrest, which appears to have been mainly promoted by a more effective central government. Such secular grievances as the nobility had in the sixteenth century were as nothing compared to those which developed in the first half of the next century, when their fiscal privileges came under systematic attack from a royal government intent on harnessing the resources of the nation more effectively than it had ever done in the past.[56]

54 Garrisson, *L'Édit de Nantes et sa révocation*, pp. 88–90, 92–9, 108.

55 A. Jouanna, *Le devoir de révolte: La noblesse française et la gestation de l'état moderne, 1559–1661* (Paris: Fayard, 1989), p. 206.

56 R. Bonney, 'The French Civil War, 1649–53', *European Studies Review*, 8 (1978), 71–100; R. J. Knecht, *The Fronde* (London: Historical Association, 2nd edn 1986), pp. 23–7.

CONCLUSION

Three major questions need to be addressed by a book concerned with the French Wars of Religion: why did they take place? Why did they last so long? And what impact did they have on the French nation and its people?

No perfect answer can be given to the first question for the simple reason that human motivation, even if it can be identified, can never be quantified. Some of the people who fought in the wars may have done so for confessional reasons. They may have believed that Catholicism or Calvinism was the only true faith and that its defence was vital to personal salvation. There is ample evidence that heresy was seen by many people, not merely as wrong belief, but also as a social pollutant which could have dire consequences for everyone and, therefore, needed eradication. Others may have joined the struggle for less high-minded reasons, possibly because they wanted a pretext to seize someone else's property or to pay off an old score. Again, the recent attention given by historians to local history in sixteenth-century France, particularly that of towns, has revealed the potency of personal jealousies or hatreds in releasing violence. We simply cannot be sure. All that is certain is that the wars did not have a single cause. The notion once favoured by historians that they were a movement of aristocratic discontent seeking respectability by sheltering under 'the cloak of religion' is no longer generally accepted. Mack P. Holt is certainly correct in his contention that religion was 'the fulcrum upon which the civil wars were balanced'.[1] By 1562, when the first war broke out, France was already religiously divided, and violence had become the order of the day as the crown tried to stamp out dissent by force. The wars were, in a sense, an extension of the martyrdoms and massacres which had preceded them.

If religion was important, however, so was aristocratic discontent. Royal authority in sixteenth-century France was heavily dependent on the support of the nobility. In the absence of a standing army and of a large civil service, the king needed the support of the richest and most powerful social estate to carry out his policies. The old nobility – often called 'the nobility

1 M. P. Holt, *The French Wars of Religion, 1562–1629* (Cambridge, 1995), p. 2.

of the sword' – provided the captains of the *gendarmerie* companies, or heavy cavalry, which was the flower of the army in wartime. During the Italian Wars in the first half of the century, it had been actively engaged fighting for the king beyond the Alps. Nobles also played a leading role in local government, serving as provincial governors or lieutenants-general. Their relatives and friends constituted more or less powerful clientèles on which they relied to support their interests. But the relationship between crown and nobility was one of mutual dependence, for royal patronage was the nobility's life-blood: it drew strength from the gifts and favours dispensed by the crown in the form mainly of remunerative offices or gifts of money or land. Exclusion from such patronage spelt ruin to a nobleman. Under Francis I and Henry II, both of them strong kings, the nobility had been, so it seems, satisfied with its lot. In 1559, however, a serious financial crisis obliged Henry II to bring the Italian Wars to an end by signing the peace of Cateau-Cambrésis. This treaty was extremely unpopular with many French nobles, who viewed it as an unjustified national humiliation. They also deeply resented their loss of military employment. The idea that the Wars of Religion were, in a sense, intended to replace the Italian Wars as an outlet for the nobility's martial propensities ought not to be too lightly dismissed. The nobility was the profession of arms, and if deprived of war it lost its *raison d'être*. Admiral Coligny firmly believed that a sure way of persuading French nobles to stop fighting each other was to redirect their energies in a foreign war, preferably against Spain in the Low Countries.

Henry II's accidental death also plunged the kingdom into a grave constitutional crisis. As the king left only a child to succeed him, power necessarily passed into the hands of the king's widow, Catherine de' Medici, who, lacking political experience, turned for advice to the late king's ministers, members of the aristocratic house of Guise. They introduced stringent economy measures while using royal patronage in the interest of themselves and their clients. Nobles outside their circle felt aggrieved, particularly members of the house of Bourbon, who, as princes of the blood, claimed that they were entitled by law to advise the monarch. The crisis was further complicated by the fact that the Guises were foreigners by origin and championed Catholic orthodoxy, while the Bourbons were wholly French and supported the Protestant Reformation. Thus aristocratic, religious and even nationalistic passions became fused. One of the earliest manifestations of that fusion was the Tumult of Amboise.

The second question needing to be addressed is even more difficult than the first. Several reasons may be offered for the extended duration of the wars. Perhaps the most important was the chronic weakness of the government, which proved itself incapable of imposing a lasting settlement. As Wood has clearly demonstrated, the crown lacked the means to keep an army in the field for long enough to impose a lasting settlement. Although the kings of France were envied abroad for their fiscal powers, these were, in effect, inadequate given the steeply rising costs of early modern warfare. In the absence of a national standing army made up of cavalry and infantry, the king had to hire foreign mercenaries, mainly Germans or Swiss, who insisted on being paid on the nail. Artillery was also becoming a costly item. The French tax system, riddled as it was with exemptions and anomalies, was wholly inadequate to meet the crown's wartime needs. Resorting to various kinds of expedients, such as the sale of offices or the alienation of royal lands, was only a partial solution. Turning to foreign powers for assistance, military or financial, often proved more tiresome than helpful as loans needed to be repaid, often with interest. Every now and then, the king had to lay down his arms, not because he had been defeated in battle, but because his coffers were empty and he needed a break to replenish them. Unpaid armies living off the countryside and terrorizing the peasants were a regular feature of French life in the second half of the century. The civil wars were far from tidy or contained within bounds laid down in peace accords; they spilt out all over the kingdom in acts of violence by mutinous or abandoned soldiers. Desertion was an everyday phenomenon.

In issuing edicts of pacification the crown may have sincerely hoped to end the fighting for good; but there was never any intention on its part of allowing two religions permanently to co-exist in the kingdom. The aim was always to patch things up until religious unity could be restored. Catherine de' Medici's attempt to achieve this peacefully at Poissy in 1561 had failed miserably, leaving force as the only alternative, but the crown lacked the necessary means to use it decisively. All the edicts of pacification, however sincerely intended, were but compromises grudgingly conceded. They contained conditions likely to offend one side or the other as excessively generous. Thus, the provision that Huguenots could worship outside certain towns provoked fierce disputes as to where their places of worship should be situated, and offered Catholic mobs opportunities of molesting Huguenots on their way to and from such places. Protestants, on the other hand, vigorously resisted demands to readmit Catholics to areas under their control and to return the churches and property that they had taken from Catholics. These were the sorts of problem which royal commissioners had to deal with on their rounds of the kingdom to enforce the edicts. Though pacification may have been intended, it was seldom achieved even in the short term. An edict which was generous to the Huguenots immediately provoked Catholic resistance and vice versa. The setting up of security towns helped to fuel further conflicts by giving the Huguenots bases from which they could operate militarily and divert royal revenues into their own war-chests.

The wars were also fuelled by certain acts of violence which they generated. The murder of the second duc de Guise by a Huguenot nobleman in 1563 ignited a vendetta between the houses of Guise and Châtillon, which the crown proved quite unable to smother. Royal declarations clearing the Huguenot leader, Coligny, of responsibility for the crime carried absolutely no weight with the duke's widow and the hired assassins in her service. The vendetta ran through the wars like a scarlet thread regardless of pacifications until Coligny was murdered, probably at the instigation of the Guises, in the Massacre of St Bartholomew. Another event which triggered a new wave of civil conflict was the *Surprise de Meaux*, when the proximity of a Spanish army heading for the Netherlands prompted a pre-emptive strike by the Huguenots on the French court. The event, which led to the blockade of Paris, shattered Catherine de' Medici's illusion that her Grand Tour of France in 1565–6 had brought lasting peace to France. The Peace of Longjumeau, which the Huguenots interpreted as a deceitful ploy by the crown to avenge the *Surprise de Meaux*, caused their leaders to flee from their homes to the relative safety of La Rochelle, which became their principal base for the rest of the wars. Whatever lay behind the marriage of Henri de Navarre and Marguerite de Valois in August 1572, it led to the Massacre of St Bartholomew which poured yet more petrol on the flames of civil strife by destroying whatever credibility the Valois monarchs had retained among their Huguenot subjects. Rightly or wrongly (the truth will never be known), they were accused of having planned the massacre. Historians now believe that the crown may have wanted only to eliminate the Huguenot leadership and that the massacre was an expression of mob hysteria. Be that as it may, the massacre served to undermine any trust which the Huguenots may have retained in the house of Valois. Although they did not embrace republicanism, as many historians have suggested, the massacre caused Huguenot thinkers to justify forceful resistance to a monarch who had become in their eyes a tyrant. Even regicide became an acceptable doctrine which, working upon fanatical minds, led to the assassinations first of Henry III, then of Henry IV. Another crucial event exacerbating civil conflict in France was the death of the duc d'Anjou in 1584 which created the prospect of a Protestant becoming king of France under the Salic law. To counter this threat Catholic zealots, now strongly backed by Spain and the papacy, set up the Catholic League which, by trying to force the hand of Henry III, drove him into the arms of the king of Navarre. Following the king's assassination, confessional strife became bound up with the question of royal legitimacy: could a Protestant, even one who converted to Catholicism, ever be lawfully king of France? The question was burning enough to divide both the Catholic and Protestant camps. While some Catholics – the so-called Politiques – were prepared to accept a convert as king for the sake of peace, others, such as the Sixteen in Paris, put religion before legitimacy. A similar division occurred among the Protestants. If some, like Sully, continued to serve Henry IV after his conversion, others never trusted him again.

Finally, we need to ponder the impact of the Wars of Religion on the French nation and its people. Constitutionally, the wars showed up the fundamental weaknesses of a monarchy which, for all its claims to absolute authority, depended for its effectiveness on the person of the ruler and the degree of support which he could command from his more powerful subjects. By uncovering those weaknesses, particularly the financial ones, the wars pointed to the reforms needed to cure them, many of which were eventually implemented during the reigns of Henry IV and his successors, Louis XIII and Louis XIV. Thus, indirectly, the wars and the revulsion which they caused in the kingdom at large strengthened the monarchy by forcing upon it a reappraisal of its own position. Economically and socially, the wars were generally disastrous, but they cannot be blamed for all the distress of the times. From the start of the century at least, the population of France had been growing steadily, yet food production had failed to keep pace with it. This was caused partly by technological backwardness, partly by climatic conditions. A harsh winter followed by a dry summer could wipe out a harvest for one year, tilting the balance between survival and extinction for the average peasant. Two or three successive bad harvests could cause a famine which in turn could facilitate the spread of plague and other infectious diseases. The winters of 1565, 1568, 1570 and 1573 were very harsh. And plague assumed a new virulence during the wars, especially after 1577.

Two facts need to be borne in mind when assessing the effects of the civil wars. First, they were not continuous but punctuated by periods of peace or relative peace totalling 13 years. Secondly, not all parts of France were affected in the same way. For example, if Normandy, the Loire valley, Poitou and Auvergne experienced much fighting, Brittany did not. Thus it is risky to generalize about the wars' effects. Yet they certainly caused much hardship in both the countryside and the towns by disrupting normal economic activities. We have already seen how bands of unpaid soldiers would feed off the countryside, terrorizing the inhabitants. As peasants fled to the relative safety of woods and forests, they would abandon their daily pursuits, thereby further damaging food production. Some towns were seriously hit by the wars. If one was besieged, its economic activity was, at best, badly disrupted; if it was taken by storm, it was usually sacked, but even if it surrendered it could not be sure that it would not be sacked, as happened at Issoire in 1577. A town which capitulated could expect to pay a large ransom. Lyon, which had enjoyed unprecedented prosperity in the first half of the century, was adversely affected by the Huguenot takeover in 1562. Its famous fairs had to move to other towns. Business recovered between 1564 and 1570 but more trouble occurred in the 1570s as roving war bands cut some of the city's supply routes. The wars also aggravated an existing monetary crisis which resulted in a trade depression. After 1572 many Lyon bankers went bankrupt while others moved to Paris. But regional variations applied to the towns as well as the countryside. Thus Marseille enjoyed something of a trade boom as its merchants took advantage of the Cyprus War to capture the spice trade from the Venetians, albeit briefly. Their success was reflected in a sharp rise in the yield from Marseille's harbour dues.

The impact of the wars on France's population is hard to assess as the documentary evidence is patchy. This suggests that the population rise, which had started in the late fifteenth century, continued during the wars. According to Goubert they 'in no way seriously hindered the general upward movement of baptisms . . . provided we disregard the ten years 1590–9'.[2] Another historian, Richet, has argued that the growth may have been checked in the Midi by the 1560s, but that it continued in the north for at least two decades after 1562.[3] However, town records point to a different conclusion. According to Benedict, the population of Rouen fell by more than a quarter between 1562 and 1594, though this may have been due to emigration as well as deaths. For many Protestants left the city to avoid persecution: some went to Geneva and others to England. As a number of exiles returned under Henry IV, Rouen's population almost returned to its pre-civil-war level.[4] Deaths during the civil war cannot be ascribed simply to fighting: famine and disease also took a heavy toll. It was mainly in the last 15 or 20 years of the century that France's population declined, especially in the towns. Allowing for a wide margin of error and for wide regional differences, the total fall in population during the wars may have amounted to between two and four million.[5]

It is commonly assumed that all France's problems were solved once Henry IV's abjuration had cleared his path to the throne. The truth is less simple. A measure of recovery certainly did take place, largely thanks to the skilful management of the king's finances by the duc de Sully. By 1610 he had accumulated perhaps as much as 15 million livres in the royal coffers.

---

2 D. V. Glass and D. E. C. Eversley (eds.), *Population in History* (London, 1965), p. 465.

3 D. Richet, 'Aspects socio-culturels des conflits à Paris dans la seconde moitié du XVIe siècle', *Annales E.S.C.*, 32 (1977), 764–89.

4 P. Benedict, 'Catholics and Huguenots in sixteenth-century Rouen: the demographic effects of the religious wars', *F.H.S.*, ix (1975), 232.

5 M. Pernot, *Les guerres de religion en France, 1559–1598* (Paris: SEDES, 1987), p. 363.

This was partly achieved by the dubious methods of defaulting on foreign debts and failing to pay arrears of *rentes*; but some more positive steps were also taken, expenditure being curbed and revenues maximized. As the economy recovered, the yield from indirect taxes rose. Income from the sale of offices was regularized by the creation of the *paulette*, a tax on the value of an office which allowed the holder to dispose of it freely. Financiers were also forced to disgorge large sums of money. But if an improvement in the the crown's finances did occur, the social climate of the Wars of Religion was not redressed overnight. Even after the Peace of Vervins, the great nobles remained troublesome. Henry IV's reign was punctuated with aristocratic plots. He also had to pay heavily to secure the loyalty of the rest. Sully estimated that he spent 30 to 32 million livres in treaties 'for the recovery of the kingdom'. To raise the money for such bribes, Henry had to put pressure on the traditional taxpayers, mainly the peasantry, at a time of continued economic hardship. He also had to disappoint the office-holders and the *rentiers* who had seen him as their saviour. As for the religious problem, it also survived the Edict of Nantes, which was never intended as a permanent settlement. Yet, unlike earlier pacifications, it lasted 87 years. Though they were not placed on an equal footing with Catholics, Huguenots were given a measure of security. Even so, many of their nobles chose to become Catholics out of self-interest, thereby depriving their co-religionists of leadership. Geographically, too, the Huguenots became largely confined to the west and, especially, the south of France. They concentrated their energies on defending their privileges under the edict which were being constantly whittled away. 'The militant dynamic of the sixteenth century,' writes Elisabeth Labrousse, 'gave way to concentration on survival and self-defence. Open war was replaced by cold war.'[6]

6 M. Prestwich (ed.), *International Calvinism, 1541–1715* (Oxford: Clarendon, 1985), p. 287.

BIBLIOGRAPHICAL ESSAY

This essay is aimed at English-speaking readers unable to cope with the vast mass of original and secondary sources which are available only in French. It is, therefore, highly selective and omits several major works essential to a complete understanding of the subject. Fortunately, the history of France in the sixteenth century generally, and of the Wars of Religion in particular, has attracted a considerable amount of scholarly attention in the United States and Britain in recent years, the importance of which has been recognized by French scholars. So while this list is necessarily selective, it ought not to be regarded as only a 'second best'.

The Wars of Religion had their roots in the early sixteenth century. An up-to-date, lively and perceptive survey of this formative period is D. Potter, *A History of France, 1460–1560: The Emergence of a Nation State* (London: Macmillan, 1995). Covering some of the same ground more succinctly is my own *French Renaissance Monarchy, 1559–1598* (London: Longman Seminar Studies, 1989). J. H. M. Salmon, *Society in Crisis: France in the Sixteenth Century* (London, 1975) is a standard work which has survived the test of time extremely well, but it is mainly concerned with the period after 1559 and is rather too detailed to serve as an introduction. Howell A. Lloyd, *The State, France, and the Sixteenth Century* (London: Allen & Unwin, 1983) is a fine study in which the impact of ideas on institutions, society and the economy is judiciously appraised. F. J. Baumgartner, *France in the Sixteenth Century* (London: Macmillan, 1995) is a more conventional yet sound survey of the kingdom's evolution between 1484 and 1616. It is to be preferred to Janine Garrisson, *A History of Sixteenth-Century France, 1483–1598* (London: Macmillan, 1995), which clumsily conflates two books originally published in French. The author is a leading authority on French Protestantism but is less reliable on other aspects. She makes factual errors and overlooks significant British and American contributions. My own *The Rise and Fall of Renaissance France 1483–1610* (London: Fontana, 1996) seeks to combine narrative with analysis. It gives more attention to cultural aspects than the surveys listed above. Natalie Zemon Davis, *Society and Culture in Early Modern France* (London: Duckworth, 1975) is a collection of eight original and stimulating essays. Also important is J. H. M. Salmon, *Renaissance and Revolt: Essays in the*

Intellectual and Social History of Early Modern France (Cambridge: CUP, 1987). Two compilations of variable quality, which draw on the research of mainly American scholars, are *Society and Institutions in Early Modern France*, ed. Mack P. Holt (Athens: Univ. of Georgia, 1991) and *Changing Identities in Early Modern France*, ed. M. Wolfe (Durham: Duke Univ. Press, 1997).

A number of works focus on the civil wars. Easily the best is Mack P. Holt, *The French Wars of Religion, 1562–1629* (Cambridge: CUP, 1995) which successfully vindicates the place of religion as 'the fulcrum on which the civil wars balanced'. The approach, however, is that of a social historian, not a theologian. The book also draws on the author's own research into French local history. It sets a new standard by showing that the Edict of Nantes did not mark the end of religious conflict in France. My own *The French Wars of Religion, 1559–1598* (London: Longman Seminar Study, 2nd edn, 1996) is an introductory survey with an appendix of 18 original documents translated into English. A far more comprehensive selection is offered in *The French Wars of Religion: selected documents*, edited and translated by David Potter (London: Macmillan, 1997). Also useful is *Blaise de Monluc: The Habsburg–Valois Wars and the French Wars of Religion*, ed. I. Roy (London: Longman, 1971) which contains substantial translated extracts from the marshal's vivid, if not always very accurate, memoirs.

An understanding of the Wars of Religion has to rest on a knowledge of what made France a distinctive nation among European states. Constitutionally, no institution was more important than the monarchy, which was closely associated with the church. Colette Beaune, *The Birth of an Ideology: Myths and Symbols of Nation in Late-Medieval France* (Berkeley, Cal., 1991) is a brilliant survey of the various theories and beliefs governing the actions of monarchs and their legitimacy. It is a useful complement to M. Bloch, *The Royal Touch: Sacred Monarchy and Scrofula in England and France* (London, 1973), a ground-breaking study of the miraculous powers traditionally ascribed to the kings of France. The development of the royal coronation is examined in *Vive le Roi! A History of the French Coronation from Charles V to Charles X* (Chapel Hill, 1984) and the funeral rites in R. Giesey, *The Royal Funeral Ceremony in Renaissance France* (Geneva: Droz, 1960). Various theories of monarchy, including the concept of its being a divine institution and the rise following the Protestant Reformation of a theory of resistance, are examined in Q. Skinner, *The Foundations of Modern Political Thought*, 2 vols. (Cambridge: CUP, 1978), W. F. Church, *Constitutional Thought in Sixteenth-Century France* (Cambridge, Mass: Harvard UP, 1941) and J. Franklin, *Jean Bodin and the Rise of Absolutist Theory* (Cambridge: CUP, 1973).

Two useful surveys of French government in the early modern period are E. Le Roy Ladurie, *The French Royal State, 1450–1660* (Oxford: Blackwell, 1994) and D. Parker, *The Making of French Absolutism* (London: Arnold, 1983).

Among more specialized works J. H. Shennan, *The Parlement of Paris* (Stroud: Sutton, 2nd edn 1998) is a most useful survey of the highest law court in the kingdom apart from the king's council. The relations between the king and the Parlement are considered, at times tendentiously, in Sarah Hanley, *The Lit de Justice of the Kings of France: Constitutional Ideology in Legend, Ritual and Discourse* (Princeton, N.J.: Princeton UP, 1983). Some of its ideas are challenged by Mack P. Holt, 'The king in Parlement: the problem of the *lit de justice* in sixteenth-century France', *H.J.*, 31 (1985), pp. 517–23, and also by E. A. R. Brown and R. Famiglietti, *The Lit de Justice: Semantics, Ceremonial and the Parlement of Paris, 1300–1600* (Sigmaringen: Thorbecke, 1994). N. L. Roelker, *One King, One Faith: The Parlement of Paris and the Religious Reformation of the Sixteenth Century* (Berkeley: California UP, 1996) contains useful material, but is rather long-winded. Given the crucial importance of funding the armies during the civil wars, a number of studies of the royal fiscal machine are to be noted. They include Martin Wolfe, *The Fiscal System of Renaissance France* (New Haven, Conn.: Yale UP, 1972) and, above all, for the later period, R. Bonney, *The King's Debts: Finance and Politics in France, 1589–1661* (Oxford: Clarendon, 1981). The crown depended on a network of institutions at the local level to ensure that its policies were carried out. Foremost among these were the provincial governors. Their role is examined in R. Harding, *Anatomy of a Power Elite: The Provincial Governors of Early Modern France* (New Haven, Conn.: Yale UP, 1978). Relations between the crown and the various provincial estates are the subject of several pioneering studies by J. Russell Major, the most important being *Representative Government in Early Modern France* (New Haven, Conn.: Yale UP, 1980). His obsession with absolutism is perhaps a trifle overdone.

Recent studies of the civil wars have emphasized the importance of religion as a cause of conflict. On this, see Mack P. Holt, 'Putting religion back into the Wars of Religion', *F.H.S.*, 18 (1993), 524–51, and H. Heller 'A reply to Mack P. Holt', *F.H.S.*, 19 (1996), 853–61. The corpus of literature concerned with various aspects of the Protestant Reformation is enormous. Only works mainly concerned with France can be cited here. Two valuable introductions are M. Greengrass, *The French Reformation* (Oxford: Blackwell, 1987) and the chapter by D. Nicholls in *The Early Reformation in Europe*, ed. A. Pettegree (Cambridge: CUP, 1992). *International Calvinism, 1541–1715*, ed. Menna Prestwich (Oxford: Clarendon, 1985) contains four authoritative essays on France. H. Hauser, 'The French Reformation and the French people', *A.H.R.*, 4 (1899), 117–27, was the first attempt to link early Protestantism with economic depression. Hauser has found a zealous disciple, albeit a lonely one, in H. Heller, who argues for a similar connection in *The Conquest of Poverty in Sixteenth-Century France* (Leiden, 1986) and in *Iron and Blood: Civil Wars in Sixteenth-Century France* (Montreal, 1991).

His views are seriously at variance with those of other historians who have examined religious dissent within an urban context. These include P. Benedict, *Rouen during the Wars of Religion* (Cambridge, 1981), and Natalie Zemon Davis, *Society and Culture in Early Modern France* (London, 1975). Focusing on the Lyon printing industry, the latter sees 'no significant correlation between socioeconomic position and religion in the period up to 1567'. A fascinating poll of religious opinion in Troyes is analysed by Penny Roberts in 'Religious conflict and the urban setting: Troyes during the French Wars of Religion' in *F.H.*, 6 (1992), 259–78. A useful study of religious anthropology in one French province is A. N. Galpern, *The Religions of the People in Sixteenth-Century Champagne* (Cambridge, Mass.: Harvard UP, 1976). The role of women in assisting the spread of Protestantism is considered in N. L. Roelker, 'The appeal of Calvinism to French noblewomen in the sixteenth century', *J.I.H.*, 2 (1971–2), 391–413, and 'The role of noblewomen in the French Reformation', *A.R.*, 63 (1972), 168–95. See also Natalie Z. Davis, 'City women and religious change' in her *Society and Culture in Early Modern France* (London, 1975), pp. 65–95. Davis also considers the goals of popular violence on pp.152–87. One of the greatest works on religious violence in sixteenth-century France is Denis Crouzet's *Guerriers de Dieu: la violence au temps des troubles de religion*, 2 vols. (Paris: Champ Vallon, 1990). Students who cannot grapple with its highly idiosyncratic French can get an idea of its contents along with a critical analysis in M. Greengrass, 'The psychology of religious violence', *F.H.*, 5 (1991), 467–74.

The French nobility in the sixteenth century has received a considerable amount of attention from historians in the USA and Britain. A useful introduction is Jonathan Dewald, *The European Nobility, 1400–1800* (Cambridge: CUP, 1996). See also his *Aristocratic Experience and the Origins of Modern Culture: France 1570–1715* (Berkeley, 1993). Other books on the subject include Ellery Schalk, *From Valor to Pedigree: Ideas of Nobility in the Sixteenth and Seventeenth Centuries* (Princeton, 1986); Kristen Neuschel, *Word of Honor: Interpreting Noble Culture in Sixteenth-Century France* (Ithaca, 1989); and J. Russell Major, *From Renaissance Monarchy to Absolute Monarchy: French Kings, Nobles and Estates* (Baltimore, 1994). D. Bitton, *The French Nobility in Crisis, 1560–1640* (Stanford, Cal., 1969) presents a view of the nobility in decline under inflationary pressures which has been decisively refuted by J. B. Wood, *The Nobility of the Election of Bayeux, 1463–1666: Continuity through Change* (Princeton, N.J., 1980) and 'The decline of the nobility in sixteenth- and early seventeenth-century France: myth or reality?', *J.M.H.*, 48 (1976). Among a host of articles the following stand out: J. Russell Major, 'Noble income, inflation and the Wars of Religion in France', *A.H.R.*, 86 (1981), 21–48: M. Greengrass, 'Property and politics in the sixteenth century: the landed fortune of the constable Anne de Montmorency', *F.H.*, 2 (1988), 371–98; D. Potter, 'The

Luxembourg Inheritance: the House of Bourbon and its lands in Northern France during the sixteenth century', *F.H.*, 6 (1992), 24–62; and W. A. Weary, 'The house of La Trémoïlle, fifteenth through eighteenth centuries: change and adaptation in a French noble family', *J.M.H.*, 49 (1977). The traditional view of conflict between sword and robe is challenged by J. Dewald, *The Formation of a Provincial Nobility: the Magistrates of the Parlement of Rouen, 1499–1610* (Princeton, N.J., 1980). On aristocratic clientage, see J. Russell Major, 'The Crown and the Aristocracy in Renaissance France', *A.H.R.*, 69 (1964), 631–48; and '"Bastard Feudalism" and the kiss: changing social mores in late medieval and early modern France', *J.I.H.*, 17 (1987), 509–35; Sharon Kettering, 'Clientage during the Wars of Religion', *S.C.J.*, 20 (1989), 221–39; 'Gift-giving and patronage in early modern France', *F.H.*, 2 (1988), 131–4; 'Patronage and kinship in early modern France', *F.H.S.*, 16 (1989), 409–18; and 'Friendship and clientage in early modern France', *F.H.*, 6 (1992), 139–58. The role played by the House of Guise and its clients, particularly in Normandy, is considered in depth by Stuart Carroll, *Noble Power during the French Wars of Religion: the Guise Affinity and the Catholic Cause in Normandy* (Cambridge: CUP, 1998). See also his 'The Guise affinity and popular protest during the Wars of Religion', *F.H.*, 9 (1995), 121–51. On the lesser nobility, see G. Huppert, *Les bourgeois gentilhommes* (Chicago UP, 1977). On duelling, see F. Billacois, *The Duel: Its Rise in Early Modern France* (New Haven: Yale UP 1990).

The role of Genevan missionaries in France is examined in R. M. Kingdon, *Geneva and the Coming of the Wars of Religion in France, 1555–1563* (Geneva: Droz, 1956). Some important articles on France by the same author are gathered together in his *Church and Society in Reformation Europe* (London: Variorum, 1985). On the affair of the rue Saint Jacques, see D. R. Kelley, *The Beginning of Ideology: Consciousness and Society in the French Reformation* (Cambridge: CUP, 1981), pp. 91–5. Royal legislation against Protestants is critically examined in N. M. Sutherland, *The Huguenot Struggle for Recognition* (New Haven, Conn.: Yale UP, 1980). See also her *Princes, Politics and Religion, 1547–1589* (London, 1984). On Antoine de Bourbon, see her 'Antoine de Bourbon, king of Navarre and the French crisis of authority, 1559–62' in *French Government and Society, 1500–1850. Essays in memory of Alfred Cobban*, ed. J. F. Bosher (London, 1971).

Recent scholarship has focused on the Wars of Religion as they affected certain towns. An extremely important collection of essays on various towns (Paris, Montpellier, Dijon, Aix-en-Provence, Toulouse) is *Cities and Social Change in Early Modern France*, ed. P. Benedict (London: Unwin Hyman, 1989). P. Benedict, *Rouen during the Wars of Religion* (Cambridge: CUP, 1981) and Barbara Diefendorf, *Beneath the Cross: Catholics and Huguenots in Sixteenth-*

Century Paris (Oxford: OUP, 1991) are both excellent. Penny Roberts, *A City in Conflict: Troyes during the Wars of Religion* (Manchester UP, 1996) focuses on the fortunes of the Protestant minority in a town situated within the Guise orbit. She uses a rich and still unpublished source: Nicholas Pithou's *Histoire ecclésiastique de l'église de Troyes*. On Toulouse, see M. Greengrass, 'The anatomy of a religious riot in Toulouse in May 1562', *J.Ecc.H.*, 34 (1983), 367–91, and J. M. Davies, 'Persecution and Protestantism: Toulouse, 1562–1575', *H.J.*, 22 (1979), 31–51. On Tours, see D. Nicholls, 'Protestants, Catholics and Magistrates in Tours, 1562–1572: the making of a Catholic city during the Religious Wars', *F.H.*, 8 (1994), 14–33. On Châlons-sur-Marne, M. Konnert, 'Urban values versus religious passion: Châlons-sur Marne during the Wars of Religion', *S.C.J.*, 20 (1989), 387–405 and 'Provincial governors and their regimes during the French Wars of Religion: the Duc de Guise and the City Council of Châlons-sur-Marne', *S.C.J.*, 24 (1994). On Dijon, James R. Farr, *Hands of Honor: Artisans and their World in Dijon, 1550–1650* (Ithaca: Cornell UP, 1988).

There is no biography in English of King Charles IX, but his mother, Catherine de' Medici, has received attention. On her see N. M. Sutherland, *Catherine de Medici and the Ancien Régime* (London: Historical Association, 1966), a valuable introduction which challenges the so-called 'Black legend'. It is reprinted in the same author's *Princes, Politics and Religion, 1547–1589* (London: Hambledon Press, 1984). Sutherland's *The French Secretaries of State in the Age of Catherine de Medici* (London: Athlone, 1962) is an excellent study of the queen-mother's working methods and of the ministers who served her. My own *Catherine de' Medici* (London and New York: Longman, 1998) seeks to be fair to the lady without whitewashing her. On Michel de l'Hôpital, see Seong-Hak Kim, *Michel de L'Hôpital: The Vision of a Reformist Chancellor during the French Religious Wars* (Kirksville, Mo.: Sixteenth Century Journal, 1997). See also her 'The Chancellor's crusade: Michel de l'Hôpital and the *Parlement* of Paris', *F.H.*, 7 (1993), 1–29; 'Michel de l'Hôpital revisited', *P.W.S.F.H.*, 17 (1990), 106–12; and '"Dieu nous garde de la messe du chancelier": the religious belief and political opinion of Michel de l'Hôpital', *S.C.J.*, 24 (1993), 595–620. See also Sylvia Neely, 'Michel de l'Hôpital and the *Traité de la réformation de la justice*: a case of misattribution', *F.H.S.*, 14 (1986), 339–66. The best account of L'Hôpital's politics remains J. H. M. Salmon, *Society in Crisis: France in the Sixteenth Century* (London, 1975), pp. 51–62. See also J. Russell Major, *The Estates-General of 1560* (Princeton, N.J., 1951). On the Colloquy of Poissy, see H. O. Evennett, *The Cardinal of Lorraine and the Council of Trent* (Cambridge, 1930); D. Nugent, *Ecumenism in the Age of the Reformation: The Colloquy of Poissy* (Cambridge, Mass., 1974); and N. M. Sutherland, 'The cardinal of Lorraine and the *Colloque* of Poissy:

a reassessment', *J.Ecc.H.*, 28 (1977), 265–89. On the Edict of January see A.-C. Keller, 'L'Hospital and the Edict of Toleration of 1562', *B.H.R.* (1952), 301–10. Nancy L. Roelker, *Queen of Navarre: Jeanne d'Albret, 1528–1572* (Cambridge, Mass., 1968) sheds valuable light on Huguenot activities leading up to the massacre of St Bartholomew. See also D. M. Bryson, 'The Vallant Letters of Jeanne d'Albret: fact or forgery?', *F.H.*, 13 (1999), 161–86. On Coligny, see J. Shimizu, *Conflict of Loyalties: Politics and Religion in the Career of Gaspard de Coligny* (Geneva: Droz, 1970), and A. W. Whitehead, *Gaspard de Coligny Admiral of France* (London: Methuen, 1904).

The military history of the Wars of Religion has not received as much attention as their socio-political context. Useful surveys of the army in the period leading up to the wars are P. Contamine, *War in the Middle Ages* (Oxford: Blackwell, 1984) and the introduction to Fourquevaux, *Instructions sur le Faict de la Guerre,* ed. G. Dickinson (London: Athlone, 1954). By far the most important recent contribution on the wars themselves is James B. Wood, *The King's Army: Warfare, Soldiers and Society during the Wars of Religion in France, 1562–1576* (Cambridge: CUP, 1996). The book is a valuable pioneering study, the chapter on the artillery being particularly important. Unfortunately, the book is confusingly structured and mangles many French place-names. The same author's 'The royal army during the early Wars of Religion, 1559–1576' in *Society and Institutions in Early Modern France,* ed. Mack P. Holt (Athens: University of Georgia, 1991) is a useful summary. An excellent study of military organization in the period leading up to the religious wars is contained in D. Potter, *War and Government in the French Provinces: Picardy, 1470–1560* (Cambridge: CUP, 1993). See also his excellent study of the mercenary market in 'The international mercenary market in the sixteenth century: Anglo-French competition in Germany, 1543–50', *E.H.R.* (1996), 24–58. No comparable study exists of the Huguenot armies, though some useful insights for the later period are provided by D. Buisseret, *Henry IV* (London: Allen & Unwin, 1984). Sir Charles Oman, *A History of the Art of War in the Sixteenth Century* (London, 1937) remains a valuable source of information on fighting methods and on the main battles. J. W. Thompson, *The French Wars of Religion* (Chicago: Chicago UP, 1909) remains useful as a narrative account of the various military campaigns, but it stops in 1576. Sixteenth-century warfare has been the object of several lively and illuminating works by the late Sir John Hale. They include *War and Society in Renaissance Europe, 1460–1620* (London: Fontana, 1985), *Renaissance Fortification: Art or Engineering?* (London: Thames & Hudson, 1977), *Renaissance War Studies* (London: Hambledon, 1983), and *Artists and Warfare in Renaissance Europe* (New Haven: Yale UP, 1990). The student of France can also pick up many useful ideas from G. Parker, *The Military Revolution: Military Innovation and the Rise of the West, 1500–1800* (Cambridge: CUP, 1988) and his *The Army of Flanders and the Spanish Road, 1567–1659* (Cambridge: CUP, 1972). See also J. A. Lynn, 'Tactical evolution in the French army, 1560–1660', *F.H.S.*, xiv (1985), 176–91. The religious wars threw up some important military autobiographies. These are examined in R. J. Knecht, 'Military autobiographies in sixteenth-century France' in *War, Literature and the Arts in Sixteenth-Century Europe*, ed. J. R. Mulryne and Margaret Shewring (London, 1989), 3–21, and 'The sword and the pen: Blaise de Monluc and his *Commentaires*', *R.S.* 9 (1995), 104–18.

Certain key events and problems are highlighted in various works in English. On the Tumult of Amboise, see N. M. Sutherland, 'Queen Elizabeth and the Conspiracy of Amboise, March 1560', *E.H.R.*, 81 (1966), 474–89; on the assassination of the second duc de Guise, see N. M. Sutherland, *Princes, Politics and Religion, 1547–1589* (London, 1984), pp. 139–55; on the difficulties faced by commissioners sent out by the crown to enforce the Edict of Amboise of 1563 see Penny Roberts, 'The most crucial battle of the Wars of Religion? The conflict over sites from Reformed worship in sixteenth-century France', *A.R.*, 89 (1998), 292–311; on Charles IX's progress through France, see V. E. Graham and W. McAllister Johnson, *The Royal Tour of France by Charles IX and Catherine de Medici: Festivals and Entries, 1564–66* (Toronto, 1979). The Massacre of St Bartholomew's Day has received a great deal of attention from English-speaking historians. The situation in Paris on the eve of the massacre is examined in B. Diefendorf, 'Prologue to a massacre: popular unrest in Paris, 1557–72', *A.H.R.*, 90 (1985), 1067–91; 'Simon Vigor: a radical preacher in sixteenth-century Paris', *S.C.J.*, 18 (1987), 399–410 and her *Beneath the Cross* (cited above). N. M. Sutherland, *The Massacre of St Bartholomew and the European Conflict, 1559–1572* (London: Macmillan, 1973) places the event in its international context. *The Massacre of St Bartholomew*, ed. A. Soman (The Hague: Brill, 1974) comprises various reappraisals and cites two contemporary Italian accounts. The wider impact of the event is considered in P. Benedict, 'The St Bartholomew's massacres in the provinces', *H.J.*, 21 (1978), 201–25. R. M. Kingdon, *Myths about St Bartholomew's Day Massacres, 1572–76* (Cambridge, Mass.: Harvard UP, 1988) focuses on the collection of pamphlets assembled by the Calvinist pastor, Simon Goulart. Mark Greengrass points to the discrepancies between the official accounts of massacres and the recollections of survivors in 'Secret histories and personal testimonies of religious violence in the French Wars of Religion' in *The Massacre in History*, ed. M. Levene and Penny Roberts (New York: Berghahn, 1999), pp. 69–88.On the Huguenot theory of resistance which was boosted by the massacres see Q. Skinner, *Foundations of Modern Political Thought*, vol. 2 (Cambridge: CUP, 1978) and M. Yardeni,

'French Calvinist political thought, 1534–1715' in *International Calvinism*, ed. M. Prestwich (cited above). See also D. R. Kelley, *François Hotman: a revolutionary's ordeal* (Princeton, N.J.: Princeton UP, 1973).

The best account of Charles IX's troublesome younger brother is Mack P. Holt, *The Duke of Anjou and the Politique struggle during the Wars of Religion* (Cambridge: CUP, 1986). The duke's involvement in the Netherlands is chronicled in P. Geyl, *The Revolt of the Netherlands, 1555–1609* (London, 5th edn 1980) and G. Parker, *The Dutch Revolt* (London, 1977), and his courtship of Elizabeth I in W. T. MacCaffrey, 'The Anjou match and the making of Elizabethan foreign policy' in *The English Commonwealth, 1547–1640*, ed. P. Clark *et al.* (Leicester, 1979). Links between the Huguenots and the Dutch rebels are examined in H. G. Koenigsberger, 'The organisation of revolutionary parties in France and the Netherlands in the sixteenth century', *J.M.H.*, 27 (1955), 335–51. The Estates-General of 1576 have been studied from several angles. See M. Greengrass, 'A day in the life of the third estate, Blois, 26th December 1576', in *Politics, Ideology and the Law in Early Modern Europe: Essays in honor of J. H. M. Salmon* (Rochester, 1994); M. P. Holt, 'Attitudes of the French nobility at the Estates General of 1576', *S.C.J.*, 18 (1987), 489–504; and O. Ulph, 'Jean Bodin and the Estates General in 1576', *J.M.H.*, 19 (1947), 289–96.

There is no biography in English of Henry III. The most recent survey of the king's controversial reputation is D. Potter, 'Kingship in the Wars of Religion: the reputation of Henri III of France', *E.H.Q.* 25 (1995), 485–528. Earlier assessments are K. Cameron, *Henry III: Maligned or Malignant King?* (Exeter: Exeter UP, 1978) and his 'Henri III – the Antichristian king', *J.E.S.*, 4 (1974), 152–63. See also S. Anglo, 'Henri III: some determinants of vituperation' in *From Valois to Bourbon*, ed. K. Cameron (Exeter: Exeter UP, 1989). E. H. Dickerman and Anita M. Walker, 'The language of blame: Henri III and the dismissal of his ministers', *F.H.*, 13 (1999), 77–98 focuses on the king's tendency to deflect criticism. His religiosity is viewed sympathetically by Frances A. Yates, *The French Academies of the Sixteenth Century* (London, revised edn 1988). See also Lynn Martin, *Henri III and the Jesuit Politicians* (Geneva: Droz, 1973) and R. J. Sealy, *The Palace Academy of Henry III* (Geneva: Droz, 1981). A fascinating examination of Henry's household reforms is provided in D. Potter and P. R. Roberts, 'An Englishman's view of the court of Henri III, 1584–5: Richard Cook's "Description of the Court of France"', *F.H.*, 2 (1988), 312–26. The 'Magnificences' for the marriage of the duc de Joyeuse and religious processions in 1583–4 are critically examined by F. Yates in *Astraea* (cited above), 149–207. Ministers who served two kings in succession are the subject of E. H. Dickerman, *Bellièvre and Villeroy: Power in France under Henry III and Henry IV* (Providence, R.I., 1971). Henry III's efforts to clear his name in Rome after the Blois murders and Guise counter-moves are examined in R. Cooper, 'The aftermath of the Blois assassinations of 1588: Documents in the Vatican', *F.H.*, 3 (1989), 404–26. Regional perspectives are offered by M. Greengrass, 'The later Wars of Religion in the French Midi' in *The European Crisis of the 1590s,* ed. P. Clark (London, 1985), pp. 106–34; E. Le Roy Ladurie, *Carnival: A People's Uprising at Romans, 1579–1580* (London: Scholar, 1980); and J. H. M. Salmon, 'Peasant revolt in the Vivarais (1575–80)', *F.H.S.*, 11 (1979), 1–28. F. C. Palm, *Politics and Religion in Sixteenth-Century France: Henry of Montmorency-Damville. Uncrowned King of the South* (Boston, Mass., 1927) is now dated. It needs to be supplemented by M. Greengrass, 'Noble affinities in early modern France: the case of Henri I de Montmorency', *E.H.Q.*, 16 (1986), 275–311, and J. Davies, 'The duc de Montmorency, Philip II and the House of Savoy', *E.H.R.*, 105 (1990), 870–92, 'Neither Politique nor patriot? Henri duc de Montmorency and Philip II, 1582–89', *H.J.*, 34 (1991), 539–66, and 'The politics of the marriage bed: matrimony and the Montmorency family, 1527–1612', *F.H.*, 6 (1992), 63–93.

The complicated history of the Catholic League and its various Parisian and provincial manifestations has been the subject of a number of recent articles. These include M. Greengrass, 'Dissension in the provinces under Henry III, 1574–85', in *The Crown and Local Communities in England and France in the Fifteenth Century,* ed. J. R. L. Highfield and Robin Jeffs (Gloucester: Sutton, 1981), pp. 162–82; 'The *Sainte Union* in the provinces: the case of Toulouse', *S.C.J.*, 14 (1983), 469–96; and N. Le Roux, 'The Catholic nobility and political choice during the League, 1585–1594: the case of Claude de La Châtre', *F.H.*, 8 (1994), 34–50. An excellent introduction to the Parisian League is M. Greengrass, 'The Sixteen: radical politics in Paris during the League', *H.*, 69 (1984), 432–9. See also J. H. M. Salmon, 'The Paris Sixteen, 1584–1594: the social analysis of a revolutionary movement', *J.M.H.*, 44 (1972), 540–76. Barbara Diefendorf writes on 'An Age of Gold? Parisian women, the Holy League, and the roots of Catholic renewal' in *Changing Identities in Early Modern France* (cited above), pp. 169–90. On Spanish involvement in the League's activities see De Lamar Jensen, *Diplomacy and Dogmatism: Bernardino de Mendoza and the French Catholic League* (Cambridge, Mass.: Harvard UP, 1964). See also his 'French diplomacy and the Wars of Religion', *S.C.J.*, 5 (1974), 22–46. Another useful article is R. R. Harding, 'The mobilization of confraternities against the Reformation in France', *S.C.J.*, 11 (1980), 85–107. The political ideas of the League are examined in F. J. Baumgartner, *Radical Reactionaries: The Political Thought of the French Catholic League* (Geneva, 1976). See also F. S. Giese, *Artus Désiré, Priest and Pamphleteer of the Sixteenth Century* (Chapel Hill, N.C., 1973). J. Powis, 'Gallican liberties and the politics of later sixteenth-century France', *H.J.*, (1983), 515–30 suggests that most Gallicans were committed to upholding royal authority rather than compromising with the Protestants, as some historians have suggested.

An excellent survey of the reign of Henry IV is M. Greengrass, *France in the Age of Henry IV: The Struggle for Stability* (London: Longman, revised edn. 1994). David Buisseret, *Henry IV* (London: Allen & Unwin, 1984) is also first-rate: though succinct, it is informative and perceptive, especially on military matters, and contains some most helpful maps of campaigns and battles. Howell A. Lloyd, *The Rouen Campaign, 1590–1592: Politics, Warfare and the Early Modern State* (Oxford: Clarendon, 1973) is the best account available of a major campaign, drawing on a wealth of English and French primary sources. M. Wolfe, *The Conversion of Henry IV: Politics, Power and Religious Belief in Early Modern France* (Cambridge, Mass.: Harvard UP, 1993) points to the tricky balance which the king had to achieve in order to retain the loyalty of both confessions. See also his 'Piety and political allegiance: the duc de Nevers and the Protestant Henry IV, 1589–93', *F.H.*, 2 (1988), 1–21. The methods used by Henry IV to regain the allegiance of towns which had supported the League are investigated by S. Annette Finley-Croswhite, *Henry IV and the Towns: The Pursuit of Legitimacy in French Urban Society, 1589–1610* (Cambridge: CUP, 1999). R. Mousnier, *The Assassination of Henry IV* (London, 1973) measures the king's record against the theory of tyrannicide. An excellent study of the king's principal minister is D. Buisseret, *Sully* (London: Arnold, 1978). Its findings need to be compared with the analysis of the minister's achievement in R. Bonney, *The King's Debts: Finance and Politics in France, 1589–1661* (Oxford: Clarendon, 1981).

In 1997 a colloquium in Amsterdam set out to compare the Dutch Revolt and the French Wars of Religion. Most leading authorities in the field took part and their valuable contributions are contained in P. Benedict, G. Marnef, H. van Nierop and M. Venard (eds.) *Reformation, Revolt and Civil War in France and the Netherlands, 1555–1585* (Amsterdam: Royal Netherlands Academy of Arts and Sciences, 1999).

GENEALOGIES

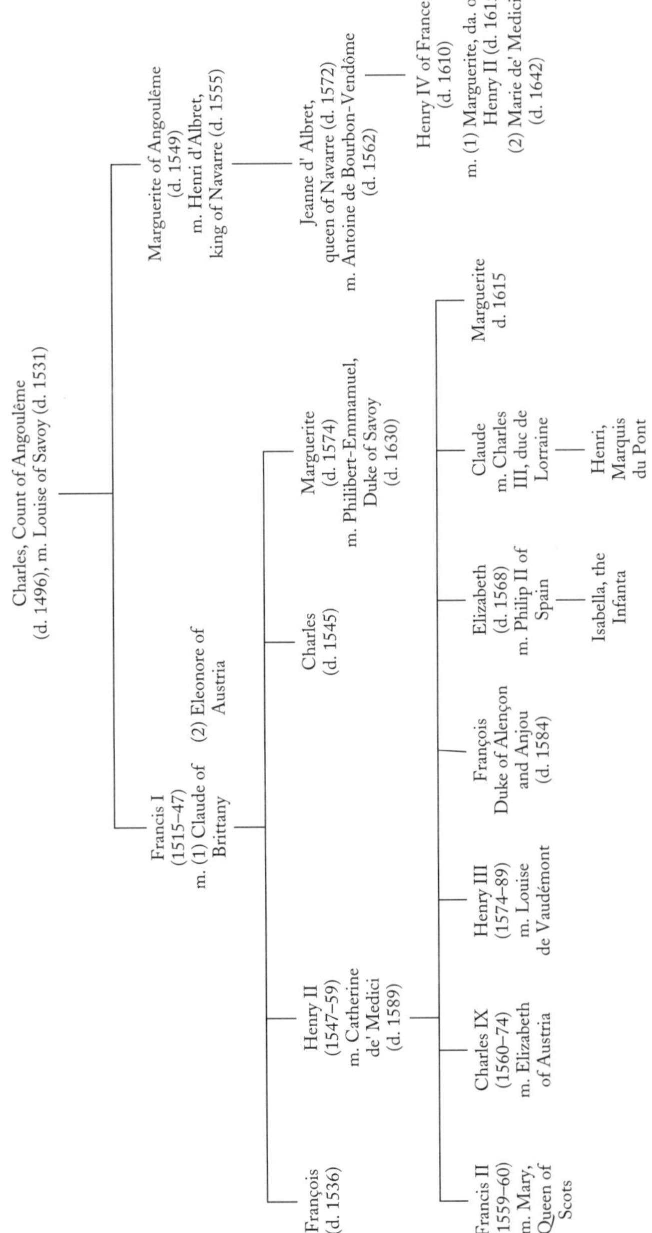

The later Valois

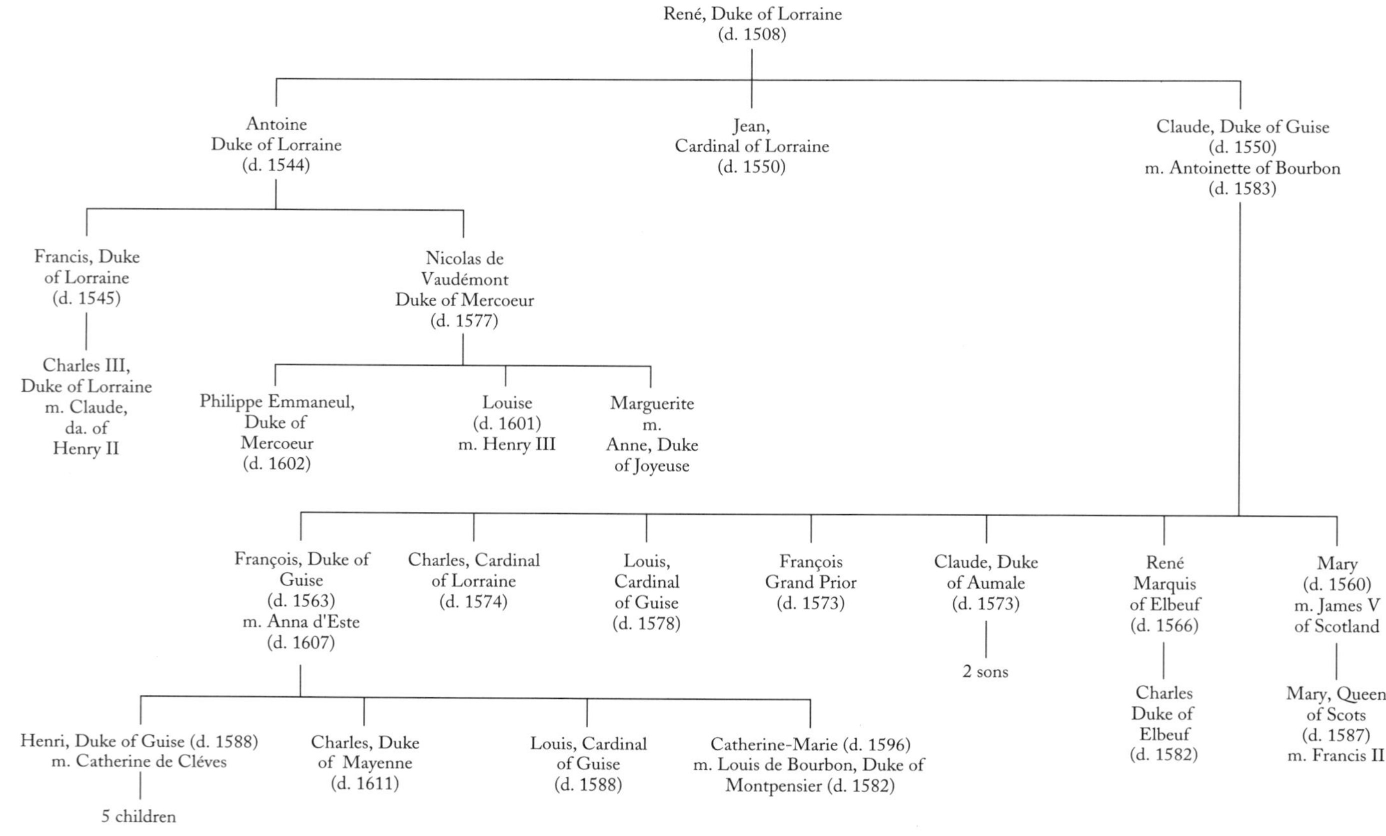

The house of Guise-Lorraine

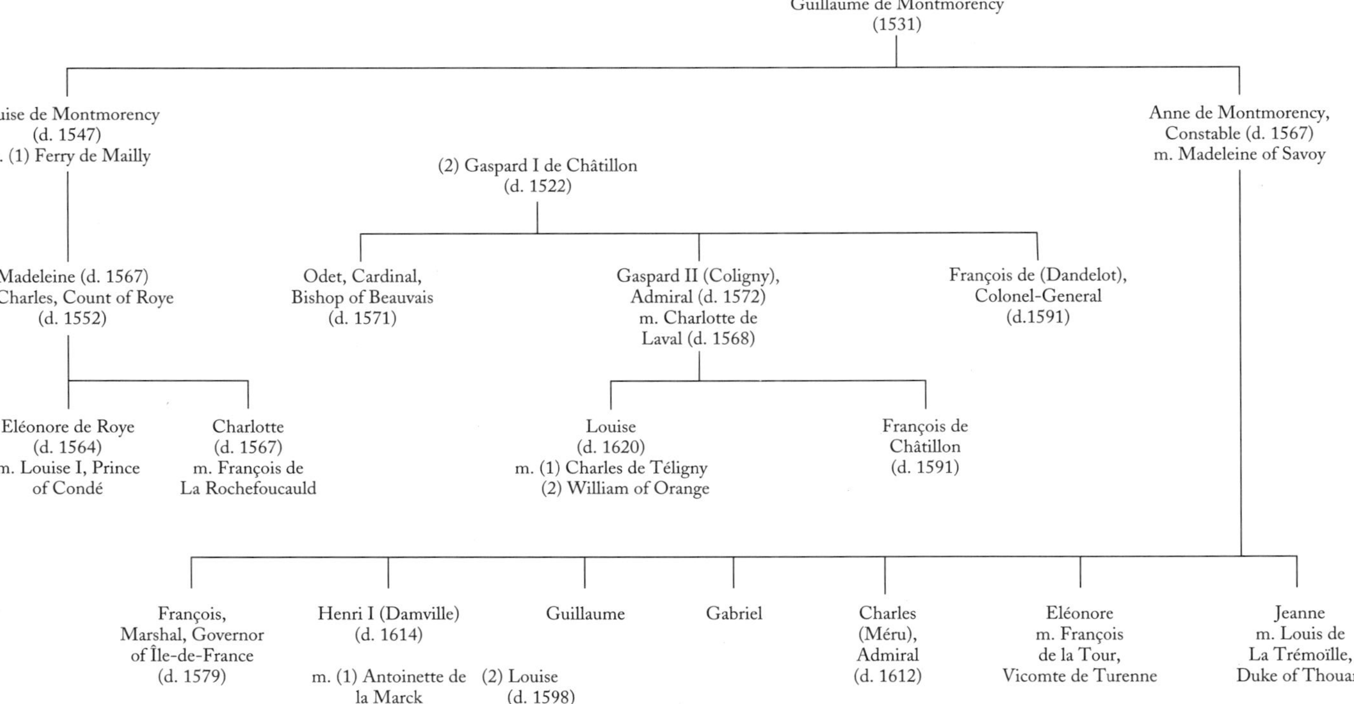

The house of Montmorency

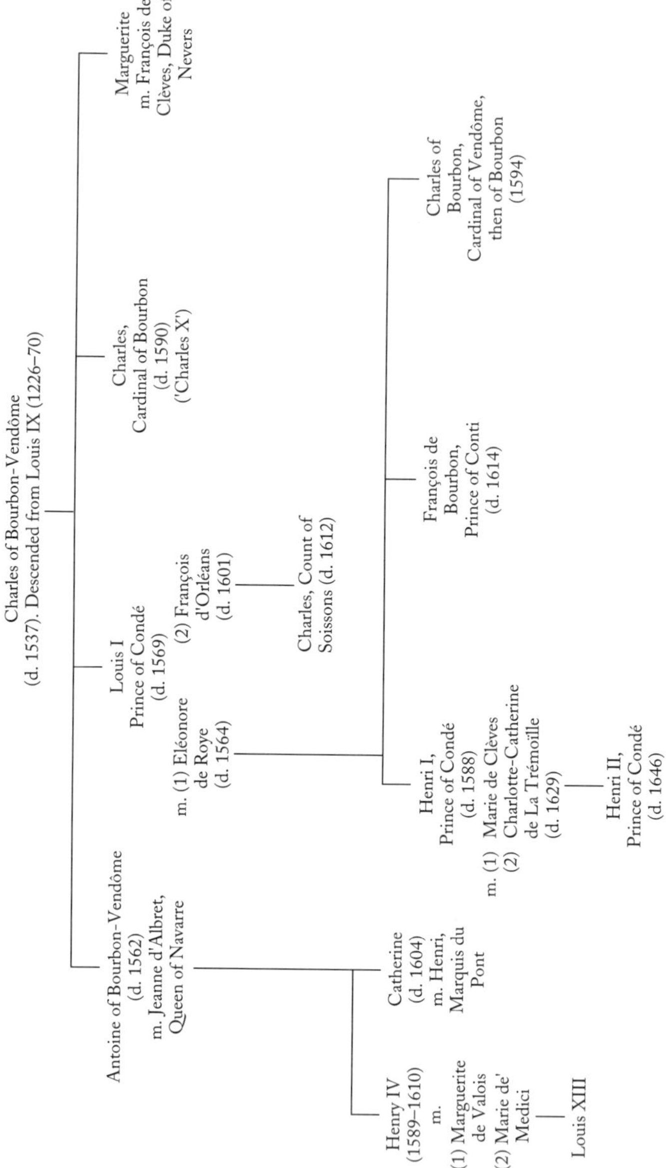

The house of Bourbon-Vendôme

LIST OF PROVINCIAL GOVERNORS, 1559–1598

Brittany

Jean de Brosse, duc d'Étampes (1543–65)
Sébastien de Luxembourg, vicomte de Martigues (1565–9)
Louis de Bourbon, duc de Montpensier (1569–82)
Philippe-Emmanuel de Lorraine, duc de Mercoeur (1582–98)
César de Vendôme (1598–1626)

Burgundy

Claude de Lorraine, duc d'Aumale (1550–73)
Charles de Lorraine, duc de Mayenne (1573–95)

Champagne

François Ier de Clèves, duc de Nevers (1545–61)
François II de Clèves, duc de Nevers (1561–3)
François de Lorraine, duc de Guise (1563)
Henri de Lorraine, duc de Guise (1563–88)
Charles Ier de Gonzague, duc de Rethelois (1589–1631)

Dauphiné

François de Lorraine, comte d'Aumale (1547–63)
Charles de Bourbon, prince de la Roche-sur-Yon (1563–5)
Louis de Bourbon, duc de Montpensier (1565–7)
François de Bourbon, prince dauphin d'Auvergne (1567–88)
Henri de Bourbon, prince de Dombes (1588–92)

Guyenne

Antoine de Bourbon (1555–62)
Henri de Bourbon, king of Navarre (1562–96)

Île-de-France

François de Montmorency (1556–79)
René de Villequier, baron de Clairvaux (1579–87)
François d'O, seigneur d'O (1587–94)

Languedoc

Anne de Montmorency, baron de Montmorency (1547–63)
Henri de Montmorency, seigneur de Damville (1563–1614)

Lyonnais

Jacques d'Albon, seigneur de Saint-André (1550–62)

Jacques de Savoie, duc de Nemours (1562–71)
François de Mandelot, seigneur de Pacy (1571–88)
Charles-Emmanuel de Savoie, duc de Nemours (1588–95)

Normandy

Henri-Robert de La Marck, duc de Bouillon (1556–74)
Jean de Mouy, seigneur de La Meilleraye (1574–83)
Jacques de Goyon, seigneur de Matignon (1574–83)
Tannequy Le Veneur, seigneur de Carrouges (1574–83)
Anne de Joyeuse, duc de Joyeuse (1583–7)
Jean Louis de Nogaret de La Valette, duc d'Épernon (1587–8)
François de Bourbon, duc de Montpensier (1588–92)

Picardy

Gaspard de Coligny (1555–9)
Charles de Cossé, seigneur de Brissac (1560–61)
Louis de Bourbon, prince de Condé (1561–9)
Léonor d'Orléans, duc de Longueville (1569–73)
Henri de Bourbon, prince de Condé (1573–88)
Louis de Gonzague, duc de Nevers (1588–9)
Henri d'Orléans, duc de Longueville (1589–95)
Henri II d'Orléans, duc de Longueville (1595–1618)

Provence

Claude de Savoie, comte de Tende (1525–66)
Honorat de Savoie, comte de Tende (1566–72)
Gaspard de Saulx-Tavannes, baron de Sully (1572–3)
Albert de Gondi, comte d'Oyen (1573–8)
François de La Baume, comte de Suze (1578–9)
Henri d'Angoulême (1579–86)
Jean-Louis de Nogaret de La Valette, duc d'Épernon (1586–90)
Bernard de Nogaret de La Valette, seigneur de La Valette (1590–2)
Jean-Louis de Nogaret de La Valette, duc d'Épernon (1592–4)
Charles de Lorraine, duc de Guise (1594–1631)

GLOSSARY

Aides	A sales tax.
Aisés	The well-to-do.
Arquebus	An early form of portable firearm used on a forked rest. An arquebusier was an infantryman armed with such a weapon.
Arrêt	Decree or judgment pronounced by a court.
Assemblée des notables	(Assembly of Notables) A consultative assembly drawn from the church, nobility, office-holders and municipal governments, usually by royal summons.
Aventuriers	French infantry volunteers.
Bailliage	The basic unit of royal administration at the local level, administered by the *bailli.*
Ban et l'arrière-ban	The feudal levy.
Brevet	A royal decree conceding a privilege.
Bureau des pauvres	A secular office for poor relief.
Cahiers de doléances	Lists of wishes and grievances drawn up locally by each order and supplied to deputies to national or provincial estates. In the estates, one general *cahier* was drawn up for each order for presentation to the king.
Chambre de justice	A special court set up to look into some abuse, usually in the fiscal administration.
Chambre des comptes	The Paris *chambre des comptes* was an offshoot of the king's council with a special jurisdiction over fiscal affairs. There were also provincial *chambres des comptes* with similar functions.
Chambre mi-partie	A chamber within a parlement, comprising an equal number of Catholic and Protestant judges, who were to try cases between members of the two religions. Also called *chambre de l'édit.*
Chevau-légers	Light cavalry.
Compagnies d'ordonnance	The armoured cavalry of *gens d'armes* (hence its other name, *gendarmerie*) in which the nobility of the sword served.

Conseil privé — The king's council (also called *conseil des parties*).
Conseiller — One of the chief legal officers in a parlement.
Constable of France — The operational head of the armed forces in the king's absence.
Cornette — A cavalry standard. The standard-bearer was called *le cornette.*
Curé — A parish priest.
Échevin — An alderman in a municipal government.
Écu — A gold crown. In 1515 it was worth 36 sous 3 deniers, or about 4 English shillings.
Édit (Edict) — A royal act on a single matter as distinct from an *ordonnance,* which ranged more widely.
Élections — Courts responsible for the local administration of the *taille* and other taxes; also the areas with which they dealt. The officials in charge were called *élus.*
Épargne — The central treasury. Its full name was *Trésor de l'Épargne.*
États-généraux (Estates-General) — The national representative body, comprising elected representatives of the three orders of clergy, nobility and third estate. During the Wars of Religion they met in 1560–61, 1561, 1576–7, 1588–9 and 1593.
États particuliers — Representative assemblies held in a few regions within the *pays d'états.*
États provinciaux (Provincial Estates) — Assemblies of elected representatives of the three estates – nobility, clergy and third estate – which met in a number of provinces, called *pays d'états* (e.g. Brittany, Burgundy, Languedoc and Provence). They were called by the king and met usually once a year.
First president (*Premier président*) — The senior magistrate in a parlement.
Gabelle — The tax on salt.
Gallican — A member of the French church who stood for the defence of its 'liberties' against the claims of the papacy.
Généralité — One of 17 fiscal regions outside the *pays d'états*, each with a *recette générale.* The officials in charge were called *receveurs-généraux.*
Gens d'armes — Men at arms serving in the heavy cavalry.
Gentilhomme campagnard — A member of the rural nobility.
Gouvernement — A provincial governorship.

Gouverneur — Provincial representative of the king at the head of a *gouvernement.*

Grand Conseil — A judicial offshoot of the king's council. Though an independent 'sovereign court', it continued to follow the king on his travels.

Grand maître — Officer in charge of the royal household.

Grand Parti — A syndicate of Lyon bankers formed in 1555 to consolidate royal debts by means of regular amortisement.

Lance — A cavalry unit originally comprising four combatants: a man at arms (*homme d'armes*) two archers and a *coutillier.* By the reign of Francis I it had become a fiction. A standard company consisted of 40 lances: i.e. 40 *gens d'armes* and 60 archers.

Landsknechts — German mercenary infantry.

Lieutenant-général du royaume (Lieutenant-general of the kingdom) — A title conferring general command of the kingdom. It was given in 1557 to François, duc de Guise; in 1561 to Antoine de Bourbon; and in 1588 to Henri, duc de Guise. During the League, the duc de Mayenne became *Lieutenant-général* of the state and crown of France.

Lit de justice — A session of the parlement in the king's presence, usually to enforce registration of an edict.

Livre — The principal money of account in sixteenth-century France. 1 livre = 20 sous; 1 sou = 12 deniers; worth about 2 English shillings.

Maître des requêtes — A senior office-holder in a sovereign court, above the *conseillers* but below the *présidents.* The masters of requests deputized for the chancellor, served the council and were often sent on missions to the provinces.

Marshal of France — The highest military dignitary with his own jurisdiction exercised in a court called *table de marbre.*

Menu peuple — The lowest rank in society: the populace.

Mignon — A term of abuse, implying effeminacy, for one of Henry III's favourites.

Noblesse d'épée (nobility of the sword) — The nobility owing its rank to military prowess and rank.

Noblesse de robe (nobility of the robe) — Nobility acquired through the holding of an office.

Notables — Important persons drawn from the magistracy or municipal government.

Office	A permanent government post (as distinct from a commission, which was temporary). It was often sold and could entail a measure of ennoblement.
Ordonnance (Ordinance)	A law whose coverage was wider than that of an edict.
Parlement	The highest court of law under the king, also responsible for registering royal edicts and with administrative duties. Apart from the Parlement of Paris, there were seven provincial parlements (Aix-en-Provence, Bordeaux, Dijon, Grenoble, Rennes, Rouen and Toulouse).
Parlementaire	A magistrate serving in a parlement.
Pays d'états	Provinces which retained their representative estates as distinct from the *pays d'élections* which had lost theirs.
Picorreurs	Lightly armed infantry or skirmishers.
Pionniers (pioneers)	Soldiers specializing in heavy labour, such as digging trenches or hauling cannon.
Place de sûreté (surety town)	A fortified town which the Protestants were allowed to garrison. Under the Peace of Saint-Germain (1570) they obtained four such towns (La Rochelle, Cognac, La Charité and Montauban) for two years. The number was raised to eight in the Peace of Monsieur (1576) and to about 100 in the Edict of Nantes (1598).
Politique	A moderate during the civil wars, who was equally opposed to Catholic or Protestant extremism and supported the crown.
Présidiaux (Presidial courts)	Courts set up in 1552 between the provincial parlements and the *bailliage* courts.
Prévôt des marchands	The mayor of Paris.
Prévôt des maréchaux	Military magistrate appointed to control vagabonds, deserters etc.
Procureur	A solicitor. In every royal court there was a *procureur du roi*, known in the parlement as the *procureur-général.*
Receveur	A tax-collector acting on orders from the *élus.*
Reiters	German mercenary cavalry, usually armed with pistols.
Remontrance	A petition listing grievances.
Rente	A government bond issued on the security of municipal revenues. A *rentier* was a person living off such an investment.

Sacramentarianism A body of Protestant thought, held mainly by Zwingli and his followers, which rejected the doctrine of the Real Presence of Christ in the Eucharist.

Sacre The French coronation ceremony.

Salic Law One of the so-called fundamental laws of the French kingdom whereby females were excluded from the royal succession. Another was the law of inalienability, forbidding gifts or sales of land from the royal domain.

Sea Beggars Dutch Calvinist rebels against Spain who operated mainly at sea.

Secrétaire d'état (Secretary of state) One of the king's principal ministers whose importance grew during the sixteenth century.

Seigneurie The basic economic unit in rural France. The obligation of tenants to the *seigneur* involved a complex of rights, services and dues. A *seigneur* enjoyed rights of jurisdiction of varying degrees (called 'high', 'middle' and 'low') within his lands, albeit subject to appeal to a royal court.

Sénéchaussée Another name, used mainly in southern France, for a *bailliage*. The equivalent of the *bailli* was the *sénéchal*.

Setier A measure of capacity of grain. Roughly half a litre.

Sorbonne Strictly one of the colleges of the University of Paris but commonly applied to the university's Faculty of Theology.

Sovereign courts Courts which had once formed part of the royal court [*curia regis*] (e.g. the Parlement of Paris) and had since 'gone out of court' and become fixed in Paris.

Surintendant des finances The minister responsible for the general supervision of the fiscal system. O was appointed in 1578.

Taille The principal direct tax, levied in one of two ways: the *taille personnelle,* levied on the unprivileged in the north, and the *taille réelle,* levied on non-noble land in the south.

Taillon A tax on certain towns and villages, created in 1549 and designed to replace the burden of providing lodging and maintaining troops. At first it was an extraordinary levy, but in time it became a more regular tax, even in peacetime. By 1567 it was set at about 1.2 million livres.

Trésorier de France	One of ten fiscal officers staffing each *bureau des finances*.
Venality (*vénalité*)	The sale of offices.
Vicomté	In local government a jurisdiction below the *bailliage* and equivalent to a *prévôté*.

INDEX

4408